For Adam,

The Correspondence of Myles Dillon, 1922–1925

Myles Dillon

The Correspondence of
Myles Dillon
1922-1925

Irish-German Relations and Celtic Studies

EDITED BY

Joachim Fischer and John Dillon

FOUR COURTS PRESS

Set in 10.5 on 12.5 point Ehrhardt for
FOUR COURTS PRESS LTD
Fumbally Lane, Dublin 8, Ireland
e-mail: info@four-courts-press.ie
and in North America
FOUR COURTS PRESS
c/o ISBS, 5804 N.E. Hassalo Street, Portland, OR 97213.

A catalogue record for this title
is available from the British Library.

ISBN 1-85182-409-X

Printed in Great Britain
by MPG Books Ltd, Bodmin, Cornwall

Æ asked me about your dissertation, and I said you had been investigating the problem of the agreement of the subject and the predicate, at which he sighed deeply.

Osborn Bergin in a letter to Myles Dillon

John Dillon

CONTENTS

ILLUSTRATIONS

PREFACE

Myles Dillon was one of the foremost Celtic scholars of this century in Ireland. As Senior Professor and then Director of the School of Celtic Studies in the Dublin Institute of Advanced Studies he exercised a major influence on the direction of Celtic Studies in Ireland in the second half of this century. He came from a family which during the last 150 years has had a major impact on Irish political and intellectual life. Myles' grandfather was the Young Irelander John Blake Dillon, co-founder of *The Nation* and later M.P. for Tipperary; Myles' father John Dillon, whose letters make up almost half of the correspondence presented here, was, as the successor of John Redmond, the last leader of the Irish Parliamentary Party and would most probably have been the leading politician in Ireland, had not the Easter Rising changed the course of Irish history irrevocably, moving it into a new direction, which John Dillon was not prepared to follow. Myles' brother James was to become leader of Fine Gael in 1959; other family members also left their mark on the intellectual and religious life of the country. For these reasons alone, the correspondence presented here is of more than merely family interest; it can be regarded as a document of considerable significance in the context of Irish political, social and cultural history.

In late October 1922, at the age of twenty-two, Myles Dillon set off for Germany to take up a travelling scholarship awarded to him by University College, Dublin. He had just graduated with first class honours in Celtic Studies, and now he was heading for what was still the undisputed centre of higher learning in this field, as in so many others. He was not to return, except for holidays, until the spring of 1927, by which time he had spent three academic years in Germany (studying in Berlin, Bonn and Heidelberg), and two more in France (studying at the Sorbonne, in Paris). This book comprises an epistolary record of his adventures and reflections during the first part of that period. It reproduces Myles' extensive correspondence, primarily with his father in Dublin, but also letters from other members of the family and from friends and colleagues to Myles written between autumn 1922 and autumn 1925. The correspondence thus contains a multiplicity of Irish perspectives on Ireland, Germany and the wider world during the early years of independent nationhood.

Myles left behind an Ireland which appeared to be sinking into chaos (observed closely in this process by the malevolent eyes of his father, who had been swept from power in the election of November 1918), and he was heading for a Germany which was also approaching at least economic chaos, brought on by the exorbitant and relentless demands for reparations from the victorious Allies, in particular the French, who were in occupation of the Rhineland.

The correspondence reproduced here is thus of interest beyond Ireland; it is a record of a particularly turbulent time in European politics, a perceptive comment on two countries *in extremis*. The letters yield fascinating insights into the nature of Irish-German relations during the early 1920s. Both countries had much in common, then; they were both experiencing major crises and both where involved in the process of building up something completely new, a (largely) independent Free State in Ireland and a new democratic republic in Germany. The letters are proof of a relative openness towards Europe which existed in Ireland during those formative years of the early 1920s. This phase, however, did not last long. Towards the end of the decade Ireland had retreated into a self-made insular Catholic-Gaelic nutshell from which it was not to emerge until the early 1960s. The position of German in Irish schools is a small but significant indicator in this respect: between 1919 and 1930 the number of pupils learning German dropped from 893 to 40. This tendency is already foreshadowed in the letters.

In reading Myles' letters it should be borne in mind that he was writing to his father; this was bound to have an effect on the content. Very few letters from other family members have survived (the majority of these we include), and none from Myles to them. John Dillon had very strong views on almost everything, especially on anything of a political nature, and it is very likely that Myles preferred to remain quiet about certain things which he experienced—as most young people would tend to present a somewhat sanitised version of their adventures to their parents. Especially, about matters of the heart, Myles' letters tend to be noticeably low-key; the letter from an American woman whom Myles met in Heidelberg seems to suggest that there may have been more than just a passing acquaintance between the two, which, but for this letter, included here, we would never have known. However that may be, the views expressed in the letters yield a good insight into a young Irish mind of the 1920s confronted with a very different and therefore challenging cultural environment in mainland Europe, even though one would hesitate to regard Myles' views as either typical or representative.

Certain family details may be conveniently presented at the outset.[1] John Dillon had six children: John Mathew (1896-1969), known as Shawn; Ann Elizabeth (1897-1986), known as Nano, who, during the period of this correspondence (in 1923), married a prominent Dublin surgeon, P.J. Smyth, and produced a son, Nicholas; Theobald Wolfe Tone (1898-1946), later Professor of Pharmacology at University College, Dublin; Myles Patrick (1900-1972), the

---

1 Short biographies of the members of the Dillon family mentioned in these letters are to be found in the Biographical Notes.

author of one side of this correspondence; James Mathew (1902-1986), who went on to become leader of Fine Gael, and Brian (1905-1979), who is during the period of these letters still a student, pursuing the law, but who later abandoned a very promising career as a barrister to become a Benedictine monk in Glenstal Abbey, and was headmaster of Glenstal School.

The mother of these children, Elizabeth Mathew (1865-1907), died, tragically, when they were still very young, and they were brought up by a faithful nurse, Maria O'Reilly (known for some reason as Lia), who was really a mother to them. Only Shawn and Nano retained any very clear memory of their mother.

The Mathews were originally from Thomastown, in Co. Tipperary (Fr Theobald Mathew, the 'Apostle of Temperance', was a grand-uncle), but Elizabeth's father, Sir James Mathew (1830-1908), after graduating from Trinity College, Dublin, had come over to London to practise at the Bar, and had in due course become a High Court judge and then Lord Justice of Appeal. He had five children, two sons, Theobald (Theo) and Charles, and three daughters, Elizabeth, Mary and Katherine (Kathleen). All of these, except Myles' mother, come into the story in one way or another, as does his wife, Elizabeth (*née* Biron). Theobald's family lived in Cornwall Gardens, Kensington and Charles' lived in Albert Hall Mansions, South Kensington. Theobald had five sons, Theobald (Toby) (1898-1950), James (1900-1960), Charles (1903-1968), Robert (1906-1954), and Francis (1907-1965), three of whom appear in this correspondence. Charles, who was a barrister, but interested in politics, died tragically on 8 January 1923, near the beginning of this correspondence, just after being elected Labour M.P. for St George's and Wapping, one of a crop of middle-class recruits who were elected for Labour in this election. It was felt that he had a good chance of becoming Attorney-General in any future Labour government. His wife was Anna (*née* Cassidy). They had three children, who do not enter this story (though his eldest son, Theobald (1898-1964), went on to become Director of Public Prosecutions from 1944 to 1964). Both Myles and his brother James had much opportunity to enjoy their grandmother's hospitality at her home in Queen's Gate Gardens.

We present the letters more or less as we found them in the Dillon family archive.[2] It seemed best to divide the correspondence, not into calendar years, but rather into academic years, running from October to the following September, since this was the prevailing rhythm of Myles' life at the time. Each chapter begins with a brief introduction which provides the historical context; copious annotation provides further background material.[3] We also provide brief biographical sketches of people who are of particular importance in this corre-

2 For the few minor changes, see Editorial Note. 3 It should be pointed out that we were not able to interpret all remarks by the letter writers nor was it possible to identify all persons mentioned in the letters. Perhaps some of our readers can shed further light on some of the unsolved problems.

spondence. The Appendix contains the full text of Myles Dillon's articles on Germany which he wrote for the *Irish Statesman* during his time in Germany and frequently referred to in the letters. An open letter by John Dillon summarizing his views of the Irish situation in 1922-3 which appeared in the *Freeman's Journal* of 12 May 1923 is also appended. It provides the ideological context to the political remarks made in his letters.

The editors would like to express their thanks to all individuals and institutions who have so generously contributed the information to be found in the footnotes and the Biographical Notes, in particular Dr Donal McCartney (for details connected with U.C.D.), Fr Liam Redmond (for information about members of the Jesuit Order), and Dr Brian Murphy (for information on Fr Sweetman and Mount St. Benedict). We would like to thank Dr Tadhg Ó hIfearnáin, University of Limerick, who helped with the letters written in Irish. We are also indebted to the University of Limerick and Trinity College Dublin for their generous financial support towards this publication.

Joachim Fischer
John Dillon

EDITORIAL NOTE

We present the letters more or less unaltered. They are arranged and numbered according to the dates they were composed. However, certain changes have been made, as indicated below.

We have cut out some purely personal matters, such as recurrent arrangements about sending money, which can be of no interest to the reader. The places where cuts have been made are marked.

The addresses at the beginning of each letter have been standardized.

The punctuation has been regularized and obvious spelling errors have been corrected. This does not apply to German words. Incorrect German forms and spellings of names where they occur have in general been retained so as not to affect the flavour of Myles' letters; Myles, it should be remembered, had almost no German when he arrived in Berlin.

We have preserved italicisation more or less as we found it in the letters which means that words or passages in other languages are not marked if they were not underlined in the originals.

The * after some names indicates that a brief sketch can be found in the Biographical Notes. The names of members of the Dillon family, however, are not marked in this way.

The key to the abbreviations used in the references to footnotes is supplied in the Bibliography.

Year 1
October 1922–September 1923

INTRODUCTION

Some general information on the situation in Germany during the post-World War I period may be helpful for a better understanding of the letters. After an initial period of revolutionary turmoil following on Germany's defeat in November 1918, what is known as the "Weimar Republic" was inaugurated by elections in January 1919.[1] The leader of the Social Democratic Party of Germany (SPD), Friedrich Ebert (1871-1925), was elected President, and a coalition government was formed under Philipp Scheidemann (1865-1939), the Social Democrats, who were the largest party, but without an overall majority, combining with the Centre Party and the right-of-centre German Democratic Party.

This Government hit a crisis in May 1919, when the terms of the peace treaty were handed to the German delegation. They were so harsh, both as regards the loss of territory and the payment of reparations, that on 19 June the cabinet rejected the treaty and resigned. Germans seriously contemplated going to war again, but the advice of Hindenburg and the General Staff was that this would be hopeless. A new government of Social Democrats and Centrists was formed under Gustav Bauer, the former SPD Minister of Labour, and on 22 June the Assembly, by 237 votes to 138, authorized the Government to sign the treaty. This was accordingly done at Versailles on 28 June.

In terms of territory relevant to these letters, Germany lost Alsace-Lorraine to France, the left bank of the Rhine and a fifty-kilometer strip on the right bank were permanently demilitarized, and, in compensation for mines in France deliberately destroyed by the Germans as they retreated, the French were allowed to exploit the coal mines and plant of the Saar basin, the Saarland being separated from Germany and placed under a League of Nations commission for fifteen years. Territory was also ceded to Belgium, Denmark, and in the East, to Poland (extensively) and to Lithuania. All her overseas colonies were also confiscated. As a result of these dispositions, Germany lost 75 per cent of her iron ore, 68 per cent of her zinc ore, and 26 per cent of her coal.

On top of these territorial losses, Germany was required to surrender or destroy all heavy weapons, and to dismantle all fortifications in the Rhineland

1 It received this title because it initially met in the new theatre in Weimar, since conditions in Berlin at the time did not seem to be conducive to calm deliberation, a Communist-led uprising having been just bloodily put down by the army. Weimar was also regarded as the cultural capital of Germany; the collaboration of Goethe and Schiller in Weimar had produced the undisputed high point of German literary culture (the *Weimar Klassik*) and the new republic wanted to link itself to this great national tradition and thus be seen as truly German.

17

and on Heligoland. The General Staff was dissolved, and conscription forbidden. Only a small professional army of 100,000 was permitted, to preserve order at home, and Germany was forbidden to manufacture tanks, gas, aircraft for military purposes and submarines. The navy was drastically reduced to 15,000 men, six battleships and a few smaller craft.

In addition, Germany was required to pay an unspecified sum in reparation to the victorious powers, comprising compensation for damage caused to allied civilians and their property—a dangerously vague and open-ended demand, and vastly more than the country could possibly afford. This was to prove a major source of aggravation, and, together with the humiliating circumstances in which the settlement was imposed, guaranteed a mood of bitter resentment which was ultimately to lead to the fall of the Weimar regime and the rise of Hitler and National Socialism. There is no sign of the latter, it must be said, in these letters, although Hitler was already on the move. But Hitler's main base was Munich and Bavaria, which Myles Dillon was not much concerned with. Of the former, however, the spirit of resentment, we hear much, and it is amusing to observe, in view of his later love of Paris and the French, to what an extent Myles adopts the German attitude to France, especially after he moves to Bonn, where they are in occupation.

In the three years following the Treaty of Versailles, governments, usually consisting of the same figures in different combinations, came and went with almost Italianate rapidity, since any reparations crisis, of which there were many, was enough to bring about the resignation of the reigning cabinet. Most of the governments included the Social Democrats as a component, but in November 1922, only days after Myles' arrival in Berlin, a Centre-Right coalition under the leadership of Wilhelm Cuno (1876-1933) formed the government.

At this time, relations with France in particular were becoming worse and worse, since France was most uncompromising in extracting its pound of flesh. Germany's Rapallo Pact with the Soviet Union, in the middle of the European Economic Conference at Genoa in April 1922, had not helped here, though it solved the problem of Russian reparations. It greatly increased French suspicions of Germany's purposes, however, and, when Germany requested further moratoria on repayments for July and August, France refused, unless she was given "productive guarantees", including the right to exploit the Ruhr coal-fields. In December, the Reparations Commission, against the protest of the British member, announced that Germany was technically in default in her deliveries of timber (she had failed to deliver a consignment of telephone poles to France). This supplied the French prime minister Raymond Poincaré with an excuse for intervention. A last-minute attempt to reconcile Britain and France at a conference in Paris in January 1923 (referred to by John Dillon in Letter 37) ended in complete failure. On 9 January the Reparations Commission announced that Germany had deliberately defaulted over coal deliveries, and two days later French and Belgian troops entered the Ruhr, ostensibly to protect a Franco-Belgian control commission sent in to supervise reparations payments. Britain and America protested, and the latter actually withdrew her occupation forces from the Rhineland.

On 11 January 1923 French and Belgian troops entered the *Ruhrgebiet* in order to supervise and ensure reparation payments. French troops also occupied large tracts of the Rhineland. Bonn was originally under British control, but had been handed over to the French as early as February 1920, a move which was very much resented by the population. The British did however hold on to Cologne, which explains the frequent references to the two Irish military chaplains in Cologne whom Myles started to visit soon after his arrival in Bonn. Myles comments on the rather positive image of the British at this time; indeed he himself believed that the Germans made rather too much of the British-French disagreements (Letter 43). Katherine Tynan in her autobiographical account of her year in Cologne round about the same time, *Life in the Occupied Area* (1925), very much supports Myles' impressions. The behaviour of the French troops did not endear the occupying forces to the population. The Germans felt particularly offended by the presence of North African troops which France decided to use in the occupying forces, less as an act of deliberate provocation than in order to allow the demobilization of French troops. The French also supported a separatist movement in the Rhineland whose expressed aim was to break away from the Reich and establish an independent Republic under the protection of the French government (see also p. 150 below).

In the Ruhr industrial belt, the German government actively supported a policy of passive resistance. They called on the workers not to co-operate with the occupying forces. Myles attended a protest demonstration in Berlin on 14 January 1923 in which he got a fair impression of the national fervour which the Ruhr occupation aroused all over Germany. However, the financial support required for the population in the Ruhr and the increasing social expenditure among other factors had very serious consequences for the German economy: the value of the German Reichsmark went on a downward spiral and the ensuing inflation reached its high point in November 1923 when US$1 was worth 4.2 billion Reichsmark. Employees on fixed incomes including civil servants were particularly badly hit by the collapse of the currency; their salaries never kept up with the rate of inflation. Myles comments extensively on the plight of university professors who often could not find the wherewithal to feed themselves and their families, let alone buy books. The Reichsbank finally managed to bring inflation under control in November 1923 by introducing a new currency, the *Rentenmark* (equalling one billion old Reichsmark).

Myles Dillon arrived in Berlin on 31 October 1922 and stayed there until 23 April 1923, interrupted only by a number of journeys he undertook to various places in Germany. In Berlin he stayed first with Baronin Sophie von Bolschwing in Wilmersdorf, of whom we know very little except that she must have been friendly with some members of the royal family in Berlin in happier times for the German nobility. However, Myles felt much more at home in a guest house on Karlstraße (today Reinhardt-Straße) which he moved to after Christmas. The Baronin however introduced him to a friend in Bonn, Gräfin Mathilde Beissel von Gymnich, with whom Myles stayed in Bonn in 3 Schedestraße.[2]

Berlin in the 1920s was by general consensus one of the naughtiest capital cities in the world. The moral decline was fuelled by the economic and social problems which forced many to sell the last thing they had left, that is, their own body, and allowed others "to dance on the volcano". Life in Berlin has been described elsewhere, notably by such writers as Christopher Isherwood and Sefton Delmer, but also by the distinguished Soviet writer Ilya Erenburg in his memoirs, *People and Life*. There is a good collection of impressions preserved by Alex de Jonge in his book *The Weimar Chronicle* (London, 1978). Dillon, by reason of both temperament and upbringing, was radically out of sympathy with much of this activity, as also with the various avant-garde developments in music, art and literature that went with it. Also, he did not at this time yet know much German. So we must not expect from him a great degree of insight into the life of the capital. And yet his comments are most interesting, even if those of a rather disapproving outsider: "[...] the utter dependence on music and light and kisses is rather desperate", he writes home on 8 April 1923 (Letter 70); what better way to describe Berlin in those years? We hear of the strong Russian influence on the cultural life of the capital. After the Rapallo Treaty of April 1922 relations between Germany and Soviet Russia improved considerably and cultural exchanges were encouraged from both sides. The First Russian Art Exhibition of 1922 introduced Berlin to Russian Constructivism, and Russian theatre companies came to Berlin to produce plays by Tchekhov and other Russian playwrights. Myles went to several Russian theatre productions and was quite impressed. Most importantly, though not mentioned in the letters, Russian films of the Soviet avantgarde were shown in Berlin. Perhaps Myles disapproved of this rather proletarian art form.[3] We also catch other occasional glimpses of the Berlin theatre scene; in particular, Myles comments briefly on the theatre strike of November/December 1922 (Letter 22).

It may also be of interest to briefly describe the Irish presence in Berlin at the time, because Myles would have met most members of the little Irish commu-

2 The house was badly damaged during World War II and eventually levelled. In 1996, the site was occupied by the representation of the Land Brandenburg in Bonn. 3 The openness towards Soviet art, very much welcomed by left-wing intellectuals in the city, however, did not last for long: when Sergei Eisenstein's revolutionary epic *Battleship Potemkin* was shown in April 1926 and subsequently hailed as a masterpiece by left-wing and Communist critics, the authorities took fright and decided to ban the film. The ban was lifted only after it had been severely cut.

nity in the German capital while he was there. Since 1920 Irish Nationalists had made use of the political and economic confusion in Germany and had bought shiploads of weaponry in Germany which was subsequently smuggled into Ireland to be used against the British during the Anglo-Irish War. The Germans were only too ready to make deals with the Irish rebels; for high-ranking ex-generals it seemed a profitable—albeit illegal—way of getting rid of surplus weapons and of laying their hands on hard currency; creating trouble for the British was—especially in those early years after the war—a welcome side-effect. A recently published article by Troy Davis (1994) proves that attempts to procure weapons from Germany continued during the years of the civil war: precisely during the months which Myles spent in Berlin, Irish agents on the anti-Treaty side arrived in Berlin to negotiate an arms deal. The mission was finally called off when the truce was declared back in Ireland; however, in the light of developments two decades later it is worth noting that one of the negotiators, Commandant Seán Moylan, met a top-ranking member of the National Socialist Workers' Party of Germany (NSDAP), a close aide of Adolf Hitler, who indicated that the future Führer might have weapons to sell. In any case, these developments show that John Dillon's worry about his son getting caught up in some shady political dealings (Letter 4) was not unfounded.

On a more official level was the Irish diplomatic representation in Berlin which was established in 1921. Nancy Power, a (former) doctoral student of Myles' supervisor Rudolf Thurneysen,* arrived in Berlin in April 1921 to set up the office. Nancy Power was the daughter of Senator Jennie Wyse Power who is mentioned in one of Nano Dillon's letters (No. 27) when her shop was burned down by the I.R.A. in December 1922 only days after her appointment to the Senate by the Free State government. One of Power's first tasks was to publish and distribute a bi-weekly *Irish Bulletin*. In this she was assisted by Professor Julius Pokorny,* Myles' professor in Berlin. Together with a student of his, Michael O'Brien,* Pokorny had been involved in many of the German-Irish activities in Berlin since the war, both legal and illegal, it would appear. The first Irish envoy to Germany, John Chartres, arrived in Berlin in June 1921. In October, Charles Bewley was appointed Trade Consul to the Berlin office. Unfortunately, the relationship between Bewley and Chartres was fraught with difficulties right from the start, and, eventually, indiscretions from Bewley about Chartres alleged anti-Treaty leanings ensured that he was recalled from his post in November 1922; his assistant Nancy Power, also under suspicion, was transferred to the Home Service. It was during his last days in Berlin that Myles made Chartres' acquaintance; from the letters, however, it is impossible to deduce whether Chartres intimated in any way what the situation in the Irish office was like. Chartres left Berlin on 4 December 1922. The Department of Foreign Affairs under Desmond Fitzgerald clearly favoured Bewley and had already promoted him to the post of Trade Commissioner in November 1922.

He took over the Irish office after Chartres' departure, but, strangely enough, Bewley did not outlast Chartres long: he resigned from his post in Berlin on 10 February 1923, stating later in his autobiography that he was fed up acting as an "unaccredited representative of a half-independent state" (Bewley 1989). Bewley's assistant, Cornelius Duane, also appears in the letters. Myles, it seems, became quite friendly with him and Duane joined himself and Harold Quinlan on their Christmas holidays in the Riesengebirge. Duane was finally given the unenviable task of closing down the Irish office on 2 January 1924. As if to prove Bewley right, the Free State government announced after Duane's departure that all future business relating to Ireland would be "handled through the British Consulate". Surprisingly perhaps, Myles never appears to have met Corkman Liam de Róiste who spent December 1922 and January 1923 in Berlin. De Róiste's account published in the *United Irishman* in a series of articles from April to July 1923 shares many of the impressions and sentiments we find in Myles' letters from Berlin.[4]

Myles did however briefly meet Thomas McLaughlin shortly after the latter arrived in Berlin in December 1922; we can infer this from Harold Quinlan's (92) and Dr Michael Hickey's (31) letters. McLaughlin had been a Lecturer in Physics at University College, Galway, but he left this post to take up the offer of the huge electrical firm Siemens-Schuckert in Berlin, to continue his training in electrical engineering in Germany. McLaughlin was to have a major impact on the economic development of Ireland when he brokered the agreement between his employer and the Free State Government to build a hydro-electric power station at Ardnacrusha on the Shannon in order to supply the Free State with electricity. Work on the "Shannon Scheme" did not begin until September 1925, which is precisely the point where this correspondence ends. Nevertheless the Shannon Scheme comes briefly into the correspondence in Year 3.

Understandably it was university life which concerned Myles most. The plight of German professors is frequently referred to, and Myles tried to do his bit to help: together with his father he devised a scheme by which the Free State Government could support work in Celtic Studies in Germany (Letter 10). This came to nothing, though the Government did occasionally support publication projects of Thurneysen's and Pokorny's, but this had nothing to do with the Dillons' interventions (see Letter 41).

We learn from Myles' letters that the professors from whom he took lectures in Berlin, apart from Julius Pokorny in Celtic, included Wilhelm Schulze in Comparative Philology, Gustav Roethe in Gothic, and Felix Hartmann in Greek. In Bonn, the great Celtic scholar Rudolf Thurneysen, who was later to supervise

---

4 Fischer 1996(b) deals with the Irish perception of Berlin during those years in a more detailed fashion. See also O'Neill (1985) for a broader picture.

his doctoral thesis, was his teacher in the area of Celtic Studies; famous philologists like the Sanskritist Willibald Kirfel, the Germanist Rudolf Meissner, later Wilhelm Meyer-Lübke (Romance Philology) and Thurneysen's successor Ferdinand Sommer were among his professors in other philological subjects. It is perhaps somewhat surprising that Myles went to Berlin rather than straightaway to Bonn. The reason might have been that Myles originally intended to study Comparative Philology rather than Celtic, which would explain his contact with Schulze before he met Pokorny. Myles' mentor Osborn Bergin had been a student of Thurneysen's himself and it is unlikely that he would have sent Myles to study with Pokorny. There was no doubt that Thurneysen was the chief authority in the area of Celtic Philology.[5] Some letters in this correspondence refer to the difference between Pokorny and Thurneysen (see, for example, Letter 50): not only in terms of scholarship one cannot but notice a contrast between the two; the political wheelings and dealings of Pokorny would also have been anathema to Thurneysen whose correctness, reliability and obliging manner is emphasized by several letter writers. In political outlook, of course, both would have been on the conservative side, as were so many German university professors of the time, who had gained their academic credentials under the Kaiser. In this respect, Myles fitted in reasonably well into the intellectual climate prevalent at German universities: no love was lost between the Irish visitor and the German left; in fact, in the letters we hear as little of it as Myles would have heard of it from his university professors and fellow students. This, it should be borne in mind, slightly falsifies the image of Germany in his letters: what we call nowadays "Weimar culture" was largely dominated by left-wing intellectuals and artists.

One feature manifesting itself in a number of the letters (for example, 8, 13, 62) that will jar on contemporary sensibilities, is a certain degree of anti-Semitism (such as would greatly have distressed Myles Dillon in later years), but it must be borne in mind, firstly, that such sentiments were, sadly, very widespread in Gentile circles prior to the horrors of Hitler's "final solution" becoming known, and secondly, that many well-off Jews in post-war German did (excusably, but counter-productively) behave in the provocative manner described in Letter 8, which made them easier targets for Nazi propaganda.

Meanwhile, back in Ireland, the Civil War ground on, bringing a seemingly endless chain of destruction, atrocity, and reprisal in its wake. John Dillon's reaction to events may seem excessively apocalyptic, and was no doubt coloured by a certain gloomy satisfaction in observing what a mess Sinn Féin had got themselves

---

5 Indeed, when it came to filling Kuno Meyer's chair in Berlin, it was Thurneysen who was placed first. It was only because of his advanced age that the committee decided to give the chair to the third-placed Pokorny (Lerchenmüller 1997).

into, but if one reads through the newspapers of the period, one can certainly see sufficient reasons for any rational and impartial observer to feel that the country was sliding inexorably into economic and social chaos. The Irregulars, having been soundly beaten in the field, and having no realistic hope of prevailing militarily, seem from October 1922 on to have turned their energies vindictively to wreaking the maximum destruction and misery on a regime which they claimed had betrayed the ideal of the Republic. The result was that the fledgeling state, which might have started its independent life in reasonably favourable economic circumstances, was involved in enormous extra expenditure, by reason of both having to maintain a much larger army than otherwise necessary, and paying out considerable sums in compensation for malicious damage. That it recovered so relatively quickly after the final disintegration of the anti-Treaty campaign in April 1923, after Liam Lynch's elimination, is something few could have foreseen, and is much to the credit of such figures as Cosgrave and Kevin O'Higgins, for whom, it must be said, John Dillon exhibits little sympathy.

One curious item that figures in a number of the letters of John Dillon (3, 4, 7, 19, 20, 25) is the Mansion House Conference Fund, and the setting up from it of a scholarship "for the encouragement of the study of the Irish Language, Literature, and History", a matter that brought John Dillon and Eamon de Valera together in a most bizarre way. The story of it was this. As a result of the Mansion House Conference against conscription in April 1918, a national defence fund was launched to finance the resistance movement. In the event, quite a lot of this money remained unspent by the time the war ended. Most of what was left over was returned to the subscribers, but a sum of £2247 9s. 2d. was left as unreturnable, and it was decided that a group of trustees should be set up, consisting of Dillon, de Valera, and the Lord Mayor of Dublin, Ald. Laurence O'Neill, to administer it, and decide what should be done with it. By the winter of 1922 they were still undecided, though a proposal for a scholarship had been mooted. What the nature of the differences between Dillon and de Valera were on the exact nature of the scholarship is not clear from the correspondence, but, whatever they were, they were resolved by early November, though progress on formalizing an agreement was delayed by the serious illness of the Lord Mayor, and, no doubt, by the circumstance that de Valera himself was in the middle of running a civil war, and was in hiding. From Letter 20 (28 November 1922) we learn that he had appointed Fr Timothy Corcoran, Professor of Education at U.C.D., to be his representative. All was settled, however, early in the new year, and a formal deed was drawn up by solicitor Arthur Cox setting up the scholarship. Trustees continued to be Dillon and de Valera, joined by President Coffey of U.C.D., Douglas Hyde and Fr Corcoran. Laurence O'Neill bowed out. Myles had been hoping that his friend Seamus Delargy* might be eligible for the first scholarship, but this was in fact not awarded until 1924, and meanwhile Delargy had been given an Assistantship in the Irish Department of the College by Douglas Hyde. The scholarship, as it happens, still flourishes, amounting now to £1000 a year. As a curious footnote to this incident, much later, in 1952, Myles Dillon, by this time a Senior Professor in the Dublin Institute for Advanced Studies, was appointed a trustee of the scholarship by Eamon de Valera.

The Dillon family were not particularly inconvenienced or threatened by the Civil War, at least in Dublin, but in Ballaghaderreen the family house was commandeered, first by the Republicans, under Tom Carney, O/C of the East Mayo Brigade, and then, from the beginning of February 1923 (see Letters 47, 50, 55), by the Free State forces, who made it their local headquarters, and remained in occupation until the summer, doing considerable incidental damage, for which Dillon was only very inadequately compensated. Various representations to the local Free State commander, Lavin, produced no very satisfactory result, but, on the whole, once they were installed, Dillon was content that they should stay there until the cessation of hostilities, since if they had evacuated it earlier, it would almost certainly have been sacked by the Republicans in reprisal.

On the personal level, the chief excitements were the ordination to the subdiaconate of Myles' eldest brother Shawn in January 1923, and then to the priesthood in late May (Letters 36, 87, 90—in which Maria relates amusingly the débâcle about the chalice), the departure of his younger brother James to the United States, to continue his study of modern business methods in Chicago, in February (Letters 48, 64, 76), and his sister Nano's sudden engagement (in May), and then marriage (in June), to a young Dublin surgeon, P.J. Smyth, when she had generally been expected to marry her chief previous admirer, Norman Reddin (Letters 76, 77, 82, 88, 89). As for his brother Theo, afflicted by tuberculosis, he moved in May 1923 from a sanatorium on the north coast of France, at Berck-Plage, where he had spent the previous nine months (Letter 79), to one in Leysin in Switzerland, where he remained for the next four years.

THE LETTERS

1

[Myles to John Dillon] Bailey's Hotel, London SW7, Sunday night, Oct. 22
[1922]

Dear Father,

I am here safely and very comfortable. I have seen my relatives at Cornwall Gardens[6] and Kensington Square[7], and found them well and happy. This afternoon, after I had lunched with Grandmother,[8] Toby Mathew and his fiancée[9] arrived, accompanied by Elizabeth. The fiancée seemed pleasant but did not say much. Grandmother was a little tried because Kathleen left her firmly to entertain first the fiancée and later Elizabeth, and neither of them was facile.

Theo had gone to Oxford[10] when I arrived and is expected back tomorrow.

By the way, please tell Maria that I have found my degree certificate in the trunk.

I shall write again when there is news.

Tomorrow I intend to call on TP[11] and on Robin Flower* of the Museum.

With love,
Myles

2

[Myles to John Dillon] Friday, 26 October [1922]

Your very welcome letter arrived yesterday.[12] Almost at the same moment arrived the man you wrote about. However, his name is not Henderson,[13] but Heneghan,* and he is a friendly youth from Galway University, he whom I remember telling you of as having got a dole of £100 from the Mayo Council to go to Germany. He was capsized on hearing that I had communicated with Bonn, and decided not to go there. He had made no enquiries but forwarded money to Bonn and arranged for digs without any communication from

6 That is, the Theobald Mathews. 7 That is, the Charles Mathews. 8 Lady Elizabeth Mathew *née* Biron, widow of Sir James. 9 Toby Mathew's fiancée, whom he subsequently married, was Jean Milton. 10 That is, Theobald Mathew (1898-1964), son of Charles. 11 T.P. O'Connor.* 12 This letter is unfortunately lost. 13 See Letter 4.

Thurneysen.* However, he is starting today and says that if Bonn proves hopeless he will come on to Berlin. But I am glad Brian gave him my address, as he is a friend and quite innocuous.

I am still trying to decide between Dover and Ostend, Folkestone—Flushing, Harwich and the Hook of Holland, Harwich—Antwerp, and finally Croydon—Berlin by aeroplane in ten hours. Of these the first is the cheapest, the second is the most direct, of the third I know nothing, the fourth is the most beautiful and the last the most adventurous, and the most expensive. I have resolved now to go again to Cook and ask his advice as to which route offers me a through carriage into which I can clamber on landing in Europe and in which I may remain till I reach Berlin. This seems the best plan for the first experiment.

About the ticket, I find that the through ticket costs only something like £3-15, and the profit on taking a second ticket in Germany would be small. Moreover, I should have to re-register my luggage. Thus I am inclined not to mind it. Leaving here next Monday at 2 p.m. or at 8 p.m. I can arrive in Berlin on Tuesday evening at 6.15 p.m. or about 8 p.m. One route, you see, is shorter than the other. Even by Antwerp there are through connections, so that I would not have more than 20 minutes in Antwerp. Therefore the question is whether for the sake of the majestic passage up the Scheldt it is worth while going out of one's way. There is also the advantage that one gets a good sleep on board and lands in Antwerp at the seemly hour of 9 o'clock in the morning.

My stay here is very pleasant. Uncle Theo took us to dinner on Wednesday in Soho, after which we saw a play. Yesterday I visited the mss. in the British Museum, took tea in Kensington Square and dined at Cornwall Gardens. Today I am lunching with James[14] and dining at Kensington Square.

I shall not go to Oxford this time for two good reasons, the first and best being that somehow I am not inclined to go, and the second that I have no time. By the way, I saw the German consul and got my visa, price 15/-.

Is there any news of the Delargy* negotiations[15] yet?

What about Brian's exam?

3

[John Dillon to Myles] 2, North Gt. George's Street, Dublin,
Friday, 27 October [1922]

When writing on Wednesday I forgot to tell you that since you left I have received another communication from DeV.,[16] refusing to agree to my proposed

---

14 It is not quite clear whether this refers to his brother James, who was in London at this time, learning business methods in Selfridge's, or to his cousin, James Mathew. **15** Seamus Delargy* was a candidate for a scholarship out of the Mansion House Fund. See Introduction. **16** That is to say,

disposition of the Fund, and making an alternative proposal more absurd than any of his previous suggestions, so I fear poor Delargy* has no chance. I am to see the Lord Mayor[17] and talk the matter over with him.

I expected a letter from you this morning, but none has come. I am anxious to learn what decisions you have arrived at as to the date of your start for Berlin. No news of Brian's fate[18] so far.

You will see from this day's paper that the Republic has been formally declared and a Government set up.[19] This does not look as if the peace negotiations were succeeding. The Republic newspaper[20] has come out again, and has been on sale in the streets for the last three days.

4

[John Dillon to Myles] Sat., 28 October [1922]

Your letter[21] came this morning, and was very welcome. I was much relieved to learn that it was not Henderson[22] who was on your track, for I really thought you were in danger of being mixed up in some objectionable mission to Berlin.[23] I hope you got Heneghan's* address at Bonn, so that you may be able to communicate with him, and find out how things turn out there.

I think you ought to select the most direct route to Berlin, regardless of scenery, etc., and of course if you can get a through carriage it will be an immense advantage. Do not forget to make sure about your luggage, whether your trunk is registered thro'. [It] will be examined at the various frontiers. And be sure to telegraph to the Hotel in Berlin to secure a room. Send me your Berlin address before you leave London. The cost of a ticket is absurdly small—it would certainly not be worth while trying to save by taking a second ticket.

Eamon de Valera, with whom John Dillon was at this time involved in negotiations as to the disposition of the Mansion House Fund. See Introduction. 17 The Lord Mayor at this time was Laurence O'Neill. 18 Brian Dillon was at this time involved in entrance examinations to University College, Dublin, in which he was successful. 19 Following a meeting of the Republican Army Executive on 16-17 October, a Republican government was set up on 25 October, with de Valera as President. Austin Stack was Minister for Finance; Robert Barton, Minister for Economic Affairs; Liam Mellows (who was in gaol), Minister for Defence; Sean T. O'Kelly, Minister for Local Government; and P.J. Ruttledge, Minister for Home Affairs. 20 Presumably the *Republican War Bulletin.* 21 Letter 2. 22 A Republican officer called Leo Henderson had been captured by pro-Treaty forces on 26 June 1922 and the anti-Treaty forces who held the Four Courts at the time had arrested the pro-Treaty Deputy Chief of Staff, Gen. J.J. O'Connell as a reprisal. Cosgrave later gave this act as a reason for the subsequent attack on the Four Courts, which marked the beginning of the Civil War. Henderson was released later. 23 John Dillon was obviously aware of some of the under-cover negotiations which were going on between Republicans and politically influential people or arms dealers in Germany. See Introduction for more details.

I am very glad to hear that you have had such a pleasant time in London. No news of Brian's fate yet. But it must be known very soon, as the Governing Body[24] meets on Tuesday, and the recommendations of the Academic Council must be ready for that meeting.

I had a letter from Felix[25] this morning. No further fighting or firing in Ballagh, but as usual the wildest of rumours. I am going down on Wednesday.

Hyde[26] is calling here on Sunday. I have not the slightest idea of yielding. The only thing to be done now, as far as I can see, is to summon a full meeting of the Mansion House Committee and ask them to appoint two new trustees.

[PS] Do not forget my suggestion of post cards to be posted en route and immediately on your arrival in Berlin.

5

[Myles to John Dillon] Great Eastern Railway, R.M.S. "St. George", Harwich—Hook of Holland Service, Monday night, 30 Oct. [1922]

I have actually got myself so far on my journey. This is the route which most recommended itself, offering an excellent boat and a good sleep on the sea. My train travelling will be all by day, which is a great comfort, and at twenty-one o'clock tomorrow (9 o'clock at night in George's Street) I arrive in Berlin. I have wired to Pokorny,* and to the Central Hotel, to secure a room. I have forgotten no items of my outfit, not even my passport or my ticket, so things are looking hopeful. Kathleen[27] was extremely kind in helping me to arrange my journey, and came to the hotel to pack my trunk, insisting that I could not manage it. This, I confess, was a great relief, for the difficulties of packing are always great for me.

Theo leaves for Boulogne tomorrow morning, and then London is at peace. Since I last wrote we have been most festive—a play on Thursday, and actually two plays on Saturday. On Friday I attended evensong in St. Paul's and on my way home noticed London University on the left hand side, and turned in just in time for a lecture on Descartes and Liebknecht.[28] London is a wonderful

24 That is, the Governing Body of University College, Dublin. 25 Felix Partridge was the manager of the family firm, Monica Duff, Ltd, of Ballaghaderreen, and an old family retainer. Many other members of the Partridge family served the firm and the family over the years. 26 Douglas Hyde* was also involved in negotations about the Mansion House Fund. 27 That is to say, his aunt, Kathleen Mathew. 28 Karl Liebknecht (1871–1919) was a SPD member of the Reichstag since 1912 but broke away from the party in 1917 when he joined the radical left wing grouping *Spartakusbund*. In 1919 he founded the Communist Party of Germany (KPD) whose intention was to carry on the unsuccessful soviet revolution of 1919. Only days after founding the party, himself and Rosa Luxemburg, another leading member of the KPD, were assassinated by right wing extremists in Berlin.

place. Last night I dined with Mrs Preston and bade her hail and farewell. Theo and I were both at lunch at the flat and tea at Kensington Square.

The London crisis is most impenetrable.[29] No one has any idea what will happen. As you know, Uncle Charles has been adopted as Labour candidate for St. George's and Wapping, but Labour is not expecting a big sweep at the general election.[30] There seems to be a general feeling that the Wee Frees[31] are down and out. Donald McClean[32] said so himself at a private dinner the other night. On the other hand, one of their agents told Uncle Theo that the Co-Libs were flocking back to them and anxious to shake off Lloyd George.

Anna tells us an amazing story about L.G.[33]—that the immortal Gosling[34] met him at the Port of London ceremony on the Tuesday before the Thursday of the Carlton Club sensation[35] and asked whether he could safely go to Geneva. Lloyd George drew him aside and said of course he was not sure till Thursday, but that he thought it would be all right and he could go without any fear of a sudden crisis!

I shall write from Berlin on Wednesday, so with luck you should hear from me on Friday, but there may well be a day or two of delay, so do not be uneasy if no news comes till Monday.

By the way, I shall always be glad of Irish newspapers or cuttings. I have not seen a word of Irish news for over a week except Gwynn's* letter in the *Observer*. There seems to be a complete boycott in the English papers.

I regret to say that our craft is now becoming very uneven on her keel.

6

[Myles' first letter from Berlin, recounting his finding a hotel, changing money, and a conversation with a (border?) guard, has been lost. It is this lost letter to which Letter 7 is a reply.]

---

29 That is to say, the political crisis produced by the refusal of the Conservatives, at a party meeting held on 19 October, to fight the election called by Lloyd George on 10 October on a Coalition ticket with the Liberals. This led to the resignation of Lloyd George that same afternoon, and the succession of Bonar Law, the Conservative leader, on 23 October. 30 In fact, Charles Mathew was elected with a majority of 428 over a Liberal for the London constituency of Whitechapel and St.George's. Labour secured 142 seats in the election, a surprisingly good result. This election, indeed, signalled the definitive arrival of the Labour Party, and the beginning of the eclipse of the Liberals. 31 The colloquial term for the Asquithian Liberals. They came in with 57 seats, narrowly surpassing Lloyd George's National Liberals. 32 Sir Donald Maclean, leader of the Asquithian Liberals. 33 Lloyd George. 34 Presumably Harry Gosling (1861-1930), trade union leader and Labour politician. 35 That is, the meeting of the Conservative Party, which voted by 187 votes to 87 to fight the election as an independent party.

7

[John Dillon to Myles], Sat., 4 November [1922]

Your letter from Berlin arrived last night, and I must say it was an immense relief to me to learn from it that you had got over your journey successfully and were so comfortably established in Berlin. Do not be in too great a hurry to leave the Hotel. Take time to secure really satisfactory permanent quarters. Your letter was most interesting . I was greatly pleased to hear that you found yourself able to make some attempt at German. Your debate with the German guard, and your account of the amazing result of the exchange, amused and interested me exceedingly. What about the League of Nations!

When you are settling the routine of your life in Berlin, I would advise to attend some good teacher of German language and literature. Read a newspaper every morning, and frequent (decent) theatres, and before you know where you are you will be thinking in German, and able to discourse fluently. You certainly have arrived in Berlin at an extraordinarily interesting moment. I only hope the situation will not become too hot. Remember I shall be intensely interested in all details you can find time to write about, your own proceedings, and the character and views of the people whose acquaintance you may make. With regard to money, I think by far the best plan will be to arrange for you—on the same lines as Theo[36]—to open an account in the National Bank, Charing Cross, and get the Manager to send you a cheque book with ten cheques guaranteed on their Berlin correspondents to the extent of £10 each. Then you would be able to draw such sums as you think best from time to time. These guaranteed cheques may be filled for any amount not larger than that for which they are guaranteed. Send me your signature on a sheet of paper to send to the London Bank.

Here the fight goes on the old lines only more so. The Republicans have been very active during the last week, and they have scored some considerable successes, notably the capture of Clifden and all its garrison.[37] The city is simply full of rumours of approaching peace. But enclosed cutting from last night's *Telegraph* does not read like peace.[38] The Republican Dail—and rival Govt. to the Free State—have directed De Valera to appeal to Rome against the Bishops, and most scurrilous pamphlets are in circulation against their Lordships.[39]

---

36 Myles Dillon's brother. **37** This operation took place on 30 October, and resulted in the capture of eighty of the Free State garrison, including Colonel-Commandant O'Malley. O'Malley subsequently, with the help of three others, turned the tables on his captors, disarmed them, and marched six of them all the way to Oughterard. **38** This has not, unfortunately, been preserved. The *Evening Telegraph* of 3 November contained reports of raids on various post offices and of the derailing of a train near Dalkey. **39** On 10 October 1922 the Catholic hierarchy had issued a pastoral condemning the actions of the anti-Treaty forces. This prompted an immediate reaction from the latter which manifested itself in strongly worded pamphlets criticizing the bishops.

On Thursday night at 10.30, as I was sitting calmly reading my English papers, a furious fusillade broke out, apparently in the street and right opposite to our windows. I expected a shower of bullets any moment, and got between the windows. However, the firing ceased after a minute or two, and apparently no damage was done. It turned out to be a lorry coming down Denmark St. towards Parnell Sq., firing wildly. Why I cannot tell. You may note the official explanation in enclosed cutting,⁴⁰ in which it is stated the troops *did not* return the fire. They may not have *returned* the fire, but they fired previously with great vigour.

I am watching the English elections with great interest⁴¹—very much pleased, I confess, to see LG⁴² in such a tight corner. He is making a great fight, and if he succeeds in securing 50 or 60 followers, he may yet be master of the new Government.⁴³

You will be interested to hear that I got a letter from DV⁴⁴ on Monday in which he practically accepts (at last) my proposal, and I hope to settle the business within the next few days.⁴⁵

I wrote yesterday to Delargy* asking [him] to call, and just now, instead of Delargy, *Mrs* Delargy called (a *very* unattractive person) to tell me that her son had gone into the country for a week to recuperate. I fear I cannot take any step towards fixing the business up till he returns.

Brian did extremely well. He was 8th on the list, but the competition was very keen, the marks high and close together.

Write fully whenever you have time. Do not forget what I wrote you about Hayes'⁴⁶ suggestion about helping Pokorny* and the Bonn Professor.⁴⁷ Say nothing about this, but let me know your views as to how it could best be done. No letter from Theo yet, since he left London, but I hope to hear tonight.

8

[Myles to John Dillon] 19, Schaperstrasse, bei von Bolschwing, Berlin (W),
[no date]

I have now obtained rooms in Wilmersdorf, which is the Kensington of Berlin,⁴⁸ and my landlady is the Baronin von Bolschwing.⁴⁹ I shall be very comfortable

40 Not preserved, but a report of the incident which does state that "the National troops did not return the fire [...]" occurs in the *Evening Telegraph* of 3 November. 41 See above, Letter 5. 42 Lloyd George. 43 He did not achieve this. The Conservative Bonar Law won, with a majority of 80. 44 De Valera. 45 For the Mansion House Fund, see Introduction. 46 This appears to relate to Myles' request to his father to see about the possibility of Irish government support for German Celtic scholars. Michael Hayes* was at this time Ceann Comhairle of the Dáil. 47 Rudolf Thurneysen.* 48 An apt description. Wilmersdorf was (and still is) one of the most elegant districts of Berlin. The house Myles lodged in still stands and has retained its rather grand facade. 49 Little

there, but I have only taken the rooms for three weeks with an option of remaining longer, for it would suit me better to be nearer the University.[50]

I have told Maria in my letter of the luxurious living which our English money makes possible for us. All around where I live are splendid restaurants with music and excellent service, and all filled with those Germans who are still rich, and with foreigners. The former class are of course largely Jews, and it is really instructive to observe the noses at each table, hundreds of Hebrew Kriegsschieber feeding well while many are hungry. "Kriegsschieber" is the word here for war profiteer, and the only thing that casts a shade over one's bliss is that one feels a bit Kriegschieberish oneself. The war and after-war collapse has had a strange effect here, because it seems to have left many people very well off and quite well able to pay the huge sums of marks demanded, while others live on black bread and beer. War profiteers and business people and these sinister Jews have all flourished.

Another strange thing is that, while the nation is presumably poor, repairs are going on all over Berlin. Many are rebuilding and renovating their dwellings, and a new underground railway is being made under the Friedrichstrasse. Of course the actual cost of production must be small, but for a native exchequer it ought to be very heavy. I am not able to deal with that problem.[51] It is not impossible that Germany, knowing she is insolvent, goes ahead in the hope that the creditors will simply have to strike off enough to re-establish her. Thus, the more insolvent she now becomes, the more value she may ultimately get for nothing by default. And perhaps she is right.

I confess I am much impressed by the kindness and real charm of most of those whom I have met. There is no feeling against England. Indeed it is most notable how anxious everyone is to be able to speak English. Even the little pages in the hotel could talk a little. But the French are not to be mentioned. I saw three Frenchmen in the hotel trying to get some lunch, and no waiter would attend them.

I think I told you of my visit to Prof. Wilhelm Schulze, the great philologist.[52] He would be my best man here, but unfortunately he is not well and will

is known about Baronin Sophie von Bolschwing who appears to have been unmarried or widowed. But, according to Letter 12, she had had some contact with the Kaiser's family in happier times. **50** Berlin University which today houses the Humboldt University (one of Berlin's three universities) is located Unter den Linden in central Berlin while Wilmersdorf is a western district, a good 3-4 miles. away. **51** Myles here touches on an economic fact of some importance, and, despite his disclaimer, more or less hits the nail on the head. Indeed before the onset of hyper-inflation from the middle of 1923 onwards, Germany experienced almost an economic boom. There were quite a few who profited from inflation. This included the state itself because it could rid itself of any internal debts it had accumulated. German industry also profited; Hugo Stinnes, for example, built his huge industrial empire by cleverly playing the continuous depreciation of the mark. (See Kolb 1988 and Tormin 1973.) **52** Wilhelm Schulze (1863-1935) had been Professor of Indoeuropean Philology in Berlin since 1901. He was one of the foremost authorities on Tocharian, an Indo-European lan-

only lecture one hour a week. These lectures I shall attend.[53] He walked across the Tiergarten[54] with me and gave me some advice on my work, but as he could not speak a word of English much was lost.

I have so far attended two lectures in the University—one of elementary Sanskrit,[55] which was old ground, so I followed fairly well. Then last night I had an interesting experience. I went up to the University to look for the twentieth time at the notices, and saw that there would be a lecture by Prof. Hermann[56] on Gerhardt Hauptmann.[57] Not knowing who the latter person was, I resolved to attend. It was snowing outside and then five o'clock, so I waited and at six advanced to the Horsaal.[58] There I found a great crowd of students assembled of all races, sexes and ages—young boys and elderly women and men. The large hall was soon full to overflowing and many had to stand at each side. There must have been over 300 present. The lecture was *publice*, that is to say that all are welcome and it costs nothing. A pleasant youth was sitting beside me, and I at last summoned courage to ask him in German who was Gerhardt Hauptmann. I explained in excuse for such a question that I was Irish. He told me that he was a poet of the modern period, still living, and we had a brief conversation. Soon the professor appeared and was loudly applauded, and then commenced a passionate oration of which I only followed parts, but which was keenly enjoyed by the audience. Then he departed and we dispersed, but I admit I admired these people greatly, many of them really hungry, who came so eagerly to that lecture. How long will it be before the sons of Erin who matriculate in Earlsfort Terrace will flock enthusiastically to hear a lecture on a modern English or Irish poet?[59]

As regards money arrangements, one of the students here has told me of his method, which he strongly recommends, and he has been here a year. He lodges his studentship cheques with the Deutsche Bank in sterling and they forward them to London, and the money stands to his credit in English pounds. He then has an account in marks, and whenever he wants money he requests them to

guage which had been discovered in 1905. Together with E. Sieg and W. Siegling he wrote a descriptive grammar of this language. **53** These lectures were on Umbrian grammar. **54** The biggest park in central Berlin. **55** Introductory Sanskrit was taught by Dr Johannes Nobel (1887-1960), later Professor of Sanskrit at Marburg University (1928-55). **56** Max Herrmann (1865-1942), Professor of Theatre Studies in Berlin. During the winter semester of 1922/23 he gave a series of lectures providing an introduction to theatre studies (Einführung in das Studium der Theaterwissenschaft) which Myles Dillon attended. **57** Gerhart Hauptmann (1862-1946), one of most influential poets and playwrights in Germany in the first decades of the 20th century. He was the main exponent of naturalist drama, a style which incorporated a strong element of social criticism. *Die Weber* of 1892, *Vor Sonnenaufgang* (1889), *Die Ratten* (1911) and *Der Biberpelz* (1893) are his most enduring plays. *Hannele* (German original *Hanneles Himmelfahrt* of 1893) had been performed at the Abbey Theatre in Dublin in 1913. Myles was clearly unaware of this. **58** Hörsaal: "lecture hall". **59** Myles made this point again in his article in the *Irish Statesman* of 15 March 1924. See Appendix B.

sell one of his English pounds and credit the proceeds to his account in marks.[60] I will make further enquiry about this before doing anything, but it seems a very good plan. That will mean that I need not have the studentship cheques made payable to you. The document from the University has not reached me yet. However, it may have come to Kensington Square after I left, and I have not yet sent them my new address. This I shall do today or tomorrow.

I have not yet made any arrangements for lessons in German, but I intend to do so. I should prefer to get lessons from a student, because that would also enable me to become more quickly acquainted with the life of the University. I have written my Gesuche[61] and my Lebenslauf[62] and tomorrow my documents go to the Minister for Home Affairs. A fortnight later I shall be immatrikuliert,[63] but I shall start lectures tomorrow. Unfortunately Pokorny* has not yet come back. He is expected tomorrow, but now I hear he is ill in Prague. He speaks English fluently, so his assistance would have been valuable in these difficult initial operations. Moreover, I long for someone who will translate the notices to the students for me. I am sure I lose much useful information through being unable to understand them.

I have taken to drinking beer in huge glass mugs. It is good, but not so good as the wonderful Rhine wine, which costs only about seven pence a bottle.

9

[Maria O'Reilly to Myles] 7th Nov., 1922

My dearest Myles,

Today I saw your address on a letter on the hall table which your Father was sending you, so I seized the first opportunity of conveying my love and best wishes to you in Foreign Parts. I hope you like your change of country and living to your liking. How about your diet? Do you get food you like or have you to eat meat and all sorts of disagreeable things?[64]

Well, Jenny showed me your letter to her all about your pyjamas, which puzzled me greatly as I put in two in your trunk and you carried one in your bag. Perhaps in looking up your certificate you took them out and forgot to pack them again, leaving them in the Hotel. By the way, did you receive two parcels from me while staying at the Hotel in London? One was clean clothes and the other a hot water bag and a lovely pair of woollen socks, which I sent you thinking they would be very useful in case you still suffer with cold feet. I posted both parcels by letter post.

60 The reason for these elaborate arrangements, of course, was the current state of galloping inflation. In July 1922 one dollar equalled 550 marks, on 31 December 1922 it traded at 7500 marks (de Jonge 1978, p. 240). 61 "Applications". 62 "Curriculum vitae". 63 "Registered as a student". 64 There is no other indication that Dillon was a vegetarian; this may have been a passing phase.

What do you think of the Rink being burned to ashes?[65] We won't be allowed any stationary Post Office it seems now.

Your Father had a long letter from Theo. He said the Dr of the Institute[66] told him he will be all right in 2 months. Your Father has got a nasty cold, but he is wise and is taking care of himself. He was to have gone to Ballagh yesterday but postponed it.

With very best love from

Your loving and devoted Nurse,
M. O'Reilly.

10

[Myles to John Dillon] Friday, 10th Nov., '22

This morning I called at the Hotel for letters, and found a large post awaiting me, including a notice from the local post office that they had a registered letter for me. This proved to be the notice of my studentship from the University. There was also a letter from you which is the second I have received since I last wrote, so your letter (which came on Tuesday) must have escaped from the Rink before the fire.[67]

Professor Pokorny* has turned up and admitted me to his seminar, and as there are very few Celtic students here, that means that I have the room, with a very complete collection of Irish books, practically to myself as a sitting-room. I am writing this letter in the Seminar, as a matter of fact, and here I intend to do most of my work.

I am still in doubt about the money arrangement. Both your suggestion and the alternative I sent you in my last letter seem very good. Perhaps the best plan would be to lodge the money in sterling in the Deutsche Bank in London. I hear they get inquisitive and uneasy if you have too large an account in sterling here. The only reason for lodging it in a branch of the Deutsche Bank is that when they sell a pound for you in their own books I am told they give you the full Stock Exchange rate. However, the amount I have with me is so mighty a fortune here that we have plenty of time to decide. I have not spent nearly £5 since I arrived, and as the mark has fallen 100 per cent in the last fortnight English money dissolves very slowly.

I have met a most amiable person here who has asked to be remembered to you. He is living in Berlin and is Reuter's correspondent here. His name is

65 That is, the Rotunda Rink Post Office in Parnell Square. It had been raided by Republicans the previous Friday, but they were disturbed. They seem to have returned on Sunday morning, in revenge, and burned it to the ground, destroying a great deal of mail. 66 At Berck-Plage near Calais. 67 See Letter 9.

Maloney.[68] He has been five years in Persia, and some years in Egypt, and he told me that you were instrumental in having him made editor of an Egyptian nationalist propagandist paper published in English in Cairo. He is married here and has two children.

Last night the Free State emissary here[69] took me to a Russian theatre in Wilmersdorf—a most extraordinary show.[70] We all sat around tables in a café, and ate and drank during the show, which was given on a stage at one end of the room. The principal features were glittering colours and loud-throated choruses always repeating the same tune throughout each piece, and continuous movement. Everything was always going round, or swinging to and fro in rhythm with the music. The words were nearly always in Russian. We saw about ten of these musical tableaux, and drank a great deal of iced wine, and at half past twelve the show was over.

The feeling towards England here is interesting. Pokorny* tells me that it was much worse than against France during the war, but now it is quite the reverse. There seems to be a general respect for England, and even *because* she has actually defeated Germany. "Der Englander ist zähe," said one of the students to me. And when I asked a waiter in a café what that meant, he laughed and said it was quite true: *zähe,* he said, means *dauernd*—that is: "lasting", "enduring".[71] I had been pronouncing it *zehe*, which confused him, and he then explained that "Zehe" means the toe of a boot. Can Brian distinguish between those two sounds?[72]

I have not yet got into any settled way of working, but it is not easy to settle down at once. An unfortunate student here, who is cold and hungry, is to start lessons with me next week. He is a teacher in a private school in Berlin, and at the same time a student. He fought through the war and is about 27, but he looks under twenty, I suppose for want of food.

---

68 This was W.J. Maloney (1885-1968), the noted journalist. Born in Limerick, Maloney left Ireland for England, and joined Reuter's. He served as a Reuter's correspondent in many parts of the world, including the Middle East, in which capacity he had come into contact with John Dillon, one of whose interests this was. He was also a good friend of Osborn Bergin, Myles Dillon's teacher. Maloney ultimately went on to become Chairman of Reuter's, in 1937. 69 These were the last days in Berlin of the first envoy of the Irish Free State to Germany, John Chartres (1862-1927). He left Berlin on 4 December 1922 as a result of indiscretions by the Trade Commissioner at the Irish office, Charles Bewley (see Letter 92 and Introduction for further details). Bewley remained in Berlin until 1923. He returned to Berlin for a second stint as Irish envoy in the 1930s when he became notorious for his anti-Semitic views and his admiration for Hitler's Nazi Germany. 70 The Rapallo Treaty of April 1922 between Germany and Soviet Russia marked the beginning of normal diplomatic relations between both countries. This development had among other things a remarkable impact on the cultural life of Berlin: many Russian artists, especially of the avantgarde, came to Berlin and introduced the Berlin public to the best Russian and Soviet theatre and visual arts had to offer (cf. Köhler 1987, p. 882f). 71 The waiter probably said: *ausdauernd*; "dogged", "tenacious" would be better translations. 72 Myles unknowingly stumbles onto a characteristic phonetic feature of the Berlin dialect. The two sounds are indeed almost identical in Berlin. It is hardly surprising that Myles was somewhat confused.

The plight of the professors here is almost ridiculous, if it were not so very horrible in fact. Pokorny has got an increase of salary now to 30,000 marks a month, just less than £12 a year. Bergin* sent him £1 last week, and we went together and with the pound he bought a suit of clothes. Schultze,⁷³ the great philologist, has 60,000 marks a month on which to keep himself, his father, and his brother. I visited him and the place was absolutely cold, and he must have difficulty in getting food, and he is an old man and in bad health. A pound of butter costs 900 marks, but that will probably rise now that the mark has fallen.

It would be most desirable to help Thurneysen* and Pokorny,* and indeed they would be very unlikely to take offence at anything, because the conditions are so hard, and so obviously deserve to be remedied. However, two ways occur to me in these two cases. Pokorny is editor of the *Zeitschrift für celtische Philologie*, the great journal of Celtic Studies,⁷⁴ and it would be quite reasonable for Ireland to grant a salary to the editor and endow the *Zeitschrift*. A total expenditure in this direction of £50 would be munificence here, £100 would be stupendous, £200 would create a sensation. Remember that Pokorny's entire salary amounts to about £11 per annum. If the *Zeitschrift* could not only give a salary to its editor, but contribute to the expenses of German scholars (who are not a few) who write articles for it, it would be a great encouragement. However, this latter part of the scheme requires consideration. I do not know whether the *Zeitschrift* ever paid for work, and though precedents are no obstacle in this case, in the scramble for a living anything and everything might get into the journal. Bergin would be able to give an opinion on this, if Michael Hayes* thinks of doing something.

As regards Thurneysen,* he lately published a very important book which you will remember.⁷⁵ I got it unbound, and you afterwards saw bound copies in Hodges and Figgis. That book was published with a grant from Dáil Eireann, but it completes only half the work contemplated by Thurneysen. To do the rest he would have to come to Ireland to visit MSS., and in any case he can buy no books. Could not Thurneysen's work be endowed by the Irish government, his expenses to Ireland paid, if he would come, all the books he requires be provided for him, and it would be possible and profitable for him to go on with his Celtic work (and it would be most delightful for me to go then to Bonn, and perhaps assist him).⁷⁶

I will be interested to hear what you think of this, and whether there is any hope of anything being done. The sale of the motor car of any one of the brigadiers of the National Army would keep both Thurneysen and Pokorny* in

73 See Letter 8. 74 Pokorny had taken over as editor from Kuno Meyer after Meyer's death in 1919. The latter had founded the journal together with Ludwig Christian Stern in 1897. 75 Thurneysen's *Die irische Helden- und Königsage bis zum siebzehnten Jahrhundert* (Halle/Saale 1921) was published with financial support from Dáil Éireann. 76 A streak of enlightened self-interest manifests itself here!

comfort for years. Anyone who has an English pound to spare should send it out to someone here. It means a huge sum in Berlin, and one has the feeling that about half the people are hungry. It is strange to see real poverty amid all the circumstances of wealth. Splendid houses of flats, with plate-glass windows and thick red carpets, and many people inside trying to conceal the fact that they have not enough to eat. And of course these people cannot get into tenements, or change their way of life fundamentally. They just cling on, and one wonders how they do it.

Please tell Maria I got her letter. She will have got mine by now. When I start working my letters will be fewer. I am a slow scribe, and rather long-winded at this distance.

Let me know what you think wise about the money business. Maloney tells me he has these guaranteed cheques on a London bank and that it works very well. I am sending the form to the University signed with my Dublin address, for the present. This is non-committal, and in any case I may be leaving the Baroness next month, and George's Street will always know my address.

[PS] You might let me have Theo's address, when you write, please. Many thanks for the cuttings. I shall always be glad of them, whenever any new misery befalls the country. I do not hope for good news.

What about Delargy?* Is he still of a mind to come out here?

11

[Nano Dillon to Myles] Friday, [10 November 1922]

Dear Milo,

I should have answered your letter long ago, but as a flow of letters from Maria and Father seemed to be going in your direction I thought I had better wait and fill a gap.

You are a lucky wretch to be out of this dear country. It's fifty times worse now than ever before. Every night we have battles and by day now it has become the fashion to have regular battles as well as the favourite ambush.

I was dancing at the Metropole last Saturday and had only just got in when a fierce fusillade broke out in O'Connell St. My unfortunate escort returning in his car must have stepped right into it.

Shawn is reported to have had an amusing adventure a few days ago, while piloting his clerics down Grafton St. (they had been over in the University Church). Maud Gonne[77] and others, who were processing down the street with

---

[77] Maud Gonne McBride (1866-1953). She opposed the Treaty, and in 1922 organized the Women Prisoners' Defence League, based at Roebuck House, on the outskirts of Dublin.

banners about Mary MacSwiney,[78] stopped him and delivered a long harangue on priests and clerics in general, and said there were far too many in Ireland, etc., etc., so when she paused for breath, Shawn said to her, "Madam, a day may come when you will wish for a priest and will not be able to have one"— and then stalked on. This tale was told Father last night by Dr Coffey.* I haven't seen Shawn since, so it may of course be wholly untrue.

I was out with Jack Yeats' sisters[79] in Dundrum at a large reception given in honour of W.B.Yeats, who arrived looking very splendid and regal. There were about 60 people there, including Con Curran* and wife, who enquired for you.

Bills are flying in here from every side and Father is paying them all like anything, saying to me with great relish, "There will be nothing left, as far as I can see, out of your next two or three months' allowances."

John Gerald was with us for dinner a few nights ago, and ate largely and well.

Father and Maria are stricken with colds—particularly Maria—and I spend my time standing several feet away from them for fear of catching germs.

I met my admirer N. Reddin* at a dance a few nights ago and he enquired most warmly for you. I didn't know you knew him much, but he appeared to think you did.

Farewell.

Yours with love,
Nano.

12

[Myles to John Dillon] Tuesday, 14th Nov., '22

I am gradually getting into a way of life here, but the difficulty of getting books and of learning what books one should get, when everything is said and done in German, makes things rather slow. I recall Mrs Scott Baker's complaint about the misfortune of being cut off from one's fellow men by a foreign language. I long to know and converse with everyone here, and I do embark on intercourse with them, but it is misery to be left in the dark as to what they mean. The professor of Comparative Philology is a well-known scholar and a charming man.[80] He is director of the Indo-Germanic Seminar here, and as such I had an interview with him again this morning. He went through the Verzeichniss with me and gave advice as to what lectures I should attend, but indeed much of what he said in comment was lost on me. I will send you a copy of the Verzeichniss, which is a catalogue of the lectures.

Tomorrow the German courses for foreigners commence here, and these I shall attend in addition to private teaching. All Ausländer go to these courses,

78 She had been arrested on 4 November, and was on hunger strike in Mountjoy Gaol. 79 That is, Susan Mary (Lily) and Elizabeth (Lolly). 80 Wilhelm Schulze, see Letter 8.

and there is an examination in German in connection with them. I had the pleasure of helping a little Chinese youth out of his difficulties the other day. He spoke English, though he had never been in England, but not a word of German. He told me English is used as a medium for teaching all subjects in the Chinese schools, and he spoke with an American accent, as his master was an American. I am looking forward to these lectures for foreigners, because there one will meet all these Greeks, Turks, Bulgarians, Russians, Chinese, Japanese, Americans and others. I have seen a number of Russian and Greek girls here too.

Grandmother very kindly sends me the *Times Supplement*, and in it I see the announcement of an article in the November number of the *Contemporary Review* on Gerhardt Hauptmann,[81] who is the subject of a course of lectures I am attending here.[82] He is a great subject of discussion and interest here at present, and his plays are often produced. One journal is producing a special Hauptmann number shortly. If you have that number of the *Contemporary* to spare I would be glad to have it. It will make the lectures more intelligible.

I saw *Tannhäuser* wonderfully played here on Sunday night at the Staatsopernhaus. A splendid orchestra and splendid singers. The theatre was packed, so there are rich people in Berlin too. As a matter of fact, the only people who are really badly hit by present conditions are those who have fixed incomes, like my baroness and university professors and teachers, whose salaries have not risen proportionately. Business people, and also to a great extent the working people, are better off, but I happen to meet the two classes who have most suffered. The baroness was acquainted with the Kaiser (and also with his bride), and all his circle, and was invited to the royal festivities, but she told me she has now tasted no meat for three months. She lives on vegetables, and cannot even afford any milk. I am taking her to *Aida* next Sunday, and I hope to have a good dinner somewhere beforehand; but I shall leave here as soon as I can get somewhere nearer town. I do not much like the baroness, and I could do no work in her flat.

Please tell Nano I got her letter yesterday.

I have now got my own key for the Seminar, so for the moment I am still enjoying my new dignity.

Do not forget about the *Review*. I shall be glad to hear of anyone who is coming to Berlin. What about Tommy Lundon?[83]

There is some sort of political crisis on here at present between the People's Party and the Social Democrats,[84] but that is all I can gather from the *Tageblatt*.

---

81 The article in question was by A.W.G. Randall (*Contemporary Review*, Nov. 1922, pp. 637-44). Randall was not overly impressed with Hauptmann and judged that "superficiality and imitation are writ large over a great proportion of Hauptmann's work [...]". 82 These must have been the lectures given by Prof. Max Herrmann entitled "Einführung in das Studium der Theaterwissenschaft" (An introduction into theatre studies). 83 William Thomas Lundon, former Irish Parliamentary Party M.P. for East Limerick. 84 The Social Democrats were refusing to enter a grand coalition

The details involve words which I cannot understand. However, today I bought a dictionary for 3,250 marks, so I am progressing.

13

[Maria O'Reilly to Myles] 2 Nth. Gt. George's St., [Dublin], [Wednesday], 15th Nov. 1922

I was very glad to get your letter acknowledging your mistake about your sleeping suit. I trust you are not feeling lonely for the old familiar faces, but perhaps the new ones have for the present more variety. I have not got over the missing stage of your dear self and my loving Theo, and to make things more depressive I have now developed a nasty bronchitis cold which is so distasteful to Nano she forbids me to cough in her presence. Your Father's cold is much better but he still takes his breakfast in bed. He went to a lunch in the Shelbourne to see Dr Cox's[85] honours bestowed on him. He [i.e. Cox] was presented with a magnificent chalice of old silver.

I sent on your letter to Theo, as he asked me to do so. I dare say you have got news of him since I sent him a warm jersey and a rug. I dare say he requires very warm clothing as he has to remain lying on a movable couch all the time. It must be very trying on him, but please God he will get cured soon, and then have plenty of exercise.

Everything is going on as usual. Plenty of ambushes and no sign of peace that I can see. Did you hear of the young Dr Power from Vincent's shot dead while he was attacking Pres. Mulcahy's house.[86] Things are about the same in Ballagh. I had a letter from Sarah. The P.O. there was robbed on Saturday last and Kilfree Station burned down. Brian has not returned from Gorey yet. I had a line from him this morning saying he may not come back till Saturday with his Reverence.[87] Shawn has just paid us a visit. He is ordering a clerical suit at Clery's. He is in great form.

I think I have no more news, only Nan[88] came in for your address yesterday.

with the Deutsche Volkspartei and other right-wing parties under Chancellor Cuno due to profound ideological differences (*BT*, 14 November 1922). 85 Dr Michael Cox (1852-1926), distinguished physician, an old political and personal friend of John Dillon's (they had graduated in medicine together from the Catholic University School of Medicine in Cecilia St. in 1875), and for many years the Dillon family doctor. In 1911 he was appointed to the Irish Privy Council, but resigned in 1920 in protest against the activities of the Black and Tans. He had now just been elected President of the Royal College of Physicians in Ireland, and this lunch has presumably something to do with this. 86 She is confused here. General Richard Mulcahy was Minister for Defence. His home, Lissenfield House in Rathmines, was attacked on 2 November 1922. The 22-year-old medical student Francis Power was killed during the attack. 87 That is, Dom John Francis Sweetman,* headmaster of Mount St. Benedict in Gorey, Co. Wexford, and one of Ireland's more controversial educators. All the Dillon boys except Shawn (who had gone to Downside School in Somerset) had been sent to his school. 88 Unidentified.

14

[Osborn Bergin* to Myles] 61 Leinster Road, Dublin, 16. 11. 1922

My dear Dillon,

I was delighted to get your letter, and should have answered it before this but that I have had some unpleasant distractions, one of which kept me away from U.C.D. for 2 weeks. However, I am able to hobble around again this week, tho' feeling very languid.

Your own advice to yourself is very good, viz. that you should give most of your attention to German. Fr Boylan's* plan was excellent. He attended lectures all day for some weeks, which meant 7 or 8 hours free tuition every day, and thus got a grip of German which he has never lost. But until you are able to read German, this wd. not be much good. So do what you can with Irish and Sanskrit and a couple of other things. As soon as your vocabulary is in working order you could look in at anything interesting in the way of public lectures. If you were at a *pension* you could pick up any amount at meals—but no, perhaps the fare would be too much like the Barmecides' feast to stimulate conversation. If there is a lecture even on *An Tarbh Breac*, you could learn German at it. And apart from the University you will have endless chances of learning.

About Sanskrit, I imagine you will find Kâlidâsa[89] rather stiff. Your case will be like that of a German coming here, understanding very little English, starting Irish in one class, and in another following a course on Tadhg óg O Huiginn. However, I have two editions of the *Meghadûta*, one by Wilson, with verse translation and notes, and a voc. by Johnson (3rd edition, London, 1867), the other published by the Nirnaya-sâgara Press (Bombay), with commentary in Sanskrit, and English notes. If you are matriculated you shd. be able to able to borrow one or both from the Univ. Library, or the Königliche Bibliothek, or if this is impossible, I shd. be glad to lend you one. And in one library or other you would have access to Monier Williams' large Sanskrit-English Dictionary.

But here I am giving you advice, when you are in the head centre of Wissenschaft, and I am hundreds of miles away, and years behind the times. If you aren't able to teach me in a couple of years I shall be surprised. Still, you asked for it.

I haven't seen Delargy* for some weeks. He went to Belfast for a change. The following is from a notice of today's Academic Council:

---

89 The chief figure of the second period of Sanskrit literature (late 4th cent. AD). His fame rests mainly on his three plays, of which the most famous is *Sakuntalâ*, but he is also distinguished as an epic and a lyric poet. The *Meghadûta*, or *Cloud Messenger*, is his most famous lyric poem, and describes the complaint of an exiled lover, and the message he sends to his wife by a cloud. It is full of deep feeling, and abounds in fine descriptions of the beauties of nature.

AGENDA

Temporary Assistant in Irish. Professor Douglas Hyde proposes that Mr Delargy, B.A., be recommended for the Winter Session, as additional work is now arising.

The other day I met Miss Wulff* and told her you were going to read the *Meghadûta*, which is ever so much harder than the Nala. This provoked her to emulation—as wb. might have said *ét lee buith duitsin oc foglaim*,[90] and she wanted to start some Sk. text at once. However I have put her off for a week or two.

Mit herzlichen Grüssen,
Ihr
Osborn Bergin.

P.S. I don't think I was ever in your fashionable quarter. Always lodged in Steinmetzstrasse 10, near Potsdamerstrasse.

15

[John Dillon to Myles] Saturday, 18 November, 1922

Your letter of Tuesday last arrived this morning. It was most welcome, as I had not heard from you for many days. I am very much interested by your account of your adventures, your method of life, and the extraordinary variety of people you have met. By the way, I should say that I duly received your previous long letter, undated, and read it with much interest. How strange that you should meet Maloney! I had not heard of him for many years, and did not know whether he was still alive. The last I heard of him he was in Teheran. Remember me to him when next you meet him.

I was very much amused by your adventures in regard to Gerhart Hauptmann. He is a very fine German contemporary writer. I have never read any of his writings, but I had read a great deal about him.

I have the *Review*, and I shall send it to you as soon as I have finished a couple of articles for which I bought it.[91]

Now about money—I am not in favour of the Deutsche Bank plan, because if there were a real crash in Germany the Deutsche Bank would in all probability suspend payment. [...]

I should say I also received in due course your letter of Friday, 10 Nov., with details about Pokorny,* Thurneysen,* etc. I shall try to see Hayes next

90 This is an adaptation of a phrase in the Würzburg Glosses, and may be translated "Desire came upon her to learn along with you." 91 The November issue also contained an article on "The German Socialists" which would have been of interest to John Dillon.

week. He has been presiding at the Dail this week. I hope I may be able to arrange to have something done to help Pokorny and Thurneysen, but that is all that one can hope for. The Free State Government is on the rocks financially, and I am afraid it is rather rapidly losing ground in the country. My accounts are very bad. Indiscipline and drunkenness prevails largely in the Army, and the people are losing all confidence in the power of the Government to restore order, or protect life or property. Robbery and murder are rampant. Last week 40 prisoners who were in Longford Gaol walked out accompanied by their guards with rifles, etc., etc., and departed into the country to join the Republicans. The newspapers, of course, have not been allowed to publish this incident[92].

Yesterday we were all shocked by a curt announcement in the evening paper that 4 men had been executed at 7 o'c. yesterday morning.[93] The trials must have [been] conducted in strict secrecy, as there had been no hint of a trial till the official announcement of the executions. This is going beyond anything done by the British Government. I send you enclosed a cutting giving the debate in Dáil on the executions. None of the newspapers, of course, dare to comment. I expect a furious campaign of reprisal assassinations will now commence.

I find I was wrong in saying that none of the Irish newpapers dared to comment. The *Independent* does comment mildly.[94] For the last ten days the *Independent* has been hedging cautiously, trying to make friends with the Republicans.

Sunday 19.

The *Evening Telegraph*, you will see, summoned up courage last night to comment on the executions, but it is careful to leave it doubtful whether it approves or disapproves.[95]

There were rumours yesterday that some striking coup on the part of the Republicans would come off last night, and you will see from the enclosed cutting from this morning's *Independent*[96] that they did attempt a large slaughter of Government troops, but with hideously disastrous results to themselves. I have no doubt we are in for a lively week.

92 This is an extrordinary story and indeed there is no mention of it in the Irish dailies which makes it difficult to verify. 93 This refers to the executions of four prisoners in Mountjoy, James Fisher, Peter Cassidy, Richard Twohig, and James Gaffney. 94 In its leader, the paper says: "Writing as strong supporters of the Treaty, deeply anxious for the restoration or order, peace and stable conditions, we have the gravest misgivings as to the wisdom of inflicting the supreme penalty for the offences as disclosed." This seems reasonably firm. 95 The *Evening Telegraph* commented: "We have all the instinctive dislike of a long-subject people to government imposed by forceful measures. Its methods are sentimentally unpopular, even if our reason and logic are sometimes compelled to sanction them" (18 November 1922). 96 The *Independent* of 20 November 1922 contained a report with graphic details of an explosion which blew four men to pieces while they were trying to deposit a mine outside the Free State army barracks on the Naas Road just outside Inchicore. One of the men accidentally triggered the mine with horrific results.

This is a horrid chill rainy day here. I wonder what kind of weather you are experiencing in Berlin. Write soon again and give me full details of your studies and of the people you meet. These details interest me very much. When you have arranged for new quarters, do not fail to send on the new address immediately.

16

[Theo Dillon to Myles] Pas de Calais, Institut Francois de Sales. Sunday,
[19 November 1922]

Dear Myles,

It is quite true that I have plenty of time to write, but unfortunately damned little to write about. I think I mentioned in my last letter that our only amusement was the Sunday cinema, for which I am religiously setting out in ½ hr. Very dull it is, but one goes as a matter of course; otherwise, even I, with my well-known leaning to the film, would not face it.

I should think by the time this letter reaches you you will find the language difficulty melting away. last week it started melting in my case; and now I can face the world in French, guaranteed as to quantity, though of doubtful quality.

The Maloney[97] man had, I think, some connection with Scawen Blunt.[98] I seem to remember his being mentioned in the diaries. He should be an interesting kind of acquaintance.

I got a letter from Brian, which I enclose.[99] You heard of course the news of Ralph [Barry]'s* success—3rd in the Brook, and 2nd in the Mod., with a Senior Mod. and Gold Medal.

You will have seen by this time the success of Charles.[100] It pleases me extremely, more particularly because of the critical atmosphere in Cornwall Gardens with regard to the expense of the election.

You may tell Harold Quinlan,* if he enquires, that he is not likely to see me in Germany for the best part of a year. I should think I shall be stuck here for 5 months at least. It is not that I am any worse than I supposed, but that Calot thinks—and thinks rightly—that convalescence is the most important, and that one should continue treatment for some months after any symptoms have dis-

97 See Letter 10. 98 Wilfrid Scawen Blunt (1840-1922), English poet and publicist, and supporter of unpopular causes, including that of Irish Home Rule, which brought him into contact over many years with John Dillon. He involved himself in the Plan of Campaign, and was actually imprisoned in Kilmainham Gaol for two months in 1887 for agitation on the Clanricarde estate. Another of his interests was the Middle East, where he violently opposed British imperialist policy, and this would have brought him into contact with Maloney. 99 Letter 16A. 100 That is, in the recent British General Election (see Letter 5). The family lived in Cornwall Gardens.

appeared. I think it an excellent idea that you should move into his pension. You will find him a very charming, easy-going person.

Do you see any Irish news? In case you do not, I may tell you that they have shot 4 men on Friday last for the possession of loaded revolvers; and that Childers, who was arrested some time ago, is on secret courtmartial, it is believed, in danger of the death sentence.[101] All this, of course, under the powers which the Dáil gave them some two months ago.

Mary McSwiney, as you no doubt have see, is still hunger-striking.[102] If all this is stale, you will excuse a well-intentioned effort.

Theo.

16A

(Enclosed in 16)

[Brian to Theo Dillon] [2 North Great George's St., Dublin, Friday], 17. 11. '22

Dear Theo,

Your letter awaited me yesterday on my return from the Mount. Your needs need consideration and possibly consultation. I will send books as soon as possible. Myles writes from Berlin the most encouraging reports of life there. George[103] and I have planned to visit him there at Christmas or Easter. I fear the matter will go no further.

The tale of my "all but arrest" is a poor one. I was walking up Earlsfort Terrace with young O'Rahilly[104] and Dermot[105] when a lorry, seeing us, pulled up and called on us to halt. We did so and they recognized O'Rahilly and arrested him. One of the soldiers recognized me and said he would vouch for me. They were very desirous of taking Dermot, but we finally induced them to refrain. The lorry then bore away O'Rahilly to Beggars Bush.[106] Meeting an officer there, he burst into tears, and the officer was so moved that he at once ordered him to be released.

You will be touched to hear that Kane Smith[107] expresses a great desire for your medical advice. He asked me what was your fee. I promised him free advice

---

101 The first item repeats what has already been reported by his father, in Letter 15; the latter rumour, of course, turned out to be true. 102 Mary MacSwiney, sister of Terence. Her hunger strike lasted from 4 to 28 November, when she was released. Her sister Annie had also been on hunger strike outside Mountjoy since 17 November. See also Letter 19. 103 George Kenny, a school friend. This visit never came off. 104 Presumably Raghnall O'Rahilly, son of The O'Rahilly, a school friend. See Letter 23 below. 105 Dermot Murphy, also a school friend from Mount St. Benedict. 106 The army barracks. 107 Another school friend who, as we hear in a later letter, spent a while in Downside, Somerset in order to become a priest. See Letter 118. 108 Francis Joseph Lavery (1899-1993), educated at Mount St. Benedict and U.C.D. where he studied medi-

on your return. He is said to have a weak heart, but Frank[108] denies it absolutely.

We brought down an Old Boys team last Sunday. Jack Peart[109] was there. Some of us stayed for a couple of days, but the intimacy which sprang up between Pat, Bill Sweetman,[110] Dermot Murphy and Miss Power (an Irish teacher, aged about 24) was so strongly disapproved of by His Reverence that the visit was a little troubled. They left on the Tuesday. No mention of the affair was made to them, but John Sweetman[111] was requested by His Reverence to speak about it. George is in great contentment down there. I imagine he will stay a couple of years. He tells me that he is greatly relieved by the absence of all financial worry. Massey is now living there, and enquired tenderly for you and Myles. Lonan,[112] as you probably heard, went back and intends to stay out the year. He is now a prefect and is in partnership with George. Ralph [Barry*] has one case, I am told.

There are now 40 boys and 9 teachers in the Mount.

We were unable to discover whether the Captain Joyce of the Clifden battle was the man you know or not. Did you hear of Nevin Jackson's death? He was shot by Free State troops as he was driving in a motor car. They called on him to put out the headlights. He did not hear, and they shot him dead.

Malachi[113] leaves for America tonight. I do not know whether he intends to return at all, but certainly not for some years. Things are a good deal more so in Dublin and elsewhere. It is commonly held that the end is near.[114]

Brian.

I will send the books as soon as possible.

17

[Toby Mathew[115] to Myles] Minden i. W., Wilhelmstrasse 1, 20. 11. 22.

My dear Myles,

Many thanks for your letter. Correspondence is apt to be difficult between those who are virtually unknown to one another, so I hasten, at all events partially, to reveal myself.

cine. In 1928, he started a practice in ophthalmology in Dublin. Montgomery Lecturer in Trinity College in 1930, from 1943 to 1971 Professor of Ophthalmology in U.C.D. and consultant ophthalm. surgeon in Jervis St. Hospital and the Royal Victoria Eye and Ear Hospital. 109 John Peart, a school friend from Mount St. Benedict. He later joined the Indian Army, and rose to the rank of Colonel before retiring back to Ireland in 1948 after Indian independence. 110 William Sweetman, son of John Sweetman, M.P., journalist. From 1937 to 1951 he was editor of the *Irish Press*. He left this position to become a District Judge. 111 Another son of John Sweetman of Drumbaragh, M.P. 112 Lonan Murphy, brother of Gerard Murphy,* and later a solicitor in Clones, Co. Monaghan. 113 Malachi Sweetman, also a school friend. A relation of Fr Sweetman's, he had Republican sympathies. His father, John Sweetman, arranged for him to go to America at this time. 114 Sc. of the Free State regime. A further example of wishful thinking. 115 He was in Minden,

First with regard to Christmas. My hosts will be delighted to see you here. Accommodation is somewhat limited, but if you do not object to sharing a very large bedroom with me there is no difficulty in this respect.

I myself am emigrating to Berlin in January. My purpose is to write an "Arnold" essay[116] upon the somewhat depressing theme "Victor Amadeus II of Savoy." I may possibly attend some lectures, but I, personally, have always found that they are a most unsatisfactory form of intellectual food. My hostess here is under the necessity of going to Berlin, so I am leaving her to make all necessary arrangements.

You will have no doubt heard by now that Uncle Charles was successful in his election[117]—a majority of 700 or so. I cannot say that I found the election news sensational. One was prepared for the defeats of Lloyd Georgians all over the country. Personally I thought that the Asquith-Grey Liberals could not hope to do better than they have done. Fighting with a divided party on two fronts is tough work. I was glad to see that John Simon[118] had won Spen Valley against Labour and Tory candidates. I helped him there in a bye-election in 1919.

I am extraordinarily glad that Asquith scraped home. Men of his calibre cannot be replaced—I am afraid that I cannot always think of a politician in terms of Ireland. I need hardly say that the fate of such as Greenwood fills me with delight.[119]

With regard to your diagnosis of the political situation, I think that you may have misunderstood my references to Bolshevism. Of course there is no question of a Communist government being formed. The way of the Proletarian Revolution is not, and never was, by the path of constitutional government. But it is conceivable that, if the allied insanity with regard to Reparations continues, you will have universal collapse in Germany. Owing to the continued fall of the mark, factories are finding it impossible to purchase raw materials abroad. This,

---

staying with a family, to study German. 116 An Oxford literary prize. 117 He was elected to parliament as Labour M.P. for Whitechapel and St. George's (see Letter 5), but sadly died shortly afterwards. 118 Sir John Allesbrook Simon (1873-1954), British politician and lawyer. After a distinguished career at Oxford, where he became President of the Union, and subsequently a Fellow of All Souls, he was called to the Bar in 1899, and took silk in 1908. He went into politics, and was elected as a Liberal for Walthamstow in 1906. Made Solicitor-General by Asquith in 1910, and was knighted the same year. Was a member of the wartime coalition government, but declined the offer of the Lord Chancellorship in 1915, preferring to remain in the Commons, and took the post of Home Secretary instead. Next year, however, he resigned on the issue on conscription, and resumed his practice as a barrister. On the split between Asquith and Lloyd George, he sided with the former. Lost his seat in the election of 1918, but was returned for Spen Valley in 1922. 119 Sir Hamar Greenwood (1870-1948) was defeated in the general election of November 1922. Between 1920 and 1922 Greenwood was the last Chief Secretary for Ireland. He was responsible for sending the Black and Tans to Ireland and defended their actions in the British House of Commons where he stated categorically: "I have yet to find one authenticated case of a member of this Auxiliary Division being accused of anything but the highest conduct characteristic of them."

of course, entails that a large number of factories must close down, and a large number of workmen be thrown out of employment. There is no money to adopt a policy of doles. You will therefore get hunger riots on a large scale. The military and police are inadequate to suppress an outburst of disorder on a large scale, and so, your Bolshevist may get his opportunity.[120] I only hope that the Hambourg and Amerika man[121] succeeds in forming a strong government. Financial sanity can only be gained through the medium of the Volkspartei.[122] Such pronouncements as Poincaré's last speech[123] fill one, however, with despair.

Of course the truth of the matter is that the French politicians are terrified publicly to say what privately they know to be true, namely that for a period of years Germany cannot pay a cent.

The lot of the middle classes today is pitiable. I know of two old ladies whose yearly income is 10,000 marks.[124] This case can be indefinitely multiplied.

I am leaving here for ten days or so on Nov. 28th. My address will be: bei Herrn Hauptmann von Campe, Carlshaven a.d. Weser.

With love,
Toby.

18

[Myles to John Dillon] Berlin W15, Schaperstrasse 19, Friday, 24. xi. '22

Your letter was most welcome. I was beginning to feel restless at the interval in correspondence from Dublin. Berlin is so far distant, and so much can happen in my native city that it is easy to feel alarmed. I was most grateful for the cuttings you enclosed. I hardly ever hear a word about Ireland here, and have not seen an Irish paper since I left Dublin. The English papers are on sale here, but I avoid them for the sake of German, and they have no Irish news. Moreover, their price in marks sounds so absurd. The *Times* costs 380 marks, the *Daily News* 260. However, Kathleen very kindly sends me a paper if there is any special interest. I only heard of Uncle Charles' success from Toby Mathew, who wrote to me from Minden.[125]

---

120 He was right about some of this, but wrong about the inability of the military, if not the police, to repress left-wing unrest. 121 On 16 November 1922, President Ebert had asked Wilhelm Cuno, director of the Hamburg-Amerika-Linie shipping company, non-party, to form a government. 122 This shows Toby Mathew's conservative leanings. 123 Poincaré demanded a tougher line towards Germany. He said that if Germany was unable to pay in terms of money it should pay by means of labour and goods (*BT* 18 November 1922). 124 The equivalent of seven shillings. The dismal economic situation and its impact on research and scholarship is highlighted by an article in the *Berliner Tageblatt* of 16 November in which the Centre Party deputy Dr Schreiber pointed out that due to the galloping inflation, the purchase of a single English publication would at present swallow up half the budget of an ordinary library. 125 See Letter 17.

Deutsches Institut für Ausländer
an der Universität Berlin

Herr *Myles Dillon*

aus *Ireland*

hat in der Prüfung am *24. Nov. 22* nachgewiesen, daß er ausreichende Kenntnisse in der deutschen Sprache besitzt, um den Vorlesungen an einer deutschen Hochschule mit Verständnis folgen zu können.

Berlin, den *25. November 22*.

Certificate from the German Institute for Foreigners of the University of Berlin stating that Myles had sufficient German to follow the lectures.

I have just now finished my examination in German for matriculation, and I believe with success. However, that is only a guess. If I am adjudged unfit, I cannot matriculate until next Semester. But as my disqualification would be not academic but only a matter of German, I could attend lectures as a Gastzuhörer,[126] and would get credit for my attendance. So it would really make no difference, except as regards my status here this Semester.

I am still rather locked out from the familiarity of my fellow-students by being unable to speak their language fluently, but this I hope will not last long. There is a swimming club here which I hope to join, and I am also arranging to join a Vincent de Paul Conference.

Maloney was greatly pleased with your message. He is a most charming person, and my only source of news here. I am going to dine with him some night this week or next week.

126 *Gasthörer*: "guest auditor".

Theo wrote to me enclosing a most interesting missive from Brian which I was very glad to get, with news of the Mount[127] and of Dublin too. I hope he will be inspired to communicate with me at his leisure, and I beg that he send me the Homer as soon as convenient.

The only things which are almost dear here are books. There are fascinating bookshops, but if they perceive you are an Auslander, some are inclined to multiply prices. One publisher will only accept the sterling of the country you come from. however, a friendly German student is dealing with him for me, which is a solution of our difference.

I have started the course in German provided by the University for foreign students, and as it includes three lectures a week of two hours each, that will be the chief feature of my work for the present. I am taking courses here in Sanskrit, Umbrian Grammar, Gothic, and Homeric Greek, in addition to lectures on Irish.[128] However, I cannot really do much till I know more German. I attend the lectures and try to read the textbooks, and will continue to do so, but at first it seems a rather fruitless proceeding.

I believe there will be about three weeks or less at Christmas, and I am thinking of going into the mountains for sports with some other Dubliners here. Oberharz, in the Harz Mountains, which are not very far from here, has been suggested. It would not be worth while going to Ireland, unless some special reason appears before then. The longer vacation comes at the end of the Semester, in March, when there is over a month's holiday.

Pokorny* has offered me some collected material left by Kuno Meyer[129] to edit while I am here. This would be a most pleasing work to be allowed to do, but I doubt whether it might not prove a rash venture. However, I shall work under direction, and refuse to publish anything unfit for publication.

I enclose my signature in accordance with your advice. I dare say that is the best arrangement.

Many thanks for your promise of the *Review*.

I am always anxious to hear whether everyone is still alive, and how the Republic stands. Brian spoke of Malachi Sweetman[130] going to America. Is this a flight before the anger of the Free State? What is happening to Childers?[131]

---

127 That is, Mount St. Benedict, where Dillon had been at school. 128 Apart from Pokorny, Wilhelm Schulze and Johannes Nobel his teachers were Gustav Roethe (1859-1926), Professor of German and Felix Hartmann, Professor of Ancient Classics. 129 (1858-1919). Great German Celtic scholar, who had devoted himself to the study of ancient Irish language and culture. In 1903 he had founded the School of Irish Learning in Dublin, and the journal *Ériu* in 1904. In 1911 he was appointed to the chair of Celtic in the University of Berlin, a position which he held until his death. Pokorny succeeded Meyer as Professor of Celtic. What the material Myles mentioned was is not clear, since the project appears to have come to nothing. 130 See Letter 16A. 131 Erskine Childers was captured on 10 November at his cousin Robert Barton's house in Annamoe, Co. Wicklow, with a small revolver in his possession. On foot of this technical offence, he was executed on 24 November. See John Dillon's letter 19 below.

I will be interested to hear whether the imprudent young lady at the Mount is the lady whom I was asked to interview, or not.[132]

[PS] Maria's letter arrived on Saturday or Sunday, but I had written to her some days before. My letter should have been in Dublin on Monday.

Another service the Free State might do for Celtic Studies here is to make a grant for books. Our students in Bonn are always in difficulty because there is no Celtic Library in Bonn, and Thurneysen* has to lend his own books. But of course he can buy nothing now. The library here is very good, but of course some things are missing, and here in Germany these books, most of which are German, could be bought for next to nothing by Germans.

19

[John Dillon to Myles] Sat. 25 November, 1922

My dear Myles,

Enclosed are (I) Letter from University with cheque for £50. Please write your name on back of cheque and send it to me. [...]

Enclosed is also a threatening notice from Falconer.[133] It came this morning. How does the matter stand? Also some notices from the Belvedere Union.[134]

Your letters have been very interesting, and very pleasant, and I hope soon to receive another. I expect you are getting quite at home in the German tongue by this time. Are you able to follow the lectures? I shall send the *Contemporary* in a day or two. There are 3 or 4 very interesting articles I want to read and I have not yet finished them.

We are having a devil of a time here, as you will gather from the cuttings enclosed.[135] Thursday night was one of the worst since the battles of June. The firing went on furiously for two hours, and it extended to all parts of the city. When the firing commenced, Nano was at a Cinderella at Leggett Byrne,[136]

132 That is, Miss Power (see Letter 16A above). No doubt, the Miss Power Myles interviewed in Berlin was Dr Nancy Wyse-Power (1889-1963), John Chartres' assistant (see Introduction). The two women are definitely not identical, since Nancy Power was almost ten years older than the Irish teacher mentioned in Letter 17. Nancy Power had by now returned to Ireland and had been transferred to the Dept. of Industry and Commerce (Murphy 1995, p. 149). She remained in the civil service until 1954 and retired as principal officer, one of the first women to reach this rank. She was always particularly interested in the rights of women in the civil service. 133 This was in connection with *An Reult*, the journal of the U.C.D. student Gaelic Society, of which Falconer was the publisher. See letter 24 below. 134 Dillon had attended Belvedere, before going to Mount St. Benedict. 135 These do not survive, but there is a report of the incident in the *Independent* for 24 November: "A heavy outburst of firing took place in Dublin last night, machine-guns, rifles and revolvers being in action for over two hours. Wellington and Beggar's Bush barracks, the City Hall, and Oriel House were amongst the many places attacked." 136 Mr and Mrs Talbot Leggett Byrne had a dancing school at 27 Adelaide Road.

Brian at the Abbey, and Jennie[137] at her mother's, so you may imagine my feelings. Maria was wandering about like a ghost, lamenting. At last the telephone rang—Jennie to say she was afraid to come home, as there was a terrible battle going on round the King's Inns. I rang up Nano. She told me that confusion and alarm prevailed at the dance, as the firing over there was very violent, so I told her to order a taxi and gave her directions how best to get home. All the taxi places in Dublin were refusing to send out cars, but the faithful L.S.E.,[138] when informed that the taxi was required for Miss Dillon of North George's St., said they would send a car, with two drivers in case one should be wounded. So Nano arrived safely with her party. Meanwhile Brian had arrived safely, tho' he had to pass thro' a considerable amount of fusillading. The battle lasted for three hours, all over the city, but as usual *no one was hurt*. John MacNeill's great saying is being splendidly vindicated.[139]

We are, however, expecting terrible work in Dublin this week as a consequence of the executions of Childers and the four others,[140] and the hunger strike of Miss McSweeney.[141] There was a meeting at the gate of the Gaol yesterday, and it was expected that the Govt. would disperse it, but they did not interfere. However, the newspapers are evidently forbidden to publish the proceedings. Enclosed is cutting from this day's *Irish Times*, giving Childers' dying statement. His fate has been really a very great tragedy. He was I have no doubt a perfectly sincere man, and an extremely good writer, but even in his ... [*illegible*] a hopeless crank—always and at all times going for the impossible. The amount of mischief that men of this type do in this very imperfect world is incalculable.

Enclosed is also a copy of Saturday's *Republic*.[142] You will see from it what the programme is. The "Murder Members" are to be "punished". It is a nice outlook.

This is Monday, on which I am finishing this letter. I am sending the *Contemporary* today. I finished all the articles I wanted to read last night. I see in this morning's papers that the actors in Berlin struck in all the theatres—they were so bored playing Hauptmann! Have you seen any of his plays?

De Valera has at last agreed to my scheme,[143] and the scholarship is to be funded at once. I expect you have heard from Delargy of his appointment.[144] He was here last week and I gave him your address. He looked cheerful, and I expect he is much better off than if he had got the studentship.

It is a good while since I got a letter from you. I am looking for one.

137 The housemaid, Jennie Penderneath. 138 LSE Motor Co., automobile engineers and taxi cab proprietors, had their premises at 35 North Frederick St. 139 This is a reference to John Gordon Swift MacNeill (1849-1926) Irish Party M.P. for South Donegal from 1887 to 1918, and Professor of Constitutional Law in U.C.D. from 1909 to his death. It is not clear what his saying was. 140 See Letters 15 and 18. 141 See Letter 16. 142 The anti-Treaty news-sheet. 143 The Mansion House Fund. See Introduction. 144 To an assistantship in the Department of Celtic at U.C.D. See Letter 21.

20

[John Dillon to Myles] Tuesday, 28 Nov., 1922

Your letter of Friday 24th arrived yesterday by a midday post, just after I had sealed my letter to you. Let me know whether the *Contemporary* which I posted yesterday reaches you safely.

I am much interested to hear the courses you are taking. You certainly are going fundamentally to work in Philology. Umbrian is a language traces of which have been only recently recovered.[145]

I heartily approve of your proposal for the Christmas Holidays. We should all be glad to see you here, but it would be foolish to return to Dublin for so short a holiday—and Dublin at Christmas, especially in its present condition, would not be a pleasant place to spend a holiday. An excursion to the Harz Mountains ought to be most delightful.

Brian has, I think, written to you about the Homer. I am to see Father Corcoran[146] today at 3.30 to make final arrangements about the Scholarship. De V. has requested and authorised Father Corcoran to act for him. I have not yet seen Hayes, but I hope to interview him this week. Money is I understand desperately scarce in the coffers of the Free State. However, the sum in which we are interested is so trifling that it may get thro'.

Every day the most sensational and startling rumours reach me as to the impending collapse of the Free State. Enclosed is a statement from Cosgrave, from this morning's F.J.,[147] which puts the other side of the case. All is quiet in Ballaghaderreen and business fairly good.

[...]

21

[Douglas Hyde* to Myles] 1 Earlsfort Place, Dublin, 30, '22[148]

A Maolra, a chara,
   Bhí áthas orm do litir d'fhághail agus fhios a bheith agam go rabhais go compórtamhail agus loistín maith agad agus go raibh tú ag fághail do sháith de

---

145 John Dillon probably mixes up Umbrian with either Tocharian or Hittite. The Iguvine Tablets which represent the main body of text for the Umbrian language were discovered as early as 1444. 146 Timothy Corcoran, S.J. (1872-1943). Professor of Education at U.C.D. from 1909 to 1942. 147 In the *Freeman's Journal* for 28 November 1922 Cosgrave defended the executions once again and declared that the Government was in total control of the situation. He also emphasised that the Free State's finances were continuously improving. 148 Translation: 30 November 1922 • Dear Myles, • I was delighted to get your letter and to know that you are comfortable and have found good lodgings and that you are getting your fill of good food and drink so cheaply. It is a pity that

1 EARLSFORT PLACE,
DUBLIN.

Facsimile of letter from Douglas Hyde, 30 November 1922

dhéigh-bhiadh agus de dhéigh-digh chomh saor sin. Is truagh nach bhfuil mé leat ar feadh beagáin amsire go bhfeicfinn gach rud, agus go mblaisfinn d'e'n fhíon san!

Nach iongantach ar fad an méid sin mac léighinn ó thíorthaibh eile do bheith ag teacht go Bérlin fa láthair! Ní fheádaim thú fheiceál im' aigne id' idirmhínightheóir 'na measg!

Is maith liom go bhfuil Pokorny* go maith. Tabhair an litir seo istigh ann so dhó le do thoil. Tá me ag tabhairt buidheachais dó fá n-a leabhair deiridh do chuir sé chugam, Sgéalta aiseirighthe ón nGaedhilg.¹⁴⁹ óir ní'l a sheóladh ceart agam.

Thuit Úna ní Fhaircheallaigh* ar an staighre insan oidhche timcheall seachtmhain ó shoin agus ghearr sí a mala. B'éigin do'n dochtuir greim do chur ann, agus ní tháinig sí amach chun an choláiste fós, acht tá biseach uirrthi. Bhéarfaidh mé do sgéala dí.

Fuair mé cead ón gComhairle Acadamhail Mac Ui Dubhlairge* do ghlacadh mar chongantóir go tosach Márta nó mar sin, agus gheobhaidh sé céad punta faoi sin do dheanamh. Ní bhfuair sé acht £50 mar gheall air a studentship. Dearfaidh mé leis scriobhadh chugad agus bearfadh do sheóladh dhó.

Do chuir an Saor-Stát Erskine Childers chun báis ó scriobh tú, is triúr eile ar maidin indiú.

Tá an Rialtas fá bhreith báis ag na NeamhRialtachaibh ach ní féadfaidh siad an bhreith sin do chur, i bhfeidhm!

Beir na mílte buadh agus beannacht úainn go léir agus tabhair aire dhuit féin.

Mise do chara

An Craoibhín

Tá an Bolbh ar ais ann so arís is í ag obair ar a tráchtas. Féachann sí go maith.

I am not there with you for a little while to see everything, and to taste some of this wine. • Isn't it truly amazing how many students from other countries are coming to Berlin these days. I can hardly picture you as a mediator among them. • I am glad that Pokorny is well. Please give him the enclosed letter. I want to thank him for his latest book which he sent me, Stories translated from Irish, but I don't have his address. • About a week ago, Agnes O'Farrelly* fell on the stairs during the night and she cut her brow. The doctor had to stitch it, and she hasn't come back to college since, but she is getting better. I will give her your message. • I was given permission by Academic Council to employ Delargy as an assistant until March or so, and he will earn £100. On his studentship he only got £50. I will ask him to write to you and I will give him your address. • The Free State executed Erskine Childers since you last wrote, and three others this morning. • The Irregulars have put the Government under a death sentence, but they will not be able to carry out this sentence. • Best wishes from all of us and take care of yourself. • Yours • An Craoibhín • [Winifred] Wulff* is back again and is working on her thesis. She is looking well. **149** *Die Seele Irlands* (Halle: Niemeyer, 1922) contained translations of short stories by Pádraic Pearse, Pádraic Ó Conaire and Pádraic Ó Siochfhradha.

22

[Myles to John Dillon] Berlin W.15, Schaperstrasse 19, 1. xii. '22, Friday

I arrived home late last night to find both your letters awaiting me, and so I had a feast of reading and re-reading till two o'clock this morning. Thanks very much for the cuttings, which I read with great interest. These executions were horrible, but from the Free State point of view, I think, reasonable. But it is a rather ghastly duty to execute one's own disciples for being faithful, when the apostles flee. This is, perhaps, a rather unfair presentation of the position, but I have always thought the Irregulars could make a good case that way.

I should like to hear more of the condition of Free State morale. I do not see why they should collapse now, if it is true that the war is almost at an end, as one hears. However, your cuttings do not look like that.

I have just written to the University requesting them to make the cheques payable to you. I had intended to do so before, but put it off till we should have made some definite arrangement. I enclose the cheque, endorsed. I am not registering the letter as I do not know the German word for registration, and in any case, if it were lost, would the post office be likely to pay me fifty times thirty-eight thousand marks? Therefore I shall be anxious to hear that it has arrived safely.

I have not heard a word from Delargy* yet. I take it from what you say that even if the scholarship is founded, he will not seek to have it awarded this year to him.

Tell Nano I have never weakened in my resolution to write to her, but somehow the opportunity has not yet arisen. My professor has found me a dancing school, and urges me to learn fencing also. This I do not propose to do.

The theatre strike was a strange affair, but it is now settled.[150] I went the other night to a very wicked but very amusing play and followed it rather better than I expected. I am reading an excellent play of Strindberg at present which is being played in one of the theatres,[151] and I have also got two of Hauptmann, but he is difficult. However, I am following the lectures here on him with huge delight, though I only rarely know what is being said. But the little professor waves his arms and reads charming passages from poems, and everyone is impressed.

With much love and thanks,
Myles.

The *Contemporary* arrived this morning. Many thanks.

150 The theatre strike began on Saturday, 25 November 1922. While it might be strange to think of actors striking, the reasons for the strike can hardly surprise us: the actors' salaries did not grow as fast as the inflation rate, and many were on the breadline. The famous Berlin theatre critic Alfred Kerr supported the strikers. The strike ended on 9 December when the theatre directors agreed to a substantial increase in salaries. 151 This was *Totentanz* which played in one of the theatres the striking actors decided not to picket.

QVOD FELIX FAVSTVMQVE SIT

RECTORE

ARTHVRO HEFFTER

MEDICINAE ET PHILOSOPHIAE DOCTORE ORDINIS MEDICORVM PROFESSORE PVBL. ORD.

Studiosus *phil.*

data dextra iurisiurandi loco legibus magistratibusque academicis fidem oboedientiam reverentiam pollicitus numero civium Vniversitatis Fridericae Guilelmae Berolinensis legitime adscriptus est. Cuius rei testes hasce litteras sigillo Vniversitatis munitas et Rectoris manu subscriptas accepit.

D. Berolini d. 27. mens. *Novembris* anni MDCCCCXXII.

Gebühr   *Mark.*

Registration certificate from the University of Berlin

23

[Brian Dillon to Myles] [2 Nth. Gt. George's St., Dublin.], 1. 12. '22

Dear Myles,

Your letter arrived and I was indeed amazed at the German. I have neither the energy nor the courage to attempt to rival it. I have not seen Gerard* since you left. He never called for various copies of the *Reult*.[152] I gave Dermot[153] a message for him about them. When next I see Dermot I will mention the Dictionary also.

I gather that the Republic objected to Raghnall[154] on the ground that while not a member of the Regular Army he went out once or twice a week to do night duty. He was inclined to join the Regular Army in reply to the Republican request, but his father persuaded him to go. He is in England, but I know no more than that. I gather that Malachi[155] has abandoned Republican activities out of consideration for his parents, and then being in constant danger of arrest and having nothing to do here decided to seek his fortune in America. Whether he intends to return or not I don't know.

---

152 *An Reult*, the journal of the U.C.D. Gaelic Society, founded by Gerard Murphy in 1920. See Letter 19. **153** Dermot Murphy, Gerard's brother. **154** Raghnall O'Rahilly; see Letter 16A. **155** Malachi Sweetman, school friend from Mount St. Benedict.

O'Reilly[156] has applied for a commission in the Civic Guard. He had an interview with O'Duffy[157] the other day, and expects to be called up for training some time this month.

I am surprised that you gathered from my letter that there was a revival at the Mount. The staff is certainly greatly improved, but there are barely 40 boys there. Miss Power is not the lady whom you interviewed. She is aged 25, a fierce Republican, an enemy of Miss Alexander's, and unattractive.[158] She does not intend to stay permanently. Harkin, the mathematical master, is a Republican Bolshevist and intends to leave as soon as he can get a job. He comes from Tyrone and is rather pleasant. Miss Alexander hostile. Desmond Murphy[159] will resume his duties there next term. Our opinions would differ as to the advantages of that. I say the staff has improved because they all have degrees, but Lonan,[160] for whose opinion I have a great respect, does not approve of either Miss Power or Harkin as teachers. George attends an Irish class each day.

I attended the Dáil on Tuesday and Wednesday last under the patronage of Alfie Byrne.[161] There were exciting scenes. These gentlemen seem determined to execute everybody they come across. Mulcahy declared that all people found in possession of firearms, etc., or found guilty of destroying or looting public or private property or of trenching or otherwise impeding roads or railroads would be at once executed.[162] Great replies are expected from the Republicans, but nothing has occurred so far. Three men were executed yesterday in connection with the attack on Oriel House.[163]

Shawn is to be made sub-deacon on Dec. 23rd. He will not come home till the 24th. It is not yet known whether James will be home for Christmas or not.

I find the College[164] dreary and its societies shocking, with the exception of the Chess Club, in which I am placing all my hopes at the moment. The L and

---

156 Possibly Michael "Ginger" O'Reilly, later a manager with Guinness. 157 Eoin O'Duffy (1892–1944), first Commissioner of the Civic Guard. Sacked by de Valera in 1932, he founded a Fascist organisation in July 1933, the National Guard, which came to be known as the Blueshirts. In September 1933 became the first President of Fine Gael, which was created out of the amalgamation of Cumann na nGael, the Centre Party and the National Guard, but resigned in Sept. 1934, and the Blueshirt movement faded. In 1936 he organized an Irish Brigade to go and fight for Franco in the Spanish Civil War, but declined into obscurity after that. 158 See Letter 19. 159 Later founder and headmaster of St. Gerard's School, Bray. 160 Lonan Murphy; see Letter 16A. 161 Alfred Byrne (1882–1956), later long-serving Lord Mayor of Dublin (1930–9), had been elected an independent T.D. in 1922, and continued to serve in the Dáil until 1928, when he was elected to the Seanad. His political sympathies would have been broadly with the old Irish Party. He re-entered the Dáil in 1931 and served as a T.D. until his death. 162 It must be said that this was in response to a formal letter from Liam Lynch, Republican Commander-in-Chief, to the Ceann Comhairle, threatening comprehensive reprisals. 163 This refers to the executions of Joseph Spooner, Patrick Farrelly and John Murphy on 30 November. They had been arrested trying to blow up Oriel House, headquarters of the C.I.D., on 30 October. 164 That is, U.C.D., which Brian had entered that autumn.

H, which I attended about 4 times, in unbearable.[165] I have not yet had the courage to attend the German Society. It is composed of ladies with one exception, and I can hardly see myself shining in such a circle.[166] I find the lecturers shockingly bad also. I am afflicted with Mrs Kelly[167] twice a week and she tries me very much. Miss McGrane[168] I attended faithfully for some time, but lately my heart has failed me. Semple,[169] however, is charming, and Chauviré.[170] Shine[171] I am devoted to, though I find his subject unbelievably dull.

I applied for a permit for cartridges 6 weeks ago and no reply has been made. I intend to make a further appeal in view of the Christmastide, though as the Republicans have blown up all the bridges afresh it will be a little difficult to get at the pheasants.

[No signature]

24

[Myles to John Dillon] 4. xii. '22

Those bills you sent me from the "Reult" printer[172] were an unhappy reminder. I am forwarding them to Gerard [Murphy],* whose business it is to look after them, but I fear he is actually a worse businessman than I am.

I am in haste. A man from Dublin has lately arrived here, and I have been proudly introducing him to what I know of Berlin and the German language. He is waiting for me now.[173]

25

[John Dillon to Myles] Tuesday, 5 December, 1922

Your letter of Friday with cheque enclosed arrived quite safely this morning. I think you did wisely not to register the letter. [...]

165 In fact, by the next year he had been elected to the Committee of the L and H, following in the footsteps of his father and his brother James. **166** The U.C.D. College Calendar gives the Professor of German, Mary Macken, as President of the German Society and Mary Bowen as Vice President. As to the preponderance of female students in German at university level, not much has changed since 1922. **167** Presumably Mary Kate O'Kelly (née Ryan, wife of Sean T. Ó Ceallaigh, and sister of James Ryan, T.D.). She had been appointed Assistant in French in 1911. She died in 1934. **168** Eileen McGrane (later Mrs Eileen MacCarville), Assistant in the English Department. **169** Patrick Semple, Professor of Latin, 1909–47 (died 1954). Also Dean of the Arts Faculty for all of this period. **170** Roger Chauviré, Professor of French, 1919–48 (died 1957). **171** Mgr John Shine, Professor of Logic and Psychology, 1909–48 (died 1960). **172** John Falconer, Dublin. It looks as if the printing bill for *An Reult* was not being paid. See Letter 19. **173** This would have been Thomas

Here we are on the eve of the crisis. If the Republicans do not carry off some very dramatic coup within the next fortnight, the present Government may pull thro', but the country is so horribly demoralised that at least it will take a long time to reestablish any decent order. Jobbery and corruption are *rampant*, but they are lesser and more curable evils than the utter breakdown of the moral law.

What do you think of our new Governor General?[174] It is a very funny ending to Tim's career. I am sure he thinks he can make peace between the contending factions, otherwise he would hardly have accepted the post. And he has of course the advantage of having kept up pretty close relations with both sides. However, I confess I cannot see on what basis peace is possible.

You will see from enclosed cuttings that we had a lively time in Dublin yesterday.[175] We had heard nothing and were under the impression that the day had passed off perfectly quietly. The searching of everyone in the street has been going on for the last three days on a scale far beyond anything known in the days of the Black and Tans. There is a terrible lot of truth in Carson's savage oration.[176]

Father Corcoran and I have had a most amiable interview, and we have settled all the details of the scholarship.[177] We are now only waiting on the Lord Mayor to complete the job. The poor Lord Mayor is, I fear, *very* ill.

Cosgrave's wife is dying,[178] and I think Cosgrave himself will break under the strain. Tragedy appears to dog all who were concerned in this movement.

I see from the papers that the situation in Germany is becoming very critical.[179] I hope Berlin will remain tranquil. You ought to be very careful. I read with much alarm, in your letter to Brian, of your nocturnal prowlings in the Tiergarten.

What you tell me of Hauptmann and Strindberg is very interesting. Strindberg was a lunatic, and a horrible person in every way, but I believe his writings are very powerful.

McLaughlin. See Introduction and Letter 92. **174** John Dillon's old Parliamentary Party colleague, and latterly bitter adversary, Timothy Healy, was appointed Governor-General of the Irish Free State on 6 December 1922. See Letter 26. **175** There are reports in the *Irish Independent* of National troops searching civilians, and the Dublin to Kells mail van being held up and burned, which on the scale of things was nothing very remarkable. **176** Lord Carson, leader of the Ulster Unionists, had made a fierce attack on the Irish Constitution Bill in the House of Lords on 1 December, describing it as a "gigantic farce". It was a most intemperate tirade. **177** I.e. the result of the long-running negotations on which he was engaged with de Valera. See Introduction. **178** Louise Cosgrave recovered and lived until 1959. **179** On 5 December, the *Irish Times* carried a leaderette entitled "A German crisis" which described the rage which was felt in Bavaria after the French demanded a fine of half a million gold mark, because officers of the Allied forces had been insulted in the towns of Passau and Ingolstadt. The article also mentioned riots in Dresden. On the whole, the *Irish Times* followed very much the British line and argued for allowing Germany to recover economically in order to preserve peace in Europe.

Have you made the acquaintance of any Catholic priest? How does the Catholic community stand in Berlin?[180]

Miss ... [*illegible*] lunched here yesterday and was inquiring for you most affectionately.

Your loving Father,
John Dillon.

All quiet in Ballaghaderreen. Miss Moloney has gone to America. Deo Gratias.

26

[John Dillon to Myles] 11 December, 1922

Your letter of 4 Dec., with warrant enclosed, arrived on Thursday. This is only a short note to acknowledge receipt. I am expecting a letter from you and shall write at greater length when it arrives.

We have had terrible times in Dublin for the last week. Enclosed are cuttings giving you latest developments. The executions of Rory O'Connor and his companions have shocked the public very much. [...][181] Whether they will have a deterrent effect on the assassins remains to be seen. *All* the newspaper men in Dublin are under sentence of death. Some are living as prisoners in their offices under guard. This is a hideous state of affairs.

What do you think of the appointment of T. Healy?[182]

All well here. So far we have been left in peace, and from Ballagh I get satisfactory reports.

[PS] Mr McBride's appeal to the law of Christ under all the circumstances is audacious.

Let me know whether you have been able to cash cheques without difficulty.

180 Myles does indeed not go into this aspect of Berlin life at all. Liam de Róiste, however, who was just about to arrive in Berlin, does tell us something about the half-million strong Catholic population of the predominantly Protestant capital of Germany. Surprisingly enough it seemed to him, around Christmas at any rate, that the Catholic faith "is not an exotic plant here, but is deeprooted in the traditions of the people" (de Róiste 1923). 181 On 8 December Liam Mellows, Rory O'Connor, Joseph McKelvey and Richard Barrett were executed as a reprisal for the assassination of Seán Hales, T.D. All four had been in prison since the capture of the Four Courts back in July. 182 Tim Healy (1855-1931) had emigrated to England during the 1870s and had worked as a journalist for the *Nation* before entering politics. In 1880, he was elected Nationalist M.P. first for Wexford and subsequently for other Irish constituencies. After the Parnell split he joined the anti-Parnellites, but due to increasing tensions between him and other leading members of the Party (including John Dillon) he was expelled from the Party in 1902, but remained in Parliament as an Independent. In 1918 he vacated his seat so that an imprisoned Sinn Féin candidate could be elected. He had been converted to Sinn Féin ideals during the Rising and the Free State rewarded his conversion by appointing him first Governor General in 1922. He left office in 1928.

27

[Nano Dillon to Myles] 2 North Gt. George's Street, Dublin, Thursday, 14th
[December 1922]

Dear Milo,

Your letter was most welcome and very many thanks for your munificent gift.

The revolting news you heard was perfectly true, and shocked, horrified, and disgusted everyone—with the exception of our mutual friend Dr Cronin, who thinks the Free State can do no wrong. Four men, Rory O'Connor, Liam Mellows, Barrett and McKelvey, were all taken out and murdered without trial as reprisals. Was such a thing ever heard of before? I send you their letters, as they may interest you.[183]

The I.R.A. burned Mrs Wyse Power's[184] shop and set fire to O'Donoghue's[185] home (Sec. to an Dáil), and also burned Capt. Sean McGarry's[186] house a few days ago, and his wife and children were badly burned and are in hospital. Then yesterday they set fire to Kenneth Reddin's[187] offices in D'Olier St., and Corrigan's and a man named Mahon's, but the Fire Brigade arrived promptly, and, though some papers were burned, the buildings weren't destroyed.

I tell you these items of news as I suppose you don't see Irish papers at all, and it may interest you to know the gentle deeds of our fellow men.

I was out at a dance a few nights ago (only a Cinderella) and both forces tried using up all the ammunition they possessed. It seemed as if the whole city was in a battle. No taxi garage would send out cars and there was rather a panic for a bit. Finally, Kevin Smith, the proprietor of L.S.E. (whom I know) sent me a taxi with *two* drivers, in case one might be shot, and we got home all right.

You lucky being! I wish I could fly to the Harz Mountains for the sports. I envy you plunging about in the snow. I'm devoted to snow.

Father is in amazing spirits, and grows younger daily in spite of all adversity. He has been trying to fly to Ballagh for weeks, but now has, I think, abandoned the idea till after Christmas, as the I.R.A. seem to spend their time derailing the Mayo trains and in setting fire to them as the spirit moves them. They set fire to one passenger train coming up to the Broadstone some days ago and all the passengers were in the train, and they set it going and told them to jump out. Some got badly hurt, but no one was killed.

183 These have not survived. 184 Senator Jennie Wyse Power (1858-1941). She had been an executive member of the Ladies' Land League in Parnell's time, a member of the Gaelic League since its inception, and one of the founders of Sinn Féin. She had a business premises in Camden St. Republicans hurled three bombs through her shop window only days after she had accepted her nomination as Senator by W.T. Cosgrave (O'Neill 1991, p. 146). 185 In fact, M. MacDonnachadha, Secretary to the Government. 186 Sean McGarry, Cumann na nGaedhal T.D. His house was burned on 10 December, and his young son, aged seven, died in hospital from burns a week later. It was a particularly nasty incident. 187 Brother of Norman Reddin, Nano's current boyfriend.

Dear James will not be with us till the 31st.[188] We are trying to bear this cruel blow with fortitude. He has turned into a "dancer" now, and takes the floor three times a week on average, generally with nothing lower than Countess or Marchioness.

Dermot Murphy is often with us, silent and peaceful, but seeming to enjoy himself.

Dr Lister[189] of the Library is dead, so Gerard Murphy,* I suppose, is one step higher.[190] The poor old gentleman died quite suddenly yesterday.

I was at an all night dance at La Scala on Friday night last and met Baldwin Murphy[191] there and Frank Lavery[192] and Jack McCann[193] and Dorothy. Jack was in great form. I had two dances with him and he enquired for you with the deepest affection. Dorothy was not very sparkling. She has grown stout of form and seemed a little heavy of wit.

Alice Meade (erstwhile Rooney) has taken me to her bosom once more and invited me to her dance next Thursday in a very friendly letter, so I am going with all due ceremony.

I met Con Curran* at Miss Purser's* At Home last week, and a few days after that I saw him at the Yeats' At Home, and his enquiries for you were warm and fervent. He is going to write to you.

The O'Farrellys were in here to lunch on Sunday—Agnes brilliant as ever and Alphonse booming as usual. Ismé was also with us, and prodded "Al" with her thumb from time to time—an attention which he did not appear to appreciate. I enclose a poem of dear Agnes' which I know will bring tears to your eyes. It appeared in the *Independent* yesterday.[194] How *can* she do such things! Oh, I must tell you what she did three weeks ago. She was roused at 2 o'c. in the early morn by sounds which she thought suggested a burglar. She sprang from her bed and, candle in hand, advanced to the staircase, stepped falsely, and went hurtling down the stairway, grabbing sundry pictures in her flight and carrying them along with her. At the bottom she rose and discovered that she had cut her head open, so she staggered up and entered Al's boudoir and made him bandage her head, and she had to stay in bed for a week, and have stitches put in her head—so there was an adventure for you![195] And as soon as she recovered she produced the enclosed poem.

Maria is still but twenty-one, and Jenny is only sixteen. Mary as the cook is excellent, and "Doran" continues to be a comfort and joy.

188 He was still in London, as an apprentice manager at Selfridge's. 189 T.W. Lyster (1855–1922), Librarian of the National Library. 190 Gerard Murphy was at this time employed in the National Library, where he worked with R.I. Best, until in 1925 the onset of TB forced him to join Theo Dillon in Switzerland. 191 Brother of Gerard. Later a solicitor in Clones. 192 See Letter 16A. 193 John McCann, later a solicitor, and senior partner in the firm of McCann, White and Fitzgerald. 194 This was entitled "The Motherland", and is indeed pretty awful. 195 Douglas Hyde* refers to the same incident in his letter (21).

I shall write soon again and give you what news there is. Shawn is getting his orders on Saturday week and we are all, of course, flocking to the ceremony.

Poor old Lady Fottrell[196] is very feeble and now has a hospital nurse in constant attendance. Farewell. I hope you will be able to read some of this.

Love from
Nano.

28

[Maria O'Reilly to Myles] 2 North Gt. George's St., Dublin, Sunday, [17] December, 1922

My dearest Myles,

Fearing my letters have not reached you, I write again to wish you a joyous and happy Xmas. I fear I forgot to put the numbers 19 and 15 in their respective places on my last two letters. In one I sent you a group of Pat and his bride and myself. I was so glad to get your photo and have it on the mantlepiece so I can have a look at you every so often. Shawn was home on Thursday and stayed till Saturday, when he went to Milltown Park for a retreat preparatory to his ordination, which will take place on 23rd at Clonliffe College. Thank God, he went off very happy. He got a nice clerical suit which he looks well in.

Poor Lady Fottrell[197] is very ill and her family are very anxious about her. She is greatly to be pitied, as she can't keep quiet for one moment and she is so unhappy.

I had a letter from Sarah[198] in which she said the Free Staters passed through the town and got fired at from Lea Street on their way to Charlestown. Your Father is not going down till after Xmas. He is wise, as Sarah said there might be a battle any day, as the troops were returning from Charlestown. The newest plan the Irregulars have started is to burn ...[199]

I had a very nice letter from Theo. He seems pretty comfortable and is learning all sorts of languages. He is in good spirits and content to absent himself from us at Xmas. He told your Father in his letter the Dr. who took the head Dr.'s place while he went to Paris told him he would be well in April,[200] but advised him to remain there till June.

With fondest love,

I am your loving nurse,
Maria O'Reilly.

196 Wife of Sir George Fottrell, K.C.B., old friend of John Dillon's and one-time chairman of Dublin Gas Co. He had offices in 8 North Great George's St. 197 See preceding note. 198 Sarah Partridge. The town is, of course, Ballaghaderreen. 199 A line is omitted here. She must have gone off the page. She refers to the burning of houses of members of the Senate. 200 This, as things turned out, was absurdly optimistic.

29

[John Dillon to Myles] Thursday, 21 December, 1922

I hope you have left directions for forwarding letters, or they may not reach you till you return from the mountains. If it does reach you, send by return your address in the mountains, and also the date on which you propose to return to Berlin.

I see the Mark has slumped again.²⁰¹ What you tell me about the rise in prices is very interesting. The fact is that prices always lag behind an expanding currency. The real time of woe is when the currency begins to contract, and prices fall, as we have experienced to our grief during the last two years. I trust you had no difficulty in cashing your cheque. You should have called in the aid of Maloney, who I am sure could easily arrange the matter for you. I fear you cashed [the] cheque at the moment when the exchange was at its worst. However, I suppose it was only a matter of £10.

Your letter of 19th arrived yesterday.²⁰² You ought to pick up a little Icelandic from your friend from Iceland. The Icelandic Sagas are in their own kind some of the finest literature in the world. I was so enraptured by them when I first made their acquaintance that I tried to learn Icelandic, and made a little progress. It is a very easy language, with a considerable relationship to English, and the relations between the Norsemen and the Irish in the Middle Ages were very close and intensely interesting.

Your letter is most interesting, but rather brief. I hope you will write at greater length during the vacation and give me full particulars of your visit to Minden, and your adventure in the mountains. Do not be too venturesome during your stay in the mountains. You have not had any experience or training in these sports, and some of them are risky. I shall be anxious to hear how you fare.

Enclosed are some cuttings. Today's *Irish Times* gives you an idea of the blessed state of peace and order we have attained to.²⁰³ It is really appalling, and I can see no way out, altho' I understand there was a peace conference in Co. Kerry on Sunday week at which all the Southern Republican leaders were present. What the result was I don't know. I suppose the Government are of the opinion that by holding up the Kerry executions they will promote peace.

All well here, and I had a very cheerful letter from Theo yesterday. He is improving, but his doctor says he will have to stay till June. Shawn is in Milltown Park on a week's retreat preparatory to receiving orders—sub-deacon—on Saturday next. Brian has become an habitué of the Chess Club, where he occasionally meets old John Sweetman.²⁰⁴

201 On 19 December the exchange rate was 25,000 marks for £1stg., one day later it was 33,000, a drop of over 30 per cent. **202** This has not, unfortunately, survived. **203** This may refer to the assassination of former pro-Treaty T.D. Seamas O'Dwyer, in his shop in Rathmines. **204** John

I have not yet seen Hayes.* The times have been so critical that I did not care to trouble him, but I [will] communicate with [him] during the Christmas holidays.

I am forwarding to you a catalogue from Max Niemeyer.[205] Some of the books seem absurdly cheap. Of course, I assume you can now buy thro' a German friend. Write soon.

[PS] Note the cute grin of the Governor General in enclosed cutting.[206]

30

[John Dillon to Myles] Friday, 22 Dec. [1922]

Your telegram arrived yesterday afternoon. Maria is despatching usual things to Peg today.[207]

I hope soon to get your address in the mountains, and remember to be reasonably cautious and do not break your bones—a thing very easy to do in frosty weather.

It has turned cold here, and I expect you are experiencing what cold weather in Germany means. Tell me how you found Toby, and what are his surroundings like.

31

[Michael Hickey[208] to Myles] Clonliffe College, Dublin, [*postmark* 26 December 1922]

My dear Myles,

I am very glad to hear from [you] and thank you ex corde[209] for your very *kind* message of congratulations. John[210] is now Rev. Mr Dillon and is very happy. He is our Sub-Deacon to-day (Sunday) in the Pro. [Cathedral]. Had a

---

Sweetman of Drumbaragh, M.P. **205** The well-known publishing house Max Niemeyer of Halle published the *Zeitschrift für celtische Philologie* and other books of Celtic and philological interest. After World War II Niemeyer moved to Tübingen in West Germany. **206** This probably refers to a photograph of the Governor-General "leaving Buckingham Palace after a lengthy audience with King George" in the *Irish Independent* of 19 December. John Dillon's description certainly fits the photograph. Healy and John Dillon had been fierce opponents in the old Irish Parliamentary Party and his dislike of his former party colleague is still palpable. **207** This refers to a Christmas present to be sent to Mrs Margaret Heneghan of Carheen, Tourmakeady, Co. Mayo, with whom Dillon was accustomed to board when visiting the Tourmakeady Gaeltacht. **208** Dr Hickey had just been appointed President of Clonliffe College where Shawn studied for the priesthood and this letter is in reply to Myles' congratulatory note. **209** "from the heart". **210** I.e. Shawn.

letter from dr. Theo some days ago. He is quite well. When you meet Tom McLaughlin[211] give him my kindest wishes.

Omnia bona pro novo anno

Very sincerely
Michael Hickey

32

[Myles to his family in Dublin] [*Postcard*], Palast Hotel, Dresden, Wednesday [27 December 1922]

Dresden is old and pleasant. I am going now to the picture gallery, which I am told is very good.[212] This is a place where one would do well to spend some time, because it is beautiful, and one could live here for nothing.

[*Over side postcard*]

I send this postcard as I am on my way to the Riesengebirge.[213] I have managed to spend four or five hours in Dresden, and have devoted some of the time to enjoying a good lunch. I embarked at Minden at 2.26 this morning, and arrived here at 11.30. I shall be in Oberschreiberhau tonight, and I have got news that it is a delightful place. Christmas in the Minden household was a most pleasant and interesting experience. I was treated with much kindness, and given Christmas presents by everyone.

Myles.

33

[Myles to his family in Dublin] [*Postcard*] Hotel Lindenhof, Oberschreiberhau,[214] Riesengebirge, Schlesien, Saturday [30 December 1922]

The environment here does not induce to long letter writing. This is a very beautiful place, and a merrier atmosphere than Berlin. I only wish I were not only in the place but more *of* it. Our being here three makes us rather a group, and not a very interesting one. But there is a ball here tonight, after which I

211 Thomas McLaughlin (1896-1971), a former Lecturer in Physics at U.C.G., had just arrived in Berlin and had started work with the German electrical giant Siemens-Schuckert, who had invited him to Germany to continue his training as an electrical engineer. He was soon to become the driving force behind the Shannon Scheme. See Introduction and Letter 148. 212 The Dresden picture gallery housed one of the premier collections of paintings in Europe since its foundation in the 18th century by Augustus the Strong (1694-1733) and its extension under his son August III (1733-63). 213 Part of the Sudeten mountain range which seperates Silesia from the Czech Republic. 214 Schreiberhau today is a Polish town called Szklarska Poreba.

hope to be less a stranger. I have already done some sleighing, and commence skiing today. I will send photographs of our adventures. Much love,

Myles.

34

[Myles to John Dillon] 31. xii. '22

I sent you a card from here the other day to let you know where I am, and that I still live. I have had many interesting adventures since I last wrote. My Christmas at Minden was pleasant, and it was my first introduction to a German home. Toby lives there as a member of the family, with the title of "Uncle Toby". I met the grandmother and uncles and cousins of the family. We visited them and they visited us, and German was spoken all the time. It has been a great chance for Toby to acquire fluency of speech, and an intimate acquaintance with Germans. He speaks with more fluency than correctness, and understands more than I can.

These people in Minden, like my baroness, are of the old Offizierkreise,[215] who long for the return of the monarchy, and think only of the next war with France. They hope that England may be with them, and perhaps they are right.

Minden is an old fortress town, with narrow streets and red-tiled roofs, and much that is attractive. The interesting thing is the old Cathedral, which by a strange chance has remained in the hands of the small minority of Catholics. It is mostly early Gothic, but was commanded by Charlemagne, and a part of the oldest building remains.

I came here through Leipzig and Dresden, and was able to wait in Dresden for about five hours. I could only see a little, many pictures, including Raffael's *Madonna*, and the outsides of beautiful buildings, with fat cherubs at every corner. Finally, I travelled hither in the wrong train, owing to the misdirection of the porters, and arrived at a station where I had to change, to find that the next train left at three the following morning, with a change at six, arriving here at 7.45. This involved a bad dinner at Görlitz, after which I lay miserably on chairs till three, and then continued my journey. The railway part of the journey, which lasted for two nights and a day, cost less than three shillings.

Here I have progressed somewhat with the sleigh, but my experiences yesterday on skis were rather a trial. However, the snow is soft, so it is only pleasant when one falls. I came down the mountain side this evening on my sleigh at great speed, often leaping into the air, and sometimes rolling in the snow, but it was a glorious adventure.

The Apache-ball last night was at least an interesting revelation as to what people will do when the conventions are definitely disregarded. It was rather a

215 "Officer classes, or 'circles'."

wild scene, both ladies and gentlemen apparently intoxicated with joy or with wine, and I went home in rather a restless mood (I could not get a room here, so I sleep outside).²¹⁶ Tonight, New Year's Eve, the Sylvesterfeier²¹⁷ is being celebrated with another dance; but this is a much more quiet performance, and is already in progress.

Nano would be edified by the ladies' fashions. The feminine heavy-weights who skip about in check knee-britches and sweaters make me feel uneasy. One enormous woman, so attired, insisted on waltzing about a café on the mountain today when music was played, to the horror of my companion.

Other details of the life here remind me of her account of her first painting expedition. I stop to gaze over an old bridge into a mountain torrent fed by the melting snow, when an appalling smell makes us flee into the valley. In my house, this horror is, as with her, all through the house, so that I have to rush through the hall and up the stairs when I go home at night.

The pine trees and the snow and the red roofs of the houses make most delightful colour. And again at night, when the windows are all alight, it is wonderful to be here. My Celtic studies have brought quite unexpected pleasures.

My future address in Berlin will be: Pension Utke, Karlstrasse 31, N.W. 6.²¹⁸ I shall go back some day next week, so it will be better to write there for the future. I have not heard from you for some time before Christmas, but I have moved about so much that a letter may await me in Berlin or elsewhere.

My love to the family, and my salutation for the New Year.

35

[Maria O'Reilly to Myles] 2 North Great George's Street, Dublin,
2nd Jan. 1923

My dearest Myles,

Thanks very much for your most generous present which I got on Xmas day. I trust you got my gift and trust you liked it. Your Father gave me this address today off the post card you sent him. It must be lovely for you to see so many lovely places.

I had a line and a gift from Theo which travelled the city before it reached me two days after Xmas. I was a bit sad as I thought he forgot to greet me on that Day. He is getting on well, I think. I missed you both more than you could

216 He means, presumably, elsewhere in town. 217 To celebrate New Year's Eve (Germ. *Sylvester*: "New Year's Eve"). 218 The Karlstraße, a side street of the Friedrichstraße and situated in the former East Berlin, has since been renamed. It is now called Reinhardt-Straße, named after the famous theatre director Max Reinhardt (see also Letter 135). The house where Myles Dillon lodged has been demolished.

guess. I sent the parcel to Peg[219] and today I got a letter from her which I enclose[220]—also a parcel which contained 2 fat chickens. Nano agreed to have them cooked tomorrow for lunch, and Miss Kathleen O'Sullivan is coming to lunch. She is a daughter of A.M. Sullivan,[221] R.I.P., and a close relative of Tim Healy's.[222]

Shawn is now the Rev. and all his letters bear that distinction. He is delighted with himself. Poor old Lady Fottrell[223] is in a bad state. Mrs Cochrane[224] and Harold is over. John Sweetman[225] dined here last night. James is home keeping us all in order. Did you hear your friend Mr Browne[226] is arrested in Kerry? Ina's husband is up in Dublin for Xmas. He says we will have Peace in a fortnight.

I wrote to Peg to thank her. Now I think I have told you all, and hope this will reach you.

With best and fondest love,
I am

Your loving Nurse,
M. O'Reilly.

36

[Shawn Dillon to Myles] 2 North Great George's St., Dublin. Sunday,
7th January, 1923

My dear Myles,

I was really ashamed when I recollected a day or two ago that I had not, unless my memory is worse than I think it is, answered your very kind letter which reached me just as I was coming out of the Retreat preparatory to my ordination to subdeaconship. I have officiated in my new capacity two or three times at the High Mass in the Pro-Cathedral, and was subdeacon in the presence of the Archbishop at the thanksgiving service on the last day of 1922. Your gen-

219 See Letter 30. 220 This has been preserved, but we do not reproduce it. 221 Alexander Martin Sullivan (1830–1884), journalist and politician. Born in Bantry, Co. Cork. Joined the staff of the *Nation* in 1855, and became editor and sole proprietor in 1858 when Charles Gavan Duffy left for Australia. Home Rule M.P. for Co. Louth 1874–80, and for Meath 1880–1. Called to the Irish Bar in 1876 and to the English Bar the following year, when he handed the *Nation* over to his elder brother T.D. Sullivan, and went over to London to practice. His health broke down in 1881, and he resigned his seat and returned to Ireland, dying at Dartry Lodge, Rathgar, on 17 October 1884. 222 Tim Healy had married a daughter of her uncle, T.D. Sullivan. See Letter 29. 223 See Letter 27. 224 Perhaps the wife of Bourke Cochrane, distinguished Irish-American politician and friend of John Dillon's. 225 It is unclear whether this was John Sweetman M.P. or his son John, a schoolfriend of Brian's. 226 Perhaps Monsignor Patrick Browne (Padraig de Brún) (1889–1960), but, if so, it is a remarkably dismissive way of referring to him.

erous desire to mark the day I appreciate most keenly, and on tomorrow (Monday) I shall DV[227] purchase your gift to me.

I should be glad to hear some more detail than you have given as to how you found Toby Mathew. Father Langford[228] I have seen a few times at a distance, but I do not know him personally. He was a Maynooth student. We had three days' Retreat from Father Fegan S.J.,[229] and I became quite reconciled to him. As the Retreat had to be made during the first week of the Christmas vacation, we made it in Milltown Park. Father Fegan praised you most highly to me.

James and Brian have gone off to Ballaghaderreen, so the house is empty indeed—only Nano and I with my father. The days pass very rapidly. On Tuesday next I return to Clonliffe for the last time, thank God.

I am glad to hear that you will be in Ireland for my ordination, and sincerely hope that nothing will happen to alter your plans in that matter. Your vote will be required on 13th inst. to assist Miss O'Farrelly* to retain her seat on the Governing Body.[230] I intend to inquire tomorrow if your voting papers have been sent out. I said to my father that neither you nor Theobald were to be trusted to do the right thing in this election, but my father has more faith in you in this connection than I have.

What with damage to railways, bankruptcy, bomb explosions, mined roads, and complete absence of any substantial hope of improvement, you are really well out of the country.

Again thanking you heartily for your great kindness to me and wishing you every blessing for the New Year.

Yours affectionately,
Shawn.

P.S. I am glad to be able to judge from your letters that you have had an enjoyable Christmas. SD.

37

[John Dillon to Myles] 2 North George's St., Dublin. 8 January, 1923

I am sending you by this post your voting paper for the Governing Body of the College. It came only this morning. They have not given time enough for voters abroad to send in their papers, but Shawn has gone today to make an application

227 *Deo volente*: "God willing". **228** As Harold Quinlan's letter (92) shows, Fr Langford was another member of the little Irish community in Berlin and Myles had met him as well. **229** Fr Henry Fegan (1855-1933), A noted preacher, who had served for long years in Clongowes as Prefect of Studies, but was from 1909 based in Milltown Park. He was much in demand as a giver of retreats. **230** That is, of U.C.D.

to get the time extended for voters abroad, so you had better fill and send in the papers immediately on receipt. None of the candidates appear to be very desirable except Miss O'F.[231] and possibly Hogan,[232] whom I do not know, and as Miss O'F. is very ... [*illegible*] to be elected, perhaps your best course would be to vote for her—and Hogan, if you think well of him—and leave the other spaces blank.

I shall write again in a day or two. Enclosed are cuttings from this day's *Independent*. Railway travelling in Ireland is not a very safe or pleasant undertaking.[233]

38

[John Dillon to Myles] 9 January, 1923

I was in such a hurry to get off your voting papers[234] yesterday that I forgot to send on enclosed letter,[235] which has been here for some days. I have been looking over your letter of 31 Dec. again with great pleasure. Your description of your experiences at Oberschreiberhau is most interesting and amusing. I should like to have details. Did you succeed to any extent on the skis before you left? And about Toby? How did you find him? Is he content with his present situation? And is he conducting himself decently?

I see you are in the midst of a crisis in Berlin.[236] I think Bonar Law did quite right in Paris,[237] and the frank and honest statement of irreconcilable differences between the policies of the French and English governments may be the beginning of better things.

Four more executions here yesterday,[238] but these are alleged to be deserters from the Free State Army who joined a Republican column attacking Free State troops. Your friend Miss Comerford[239] was arrested yesterday in possession of a revolver. She is now in Mountjoy.

[PS] I have not forgotten our project about assisting Pokorny,* etc., but really the times have been [so] critical that I did not care to seek an interview with Hayes,* who, I assume, like all the other leaders [?], is obliged to be *strictly*

231 Miss Agnes O'Farrelly.* 232 Gabriel P.A. Hogan, B.A., B.L., was a candidate on the graduates' panel.   233 This refers to a story about the sabotage of a G.N.R. train at Killester, in which seven passengers were injured. 234 For the U.C.D. Governing Body elections. 235 Disappeared. 236 After the collapse of the Paris Reparations conference the situation was very tense in Germany due to French threats to occupy the Ruhr, as reported in the *Irish Times* of 8 and 9 January 1923. 237 He withdrew from the Reparations conference. 238 There were actually five. These were Free State soldiers who had defected during an engagement at Leixlip on 1 December. 239 Máire Comerford.* She was arrested in Loughlinstown with four others, all men. Fortunately for her, the Free State did not execute women.

guarded. The moment things settle down a little—if they do—I shall look up Hayes and remind him of his suggestion.

—Since writing above, I have received a telegram from Aunt Anna announcing sad news that your Uncle Charles died last night.[240] He had been obliged to undergo another operation last Saturday.

39
[John Dillon to Myles] 11 January, 1923

Enclosed is a letter from Brian, which he asks me to forward.[241] I got a letter from your Aunt Anna this morning, giving particulars of Uncle Charles' illness and death. Poor Anna—it is a desperate business for her. Your uncle is to be buried in England, so none of us can attend the funeral.

Enclosed is a cutting from this morning's *Irish Times*, from which you will see that the Republicans are still active.[242] They apparently proposed to shoot any member of the Dail or Senate present at the meeting.

40
[Nano Dillon to Myles] Friday, 11th [January 1923][243]

Dear Milo,

Your postcard thrilled me and filled me with envy. I should adore to be there in all that lovely snow. A reminiscent smile flitted o'er my face at your mention in one letter of certain drawbacks which went hand in hand with the beauty you enjoyed. However, all that is a detail. I'd give anything to be sleighing and skiing about.

Do you know Mrs Bithrey[244] and I are planning a tour early in April? We think of going to Italy and Venice—only for a short few weeks, but still … It would be rather glorious, wouldn't it? Father is quite keen on the idea, so it only remains with dear "Lollie" to stick to our arrangements. I gave Mr Bithrey your address. He wants to pen you a note, it appears.

240 Charles Mathew, who had just been elected to parliament as a Labour M.P. See Introduction, and Letter 5. 241 This does not survive. 242 The paper reported that four armed men invaded the Irish County Councils meeting in Dublin looking for Dáil members as hostages, or worse, for reprisal killings. Luckily, there were none present. 243 If Friday, not the 11th, but the 12th. The postmark ensures the month, but obscures the date. 244 We have little further information on Mrs Bithrey herself. She was married to John Bithrey who taught at Mount St. Benedict (McElligott 1986, p. 165) and went on to become an Inspector of Schools in the Dept. of Education. He died in 1973.

James is fairly insufferable. He is in Ballagh at the moment, D.G.

I do not know if you have been informed that Uncle Charles[245] died two days
ago. An operation was performed in Folkestone and he died from heart failure
the next day. It is tragic and was really quite unexpected because, though he
has been ill, somehow no one thought of his death.

Shawn went back to Clonliffe yesterday. Brian is down in Ballagh (being
rather bored, I fear) with James. He went down thinking to shoot, but found it
impossible. He is coming back on Saturday.

The Lamb of Ulster[246] is quivering with great expectations. The elections
for the Senate of the University take place in a few days, and the students have
nominated her.

Mrs Bithrey and I might come and see you in Berlin, if you're there. I've
just remembered that you probably won't be, as you may be home for Easter.

I've asked Eimar O'Duffy* to dinner on Wed. with his spouse. I shall write
later and tell you of their visit.

The Free State has abolished all Crown Solicitors. Doesn't that mean that
Gerard [Murphy]'s* father[247] loses his work? It's dreadful for all these unfortunate men.

Farewell. The Household flourishes.

Nano.

41

[Myles to John Dillon] Berlin N.W. 6, Karlstrasse 31, Pension Utke,
Monday night, 15. I. '23

I got your letter and the very sad news of Uncle Charles' death. I have written
to Aunt Anna and to Grandmother. The voting paper, and another enclosure
from Brian, also arrived.

My new dwelling is entirely satisfactory, and makes it much easier to work
regularly. I can eat here, which saves a great deal of time, and has withdrawn me
from the distraction and luxury of the cafés. The food is excellent, there is more
of it, and it costs less than half as much as the restaurant. My Mittagessen here,
which is a meat meal, and the principal meal of the day, costs up to the present
only 900 marks. Moreover, I am within ten minutes' walk of the University.
The manageress is a most affable dame, a Catholic, whose son is a priest, and
she plays Beethoven after our Abendessen, having previously assisted at serving
the table.

245 That is, Charles Mathew. See Introduction. 246 A reference to Miss Agnes O'Farrelly* who
used the pen-name Uan Uladh. 247 Henry Murphy, solicitor, later County Registrar for
Monaghan.

We have had the great pleasure for the last fortnight of a visit of Father Boylan* to Berlin. He is very faithful to Berlin, and has come here almost every year for the last eighteen years, and often twice a year. He always stops in a home kept by Dominican nuns, which is next door but one to this house. We have just been drinking together, and he returns to Ireland on Wednesday.

Toby has come to Berlin and is working in the Staatsbibliothek. One would think he had been rather libelled by his friends. He does not appear to be a dominating personality, but his behaviour is above reproach. We could not get him to drink any wine on Christmas Day in Minden, though the wine was a gift from him to the man of the house. I have not seen much of him yet, as he is out in Wilmersdorf, where I languished before Christmas, and we are both busy.

It is a difficult position for Germans now. I attended the demonstration on Sunday (yesterday) at the Reichstag, to protest against French aggression.[248] The students took a prominent part, and "Deutschland über Alles" and "Die Wacht am Rhein" were sung vigorously. Meanwhile a rival procession of Royalists marched past with a small body of followers, the band consisting of distinguished gentlemen, each man wearing a silk hat. The followers were fairly numerous and included all sorts of people, old gentlemen in frock coats, and poor little women shouting with enthusiasm. I feel myself very anti-French, but cannot help thanking Providence that Germany did not win the war.

Where do the Italians stand in this business? Mussolini opened up by violent declarations of his terrible purpose against Germany,[249] but now that England has halted, Italy seems to have taken fright. The Italian papers seem rather to reprove France for her conduct. Italian Weltpolitik seems to be a discreditable business.

Pokorny* has got a little money from the government to publish a book he has written.[250] This will bring him some relief. By the way, if the question of helping these men does seriously come up, it is only fair to explain that the dif-

---

248 The *Berliner Tageblatt* estimated that half a million people attended the demonstration and called it one of the biggest Berlin had ever seen. The parties of the left, SPD and KPD, did not participate and held their own protest rallies (*BT* 15 Jan. 1923). See also Introduction. 249 After his March on Rome on 27 October 1922, Mussolini had been invited by the king to form a government, and on 25 November the Parliament had granted him dictatorial powers. Mussolini first supported the severe line the French took in the reparations' question and encouraged the French when they decided to move their troops into Germany. These views were partly inspired by anti-British feelings: limiting the influence of the British empire could open up new possibilities for Italy in the wider world. When some of his anti-British remarks became known he backed down and even claimed to have opposed the occupation of the Ruhr. Italian foreign policy was indeed rather erratic in the early 1920s (cf. Smith 1993, p. 61). 250 This was *Die älteste Lyrik der grünen Insel*, an anthology of Old Irish poetry. The Irish envoy in Berlin, Bewley, had supported Pokorny's application and the Dept. of Foreign Affairs had paid the author the (then) princely sum of £30 (Murphy 1995, p. 141).

ference between Thurneysen* and Pokorny as scholars is as great as the difference between Dr Bergin and myself. That is, as far as academic claims are concerned. Of course, the claims of a human stomach can be established by every man. The University people, I suppose, are aware of that. I only say it in case you might be under a wrong impression.

I have written today to a student in Bonn to enquire what the prospects are as regards work there after Easter. If Thurneysen is agreeable, I think I will go there next Semester, and then possibly winter again here in the Karlstrasse. I have recently managed to get some of the books I wanted, two through the great kindness of Kathleen, and as my German is now commencing to walk, I hope to do something before Easter. If, therefore, fewer letters arrive, you will know it is a good sign. I have acquitted myself well in the matter of letters up to now. But I hope that George's Street will keep active.

Enclosed are some photos of the Riesengebirge. In two you will see the trees on the mountain quite snowed up. It was hard to believe that they were really trees. The figure in these two is Dr Quinlan,* a fellow student of Theo's, who is out here on an anatomy scholarship, and lives in this house. His brother is now rector of Belvedere College.[251] The third man is a member of the Irish Trade Envoyage here, named Duane.[252] He insisted on wearing a Stephen's Green costume in the snowdrifts, which often spoilt things for him. You will notice that your muffler and gloves were of great use to me. I had not enough practice to attain any skill on skis, but I did endeavour, and often failed nobly, once even splendidly—on a steep slope.

Many thanks to Nano for her letter, which came this morning. Is there any news of Theo? I would be glad to get some of his letters from you if he sends news.

[PS] I look a little determined in one of these photographs. But the family will have to forgive that.

42

[John Ryan, S.J.,* to Myles] Bonn, Hofgartenstr. 9, 23. i. '23

Dear Mr Dillon,

Thurneysen* has just passed me on your letter. Of course I am delighted to make your acquaintance even in this distant way and hope we shall have an opportunity of getting to know each other better later on. *Re* coming to Bonn, I

---

251 This was the Very Rev. Michael Quinlan, S.J. See also Letter 145. 252 Cornelius Duane was assistant to Charles Bewley in Berlin. After Bewley's departure in February 1923, Duane remained in Berlin as Irish Chargé d'Affaires until 2 January 1924 when the Irish office in Berlin was finally closed down (Murphy 1995, p. 143). It reopened again in 1929, with Daniel Binchy as the first fully accredited Irish Minister.

think you would be very well advised to do so for at least a semester. Gothic, Anglo-Saxon, Umbrian and Sanscrit are all taught here, and the differences between the professors can hardly be very great. The library here, however, is poor, or perhaps it would be more correct to say, as far as Irish studies are concerned, non-existent. Still, for anybody wishing to hear the last word on Irish Philology, it would be most unwise to let an opportunity of hearing Thurneysen pass. As a matter of fact, he is beginning to fall into age, and obviously feels very heavily the disasters that have ruined Germany, so his teaching work is nearly done. As he has not yet announced his programme for next semester, and we all have a certain shyness of asking him to divulge it beforehand, I do not know if it will be worth your while to come next term. Welsh would hardly attract you. The Vorlesungsverzeichnis will, however, be out about Feb. 20th, and I shall then let you know at once what is on. Thurneysen is just the man for your text problems, so that even if you did not come here for next term, you might do well to spend some time here with him during the Easter holidays. He is very kind and extraordinarily obliging. Miss K. Mulchrone,* Miss MacNevin,[253] Heneghan,* myself and two Germans form his class. This semester he is merely marking time with one lecture on the glosses a week, and that only by special request.

I shall ask Mr Heneghan to write to you next time I meet him. Unfortunately I have not the least idea what the number of the house is in which he lives, so I cannot give it to you now.

I fear I know very little that would be of use to you in the work you are doing, but if you let me know your difficulties, I shall try and see if anything is to be done. If you want anything looked up in Ireland, please let me know, as I hope to go back for a few weeks at end of February.

My own chief interest is early Irish ecclesiastical history, and I am trying to unravel some of the mysteries connected with the Early Irish monastic rules. It is an awful subject, with ramifications everywhere, and I have no hope of publishing anything before about 25 years.[254]

I should love to discuss a multitude of problems with you, so I hope it will not be too long until we meet.

B'fhearra liom gan amhras ar domhan, litir a chur ag triall ort ar Gaodhluinn acht ós rud é go bhfuilim im' chomhnuidhe anois le trí bliadhain go leith ar Roinn na h-Eórpa agus gan aon thathuighe a bheith agam ar an dteangain mhilis sin is eagal liom nach ró-bheacht ná ró-bhlasta í an Gaodhluinn a chuirfinn ag triall ort. Beir buadh agus beannacht is gach deagh-ghuidhe i gcóir na h-oibre ód charaid i sean-chúis tíre is teangan .i.

Eóin ua Riain C.I.[255]

253 Miss M.K. MacNevin studied in Bonn for two years before she returned to Ireland in 1924. See also Letter 148. 254 In fact he did much better than that. *Irish Monasticism* appeared in 1930, with the Talbot Press, Dublin and Cork. 255 Translation: No doubt I should have preferred to

43

[Myles to Osborn Bergin] Berlin N.W. 6, Karlstrasse 31, Pension Utke.
Thursday, 25. I. '23

Dear Sir,

[...]²⁵⁶

The crisis here is more and more interesting. The question is whether
Germany can stand the strain of the Ruhr occupation. The fall of the mark and
the coal shortage both threaten an industrial collapse, and of course a possible
revolution. The French and Belgians are leaving Berlin. A young Frenchman in
a restaurant committed to my care today a Russian lady who insists on being
escorted across the frontier by someone if life here becomes impossible. As the
Frenchman is going tomorrow, he could not maintain his promise to do it, so he
has left it to me. However, it is unlikely that anything very serious will happen.
Many people here are longing for a war with France again. They are almost too
optimistic about the disagreement of England and America with France,²⁵⁷ and
also about their own capacity to smash the French if only England would keep
out of it. It looks as if the German government are determined not to yield, and
the French can hardly go home again, so it is a nice problem.

Maloney²⁵⁸ gave us lunch today after Pokorny's lecture, and had a German
lawyer there whom he introduced as an authority on German politics. This man
greatly consoled me by his attitude to the whole position of the future of
Germany. He described the Germans as the stupidest people in the world,
people who loved the Gesetzbuch, "aber er vergisst dass dieses Gesetzbuch ist
auch von Menschen geschrieben".²⁵⁹ He attributes this to the feudal system, and
says that the defeat of Germany was good for her and for the world, and is the
beginning of her greatness in the way in which England is great, which was
impossible before. He did not mean, of course, that he welcomed the devouring
and destruction of Germany by France.

Father Boylan* was out here for three weeks, and stopped two doors away
from us. He will give you an account of our edifying life when you see him.
This location is most convenient. I can get to the University in ten minutes,
and can get all my meals here, thereby saving about fifty per cent, and valuable
hours wasted in restaurants, and the food is excellent. My room costs 1000
marks a day, dinner 1200, and breakfast and supper probably another 2000, but

send you a letter in Irish but because I have been living on the Continent for three and a half
years now without any practice in this sweet language, I am afraid the Irish I could write to you
would neither be very correct nor idiomatic. • God's blessings. Take care and all the best for your
work from your friend in the old causes of country and language, • John Ryan, S.J. **256** The first
part of this letter is of an extremely technical nature (concerning the collation of manuscripts of the
Lebor Brecc, an Old Irish text), and we omit it. **257** See Introduction. **258** See Letter 10. **259**
Trans.: "but he [that is, the German] forgets that this law-book is also written by men."

since the invasion of the Ruhr district, this has left a great deal to spend on books.

I am sending you a list of MSS references in connection with my text in case you happen to be looking at any of the MSS. I can only beg you to forgive my annoying you about my researches.

The difficulties of German are less for me now, but still considerable. I have decided to do more Sanskrit than anything else this term, and am taking a private grind with the Dozent.

I still hope to go to Bonn next term, but there is a rumour that Thurneysen will not be lecturing. If you hear anything from him, I would be glad to know, but I shall write to him myself.

Give my love to Murphy* and Miss Wulff,* and to Delargy.*

Myles Dillon.

44

[John Dillon to Myles] Sat., 27 January, 1923

On my return from Ballaghaderreen last Saturday evening, I found your letter of Monday 15 waiting for me here—to my great relief, for I had really been uneasy about you for some days, and had unpleasant visions of you having broken a limb or fallen over a precipice, etc., fluttering thro' my mind.

The death of your uncle was a real tragedy. I am extremely glad you wrote at once to your Aunt Anna and to your Grandmother. What a terrible [blow?] of Fate! For many, many years your uncle's great ambition was to get into the House of Commons. At last he got returned triumphantly for the one constituency in all England he would have selected,[260] and then comes death to end it all. Your aunt is the most to be pitied, because his death destroys her life altogether, and she must go on living. Such are the decrees of Fate—impossible to comprehend.

Your account of your new surroundings is most pleasant and satisfactory. I like the idea of your affable hostess, who is a Catholic and has a son a priest. This will bring you into touch with some of the Catholic people of Berlin.

What you tell me of Toby is very interesting and rather surprising. I trust it means a real reformation. Let me know any further developments. I had not supposed that even in his steadier moods he was the kind of youth who would work in the Staatsbibliothek.

You are in the centre of European disturbance. I hope the hostility to foreigners has not affected your position unpleasantly. The French in my opinion are acting very wrongly, and very foolishly. Whatever may be the immediate

260 That is, Whitechapel and St. George's, presumably because it was near his home. See Letter 5.

financial results, in the long run they will lose the respect and sympathy of the world, which enabled them to win the War. Be cautious about joining meetings. There may be disturbance, if attacks are made on foreigners, and you might get into trouble. I feel exactly as you do. I am dead against the French in their present proceedings, and indeed to their whole attitude since the Armistice. But thank God the Germans did not win. If they had won, we should all have been under the harrow. And they would have been a worse crowd to deal with [by] far than the French.

It is very difficult to say where the Italians stand. I doubt if they know themselves. Their position is a desperately difficult one. They do not want to quarrel with either France or England. As a matter of fact just at present no one counts in Italy except Mussolini, and altho' he talks very loud and tall, I doubt whether he has any very fixed opinions on the foreign policy of Italy.[261]

Sunday, 28 Jan.

The photographs were much appreciated by all the members of the family. I have not yet seen Hayes,* tho' I attempted to open up communication with him last week. He had been laid up and was absent from Chair of Dáil for some time. I shall remember what you say about relative merits of the two scholars, if anything can be done. I assume also that Thurneysen* is a much older man.

I am much interested to hear of your idea of possibly spending next Semester in Bonn. Much will depend, of course, on the proceedings of France. It is quite possible that even Berlin might become too hot for foreigners of any nationality, if things go on as they appear to be moving in the Ruhr. Any chance of seeing [you] at home in the Easter recess?

Here we go from bad to worse, as you may gather from cuttings from this morning's *Sunday Independent* enclosed.[262] There are very ugly rumours in circulation about the financial position of the Government, and about the condition of the Army, but it is extremely difficult, if not impossible, to ascertain the truth in such matters.

On last Wednesday week I went to Ballaghaderreen, where Brian and Jim had been for a week. Found all quiet there, and business better than could have been expected, under the awful conditions prevailing. The whole district is still controlled by the Republicans, with occasional raids from Boyle or Castlebar by Govt. troops.[263] Carney, the man in command at our house during the

261 This was perceptive. Mussolini's policy at this time was largely opportunistic. 262 The title page of the *Sunday Independent* has the following headlines: "Shot through head. Two executions. Illegal possession of arms. Alarming reports—more trains derailed. Governor General's residence attacked." John Dillon was certainly not exaggerating. 263 After the landing of the *Minerva* in Westport on 22 July 1922, the Free State troops it was carrying established themselves in various towns including Ballaghaderreen while the anti-Treaty forces retreated to bases in the countryside from which they continued their guerilla attacks. Despite their presence it never seemed as if the Government forces were really in control of the western counties. (Hopkinson 1988, p. 16of.)

Republican occupation, was shot in the Kiltimagh ambush last week, and is, I believe, dying.[264]

We had a narrow shave coming home yesterday week. The Republicans arrived at Kilfree about 10 minutes after the Dublin train left, and burned the station. It is believed that they intended to attack the Dublin train, because there were some Govt. troops on board.[265]

Write as often as the spirit moves you, and when you are too hard worked to write, send a postcard, so that we may know that you are alive and well. Your first card to Nano arrived, and was welcome.

[PS]We get very cheerful letters from Theo, but he does not give much detailed information as to how his malady is getting on. All he said was that Dr —'s assistant declared that he was very much better, and doing quite as well as he had hoped for. I shall send you the next letter I receive from Theo. Enclosed is a letter that has been sitting here for some time, which I ought to have sent before now.

45

[Maria O'Reilly to Myles] 2 Nth. Gt. George's St., [Dublin], 3rd Feb. 1923

My dearest Myles,

Your very charming and interesting letter came at last. I am glad your cousin Toby has taken to work. The poor boy suffered his own share of pain and torture after the War. Thank God none of you are inclined to be warriors, and God help the youth that are fighting here—one cannot say what they are fighting for except the love of killing their own countrymen, which is most unpardonable.

They have become much worse since you left the country. They have burnt Sir Horace Plunket's beautiful residence[266] to the ground, the Earl of Mayo's Palmerstown—your Grandmother had it one season. The Reddins'[267] lovely place out at Artane was burned also this week, and they blew up Shawn McGarry's place[268] in St. Andrew's St. last night, and poor Stephen Gwynn's residence they burned also.[269] I forget half the destruction they wrought all this week. No one knows what to do or say as there seems no hope for anything but

---

264 Tom Carney, O/C of the East Mayo Brigade.   265 This incident is reported in the *Irish Independent* of 20 January.   266 Kilteragh, Foxrock.   267 Rockfield, Artane, home of John Reddin, father of Norman Reddin* and Kenneth Reddin, a district judge, was burned down on 1 February 1923.   268 On 10 December 1922 the home of Seán McGarry T.D. had been burned down. One of his children died as a result of the fire and his wife suffered severe injuries (see Letter 27). Now, only two months later, McGarry's electrical fitting premises in St. Andrews' Street were blown up by members of the I.R.A.   269 It was destroyed by a landmine on 31 January 1923.

destruction to life and property. What sort of freedom does it mean at all? It's well James is going to America as it would be dreadful were he to get mixed up on either side, for one is as bad as the other.

Brian has taken [up] golf. He goes to Carrickmines with John Sweetman. His hands are very sore from using the sticks at present. I had a long letter from Theo which I enclose, and one from Sarah, which will give you the state of affairs at Ballagh at present.

I hope you got your Swan ink all right. I posted it from Healy's. I now enclose Koloynos [*sic*],[270] and hope you get it all right.

With my very best love, and thanks for long letter,

I am always

Your loving nurse,

M. O'Reilly.

46

[Myles to John Dillon] Berlin, N.W.6, Karlstrasse 31, Pension Utke, Sunday, 4. ii. '23

I was very glad to get your letter. I was also feeling that there had been a long silence.

Here life goes on more or less calmly, in spite of the horrible condition of things. You have no doubt seen how the mark has been behaving. Last week my money was just eight times as valuable as Christmas. Nano will wonder to hear that I got the best chocolates obtainable for about five pence a pound—4000M. However, the prices are of course leaping up every day. How the ordinary Germans live is the question. For the workers, and also for all civil servants, who in Germany are an enormous class, including university professors and others not so classed in Ireland—for these people it is not so hard, because their wages rise at once, as fast as the mint can print the money. However, the strain last week was too much for them, and it was very difficult to get any money for some days.

The French have now cut off all transport of coal from the Ruhr, which will mean not only a shortage of coal here, but of course paralysis of all work in the mines.[271] The question of feeding the population will be troublesome. These wretched French and Belgians have in some cases brought their whole families with them, and commandeered seven or eight rooms in towns where housing is scarce, so as to fatten on the starvation of Germany. This I have only read in newspapers, but it can well be true. The Allied Commission are still in the big

270 Kolynos, a brand of toothpaste. 271 This was part of the continuing French effort to extort reparations. For further details, see Introduction.

hotels here, but in the Adlon[272] the guests have objected to eating with the French General, so he has to eat in his room. But if the French go on for a week longer, and England and America can do nothing, I do not see how Germany can hold out. Most of the people I meet want to go and blow the miserable French to pieces, but that cannot be possible, and I believe the whole mass of the people are determined to do no more fighting.

The news from Ireland fills one with rage. I am much tempted to heap blame on the F.S., but it is not easy to see what you can do with such an utterly insane crowd. After these last outrages on Plunkett's house and the others,[273] I think the Government should formally outlaw these people and shoot them on sight, but I suppose that it is practically the case at present. Probably as a whole the country deserves what it is getting, which to me is an uncomfortable consolation.

I would like to go home in March, but I think for many reasons it will be better to remain in Germany till the end of the next Semester, in July. Then I will be free from July until November, and can dispose the holidays as I like. I will be able to return for awhile to Inishmaan and Tourmakeady, and save myself from perdition. I am doing Sanskrit privately with a Dozent[274] who proposes that I should remain in Berlin during March and continue my work with him, and then go down to Bonn a few weeks before the semester commences there. The holidays are from the end of February till the third week of April. This arrangement has something to be said for it, because I can also continue my labours with German. It will be a great advantage if I can finally remove the German difficulty before the next semester commences. I am now going to Berlitz lessons twice a week, and find them good and interesting. They have another interest for me, because I have tried the experiment on others with Irish, and will probably have to try it again.

Another consideration with regard to going home at Easter is that it might be difficult to get back again. The more acute the food question becomes here the stricter they will be, and it is already impossible to come unless you have some genuine reason. It would be a disaster to get caught in Dublin when I am just commencing to do something. Of course one cannot say how things will be in the Summer, but at any rate I shall have been a year here by then, and I cannot remain here for ever. Please let me know what you think of this plan.

I am assembling a great collection of philological treasures here. The names on the backs of the books make me feel learned and blankly ignorant together.

---

272 The Adlon hotel on Pariser Platz, a stone's throw from the Brandenburg Gate, was Berlin's most luxurious and expensive hotel. It was destroyed during World War II and has just been rebuilt—rather controversially—in the old style. 273 Sir Horace Plunkett's house, Kilteragh, was burned down on 20 January. Moore Hall, the ancestral home of Colonel Maurice Moore, and property of his elder brother, the novelist, George Moore, was destroyed on 1 February. 274 I.e. a lecturer. This must have been Dr Johannes Nobel (1887-1960). See Letter 8.

Yesterday I added Ugro-Finnish and Old Bulgarian to the collection. The latter is to my amazement an important member of the Indo-Germanic group.[275] However, I am going to toil at Sanskrit, Gothic and Greek for the present. I am trying to nerve myself to do some Latin again. But I can consider that when I get to Bonn. I have written to Thurneysen and to some of the Irish fellows in Bonn to find out whether it will be profitable to go there, but I have not yet had an answer.

I am going this afternoon to visit a Russian friend of Dr Quinlan's.* He had invited us to a festivity at the Russian club[276] tonight, but it cannot take place for want of a police permit. In order to economise food and light and heating, all public places of entertainment have to close now at eleven o'clock.

Partly as a result of my efforts to master the language of this country, and partly because I am, as usual, always trying to make up for lost time, I have read hardly any English since I came out here. I sometimes fear that a cloud of utter dullness will descend upon me, and that nothing may remain but the traces of philology. The library in George's Street was always an inspiration.[277]

I wonder whether Brian could be prevailed on to write to me. I really owe him a letter; but he will admit that his missive, though very welcome, was brief.

James is by now preparing for the glory of Chicago, or is it New York? It will certainly be a happier atmosphere than Berlin, though not so economical.

I held out the laurel leaf[278] to Miss O'Farrelly* in an affectionate letter, but she remains sternly silent. Perhaps Nano could explain this. I would like to hear some news of University College. I suppose James[279] has returned to the fold while in Dublin. Gerard [Murphy]* has been silent for some months.

I dined with Toby last night, an entertainment which cost 51,000 marks—not as much as it looks, but it was made less cheap by my ordering a very monotonous goose, which cost 22,000 marks,[280] and made a poor meal. Toby is well and happy. He speaks of going to Leipzig, Toronto, and Vienna, but it is uncertain which it will be.

[PS] I had a letter from Theo the other day, and actually answered it a few days ago.

---

275 In distinction from modern Bulgarian, which is simply a Slavic dialect, akin to Macedonian, Old Bulgarian is another name for Old Church Slavonic. 276 On the Russian influence on the cultural life of Berlin, see Introduction. 277 John Dillon's library, of over 10,000 volumes, was largely dispersed on the sale of 2 North Gt. George's St. in 1943, but even the little that remains is still impressive. Apart from a comprehensive collection of Irish history, his favourite authors included Scott, Shelley, William Morris, Ruskin and Sir Richard Burton. He also liked travel books. 278 To wish her luck in the forthcoming elections to the Governing Body? 279 Presumably this simply refers to his staying in 2 N. Gt. George's St. 280 73,000 marks was the equivalent of 15 shillings.

47

[Brian Dillon to Myles] [Dublin], 5. 2.'23

Dear Myles,

After a long silence I write compelled rather [by] a desire for the book which I asked you to buy for me than by any sense of duty. I now repeat my request that you should obtain for me *Wietors Deutsche Buch auf laute Sprache*,[281] either in German or in English. I am in urgent need of it, and I [am] told that it is printed in Germany and not to be had here at present.

Have you heard that I have taken up golf? Three times a week John Sweetman and I set off to the professional in Carrickmines. John, strangely enough, is a far apter pupil than I am.

The society of Old Boys is meeting next Friday. His Rev. held a conference with John Sweetman this morning. I am told that he intends to press the hostel scheme.[282] You will shortly receive a demand for 10/6. Have you heard that O'Reilly[283] is now an inspector in the Civic Guard?

We held a meeting of the L. and H. last Saturday night[284] and discussed the Ruhr Valley with Chauviré,[285] and during the meeting Lieut. Gen. O'Connell[286] stepped in in plain clothes and on request addressed the meeting.

James is setting out for Liverpool on Friday next. Father intends to go with him. Miss McKenna, whom I think you knew (of Mount fame) died at the end of last holidays. I see Delargy* slipping silently around the college. Jerry Carroll is now an officer in the Flying Corps. Basil Blewett has been released and is now in Rome.

The political situation seems much as before. It is amusing to note that despite my protests the L. and H. refuse to discuss anything connected with Irish politics on the ground that it is not safe.

I must close now.

Farewell,

Brian.

---

281 See Letter 57 for the correct title. 282 There was obviously a suggestion to open a hostel at Mount St. Benedict. 283 On "Ginger" O'Reilly see Letter 23. 284 Brian Dillon had been elected to the committee of the L. and H. There is a good account of the events of this year in the society in Flood [n.d.], p. 197. 285 Professor of French in U.C.D. 286 Lieut.-Gen. J.J. (Ginger) O'Connell was Chief of Staff of the Free State Army. He had been Deputy Chief of Staff under Michael Collins. On 27 June 1922 O'Connell had been arrested by the I.R.A. and conveyed to the Four Courts which the anti-Treaty forces held. Cosgrave gave the capture of General O'Connell as the reason for the attack on the Four Courts by the Free State Army one day later (MacArdle 1951, pp. 742f).

48

[Bob Partridge to Myles] Ballaghadereen, Feb. 5, '23.

My dear Myles,

Sara[287] received your card, and I took the liberty of dropping you a few lines as I thought perhaps you might like to hear from "Ballagh" to hear how we are all going on. Well, there are changes here since you were down with us. The F.S. troops are here now permanent, they came here a week ago and are in the Town Hall. They have taken over the top floor of the Private House also, so Sara is kept busy at present. She intends however to write to you soon. Mr Dillon and James were down here a few weeks ago. I never seen Mr D. looking as well (TG),[288] he was in great form. James was also looking forward to his USA trip. I think he was very lonely going away. I suppose he will return a full-blown "Yank" with a strong accent. He gets wild when anyone says this to him. I suppose you are delighted with your new (temporary) home. It is well for you that you are out of the "Island of Saints". If things continue, there will not be much of it left when you return.

All here are well (TG) and the Billiard table is in fine form. Do you ever have a game now? How are German marks going now? Weather here was very good all last week but it has now turned to rain. Would you like me to send you the *Roscommon Herald* each week? There is a very interesting article in Irish every week so if you would like it I could post you my copy every Saturday. It might interest you.

Ellie,[289] Sara, Ben,[290] Felix[291] all wish to be remembered to you.

With all best wishes.

Yours sincerely,
R. Partridge.

49

[John Dillon to Myles] Tuesday, 13 February, 1923

Returning home yesterday afternoon after a walk across town on one of the most miserable, depressing, characteristic Dublin days, I was immensely gratified to find a letter from you lying on the hall table. By some extraordinary vagary of the post your letter, tho' dated 4 Feb., did not arrive till yesterday.

Yes, I watch the vagaries of the Mark with much interest. The rise during the last few days has been a marvel, and difficult to explain. I see various theo-

287 Sara Partridge, housekeeper at Ballaghadereen. 288 Thank God. 289 Ellie Partridge, Bob's sister, in charge of haberdashery at Monica Duff's. 290 Ben Waldron, on the staff at Monica Duff's. 291 Felix Partridge, Bob's brother, General Manager of Monica Duff's.

ries in the English papers. I think the Germans will hold out much longer than you suggest.[292] And so far the French have gained nothing by their seizure of the Ruhr, while they are turning the public opinion of the world against them. The English are in a desperately [embarrassing?] position, and evidently find it almost impossible to make up their minds what to do. It looks as if they would find it necessary ultimately to withdraw their troops from the Rhine and leave the French a free hand.[293] It is a disgusting situation, almost as bad as our own here in Ireland.

I have read over carefully what you write about your plans, and on the whole, much as I would like to have you home at Easter, I am of opinion that your best plan will be to accept the advice of your Docent, and remain in Berlin during March. It will be a great advantage to stick to your German until you are quite at home in it. And I think you ought to go on to Bonn for the Summer Semester, no matter what reply you get to your enquiry. You would make the acquaintance of Thurneysen,* and explore the ground in Bonn. And it will be a very pleasant place to spend the early Summer in. If you find that there is not much to be learned there, you can return to Berlin or go on to Paris in November.

All the foregoing is of course subject to developments of the situation in Germany. If things become too hot for foreigners, or threaten to get too hot, or if there is immediate prospect of revolution of any kind breaking out, you should of course make a bee line for home. I am sure there is a great deal of force in what you say about the possibility of your not being allowed back to Germany, if you returned here at Easter, and that is a strong argument in favour of your staying on till July, always provided that Germany remains reasonably safe.

How are you off for money? I shall lodge more to your credit as soon as required. Enclosed is receipt for your second scholarship cheque, which you are to sign and return to McGrath.[294] You will see I have put receipt stamp on it. I forged your name and lodged the cheque to my account. I am keeping an account with you, which will show you how we stand.

I was much interested in your account of Toby and the price of your dinner. What does Toby contemplate doing in any of the various cities mentioned? Has he any plans for earning a living?

292 They did, of course, despite the catastrophic fall in the value of the mark (by August the pound was worth over twenty millions marks, and by November over sixteen billion), until Gustav Stresemann, as chancellor, called off passive resistance unconditionally on 26 September, and announced Germany's willingness to resume reparations payments. **293** The first Rhineland zone began to be evacuated towards the end of 1925, but some British troops stayed on after that. **294** Joseph McGrath, later Sir Joseph McGrath, was Registrar of the National University of Ireland.He had been a candidate for the post of president of University College Dublin when it came under the newly established National University of Ireland in 1909, but John Dillon's support for Denis Coffey was one of the main reasons why the post in the end went to the latter (cf. Morrissey 1983, pp. 299ff).

I accompanied James to Liverpool on Friday last, and saw him off on the *Celtic*. The *Celtic* is a magnificent ship. As this is a very slack season, she was half empty, and James with his usual authority got himself transferred into a palatial cabin, so he is travelling in luxury, which at other seasons would be reserved for millionaires. This morning I had a very pleasant letter from him posted at Queenstown.

James' ultimate destination is Chicago, after spending a week in New York, calling on friends of mine, and others to whom he has letters of introduction. He has a number of letters to important people in Chicago, and thro' Selfridge, who has given him an excellent letter, he is promised a post in a big store in Chicago, at a salary, so he ought to have a good time out there. And he and all of you are lucky to be out of Ireland, for it grows less and less fit for civilised human beings to live in.

It is extremely difficult to make up one's mind which side in the present disgusting mess is most to blame, or most objectionable. I am enclosing a bundle of cuttings giving you details of recent happenings. Of all the sordid incidents in this loathsome fight, I think that the treatment of Deasy by Mulcahy,[295] and the sudden discovery by Deasy, when within a few hours of his execution, that the highest national interest demanded peace and unconditional surrender, are the most shocking. It is quite impossible to say what the effect of last week's developments will be. The collapse of Deasy must be a very heavy blow to the Republicans, but so far there is no real sign of a disposition to surrender on the part of the leaders still at liberty.

Enclosed also are the Bishops' Pastorals.[296] A more melancholy and deplorable set of utterances I have never come across. When one recalls the fact that their Lordships are largely responsible for the present state of the country by their attitudes to the Irish Party and their encouragement of Sinn Fein, one cannot help regarding their present pitiable position as a well-earned nemesis.

I wonder that Miss O'Farrelly* did not reply to your letter. She and Æ* lunched with us on Sunday week, and the usual cordial relations are in full force. I suppose you heard that she was triumphantly elected to the Governing Body by the Graduates, to her very great satisfaction.

Brian is at present in Ballaghaderreen. I asked him yesterday to go down to occupy the front rooms. The Free State has had a garrison of about 100 men in

295 This refers to the manifesto issued by Liam Deasy, O/C West Cork Brigade, following on his capture on 18 January, under threat of immediate execution, calling on his Republican colleagues to surrender. Deasy was not in fact acting purely out of fear from cowardice. He believed that the continuance of the fight was futile. Richard Mulcahy was, of course, Free State Minister for Defence. 296 The Hierarchy had condemned the Republican campaign again in the strongest terms in their Lenten Pastorals, issued on 12 Febuary, Cardinal Logue was particularly scathing about de Valera's "external association" policy; Archbishops Byrne of Dublin and Harty of Cashel strongly condemned the destruction of property, while Dr Gilmartin of Tuam demanded that the decision of the majority in the country be respected.

Ballaghaderreen for the last fortnight, and have quartered several in the upper rooms in the private house. Sara[297] has been fighting a gallant battle to keep them off the 1st landing and out of the Drawing room and Dining room. Brian has gone down as a reinforcement. I have a letter from Felix[298] today telling me that at last a load of officers came in and took over a part of the old College.[299] That promises relief. I had been in a very nervous condition, fearing that they would make a regular barracks and headquarters of the Private House, and by and by evacuate the town and leave it to be burnt out.

By the way, I forgot to tell you that I found your Sanskrit book. Do you wish me to send it to you? I was much interested to hear of your literary accumulations. I wonder if you will be able to get them out without heavy duty, when you are coming home in July.

50

[Fr John Ryan, S.J.* to Myles] Bonn, Hofgartenstr. 9, 14. ii. 23

Dear Mr Dillon,

I was naturally delighted to hear that you intend to spend the coming semester with us at Bonn. As I told you before, you will not, I think, have any cause for regrets. Of course it will be a great disappointment if Thurneysen* does not read something beyond elementary grammar, but for that the assistance you can get from him privately will be adequate compensation. As I am doing history myself rather than philology, and as Thurneysen is not an authority on early Irish ecclesiastical history, the visits I paid him in his house have been rare indeed, but such as they were they left the very best impressions. He is very kind and generous in helping; also extraordinarily sharp and reliable. The last adjective could hardly, I think, be applied with much justice to your tutor of the present semester,[300] so it would be worth your while to seek a supplement in that line. Miss Mulchrone's* only objection to Thurneysen is that he takes *too* great interest in her work; in other words she feels when with him somewhat as she would feel with the Mother Prefect at the Loretto Hall.

I am sending you a Vorlesungsverzeichnis[301] so that you can have a look through and see if the lectures, apart from Irish, suit you. For the kind things you say about my knowledge of Early Irish many thanks. but alas! honesty forbade that I should lay the flattering unction to my soul. A three years' break spent mostly in slaving at philosophy ended in a complete rout of E.I. roots by metaphysical concepts, and my history work here is so heavy that the philology side does not get a chance. The learning will be all on my side.

297 Sara Partridge, who remained in service in the house until her death. 298 Felix Partridge, general manager of Monica Duff's. 299 St. Nathy's College, the local diocesan seminary. 300 I.e. Pokorny.* See also Introduction. 301 "University calendar".

How have you found German? I often regretted that linguistic republicans did not get at it with "warflour"[302] some time or other during the centuries that are passed. Even a few verbs blown away at the end of a normal (!) sentence would be a help to be thankful for. As to life here, it is of course impossible to give an absolute judgement, as so much depends on the subjective tastes of the student. In general the professors are good and the students decent. Naturally those I know best are the theologians (about 400 of the Köln theologians do their studies here) and they are good as gold (albeit practically starving at present).[303] An American with me here last year, a Presbyterian (or something similar) layman, found the students awfully nice, and your friend Mr Heneghan, as far as I can see, is getting on splendidly with them. You have every chance of striking a decent set.

The Rhine district here is delightful, so that if you are so built psychologically that nice surroundings help your studies, this is one of the nicest places you could find. Any books not here can be got from Berlin at a small cost, so in that way, too, there is not so much to be borne. The great drawback, of course, is the occupying army, including "les fils *noirs* de la grande nation".[304] If I let myself go on that point I would require a few volumes before coming to an end, but I think you feel yourself exactly what I would say. It must be said that hitherto the occupation, beyond the pain of looking at it, has interfered in no way with the life of the Univ. What the future is bringing cannot, of course, be foreseen.

The development in Ireland is unspeakably sad. To us especially who can read at first hand the evidence of our political incapacity in all ages it is heartrending to find that we are still untaught and unteachable. Go bhfóirid Dia orrainn!

You may be sure that I am not going back to Dublin for pleasure at present, but I have some important business to do which it is too hard to do by letter. With all the trains here stopped,[305] it may be impossible to get out, and if I do get out, it may not be so easy to get back. And this is the fifth year of the peace following the war to end war!

I do hope your family will come quite safely through the present troubles. Except for the ordinary accidents, from which nobody in Ireland today is exempt, you have happily nothing to fear. Stephen Gwynn* may feel fortunate that he did not meet rougher treatment during the English terror two years

---

302 Presumably the 1920s equivalent of Semtex. 303 The university of Cologne, founded in 1388 and thus the second oldest in Germany, had ceased to exist in 1798, but was refounded in 1919. Despite Cologne being one of centres of German Catholicism, its university still has no theological seminary. 304 A reference to the North African troops of the French army. See Introduction. 305 Part of the strategy of passive resistance was the non-cooperation of German railway personnel with the French occupying forces. The resulting transport difficulties, however, also aggravated the situation for the German population.

ago.[306] Aubrey,[307] when I was with him in Louvain in 1920, was expecting to hear of his murder any moment. Thank God that things did not go that far. With kindest wishes,

Ever yours,
Eoin ua Riain, C.I.

51

[Thomas Heneghan* to Myles] Dorotheen Str. 64 II, Bonn a. Rhein, Dia Sathairn [early 1923][308]

A M[h]aolmhuire, a chara,

Fuair mé do litir tá cúpla lá ó shoin, agus bhí mé díreach ag smaoineadh ar litir a scríobh chugat, mar shíl mé go ndeacha an chéad cheann amú.

Tá sé soléir ó do litir go bhfuil an-chúram ort annsin, agus nach bhfuil tú ag déanamh cinn faillighe ar do chuid oibre. Téigheann sé cruaidh go leór ormsa annso mórán buntáiste 'fháill as na léigheachtaibh sa nGearmáinís, ach tá mé cinnte nach fearracht sin leatsa é mar bhí go leór dhe foghluimithe agat ´shul ar

306 Presumably from the I.R.A. He had little to fear, surely, from the Black and Tans. **307** Fr Aubrey Gwynn, S.J. (1892-1983), son of Stephen Gwynn. Distinguished mediaeval historian. He had taken his B.A. degree in U.C.D. in 1912, and enrolled as a Jesuit novice in Tullabeg. He then took a B. Litt. in Oxford. He was teaching philosophy in Louvain when Ryan was there with him. He was ordained in 1924. In 1927 he was appointed lecturer in Ancient History in U.C.D., lecturer in Mediaeval History in 1930, and then in 1948 Professor of Mediaeval History. He was President of the Royal Irish Academy from 1958 to 1961. His major works were *Roman Education from Cicero to Quintilian*, Oxford, 1920; *The English Austin Friars in the Time of Wyclif*, Oxford, 1940; and *The Mediaeval Province of Armagh*, Dundalk, 1946. On his retirement from U.C.D. in 1962 he moved to Milltown Park, where he died at a great age. **308** Translation: Saturday • Dear Myles, • I got your letter a few days ago; I was just thinking of writing a letter to you, because I thought the first one got lost. • It is clear from your letter that you are very busy and are not neglecting your work. I am disappointed that I don't profit much from the lectures in German, but I am sure that it won't be the same for you, as you had learnt enough of it before you left Dublin. I am doing French here, and a bit of English, Latin, and Education. Not all of them interest me, but perhaps I can learn a little German that way. • As far as next term is concerned, I don't know what to say to you but I presume that you have received an answer from the Professor [Thurneysen] by now. If he hasn't decided to teach a course one would think that it would be a good idea to ask him to do it, if there are six of us. I will make it my business to ask him this question soon, next time we have a class with him. • We haven't had any news from the old country for a fortnight, due to the strike which is going on among the Germans out of hatred for the French. • If you are thinking of coming here for the next term, I hope you will be happy with the place. It is quiet and tranquil, and the French do not interfere with the students at all, because they don't bother them. • The town—or should I call it a city?—has about 100,000 inhabitants, almost as big as Cork. It is quite a popular place and it should be a nice place in the summer. There are usually a lot of visitors in the summer and it is difficult enough to find a place if you wait until you need it. I am certain that it is a good deal more expensive here than it is in Berlin. It will set you back by about $2 a week for a comfortable place. There is lots to eat and

fhág tú Baile Átha Cliath. Tá mise ag pléidh leis an bhFrainncís annso, agus ag déanamh beagán leis an mBéarla, an Laidin agus leis an Oideachas. Níl de shuim agam ionnta ar fad ach b'fhéidir go bhféadfainn beagán Gearmainís[e] a fhoghluim ar an gcaoi sin.

Mar gheall ar an gcéad téarma eile níl 's agam go ceart céard tá le rádh agam, ach is dóigh go bhfuil freagra fághta agat ón Ollamh é féin anois. Muna bhfuil sé socruighthe aige cúrsa a thabhairt, nach dóigh leat go mba mhaith an rud é má tá seisear againn ann, é do fhiafruigh dhe. Tá fúmsa ceist den tsort sin a chur air gan mórán moille an chéad lá eile a bheas rang againn leis.

Ní bhfuair muid aon sgéal le coicthidhís ón sean tír, mar gheall ar an stailc oibre seo atá ar siubhal ag na Gearmáinibh le gráin acu ar na Franncaighibh.

Má tá fút theacht annso le haghaidh an chéad téarma eile, tá súil agam go mbeidh tú go han tsásta leis an áit. Tá sé go ciúin socair, agus ní chuireann na Fr. isteach ar na mic leighinn [ar] chor ar bith, mar ní bhacann siadsan leo.

An baile seo—nó an ceart dhom cathair a thabhairt air?—tá timcheall 's 100,000 daoine ann, chomh mór le Corcaigh beagnach. Áit ghnathach í agus ba cheart gur áit deas a bhíonn ann sa Samhradh. Bíonn go leór strainséar ann sa Samhradh; agus bíonn sé deacair go leór áit fháil má fhanann tú go dtí go mbeidh sé ag teastáil uait. Tá mé cinnte go bhfuil sé go leór níos daoire annso ná tá i mBerlín. Bainntear amach timcheall 's $2 gach seachtmhain ar áit chompóirteamhail. Tá neart le n-ithe is le n-ól ann, agus is ionamh a bhíonn ganntán ins na rudaí seo.

B'fhearr liom fhéin fannacht annso sa Samhradh, mar is deise go leór é ná bheith í gcathair mhóir le teas an tSamhraidh. Má's féidir liom cuntas cruinn ar bith 'fháil roimh M[h]árta, rachaidh mé go Berlín le haghaidh na laetheannta saoire, agus tiocfa[idh] mé ar ais nuair a bheas an téarma ag tosnú annso—sé sin má's féidir liom. Má scríobhann tú chugam a' rádh go gtiocfa tú annso san Samhradh cuirfidh mé tuairisg má tá áit le fáil agat, mar beidh go leór de na mic léighinn go bhfuil aithint agam ortha ag imtheacht ón áit seo roimhe sin.

drink here and it is rare that there is a shortage of these things. • I would like to stay here for the summer, because it is nicer than being in a big city, with the summer heat. If I manage to get exact information before March, I will go to Berlin for the holidays, and I will come back when the new term starts here—that is, if I can. If you write to me and tell me whether you are coming in the summer, I will find out whether there is a place available, as there are many students who I know will be leaving here before then. • Miss MacNevin is working here in Irish and German. She went home for Christmas and she was a bit late coming back. I think she is staying here for a total of two years. • I gave her your address and your message. You can expect a letter from her any day. There are two more here—from Co. Meath as well, a girl who is doing Irish and another doing German. What about Pokorny, is he any good? I would like to hear what kind of a person he is and whether he is doing only Old Irish? Thurneysen is a friendly man and he is very obliging. Not like the fools we have as professors in Ireland. • It seems that things have been getting worse in Ireland lately, and that there is no hope for a settlement. • Tell Micheal O'Brien I was asking for him. Perhaps he remembers me from when he was in Ballinrobe? I have nothing more to write now; if I get any news about Thurneysen or about his lectures here I will send you a letter. • Kind regards • T Heneghan.

Tá inghean Ní Chuaimhin[309] annso, ag obair leis an nGaedhilge agus an nGearmáinís. Chuaidh sé abhaile le haghaidh na Nodlag agus bhí sí beagán deidheanach ag teacht ar ais. Tá sí le fannacht annso ar fad silim go ceann dhá bhliain.

Thug mé do sheóladh agus do theachtaireacht dhí. Agus tig leat beith ag súil le litir lá ar bith uaithí. Tá beirt eile annso freisin, ó Cho. na Mídhe freisin, cailín acú leis an nGaedhilge[310] agus an dara ceann leis an nGearmáinís,[311] Céard faoi Pokorny* nó an bhfuil aon ráth leis? Ba mhaith liom cloisteáil cé'n sort duine é, ná an í an tsean-Ghaedhilge ar fad a bhíos ar siubhal aige? Fear lághach é Thurneysen* agus tá sé an-oibliógoideach. Ní hionann é agus na daoine amadánaighe atá mar ollmhain againn in Éirinn.

Is docha go bhfuil an saoghal ag dul 'un donnacht[a] in Éirinn le deidheanaidhe, agus nach bhfuil aon súil acú le socrú a déanamh.

Abair le M Ó Briain* go raibh mé ag cur a thuairisg[e], b'fhéidir gur cuimhneach leis mé—nuair a bhí sé i mBaile an Rodhba? Níl nios mó le scríobh agam faoi láthair, ach má fhaghaim aon sgéul cinnte faoí Thur[neysen]* ná na léigheacht[anna] annso cuirfidh mé litir ag triall ort.

Mise agat le gean
T Ó hEighneacháin.

52

[John Dillon to Myles] Thursday, 15 Feb., 1923.

I omitted to post enclosed in my last letter. No news since I wrote on Wednesday, except the very disagreeable news that the Govt. troops yesterday seized the whole of the private house,[312] and propose to use it as headquarter barracks for a permanent occupation of the town.

Brian arrived back yesterday. He had gone to Boyle on Tuesday and seen Lavin,[313] who told him the whole matter was before the Army Council. It seems the Bishop[314] went up to town specially, and succeeded in inducing the military authorities to remove the soldiers from the old barracks, a portion of which they had occupied.

[PS] I see the Mark has jumped to 120,000, so that anyone who bought last week would have nearly doubled his money. There must be terrific speculation in Berlin.[315]

---

309 M.K. MacNevin; see Letters 42 and 148. **310** Kathleen Mulchrone.* **311** Unidentifiable. **312** That is, the house in Ballaghaderreen. **313** A local Free State army officer or civil servant. **314** No doubt Dr Morrisroe, Bishop of Achonry, who was the local bishop. **315** Since it was difficult enough for Germans to lay their hands on foreign currencies, it was especially foreigners who took advantage of the situation (see de Jonge 1978, pp. 98ff).

53

[Myles to John Dillon] Berlin, N.W.6., Karlstrasse 31, Pension Utke, Sunday,
18. ii. '23

I was very glad to have your letter. The post has become hopeless now, and
some suggest that the French delay the mail. But I imagine that mails come
through Holland, and should be quite free from their attention. Letters for
another man here, posted in Ireland on the 5th, only arrived yesterday.

I have got the catalogue of lectures for next Semester in Bonn, and am
arranging to go there. It will be a matter of some difficulty to get myself and my
books and luggage over the Allied customs boundary, and through the gentle
hands of the black troops, who I am told form part of the force there, so I could
hardly have arranged to go to Ireland in any case. The term ends here with this
month, and I shall go down to Bonn for a few days without a dwelling, and to
meet Thurneysen, and the Irishmen there. It will probably be very difficult to
get lodging on account of the occupation. Since I have left the easy accommodation of home, I have been almost enraged by the ridiculous difficulty of simply
living. If it were not for that, I believe I should have done twice as much work.
The finding of lodgings, and then the discovery that they won't do, and the
search for others, the ordering of every meal one eats, and deciding whether the
potatoes are to be mashed or roasted, and whether one will have coffee, have
worn my patience. Worst of all, perhaps, if a hole appears in a sock! And the
thing is made worse in a foreign country by the fact that one has to render an
account from time to time to the police.

Toby is in Germany for the purpose of learning German with a view to getting a job in the League of Nations.[316] He speaks French very well already. He
came to Berlin, and has brought his Minden landlady with him—ostensibly to
read in the libraries here, preparatory to entering for the Arnold Essay prize[317]
this year. This may have been only a sort of excuse, but it is a very good one,
and much more sensible than sitting in Minden from morning till night. His
essay subject involves the reading of Italian books, so he is now learning Italian,
and has suspended his work in the library. I dare say he will never write the
essay, but perhaps it is as wise not to. It gives him a thesis for the moment. But
now he is in great excitement because a wire has just come from Geneva, saying
that a vacancy is likely, and that he may be summoned for an interview. We
dine together once a week, and he treats me to very admirable Balliol conversation, and explores more and more the regions of my ignorance—not at all inten-
tionally, but so it happens. The list of books one has not read would make a
splendid library. I can only hope a day will come when I shall have hours to
read them.

316 This ambition was realised.   317 A literary prize in Oxford. See Letter 17.

I shall be glad to get out of Berlin after Easter. It is poor and sad, and very pagan. Moreover, the university is so great in numbers that one knows no one. I think there are about fourteen thousand students. In Bonn it will be much smaller, and the country is Catholic, which will make a difference. There are in the university two faculties of Theology, one for the Evangelicals, and the other for the Catholics.[318]

One of the strangest things here at present is the absolute occupation of Berlin by the Russians.[319] There is a café Unter den Linden where I sometimes lunch, and I rarely hear a word of German there. The Russians here are estimated at two hundred thousand. They occupy a very great proportion of the houses in the West End, and it is said that one hears only Russian in the streets; they have Russian theatres, and newspapers, and speak of starting a university. Most of them are Jews, and not very winning companions. Unfortunately, this Pension is almost exclusively occupied by them—I know twelve, nearly all Jews, the remainder consisting of three Germans, three Anglo-American cockneys, one Italian, and ourselves. Not an ideal household, as you can imagine, but the result of conditions such as prevail here is that the wrong people get all the money.

The "frenzied finance" due to the Valuta has never been more frenzied than since I last wrote. The mark rose in a few days nearly 200 per cent—from 225 to 76 thousand[320]—and prices in many cases rose at the same time. Thus the chocolates which then cost 4*d.* a pound, last week cost four shillings. Coffee is now dearer in Berlin than in New York. However, I confess that life still costs very little.

James is having a wonderful adventure. I would very much like to see his first letters from America, if you could manage to send them on to me. I could send them back, if you like, or perhaps first send them to Theo. It is a pity that we have all scattered at the same moment. However, the return of the pilgrims will soon commence. Shawn will be home in April, then I shall arrive in August, for a long period. And I suppose Theo and James will return shortly afterwards.

I have undertaken to edit some work left unfinished by Kuno Meyer, which I could offer for my doctorate here.[321] I am also doing M.A. work for Bergin, but if during the Autumn vacation I find that I am quite at ease with German textbooks, and that the handicap of starting again in French is not too great, it will be quite possible that I shall do my second year in Paris. French is, of course, not as big a difficulty as German.

I hear that Dr Browne of Maynooth[322] is in Mountjoy Jail. He is apparently the "clergyman" arrested in Suffolk Street. It shows how powerless the bishops

318 It may be worth mentioning that John Marcus O'Sullivan (1881–1948), Minister for Education from 1926 to 1932 who had studied in Heidelberg and Bonn during the first decade of this century, had contrasted the position of Theology in Bonn with Trinity College in an article in the *New Ireland Review* of 1905. 319 See Introduction. 320 For £1stg. 321 There is no evidence that this came to anything. 322 Dr Pádraig de Brún, or Patrick Browne (1889–1960), distinguished mathe-

have become. But in spite of all the horror of the present, I have never loved the Irish people as much as now. Having lived here and seen what is taken for granted as the normal life—and I have no reason to suppose that France or America are better, while Russia is worse—I have come to the conclusion that the Irish people are the holiest and most Catholic in the world. It may be only the result of circumstance, but I believe it is so.

P.S. The ink Maria sent never arrived. I wonder whether it is contraband. Give my love to Nano. I hope people will write often. You can well imagine that at this distance one feels uncomfortable. Thanks for the cuttings and receipt, which I forwarded. I will write later about money and the Sanskrit book.

54

[Maria O'Reilly to Myles] 2 Nth. Gt. George's St., [Dublin], Sunday,
18th Feb., 1923

My dearest Myles,

Thanks for your nice P.Card. It is good of you to think of sending it. I was glad you got my letter, also the toothpaste. [...]

This is a day when we are all praying that we may get peace, as the President's Proclamation ends today.[323] God grant they will accept his terms. Your Father does not think they will. On Wednesday night we were nearly blown out of our beds. There was an explosion on Rutland Square that shook the whole city, and on Friday another in Fleet St., and there is not a pane of glass in a house left either on the Sq. or Fleet St.[324] Poor P. O'Brien's windows suffered, and Dr Fottrell's also.

The Free State troops have taken the private house for a barrack, and though Brian went down and got a kind of promise from the Officers in Charge, they all turned in from the Town Hall and the Old College where they were staying temporary. Your Father thinks the Bishop has worked his influence in his own favour, as Sarah says he came up to Dublin, and when he returned the troops left his possessions. So there is gratitude from the clergy. Father Browne from Maynooth was arrested last week for having a revolver. He is a violent Irregular.[325]

matician, lover of the Irish language, and university administrator. At this point, and until 1945, he was Professor of Mathematics in St. Patrick's College, Maynooth, and then President of University College, Galway. Myles and he were later good friends. He was at this stage, however, a strong Republican. **323** This was an offer of amnesty promulgated on 8 February, in the wake of Liam Deasy's call to surrender. It had some effect. A number of local leaders laid down their arms, notably in North Kerry and Limerick City. Seventy prisoners in Tralee Gaol approved Liam Deasy's surrender call, and requested a parole to enable them to persuade their comrades to surrender. **324** This is reported in Saturday's *Independent*. Much damage was indeed done, but fourteen people were arrested. **325** See previous letter (53).

James is landed by now, I am sure. We are expecting a wire all day from him, but it has not come yet. Your Father went as far as Liverpool with him, but did not go on to London, though T.P. O'Connor* wired and invited him to go, but I think he was nervous in staying any time from home, owing to the state of things in Ballagh.

I gave your messages to Brian regarding the books. He has taken up golfing and has gone out to Delgany with John Sweetman[326] today. Minnie[327] came up to say goodbye to James. She is now changed to Carlow and likes it better as it is less expensive to live there, and the fare to Dublin is less than half to Waterford.

I read that all the Kerry Irr.s have laid down arms today.[328] I hope it's true. I am all alone. Nano has gone walking with the Bithreys,[329] and Jenny's gone home, so I am talking to you all I can think of in this letter.

With much love,

Your loving Nurse,
M. O'Reilly

55

[John Dillon to Myles] Saturday, 3rd March, 1923

My dear Myles,

Your extremely interesting letter of last Sunday week—18th—arrived last week, and it is more than time I should answer it. I am very pleased to learn of your plans about moving to Bonn for the Summer Semester. If you can arrange this, I am quite sure it will be a most pleasant experience, and even altho' Thurneysen* may be doing Elementary Irish, it will be valuable to make his acquaintance and you will be sure to learn something from him. I only hope things will not get too hot for any foreigner to stay in Germany. If we can believe the accounts in the London papers, the French are behaving scandalously in the Ruhr, and the situation is becoming very strained.[330] On the other hand, Lloyd George and his newspaper, the *Daily Chronicle*, are doing everything possible to insult and exasperate the French—not a very wise course. The *Daily Mail* is carrying [on] a furious campaign in support of the French seizure of the Ruhr, and reviving all the old war-time abuse of the Germans. It is as impossible to forecast what will happen in the Ruhr as it is to forecast what will happen

---

326 Son of John Sweetman, Irish Parliamentary Party M.P., and a school friend. 327 Maria's daughter. 328 This seems to be a reference to the move by the 70 prisoners in Tralee Gaol, but also to a move by a North Kerry Irregular leader named Pierce. 329 See Letter 40. 330 On 22 January 1923 all trade unions decided to join the boycott. In retaliation for the non-cooperation of the population the French took to robbing banks and passers-by on an indiscriminate basis. On 25 February they sacked the townhall in Bochum, but worse was to come: on 31 March they shot 13 German workers who attended a protest demonstration.

here in Ireland. I shall be anxiously looking out for details of your investigations in Bonn.

I can quite understand and sympathise with your troubles over the art of merely living. I suffered acutely in that respect myself when I first went to London, and for many years. Experiences of this kind make one appreciate the advantage of a settled home.

Shawn is to be ordained priest in the last week in May. He appears to be quite happy and settled in mind. We see a good deal more of him since he was ordained a Deacon. He gets an afternoon out—and sometimes two—every week.

I forget whether I wrote you of James's departure. I saw him off at Liverpool. As this is the slack time of year for going to America he got a *magnificent* cabin all to himself. On Thursday I received a very amusing letter from him, which I shall enclose in this, or send by next post. I sent it to Shawn yesterday. James evidently had a glorious time on board the *Celtic*.

What you tell me about Toby is interesting, but I am afraid not very hopeful. However, it is something if he is able to live and take care of *himself* in Germany. I trust he is taking care of himself.

I am very much interested in what you say about Berlin. I always heard that it was *very* pagan and that vice there was exceptionally coarse and flagrant. That is the nature of North Germans. Other big cities are, I dare say, nearly as bad, but there is more decency, civilisation, and grace in Paris, Vienna, and in Italy, and a larger percentage, I imagine, of really religious and good people.

I was greatly surprised and interested by what you say as to the immense number of Russians in Berlin. How, I wonder, do they manage to live? If they are mostly Jews that question is answered, for Jews can live anywhere.

Maria showed me your letter to her. I am sending on £50 to the Bank and asking the Manager to send you 25 cheques. I hope you had the good luck to change a cheque and have a good supply of marks on hand when the mark began to jump. I have been watching the phrenzied finance with interest. How the Germans managed to raise the mark from 225,000 to 90,000 and at the same time raise prices puzzles me. And it is hard to understand how the population can endure such an operation. The distress must be very acute. I see it stated in one of this day's papers that Berlin has now become as dear as London or New York. Surely that must be an exaggeration.

Your Sanscrit book goes by this post. Eimar O'Duffy* and his wife dined here last Thursday. George Kenny is in the Mount,[331] very pleased with his work, and looking much improved in health. He was here some weeks ago, on his way home for Christmas, but he rarely comes to town. Gerard[332] has been out of town—in Clones—for some weeks, recovering from a bout of influenza.

---

331 See Letter 16A. 332 Gerard Murphy.*

Enclosed are three very amusing letters from James. Send them on to Theo. The farewell dinner and the menu are splendid, and the arrival of the four reporters to interview Jim. Fortunately I warned him that this might happen. Forewarned is forearmed, so he got through the ordeal with colours flying.

Here things are as bad as ever. Thursday night was really horrible.333 To begin with there was a *terrific* storm, so violent that it reminded me of the big wind of 1903, and I expected the chimneys to crash every minute. At 8.30 an appalling explosion took place. It turned out to be in Findlater's Lane—a land mine, the beginning of an attempt to blow up all the big telephone posts in the city and destroy the telephone system. There was a panic in Marlboro' Street church, where a mission was in progress. Some people were thrown out of their seats, women fainted, etc. All through the night explosions went on from time to time, to the company of the hideous howlings of the storm. I could not get any sleep till past 4 o'c. We are treated every week now to a discourse by Mr O'Higgins,334 declaring that [all?] is going well, and that the country is settling down. This is preposterous. But so far as I can learn the Republicans are crumbling. They have never recovered from the collapse of Deasy,335 and the publication of the Miss MacSweeney document336 has hit them hard.

The private house in Ballaghaderreen is still held by Government troops. They have turned it into a regular fortress—steel shutters pierced for rifles, barbed wire all round it, and large sheets of wire netting from the roof to the barbed wire to keep off bombs. It is really a monstrous outrage, and no one even had the decency to communicate with me before seizing my house.

I suppose you will be in Bonn when this letter arrives. However, you will find it on your return. Do not fail to send on James' letters to Theo. Perhaps after all I had better send them to Theo first and ask him to send them on to you, as they might be lying in Berlin awaiting your return. So they won't be enclosed in this letter after all.

I was greatly impressed by your announcement that you had undertaken to edit work left by Kuno Meyer. I think your plan of taking next year in Paris is excellent, and I hope you will stick to it.

Monday, 5 March

I am sending a cutting from this morning's *Independent*. It does not look very peaceful. I see in another paragraph that Frenchpark337 was sacked on Saturday—£700 worth of goods were carried off.

333 There is a report of this in the *Irish Independent*. A telegraph pole was blown up, but it is stated that "little damage was done". 334 Kevin O'Higgins (1892-1927), at this time Minister for Justice and Vice-President of the Executive Council. 335 See Letters 49, 54 and Introduction. 336 Mary MacSwiney (see Letters 16 and 19), a hard-line doctrinaire Republican, consistently took an absolutist stance and was highly critical of attempts to reach a negotiated agreement with the Free State government. In the end she also deplored the ceasefire. 337 The passage referred to is probably that headed, "Reported captures in Dublin", which detailed many incidents.

Enclosed also a notice on the death of my dear friend Bourke Cockran.[338] I was greatly shocked and grieved to hear of his death. It was quite sudden. He was struck down a day or two after he had delivered one of the greatest speeches of his life, denouncing the Ku Klux Klan.

Enclosed also is a cutting about a newly discovered ancient language, which will, I think, interest you.[339]

I note with interest what you say about your recovered faith in the virtues of the Irish people. They are and have been for some years under a sad eclipse. It is to be hoped that before many years they may become so manifest again that it will not require a visit to Berlin to discover them, altho' the Cardinal in his Pastoral[340] declares that it [will] take centuries for the Irish people to recover from the degradation and demoralisation into which they have fallen—into which by the way he largely contributed to push them.

56

[Myles to John Dillon] [*Postcard*], 3. iii. '23

It has occurred to me that it might be of some use for me to write to people in Ireland if you think well of it, either to the Royal Dublin Society man or to my friend in the west. You remember he had promised to help me.[341] Let me know what you think. I go tonight to Bonn, but I will be back before your answer comes.

57

[Brian Dillon to Myles] [2 North Gt. George's St., Dublin], 4. 3. 23

Dear Myles,

I have failed to answer your post-cards for many reasons. Firstly, I started golf, to which I am now devoting about 12½ per cent of my total time. I am told that when learning golf one must devote one's whole time to it. Then I was

---

338 (1854-1923). Leading Irish-American politician and lawyer. There is an appreciation of him by Sir Shane Leslie in the *Irish Independent*. He died on 1 March. See also Letter 35. 339 This does not survive, but probably concerns Hittite. It had been discovered in 1906/7 but it was not until 1917 that Friedrich Hrozny succeeded in deciphering the inscriptions in cuneiform and identified Hittite as an Indo-European language. The Prussian State Museum in Berlin started publishing the texts in 1921. 340 Cardinal Logue issued a Lenten Pastoral on 12 February, condemning the Republican campaign of sabotage in the strongest terms. 341 The reference is to writing to people who might intervene to secure the evacuation by Free State troops of the house in Ballaghaderreen. Cf. Letter 59 below. All is explained at the end of Letter 62.

on the committee of the L. and H. and of the St. Benedict's Society. The former took a certain amount of time, the latter not so much.

Speaking of the St. Benedict's Society reminds me, firstly, that John Sweetman [Jr.] asked me for your address so that he might urge you to pay your annual subscription. I don't think I was able to give it at the time, so I don't suppose he has written, but you might well forestall his claim by sending it to him—47 Merrion Sq.

Another proposal which had reference to you was the starting of a magazine on the style of the *Belvederian*. It has always been crushed before, but His Reverence[342] is very eager about it this time. It was proposed that the material should be collected, sent out to you, and that you should get it printed, correct the proofs, and send it back complete. I defended you from this, however, and I think the proposal will die a natural death. There is a sub-committee consisting of Chris Dunn, Jack Peart and Sandy Comerford[343] dealing with the question of buying a house as a hostel. To the horror of all, they are very active, and it seems that they will buy the house. George[344] is still in the Mount. He calls in. Gerard[345] I never see, nor Ralph.[346] Eimar[347] comes in from time to time, and I go to him sometimes.

I have been greatly occupied for the last fortnight about the house. John Dillon[348] arrived back on Sunday after dispatching James from Liverpool, and found a letter awaiting him saying that the military were talking of taking over the whole house. It was decided that I should go down on the Monday, and off I went.

On arrival I found complete confusion. All the milliners were collected in Theo's and Nano's rooms, for the military had the top storey, and they were afraid to use the front rooms. When I arrived, Sarah insisted on my taking Theo's room (she held that the front rooms were too dangerous). The ladies' parlour had been taken as an officers' mess and they had to eat in the kitchen. Sarah thought it better to lock off our part of the house, so she had all the doors except the dining room door locked, and we had all to go in and out that way. On the following day I went up to Boyle to see Lavin.[349] Lavin was not very helpful, but referred me to Mitchell.[350] Mitchell said it was a matter for the Army Council, and that I would have to lay my complaint before them.

I went up to Dublin by the first train on Wednesday morning and on Tuesday afternoon I got an interview with the Adjutant General.[351] He said he would do all he could, and he rang up the other day to say that they were going

---

342 Fr John Francis Sweetman,* O.S.B., Headmaster of Mount St. Benedict. 343 Probably a brother of Máire Comerford. Chris Dunn we cannot trace. On Jack Peart see Letter 16A. 344 George Kenny, see Letter 16A. 345 Gerard Murphy.* 346 Ralph Brereton Barry.* 347 Eimar O'Duffy.* 348 An odd way of referring to his father. 349 See Letter 52. 350 Another local official. 351 This was Gearóid O'Sullivan, a former close associate of Michael Collins. He was later dismissed from the Army, in the wake of the Army Mutiny of March 1924.

to evacuate the lower part of the house and confine themselves to the top storey.

The exact name of the book I want is "Wietor's Deutsche Buch auf laute Sprache".[352] You are familiar with it as Miss Irmsinger [?] lent it to you. It was a thin bluish-grey book. I am sure, however, that "German pronunciation" will do admirably. It is merely as a book of reference that I want it, but it would be best to have a book by Wietor, so as to have his ideas on it as far as possible. Any small book would do. The one Miss Irmsinger lent you (which is the one I want) was about 100 pages long. I cannot discover the publisher because I know no one who has a copy. I will look in the College syllabus and see if they mention it.

Maria is greatly troubled about ink. We have heard nothing from James so far except a cable to say he has arrived. Shawn was ordained deacon on Saturday last and was in here all Saturday and Monday. I feel that I have now done my duty.

Brian.

The book I want is described in the college calendar as follows: Vietor, "Deutsches Lesebuch in Lautschrift (1 Teil)".

Father is sending the Sanskrit book.

58

[Myles to his family in Dublin] [*Postcard*], Bonn, 6. iii. '23

I have found Bonn a most pleasant surprise, in spite of the presence of the French and their coloured auxiliaries.[353] It is a charming town, and the people are charming. I called on Thurneysen yesterday, and his very attractive daughter gave us tea. The horrible flats of Berlin are the exception here, and most people have their own houses. And the lifeless poverty there is here unknown, or at least unseen, although things are said to be dearer. I suppose the wealth here is better distributed, and milk and eggs are perhaps more easily obtainable. The prospects of working under Thurneysen are hopeful. It seems possible that he may be able to arrange his Irish lectures for me in particular, as an aspiring beginner from Catalonia, who had a prior claim, has fled from Bonn. The Rhine looks splendid, and it should be glorious here in the summer. Unfortunately the French are behaving more and more wildly here as well as elsewhere, and a feeling of despair is growing, if no help from England or America comes.

I return to Berlin in a few days till the middle of April.

With love,
Myles.

---

352 Wilhelm Viëtor, *Deutsches Lesebuch in Lautschrift.* 2 vols. Leipzig: Teubner. Brian eventually found the correct title: see end of this letter. 353 See Introduction.

59

[John Dillon to Myles] Wednesday, 7 March, 1923

A mysterious post card from you arrived this morning. You do not say about what it has occurred to you that it might be useful for you to write to people in Ireland. Who is the Dublin Society man, and who is your friend in the West? I am wholly in the dark on all these points, and of course can give you no advice till I receive an explanatory letter.

I am glad to learn you were able to start for Bonn, and I trust you got through safely. The news published here makes one uneasy as to what may happen in Germany. If things get too hot you had better strike out for home. I hope Bonn is in the British Zone.[354]

We had another tremendous explosion here last night. Nano had been out at the Opera, and arrived home just a quarter of an hour before the explosions took place. You will see an explanation of the cause in enclosed cutting from this morning's *Independent*.[355] The news in it does not look like an early peace. Note the concluding paragraph of Cosgrave's speech on Griffith family Bill. Was there ever a more astounding challenge?[356]

I posted the Sanscrit book, very carefully packed, on Monday. James' letters have gone to Theo. I asked him to post them on to you. When read, you might send them back to me. They are very interesting and amusing.

[PS] Thursday, 8 March.
I kept this letter open till today, and I send you a cutting from this day's *Independent*. From it you will see that there was another mine explosion yesterday morning, of a more deadly character.[357] I was fast asleep and did not hear it. Last night there was a good deal of sniping and another mine explosion. On the whole the paper this morning does not look very peaceful, tho' I see that great prelate Dr Harty[358] has now started another peace move as off his own bat[?].

The news from the Ruhr is very disquieting.[359] I am anxiously awaiting your account of your experience on your journey and in Bonn.

---

354 It was in the French Zone. **355** This does not survive, but the reference was to the explosion on the Royal Canal between Blacquiere Bridge and the Broadstone Railway Station, which "broke the windows of many houses, [...] as far away as Glasnevin". **356** The Bill concerned the financial settlement for the Griffith family. The speech ended in the following words: "Si monumentum requiris circumspice" (If you seek his monument look around you) (*II*, 7 March 1923). **357** The mine destroyed the Customs and Excise Office in 4 Beresford Place and killed one C.I.D. officer. **358** Dr Harty, Archbishop of Cashel, submitted a proposal to Tom Barry and the I.R.A. which involved an immediate cessation of violence and the handing over of weapons after a General Election was held. It was rejected. **359** The Irish papers, the *Irish Times* in particular, maintained a remarkable interest in German affairs throughout this period.

60

[John Dillon to Myles] Monday, 12 March [1923]

Your post card from Bonn came this morning, to my great relief. I was beginning to get anxious about your fate, as the accounts of happenings in Germany have been very alarming. It is refreshing to hear that Bonn impressed you so favourably. I felt sure it would. You will have a delightful time there during the Spring and Summer, if the French do not make it impossible to live in Germany at all. I had hoped that Bonn was within the British Zone.

You will find many letters awaiting you on your return to Berlin. No change in situation in Ballaghaderreen, and I have now decided to take no further steps in this matter. Sara and Felix are afraid that if town were evacuated now, the Republicans would burn the house. It is stated on fairly good authority that part of the programme if fight goes on is to burn *all* houses over a certain size.

Since I wrote last, the meaning of your mysterious post card from Berlin has dawned on me, but as you will gather from this letter I do not desire you to write. We are managing to carry on the business, but I fear I shall not be able to visit Ballaghaderreen till the garrison is withdrawn. Enclosed is cutting giving you latest news.

Esmonde's house is gone.[360] He was very foolish to join the Senate. It is amazing that the Government have taken no steps to protect the houses of Senators. The last two nights with us here in Dublin have been quiet.

61

[Osborn Bergin to Myles] 61 Leinster Road, Dublin, 12.3.1923

My dear Dillon,

The sight of your second letter fills me with shame when I think of how dilatory I have been in answering the long and interesting one that came before it. Before I go any further I must settle the problem of the *Sex Aetates*—in the unlikely case of your having hitherto missed the solution in the home of Wissenschaft. It is simply a division of world-history into six periods, or an outline based on that division. I suppose it goes back, like so much mediaeval Irish scholarship, to Isidore of Seville, and I enclose an extract from his work. This division was long remembered in Ireland. Even in seventeenth century bardic poetry *na sé slúaigh, na sé líne*, etc. is common in the sense of "the human race".

360 The house of Sir Thomas Grattan Esmonde, Ballynastragh, Co. Wexford, was burned on 9 March 1923.

I will give over the books to Gearóid [Murphy]* and Delargy* as soon as they reach me. I hope they were not blown up with the Parcels Office the other day.[361] As you know, the big bangs go on every few days.

The Lehmacher controversy[362] has at last, after twelve months, appeared in *Studies*. I am sending you a copy of the number, in case you are interested in the debate. When you have done with it you might hand it on to Pokorny or anyone else you like. Looking over Fr Lehmacher's article again I seem to notice a somewhat patronizing tone. And in his reply he seems pained that none of us is eager to undertake, for the sake of two or three students in Germany, a task which we cannot accomplish for our own people. I see that my own article,[363] considerably shortened before it was sent in, ought to have contained a paragraph combating the popular heresy about the influence of literary geniuses on dialect—as if it was Cicero who induced Plautus and Terence and Julius Caesar and the rest to write Latin, or Shakespeare, so little known in his own time, who kept the Elizabethan writers and statesmen from using the dialect of Yorkshire or Devonshire. And Pânini,[364] with his *iko jan aci and aka: savarne dîrgha*: masquerading as a literary genius!

I should be glad to get a copy of Hirt's *Vokalismus*.[365] Let me know what it costs you. Meanwhile I have to confess that I have not yet gone into the problems connected with your *Scél Saltrach na Rann*.[366] No doubt you have consulted Thurneysen* about it. But of course you have far more than enough ready for the minor M.A. dissertation already. I will try during the Easter holidays to go into the whole matter.

Poor Delargy* looks very rueful, and his hair is turning grey. It is hard to see what can be done for him.

Is baolach go mbeidh an donas ar fad ar an nGearmáin feasta, agus ar mhuintir na hEórpa go léir. Tabhair aire dhuit féin![367]

Mise do ch. g. b.
Osborne Bergin.

361 4 Beresford Place which had been destroyed by a bomb (see Letter 59) also housed the Foreign Parcel Dept. of An Post. **362** This controversy concerned the standardisation of the Irish language. Fr Gustav Lehmacher, a German Jesuit and Celtic scholar, made the point that if the language is to attract learners it has to develop a standard form; fostering the dialectal variants out of an unwillingness to put one dialect over another, he argued, will be detrimental to the future of Irish as a language of culture. The *Studies* number also contained (critical) replies by Michael Sheehan, Osborn Bergin, F.W. O'Connell, Thomas O'Rahilly and Tomás Ó Máille. Fr Lehmacher was a student in Bonn when he wrote his article (1922). **363** In *Studies* 12. 1923, pp. 34-6. **364** The great Sanskrit grammarian Pânini (4th *c.* BC) defined a rigid standard for the Sanskrit language which all later users of the language adhered to. **365** Hermann Hirt, *Fragen des Vokalismus und der Stammbildung im Indogermanischen*. Straßburg: Trübner 1914. **366** Myles Dillon published an edition of *Scél Saltrach na Rann* 35 years later in *Celtica* 4. 1958, pp. 1-43. **367** Translation: "There is a danger that things are going to get worse for Germany still, and for the people of Europe as a whole. Take care of yourself!"

P.S. Could you send me the reference to the word *deichbriathar* as "the ten commandments" which occurs in your text? I've mislaid it.

[*Appendix*]
Isidori Etymologiarum V xxxvii, 5.
Ed. by W.M. Lindsay.

Aetas autem proprie duobus modis dicitur: aut enim hominis, sicut infantia, iuventus, senectus: aut mundi, cuius prima aetas est ab Adam usque ad Noe; secunda a Noe usque ad Abraham; tertia ab Abraham usque ad David; quarta a David usque ad transmigrationem Iuda in Babyloniam; quinta deinde [a transmigratione Babylonis] usque ad adventum Salvatoris in carne; sexta, quae nunc agitur, usque quo mundus iste finiatur. [368]

Then follows an outline of the history of the world down to his own time, ending with:

[Colligitur omne tempus ab exordio mundi usque in praesentem gloriosissimi Recesvinti principis annum x, qui est aera DCXCVI, ann. VMDCCCLVII.] Residuum sextae aetatis tempus Deo soli est cognitum. [369]

62

[Myles to John Dillon] Berlin N.W.6, Karlstrasse 31, Pension Utke, Monday night, 12. iii.'23

I came back from Bonn this evening, having had a most delightful adventure. The Rhineland is a charming country, and its people equally charming. It is only the more sorrowful that just these people should be the victims of the cruelty of the French. But I shall postpone that part of my story.

I believe I told you on a postcard of my visit to Dr Thurneysen.* He is a most friendly and attractive old gentleman, and I think will be able to arrange his work to suit us.

On Sunday I arrived in Köln, and, having heard mass in the Cathedral, went on to Bonn. This is only forty minutes in an electric train. There I found four Dublin students, three of them ladies, and the fourth my friend Heneghan.* I spent a few days searching for lodgings, and looking at the University library,

368 Translation: "'Age' is properly used in two senses: either as that of an individual man, as 'infancy', 'youth', 'old age': or as that of the world, of which the first age is that from Adam to Noah; the second from Noah to Abraham; the third from Abraham to David; the fourth from David to the transmigration of Judah into Babylon; the fifth from that [sc. the transmigration to Babylon] up to the coming of the Saviour in the flesh; the sixth, which is the current one, up to the time when the world shall be finished." 369 Translation: "[The whole time from the beginning of the world up to the present tenth year of the most glorious prince Recesvint, which is 696 AD, is 5857 years.] The time remaining from the sixth age is known to God alone."

and wrote to my Berlin baroness, who spent her distant youth in Bonn, asking for a promised introduction to some friends. On Thursday I went back to Köln, and spent some time wandering about, and made many visits to the Cathedral. The city is full of old and interesting things, mostly churches—Köln has more Catholic churches than any other city—and I found a good many of them. On Saturday I came by chance on a very old church near the river. I tried to get in, but everything was locked. I then tried to walk round it, but it has been built round by houses. However, I walked around the houses and found an old doorway with a gold mosaic above it which I entered, and found myself in the cloister of the church, which is as old as the hills—that is to say, before the Gothic arches commenced. Here I remained for a while, in a mood of the deepest reverence and philosophy, which was rudely shocked as I came out into a little square, by two huge glittering Union Jacks floating from a balcony, under the inscription "Officers' Club of the British Army of the Rhine".

On Saturday afternoon I came back to Bonn, to find an answer from the baroness, telling me to call on a friend of hers for assistance in finding rooms. I called on the lady, who fortunately had a very nice room free herself, which she has allowed me to have, and I have promised to take up residence there in the last week in April.

Ever since I had gone to Köln, many people had been deported from Bonn by the French, including three masters from the big school there.[370] Before I arrived they arrested the old postmaster and sentenced him to a year's imprisonment which he is now serving, for posting notices that he would accept subscriptions for the relief of distress in the Ruhrgebiet.[371] On Saturday two doctors and another post official were deported. The only reason I could get was in the case of one of the doctors. Some boys had sung songs provocatively, and were attacked and badly beaten by the French. This doctor attended them, and signed a statement as to their condition. But for the others there seemed to be no good reason. Another doctor was fined a million marks for having a forbidden newspaper, a sum which of course he had to borrow to escape imprisonment. A more unpleasant case which occurred, I believe, while I was there, was that of a man who spoke out rather plainly about the French in a friend's house. He was apparently betrayed, and shortly afterwards arrested and escorted over the border. In all these cases the wives and families have to leave in four days.

One of the things which seemed to me particularly unpleasant, perhaps unfairly, was the way in which soldiers and officers have brought wives and families, in some cases, mothers and fathers—and the officers large numbers of ser-

---

370 The *Kölnische Zeitung* of 8 March 1923 reported that Geheimrat Riepmann, Studienrat Franke and Gymnasiallehrer Franke from three different schools in Bonn and Siegburg were expelled by the French. 371 This was Oberpostdirektor Schmicke; another high post official by the name of Grüttner, from Siegburg, a town near Bonn, was also imprisoned (*KZ*, 4 March 1923).

vants, nursery maids and so on—all of whom have to be housed and fed by a town where the parents can often not afford milk for their children. A case of this kind occurred to me. I stayed with Heneghan, and the woman of the house had always milk to spare. I wondered at this, and she explained that the woman opposite had a great many children and could not afford the milk to which her card entitled her, so she sold it to our landlady in order to make a little more money to buy other things. She said this was amongst the poor. But I must say the children there do not look at all as bad as they do here.

In spite of all these unpleasant things Bonn will be a beautiful place to live in. The Rhine is splendid there as also at Köln, and in the summer the steamers will be going up to the Baden country. I only wish that a thick fog would come over the Rhine and obliterate the French, and then disperse, leaving them back twenty or thirty miles away. All along the upper Rhine they are there. Even the English would be much better. They occupied Bonn at first, and later withdrew to make room for the others.[372] The Rhinelanders are still hoping that the English will not withdraw from the territory they still hold, to leave them entirely at the mercy of the French. They are now completely isolated from unoccupied Germany by the French advance, and I read in a Cologne newspaper that the British government has protested against this.[373] One hopes that it may provoke them into some activity.

The position is just as obscure here as from outside. There is great anxiety, and this horrible persecution of rising prices, and consequent hunger and sorrow, but no one speaks of giving in, and it looks as if the French and Belgians were rather sorry for themselves. The great triumph is the wonderful and maintained improvement in the mark. This has been done by the Reichsbank, which used the money saved by refusing to pay anything to the French to improve the mark, thus effecting a double manoeuvre, with some success.[374] But it was not expected that it could stand so long. However, you have seen that the banks have promised to take over half the new loan in foreign currency, which will give the Reichsbank, or perhaps the Treasury, a new lease of life.

What you say about the great difficulty for Germans of an improving mark with a simultaneous rise in prices does not so much apply because this really only hits the undeserving foreigner like myself who lives on the exchange, and also the equally undeserving millionaire who prospers on the starvation of his country by trading in foreign money. The wages of workers, officials, university professors and so on, are fixed according to the rise in prices. I was told some time ago that the workers now get 3000 marks an hour, which amounts to nearly

372 See Introduction.   373 This was reported in the *Kölnische Zeitung* of 11 March 1923. The British complained that the French blockade would impede their own trade.   374 While US\$1 traded at 41,500 marks on 1 February 1923, the exchange rate on 1 April was US\$1 = 20,925, a 100 per cent increase in value. Hyperinflation did not set in until July 1923.

six hundred thousand marks a month, that is roughly £6 per month. This is, of course, the result of the erratic behaviour of the pound which rose enormously, causing a great rise in prices and therefore in wages, and then fell nearly 150 per cent, more than doubling the values. I believe it is true that some things, notably coffee, are actually dearer here than in New York. But you see that, if my figures are anything like correct, the workers' wages here have been for the moment propelled up to a less unreasonable level. Incidentally, they are three times as much as Professor Pokorny's salary.

The problem of how the Russians live is not capable of solution. Nobody knows—and they do not know themselves. They are nearly all Jews, and are supposed to live by selling their jewelry, which must be an everlasting treasury. I am told that they are still crowding into Berlin in thousands, but this I can hardly believe—because if now, why not four years ago, and moreover, why are these latecomers not already starving or dead?

I found a feast of letters awaiting me this evening. Please tell Maria and Brian I rejoiced to have their letters, and will write. From what I hear of Ballagh, it seems that the only thing to be done is to wait hopefully, falling back on Maria's philosophy that it is grand when it wasn't something worse. If Sarah has again succeeded in saving everything in the house, and going through that enormous labour of carrying everything all over the place, I think she deserves some valuable tribute as a reward for heroism.

By the way, there is not the least ground for doubt that Toby's behaviour is exemplary. He is now far more temperate than I am. His only drawback is a certain want of underneath (I falter at the word "foundation"); the superstructure is a mass of English literature, and Balliol politics and philosophy, which casts rather a gloom over me sometimes.

The Sanskrit book I also found here on my arrival. Many thanks. It has arrived quite safely. Thanks also for the cuttings, all of which I have not yet read.

Theo has not yet sent the letters from James, but I dare say they will come soon.

> With love to all the household,
> Myles.

Thanks for sending the money to the bank. He has sent me a book of cheques.

Tuesday: This morning your letter of Thursday came. I am sorry my postcard was unintelligible. It was written in haste, both mental and physical, the day I was going away, and was an effort to be cryptic and intelligible. Perhaps I have inherited the characteristic Ballaghadereen faculty for such performances. I think Dominick Cryan[375] would enjoy such a message greatly. I meant to suggest

---

375 An employee in Monica Duff's, in charge of the hardware dept.

that it might perhaps be of some use if I wrote to Hayes* or Lavin[376] or both, reminding them of previous promises, with a view of rescuing the house in Ballagh. And I hesitated to put all this on a postcard. However, it would probably not be of much use. From Brian's letter I gather he has done this already. And at any rate, now that they have gone so far, it is hard to say what would be better, for them to go out or stay where they are.

Thanks for cuttings enclosed.

63

[Jennie Penderneath[377] to Myles] March 13, 1923

My dear Myles,

Just a line to wish you all the blessings of St. Patrick's Day. I suppose it is not a Holiday in Germany. I am glad to hear from Maria you are doing well. I got 2 letters from you since you went away. I sent it too bad I am not going to France.[378] I got a nice letter from the Registeration of Grave Committee saying they were going to erect a memorial to soldiers who's graves could not be found. I will then have a chance of going to France. I have not much news to tell you conserning myself as Peter[379] and myself have not singed the Treaty yet. I will tell you all when it is singed. All well here. I hope you are Happy and enjoying yourself, and God watch over you.

Jennie.

64

[John Dillon to Myles] Thursday, 15 March [1923]

Theo returned enclosed letters. He says he hears that the post from France to Germany has become very uncertain and unsafe, and thinks that you never received some communication he sent to you some time ago, and which demanded an answer.

James' letters are very amusing. I have another batch, written after his arrival in New York. He was having a great time in New York. I am sending these letters to Theo and shall send them on to you when he returns them.

Here in Ireland things are going from bad to worse. All the peace moves appear to have hopelessly broken down, and the executions are in full swing again.[380] Enclosed I send you cuttings from this morning's *Independent*, which

376 See Letter 52. 377 Housemaid in George's St. We have retained the somewhat idiosyncratic spelling and syntax in her letter. 378 A close relative must have died in France during the War. 379 Her fiancé. 380 There are reports of "four executions in Tirconnaill", and two executions in

will give you a specimen of the happenings from day to day. You will see that Charlestown has been sacked.[381] In view of the desperate exasperation now existing, and the length of time that my house has been occupied, it is very difficult to know what to desire in regard to it. If the Govt. troops leave it now, there is serious risk of its being burned. Up to Tuesday—date of last letter from Felix—the situation in Ballaghaderreen remains unchanged.

The Roman mission of Mgr. Luzio is an amazing affair[382]—a desperate snub for the Cardinal and the Irish Bishops, who seem not to have been consulted or to have received any notice of his coming. The Cardinal is evidently desperately annoyed [?], but I expect he knew a great deal more about the business than he cares to admit.

The news of the operations of the French continue to be disturbing, and I am looking out anxiously for a letter from you. Are you getting any trouble in Berlin? I should like to have full details of your journey to Bonn and your experiences in that charming town. I am sorry to observe that it is within the French zone.

Enclosed is also a communication in Irish which has been here for some time. I can't guess what it is about. Also a threat from Falconer.[383] He can of course do nothing in your absence, but probably by sending the document on to G. Murphy* it might be possible to recover the money due from O'Dea, who is, I understand, flourishing about town in apparent opulence.

[...]

65

[John Dillon to Myles] 21 March 1923

Enclosed is a further lot of letters from James. They are really very interesting. I have not heard from him since letter dated 4 March, and am getting very anxious for news, as I see that the weather in America has been terrific. Chicago appears to be snow-bound.

Your letter to Brian came yesterday. Enclosed cutting will interest you. The report amused me very much, especially Magennis' stern enthusiasm for making Irish the sole official language of Ireland.[384] Interest here is to a large measure

Mullingar. 381 The report in the *Independent* states that "all the business houses in the town were ransacked, and almost every window in the town was smashed". The raiders withdrew on the arrival of Free State reinforcements. 382 In response to a delegation to the Vatican from the Republican side, a Monsignor Salvatore Luzio, who had been Professor of Canon Law at Maynooth from 1897 to 1910, was sent to Dublin as a Special Papal Envoy, to see if mediation was possible. He arrived on March 20, but was snubbed by the Irish Hierarchy and the Government, and returned without accomplishing anything. 383 This seems to concern a problem about paying for the printing of an issue of the magazine *An Reult*. See Letters 19 and 78. 384 William Magennis T.D. was Professor of Metaphysics at U.C.D. and also a member of the Governing Body of his university.

now concentrated on Monsignor Luzio,[385] who is installed in the Shelbourne. I am very curious to see how the Bishops will receive him. My private accounts from the country are to the effect that things are much worse than the Dublin newspapers are allowed to make public.

[PS] Position in Ballagh unchanged.

[...]

I find I did not acknowledge your long and *most* interesting letter of Monday, 12 March, giving a *most* cheerful account of your visit to Bonn and Cologne. It fortunately arrived on Friday afternoon, just after I had posted my letter to you. If it had not arrived on Friday, it could not have reached me till Thursday morning, as here we had no deliveries on Saturday or Sunday.

I was most interested by your detailed account of French proceedings in Bonn, and of the general situation there, and very much gratified to learn that your impression confirmed all I had said to you about Bonn. I am sure you will enjoy your time there thoroughly. Yes, the Rhine is a magnificent and most inspiring sight. Some day when you are settled in Bonn, you should get on one of the big tourist steamers—if they are still allowed to run—and spend a long sunny day going up the Rhine as far as Mayence.[386] It is a glorious and unforgettable experience. A bottle of excellent Moselle, consumed leisurely, adds to the enjoyment.

I follow the Franco-German question very closely in the newspapers, but of course one cannot believe one tenth of what one reads there.

66

[Myles to John Dillon] Saturday, 24. iii. '23

Many thanks for your letters, and for the letters enclosed from James. He has had a great adventure,[387] but that is now so long past, I am wondering where he is by now, and what he is doing. I heard he was bound for Chicago, which means that he will meet Cousin Willy and his household. When you have his address in Chicago send it on to me, and I will some day try to rouse him into correspondence.

We are enjoying the most wonderful summer weather here now. Twenty degrees of heat, and I sit before wide open windows all day. Whether as a result of the weather or the stabilisation of the mark Berlin has become a much brighter and happier-looking place. I walked about in the Tiergarten this morning, and the roads were humming with splendid motors, and everyone carrying

385 See previous letter (64). 386 That is to say, Mainz. 387 This will refer, presumably, to his crossing to New York, and his adventures in New York, which will be more extensively treated in Maurice Manning's biography of James Dillon, forthcoming.

his hat in his hand. I sat on a seat and enjoyed the *Roscommon Herald* which Bob[388] sends me regularly. And I must say I find it most amusing.

The sudden stabilisation of the exchange here, which has been maintained now for a fortnight without so much as one mark's rise or fall, must be the result of cooperation from abroad.[389] Do you think it possible that the Bank of England can have come to some arrangement? Another extraordinary development is the rapidly growing movement in England against France. Birkenhead's speech goes about as far as possible.[390] One hopes that something definite will be done.

We are in mourning here, because Moloney was suddenly summoned to London last week, and has returned with the news that he has been offered the office in India; and he is leaving here in ten days. I am sorry not to have seen more of him. He is a pleasant fellow, and has had a very interesting life. However, he will have a good time, and has the privilege of having his office wherever he likes, so he is well pleased.

I have not yet heard from Theo. I expected him to forward the other letters from James, having learned from me of the safety of the post, but the cloud of silence is unbroken.

Sanscrit, Gothic, Old Irish, and the German language are my only amusements here, and I find it rather an unhealthy diet. The position of having no one within two thousand miles who will talk about what one wants to talk about, and having very few books in a familiar language, does not agree with me. I am afraid it does not drive me to reading as much German as I should, but it merely makes me feel uncomfortable. The German cigarettes are so unspeakable, too, that when I turn to that one solace, it cheats me. The more German I read the less I understand how you, without any special opportunity, reached the point of being able to read German prose or poetry with anything like ease. I can now converse pretty freely, and generally read the newspaper, and with luck follow a play at the theatre, but to read Goethe's *Faust* would be like reading the Vedic poems. However, the literature that I require for my work is becoming easier, which is good. If I really feel free of Germany and German at the end of next semester, I shall be very much tempted to spend the second year in Paris. The only question is that of the Doctorate. It may in the end be wiser to remain here for three semesters at least (which I think will suffice for the degree),[391] and then spend some time in Paris. I need not, perhaps, limit myself too strictly to two years altogether.

388 Bob Partridge. 389 According to Köhler (1987) the Reichsbank supported the currency by selling its foreign currency reserves. (p. 835) 390 Lord Birkenhead stated in the house of Lords that "the warm friendship of France and this country was necessary to the salvation of Europe" (*IT*, 22 March 1922). It was a reaction to a growing resentment in Britain against the French actions. The British government, as we have seen, was also not favourably disposed towards France (Moore 1994, pp. 176ff). 391 He was somewhat optimistic here. The doctoral thesis was only completed in 1925, after he had transferred to Paris.

However, all this is still distant, and I shall be home in August, for which I am very thankful.

I want to write to Mrs Salkeld.392 Her son is in Cassel,393 and I thought of spending a day or two there on my way to Cologne; but I do not know his address. I have forgotten the French-Mullens'394 address in Templeogue, but Nano will remember it, and she may chance to know whether Mrs Salkeld is still living there. Please ask her to let me know.

I have given up talking about the cost of living, but the change here is now remarkable. I was feeling forlorn last night, and resolved upon a wholesome cure, by having a really good dinner. I went into a very glorious and small restaurant and ordered some sole and other things, with coffee afterwards. No soup, no sweet, no wine. The bill was 37,600 marks, which I leave to you to reckon. But it represents more than I could afford to pay for my dinner every evening. The sole had cost 27,000 marks. But it was a glorious fish, and a meal for four men, all of whom I represented, so perhaps I should not complain.

Much love. The days here now very much resemble each other, but now they are longer and beautifully fine, and we have splendid sunsets.

67

[Nano Dillon to Myles] Tuesday, 27th [March 1923]

Dear Milo,

At last I take pen in hand. I suppose you will spend Easter in Berlin surrounded by a mound of large chocolate eggs, each more bewitching than the last, and all only a 1d. Here the meanest and most disreputable egg costs a hundred guineas, and no one is buying any.

Father is young and splendid and in the very best of form. Never have I known him more jovial and gay, though our reverses are many. As you know, F.S. troops are dwelling in our house, which they refer to as "The Barracks",

392 Florence Salkeld, sister of Ernest French-Mullen (see below), and mother of the actress and writer Blanaid Salkeld and of Cecil Ffrench Salkeld (see below).   393 This was Cecil Ffrench Salkeld (1904-69), well-known Irish portrait and figure painter. After attending Mount St. Benedict, Salkeld was a student at the Dublin Metropolitan School of Art from 1919 to 1921. He then went to Kassel to study at the Kassel Academy under Ewald Dülberg (1888-1933). In 1922 he had an exhibition at the 1. Internationale Kunstausstellung in Düsseldorf, but returned to Ireland around 1924. His daughter Beatrice married the writer Brendan Behan. There is no indication that Myles ever managed to meet Salkeld in Germany.   394 Ernest French-Mullen and his wife Winifred were friends of the Dillon family. He had been a rubber planter in Malaya, and had come home to retire in the early years of the century. He was a moderate Nationalist, and had been in the British Army during the war, whereas his sister Madeleine had been involved in the Easter Rising, as a nurse with Countess Markievicz's contingent in Stephen's Green. Ernest died, rather young, in 1929, but his wife lived into the mid-1970s. (We are indebted for this information to his son Jarlath French-Mullen.)

and they are feeding largely and living generally on the "Bill System", which means no money ever leaving their hands to enter ours.

We often see the silent Dermot Murphy,[395] but Gerard shuns us. He is to be married in September. He has fixed a date, but I've forgotten it. We constantly see Eimar and Kathleen O'Duffy,* and the more I see of Kathleen the more I like her. She is a very nice person indeed.

I meet Con Curran* here and there. He always enquires warmly for you. "The Wolff"[396] still continues to invite me to tea and is more than friendly— almost affectionate—which surprises me. She doesn't enquire for you, but merely talks frivolities with me. I had an excellent tea with Nora Walshe and her a few days ago.

I'm going to Paris in the near future. I leave here on the 5th, go to Theo at Berckplage and spend the weekend with him, and then on to Paris. We've abandoned Venice, I regret to say, but it is more or less of necessity, as a plague of mosquitoes carrying some weird disease abound there at the moment, [and] it was regarded generally as madness to think of going there.

Haggie Mutton[397] and Mother Hutton are, as ever, most affectionate and bewitching, and clinging, I regret to say. [...][398]

The Lamb of Ulster[399] and "Alfons" are as fascinating as ever, and as faithful. The Lamb is writing to you, she tells me.

Maria is under twenty and Jenny seventeen. "Liam Doran" charming as ever. And there we are. Brian and I agreeing and living most amicably—Brian frequently journeying in John Sweetman's "Ford" to play golf at Delgany and other places.

Una Hyde[400] and myself and another studio girl have broken loose and set up a studio at "Lincoln Chambers", a fine room, and we hope to make some money. There's nothing like hope! Father is delighted at our impudence, and supported the motion. The rent of the room becomes small and possible when split in three, so all is well. I shall let you know when I get a commission.

Yours with love,
Nano.

68

[John Dillon to Myles] 4 April 1923

Your letter of 24 March arrived here in due course, and was most welcome. I was rejoiced to hear that you were enjoying such pleasant weather. We here also

395 Elder brother of Gerard Murphy.* **396** A reference to Miss Winifred Wulff,* like Myles a student of Osborn Bergin's. **397** A nickname for Margaret Hutton. **398** Two lines illegible here. **399** A reference to Miss Agnes O'Farrelly.* Alphonsus was her brother. **400** Daughter of Douglas Hyde.*

have had a spell of almost summer weather during the Easter holidays, but today is wet and cold again.

I am glad to hear that Moloney is doing so well. His departure will not affect you, as you yourself are also leaving Berlin. If this finds you still in Berlin, remember me very kindly to him, and say how glad I am to hear of his prosperity.

I have received a letter from James from Chicago, and I would have sent it on to you in this, but I do not know whether this will catch you in Berlin. You forgot to give your address in Bonn and to mention the date on which you had settled to leave Berlin for Bonn. Let me have your Bonn address by return.

Nano starts for Paris tomorrow with Mrs Bithrey.[401] They propose to spend a day or two at Berck-plage with Theo, and will reach Paris on Monday next at the latest. Their address will be: Hotel d'Arcade, 7-9 Rue d'Arcade, près Madeleine, Paris. It is suggested that you should run up from Bonn and join them for a week. This seems to me an excellent idea. It would give you a very pleasant opportunity of exploring Paris with a view to next year. Communicate with Nano at the Hotel d'Arcade as soon as this reaches you.

I spoke to Nano about the French-Mullens and Mrs Salkeld.[402] The French-Mullens have left their old address, and Nano does not know where they are, or any one who could tell, and she had no idea where Mrs Salkeld was. She says she cannot think of anyone who could tell her.

Goethe's *Faust* you should read, *with a good translation*. Parts of it are so difficult and obscure that it is absurd to tackle it without a translation and some simple notes. But do read it, for it is very great, and some of the finest parts are very simple and easy.

I think I mentioned that I lodged £50 to your credit the week before last. Write on receipt of this.

[PS] No fresh developments in Ballaghaderreen. But I need not give you any B. news, as you see that great journal, the *Roscommon Herald*.

69

[Shawn Dillon to Myles] Holy Cross College, Clonliffe, Saturday, 7th April, 1923

My dear Myles,

I must not neglect to send you my very best wishes for your birthday, and to wish you from my heart many happy returns. With all the racing about and spiritual activity which Holy Week entailed for us my Easter correspondence

401 See Letter 40.   402 See Letter 66.

was left unwritten. I am endeavouring in a feeble sort of way to make it now, though as the time of ordination approaches I begin to experience that sense of high pressure which you I am sure know so well. This is especially so because the examination for priesthood is, as is to be expected, a fairly severe one. Moreover, I have been experiencing a good deal of difficulty both with the professor of music and the professor of ceremonial. At last I have been pronounced as able to sing a gospel, but the Mass is giving me enough to do still. To say Mass correctly is not at all as easy as it looks.

We had a day of Retreat on the Tuesday in Holy Week conducted by Father Frank Browne, S.J., the Rector in Gardiner Street, and I was delighted with him. I do not think I ever met a finer lecturer or director. I had not an opportunity of any contact with him in an unofficial capacity during the Retreat, but I came to the conclusion that he must be well able to fill the position he has. At last I am free for some hours on Thursday, so I shall not for the future be such a stranger in George's Street as heretofore. Last Thursday I found my father deserted by all his family, Brian being at Mount Saint Benedict until Monday next, and Nano gone for a three weeks trip to France, about which you have probably heard.

The chief news from Ireland with regard to public affairs seems to be that we are to have another huge deficit on this year's budget.[403] The nation seems to be drifting rapidly into hopeless bankruptcy and it seems to me that the Free State troops are having much too good a time at the public expense to be particularly desirous of an immediate peace. There is a limit to human endurance, and I am afraid that my enthusiasm for the Free State is beginning to cool. That does not of course mean that I have become any more leniently disposed towards the Irregulars.

Monsignor Luzio[404] seems to be going about his business very quietly. Beyond the fact that he saw the Cardinal and was advised, according to the press report, not to interview the Northern bishops because in the opinion of His Eminence they had nothing to do with the trouble, and that thereupon he seems to have come straight back to Dublin, nothing appears to have been made public, as far as I know, concerning his activities. I would not have his job at any price. He will get the red hat is he sees this mission through successfully, and he will have earned it if any man ever did. I wonder how the Irish Bishops relish his presence in the country. I am sure there is great speculation as to whom he will see.

Dr Hickey[405] often enquires for you. He is now a Right Rev. Monsignor and I shall not be surprised if we see him Assistant Bishop of Dublin in a very short

403 Government expenditure for 1923-4 reached £42 million, but this was largely war-related. By 1924-5 it had come down to £32 million, and by 1925-6 to £24 million. 404 See Letter 64 above. 405 Mgr Dr Michael Hickey, President of Clonliffe College, Dublin.

time. He has handed the whole discipline of the college over to the Dean, greatly to my distress. Perhaps he thinks that it might be too pleasant to be dealing
officially with himself.

The occupation of our house in Ballaghaderreen by Free State troops appears
likely to continue, and I think my father would be just as well pleased that they
would stay there now, as were they to evacuate the house now it would probably be to leave the town, and then the chances are that the Irregulars would
burn the house to the ground.

Hoping that your birthday may be a happy one, and that the happy returns
of it may be many for you, and with every good wish for now and always,

Yours affectionately,

Shawn.

70

[Myles to John Dillon] Sunday, 8. iv. '23

I am still here in Berlin, and do not leave for Bonn till the 23rd. My address
there is Schedestrasse 3, bei von Beyssel.[406] I dare say Nano will have left Paris
by then, so I shall hardly be able to see her. I should have very much liked to
visit Paris while she was there, but I shall be working here for the next fortnight. However, if she thinks of coming to see Cologne and the Rhein before she
returns, I might meet her there. I am writing to her in Paris.

I shall be very much interested to hear of James in Chicago. He will have
interesting news of Cousin Willy and his household, and of his new work. Please
let me have his address as soon as he has found a permanent dwelling.

I have been out in the Grunewald today, a great forest to the west of Berlin.
We walked by the lake road to Schilthorn where there is one of these pleasant
cafés at which one drinks beer and looks around. Today there was a party of
youths and maidens there with banjoes and mandolines, in the fashion so popular here, so we had music with our drinks. I have the greatest admiration for
the faculty these people have for enjoyment. Wherever you go there are restaurants and beer-lokals, where anyone can afford to sit at a table, in the house or
in the garden outside, and enjoy beer and cigars. My expeditions are perhaps
too often a procession from one lokal to another.

I should like to go away to a mountain, and think about what I see here. I
used to wonder before about the social life of cities under paganism, where,
in the Greek cities for instance, there was plenty of culture very similar. From

406 Born Mathilde Schaafhausen in 1865, Gräfin Beissel had married Graf Richard Alexander
Hubert Beissel von Gymnich, Kgl. Preuß. Major with the Kürassier Regiment No. 5 in 1887 (von
Oidtmann 1908, p. 230). She died in December 1926.

the stricter moral point of view, perhaps, it becomes a classification of vice. Some are merely broad-minded, and are charming fellows, with no "morality", and plenty of honesty. And they have a gift for enjoying themselves in a pleasant sort of way, even in these difficult times. But the utter dependence on music and light and kisses is rather desperate. One gets the impression that Berlin must have more cafés than any city in Europe. Wherever one is there are ten to choose from, always music and smoke and coffee, and always crowded.

I saw the Moscow players this week in a play of Dostoievsky's.[407] They played in Russian, but an outline in German on the programme helped me to follow, and the acting was worth seeing. The audience were almost all Russians.

I am sorry, now that I am leaving Berlin, that I have not seen more of the theatres and concert halls here. But the others did not lead me to them, and I have been so pressed to learn things at first that I seemed to have little time. However, I have made good resolutions for the next fortnight. Unfortunately, I will now have to visit the fourth circle in the opera house, instead of the stalls, as before Christmas. Even this lofty discomfort will cost a half-crown, and a wait in a queue. But this I hope to suffer and endure once or twice before I go.

Moloney[408] left with his wife and children, and twenty trunks, on Thursday. Unfortunately, I did not see him again before he left. He was unapproachable owing to many other obligations; but he had entertained some of us to lunch last week.

Thurneysen* is coming to Berlin on Wednesday, so I hope to meet him, and talk about the work in Bonn next semester. If all goes well there, it is hardly likely that I shall leave Bonn after one semester. I would like very much, too, to make an excuse to spend some time in Heidelberg. I feel myself always wishing there were more than twelve months in the year, and more hours, too, in each of the days. But I suppose this is a difficulty which cannot be remedied.

I get the impression that things are somewhat quieter in Ireland now. Someone newly arrived from Dublin tells me that the general feeling of dissatisfaction with the government is very strong. He prophesied that in a year they would all be utterly discredited. It will be very interesting to see what parties will take the field at the next election.

I return James's letters, which I have much enjoyed.

[PS] I have received a notification of your lodgement in the bank. Many thanks.

---

407 According to the Berlin papers the Moscow Art Theatre only performed Tchekhov plays that week; perhaps Myles mixed up the two writers. See Introduction for more background. 408 See Letter 10.

71

[John Dillon to Myles] Friday, 13 April, 1923

Your very interesting letter came yesterday. I shall answer it in the course of a few days. Meanwhile I send you two interesting letters from James. I have another later in which he tells me Mr Kelly[409] has engaged him for $25 (£5) a week. This letter has gone to Theo. I will send it to you when it returns.

Enclosed is James' permanent address. Nano, I rejoice to say, has written a most enthusiastic account of Theo's surroundings, and both she and Mrs Bithrey declare that Theo looks very healthy, much better than when he left Dublin. This report was a great relief to me.

Things have been quieter here for the last week. The death of Lynch[410] is, I should say, a knock-out blow to the Republic as a fighting force, but the situation is frightfully complicated, and the troubles of the Government will by no means end when the fighting ceases. The recent murders in Dublin[411] have created a very bad feeling. It is not very safe to write freely on these matters, but you may take it that the report of ... recently from ... [*illegible*] is not far from the truth. Read the enclosed report of debate on control of Army. There is much more behind this than appears on surface.[412] Mulcahy's speech is very enigmatical and mysterious, but to those who know there is a great deal of meaning in it, and also in Johnson's remarks.[413] Enclosed you will also find an extremely interesting report of the inquest on the murder of Bondfield.[414] Bondfield seems to have been a student in the university. I wonder did you know him.

---

409 Mr Kelly was the proprietor of "The Fair", a large department store in Chicago. **410** Liam Lynch was shot on 10 April at Goatenbridge, at the foot of the Knockmealdown Mountains, while attending a meeting of the Executive of the anti-Treaty forces. **411** On 4 April the bullet-ridden bodies of two young men were found on Cabra Road. One day earlier Robert Bondfield (see note below) had been found. **412** Tensions had built up between the Army Council and the Free State government generally, and between the Minister for Defence, General Mulcahy, and the Minister for Home Affairs, Kevin O'Higgins, in particular. Richard Mulcahy, and his commanders felt that the army council no longer had the confidence and trust of the government, and the Council collectively tendered its resignation in early April 1923. The government refused to accept the resignation on 9 April 1923. In the ensuing Dáil debate, Mulcahy said in defence of the army that "they found themselves to-day without a national leader [...]" which could easily be understood as a criticism of Cosgrave (further details in Valiulis 1992, pp. 195ff). **413** The leader of the Labour Party, Thomas Johnson, feared that the army was not sufficiently under General Mulcahy's control. **414** On 3 April, the body of Robert Bondfield, a 3rd year dental student at U.C.D., had been found in a field in Clondalkin. During the inquest it transpired that Bondfield had been murdered only a very short distance away from President Cosgrave, who had been on his way to mass, and there was a suggestion that Cosgrave's guards may have been implicated. Cosgrave denied that he had been accompanied by guards (*II*, 11 April 1923).

72

[Maria O'Reilly to Myles] 13th April, 1923

My dearest Myles,

It is a long time since I had a line from you. Jenny got a post card from you yesterday. Your Father told me he had a letter from you which satisfies me you are all right. I hope you had a pleasant Birthday and received our small tokens of esteem on your Birthday. We posted them 5 days previous to the 11th so that you would rejoice at our congratulations.

You heard Nano and Mrs Bithrey visited Theo and Nano wrote a very satisfactory account of Theo's health which subdued my anxiety about him as there was a rumour going about that the trouble he was suffering from attacked his spine. I need not tell you how troubled I felt about him until Nano's letter arrived which gave me great comfort.

I am now sending the Gillet Blades and hope you will get them without delay. I told you of poor Mr Parsley's death R.I.P. I am a bit depressed ever since. It was a great shock to us all so soon after Uncle Ned's death.

Brian is in Gorey since Easter Saturday. The troops raided the Mount[415] and took Irregulars who were hiding there. Liam Lynch is dead Thursday. What will take place next?

With best love,
I am,

Your loving Nurse,
M. O'Reilly.

73

[Myles to his family in Dublin] [*Postcard*], Schedestrasse 3, Friday
[20 April 1923]

I arrived here last night, after a most pleasant journey. The country looked more like Utopia than Germany after the war. I only wish we had such charming towns and villages and woods in Ireland.

Here everything is beautiful too. There is a garden below my window, with wonderful trees. I wish the French were in France.

I will write soon, but I am expecting a letter from you.

Myles.

Your note enclosing James' letter arrived.

415 Fr Sweetman's* sympathies were strongly anti-Treaty.

74

[John Dillon to Myles] Tuesday, 24 April 1923

A post card to Maria arrived yesterday, and from it I gather you are not leaving Berlin till tomorrow. Enclosed are further letters from James. Is not the O'Neill mentioned in enclosed cutting your friend?[416] I fancy it is a very good appointment, from what you and Theo have told me of the man. Look over the enclosed circular from the Irish Texts Soc. and let me know your views on questions asked.

I sent to your Bonn address a few days ago a copy of Mrs Costelloe's book, on … [*illegible*] folk songs.[417] I thought you would like to see it. I shall write again soon. I am off now to the 1st meeting of the new Governing Body of the College.[418] I am glad to see that Father Cronin and Monsignor Hickey are on it.[419] Write soon.

75

[Myles to John Dillon] Bonn am R., Schedestr. 3, bei Beissel, 1. iv. '23

I have just received your letter, which has brought with it so many interesting things. I had seen about Joseph O'Neill's* appointment in a paper which came out to someone, and I am very glad of it.

The news of James is most interesting. His whole career as a merchant apprentice is very remarkable, and he certainly seems to be earning his living. I am in difficulties here too, because it is common to have lectures at eight o'clock in the morning. I rose this morning at ten past seven, and afterwards the worthy professor was absent. But I must not mix my affairs. I have never yet discovered who this man is to whom James has gone, or how he heard of him. I had heard a different name previously, and even of a possible sojourn in New York. I wonder who is "young Insull"[420] who entertained James so well.

416 Joseph O'Neill.* His appointment was to the Department of Education. 417 Eibhlín Costelloe, *Amhráin Mhuighe Seóla. Traditional Folk-Songs from Galway and Mayo.* Dublin: Talbot Press 1923. The 1st edition appeared in 1919 (Dublin: Three Candles Press). 418 He continued to be on the Governing Body of U.C.D. until his death. 419 Rev. Michael Cronin, Professor of Ethics and Politics at U.C.D., had been appointed by Academic Council, while Mgr Hickey (see Letters 31 and 69) was a Government appointee. The graduates had elected Prof. Timothy Corcoran, Patrick McGilligan T.D., Prof. John Marcus O'Sullivan, Gabriel Hogan, Agnes O'Farrelly and Prof. Michael Tierney, Prof. of Greek and later Coffey's successor as President of U.C.D. John Dillon had been appointed by the University Senate. 420 He was the son of the industrialist Samuel Insull (1854-1938), a public utilities executive, who was President of Chicago Edison, and a great pioneer of electrification. However, in 1932 he fell into disgrace, and was prosecuted on fraud charges, and ruined.

You enclosed a letter from the Irish Texts Society. They omit any reference to their volume for 1920 which has just appeared, and should be one of the best in the series. It is the first volume of the poems of Tadg Dall O h-Uiginn, edited by Miss Knott.[421] You will see a review of it, saying indeed little about the book and a lot about the subject, in the *Times Supplement* for March 29th. [...]

Tadg Dall O h-Uiginn lived at Coolavin near Ballagh in the 17th century. He went on a visit to the O'Haras, and was not entertained with sufficient generosity, so he wrote a satire on them. Thereupon they came to his house, and killed him by cutting out his tongue.

Many thanks for sending me Mrs Costelloe's book.[422] It was a most happy inspiration, because I had been asked by a German musician to obtain it for him on loan, as he is editing Irish folksongs.[423] I have a copy of the first edition, which came out two years ago, somewhere in the house, and was wondering whether I could have it found and sent out. It is a most delightful book, and I shall be very glad to have it here.

I am almost forgetting to tell you what a wonderful town this is. I sometimes feel as if I were in a sort of fairyland, till the black troops awake me. Before the war it must have been unknown happiness to live here as a student.

The term has started today, and I commenced my labours with Thurneysen, and other *Gelehrte*. It seems a pity to work too much here. The Rhine is only a few minutes away, and the steamers are going up every day; everywhere there are flowers and trees, and at night nightingales sing outside my window.

The French have crowded into Bonn like a plague of insects. They have a school here where their children are taught. Every house, almost, houses them. Hundreds of students have been driven out of their lodgings to make room for them. The Burgermeister of Bonn has been sentenced to three years imprisonment and five million marks fine, and deportations continue in large numbers from this district. One of our students saw a German led through the streets on a chain by French soldiers on Saturday.

I wish I had the time and the gift to write for some paper about these things.

You do not say whether Nano is home yet.

[PS] I hope you are not anxious to have James' letters back at once. I wanted to return you the other documents, and there is not room for more. M.

---

421 Eleanor Knott (ed.), *The Bardic Poems of Tadhg Dall Ó Huiginn (1550-1591)*. Vol. I. London 1922. Vol. II appeared in 1926. 422 See previous letter (74). 423 A letter from this man, Dr Heinrich Möller, survives, dated 21 March, 1923, from Breslau, to which he had returned from Berlin. It shows considerable knowledge of Irish folk songs. Some of these translations were published in his book *Das Lied der Völker*. Vol. 1. Mainz: Schott 1930.

76
[John Dillon to Myles] 2 May 1923

Your postcard of Friday last arrived this morning. It took a long time to come. I was much rejoiced to get it, as I had been looking out for news of you for some days, and anxious to learn how you got over your Hegira from Berlin to Bonn. I did not know but that you might meet with all kind of difficulties, and possibly be arrested by the French authorities as a Bolshevist agent. So I am happy to learn that you are safely launched in Bonn, and like the place so much. I have not the slightest doubt that you will enjoy your stay there during the next three months immensely.

I have an interesting piece of family news to give you. Nano is engaged to be married, and the marriage will take place some day in June. Her future husband is a young doctor named P.J. Smyth,* one of the staff surgeons at the Mater. I have had an excellent character of him, and am satisfied that Nano has made a good choice. It was only quite recently they met—about two months ago—but Dr Smyth had for a long time been a devoted admirer, and had sought thro' various channels to be introduced to her. Shawn is to be ordained next Saturday three weeks, so that the next few weeks will be an eventful time in the family.

Enclosed is a further letter from James. I have had two letters since date of enclosed. They have gone to Theo, and I shall send them to you when they return. He seems to be getting along most prosperously in Chicago, but I do not expect he will enjoy that city when the heat sets in. It is desperate in a really hot spell.

I was very much interested by your letter from Berlin of 8 April. Your description of life in the Grunewald was most cheerful. In these respects people of all nations on the Continent are able to enjoy the simple pleasures of life in a fashion that the English seem to be incapable of. And yet when English people go to these countries they fall into those ways—at least many do—with the keenest delight. It is strange. Light and music are excellent. The kisses in Berlin I have no doubt hold much too large a place in the social enjoyment. Let me know some details of your last fortnight in Berlin. Did you carry out your good intention and make an exhaustive round of the theatres, music halls, etc.? Did you ever visit the great Art Gallery or the Museum?[424] I have always understood that they are extremely fine. Did Thurneysen* turn up in Berlin, and did you have any talk with him?

424 The Picture Gallery, then housed in the Kaiser-Friedrich-Museum, had one of Germany's finest collections of Old Masters before World War II, when many of its best pieces were dispersed or distroyed by fire. Which one of the many Berlin museums John Dillon meant is unclear; the most famous collections were probably those of ancient Egyptian art and of classical antiquity, the latter included the Pergamon altar. Since all museums were located on the Museumsinsel, the whole complex may have been perceived as one huge institution.

If you do get a chance by all means spend some time in Heidelberg. It is a most fascinating place. It has sometimes occurred to me that if you make a name as a successful scholar, it might be possible to get the Senate to extend your studentship for another year. What do you think of that idea? Enclosed is your quarterly cheque, which please endorse where I have written "signed", and return to me in registered letter. I have proper stamps on the receipt which you have to send to the university. Give me timely warning when you need a further lodgement to your bank account.

I need not tell you that Maria is [in?] tremendous activity getting ready for the double event.

The political situation here is most tangled and complicated. The fighting is I think practically over, altho' we had some bad explosions in Dublin last week, but De Valera's last proclamation has put the Government in a position of considerable difficulty, and it is strongly rumoured that there is keen difference of opinion amongst the members of the Government as to the reply to be made to it.[425] Moreover, the Luzio Mission,[426] and the interference of Rome, has increased the difficulty of the Government very much. Many things have conspired to make the Government thoroughly unpopular, and the informant from Dublin mentioned in your letter was not far out in his estimate of the position of the Government.

I shall expect a good long letter soon.

77

[Nano Dillon to Myles] Wed., 2nd [May 1923]

Dear Myles,

Don't be too startled when you hear that I am about to wed. I am engaged to a certain surgeon named Smyth,* and we are to be married in June, and should you return here in the autumn, you will find your sister an elderly married woman, living in a flat in 26 Lr. Fitzwilliam St. I hope that thrills you. I shall be quite near Eimar O'Duffy* and his wife. Father approves of everything, and is, I think, very much pleased, which is of course very pleasant.

I shall write more anon. At the moment, as you may imagine, I am rather fluttered. We have a car, small but beautiful, which I can now drive.

My love to you, and kindly pray for us both,
Nano.

425 On the same day as Frank Aiken issued a cease-fire order, de Valera issued a proclamation to the Republican army, declaring "Further sacrifice on your part would now be vain and continuance of the struggle in arms unwise in the national interest. Military victory must be allowed to rest for the moment with those who have destroyed the Republic." This was naturally regarded by the government as a less than wholehearted renunciation of violence, but was ultimately accepted. **426** See above, Letters 62 and 63.

78

[Myles to Osborn Bergin] Bonn a.R., Schedestrasse 3, bei Beissel,
Wednesday, 2. v. '23

Dear Sir,

I came down here last week, and we have commenced the lectures yesterday. Thurneysen is reading *Elemente der Sprachwissenschaft* four times a week,
and *Keltische Übungen*, so that I hope to learn a great deal from him before
August. I shall go on with Sanskrit with Kirfel,[427] who is reading *Visnupurâna* V
and Kalidâsa's *Raghuvamsa*. I have promised to attend both, but if I can afford
to skip the *Visnupurâna* I shall do so. The only other very useful lecture here
this Semester is Alt-hochdeutsch with Übungen, by Hempel.[428] However, I have
put the *Niebelungenlied*,[429] and Pädagogik,[430] and the Renaissance in Art,[431] and
something about Sonatas,[432] and about das Wandern (a strange Kollegsubject),[433]
into my Stundenplan.[434] Jacobi's[435] *Buddhismus* is too much for my Sanskrit.

I am still in the newness of rejoicing at the charm of Bonn. It is hard to
imagine a more delightful University town. I am trying to forget that I have
ever been in Berlin. But, unfortunately, being a solitary beast, the pleasant life
which surrounds me sometimes makes me lonely.

I have made the acquaintance of John Ryan,* who arrived back on Saturday.
He is a peacefully-minded man, but he seems not to regard Irish as his chief
concern. He tells me he met you in Dublin. We walked together along the Rhine
today in the most glorious sunshine. I was longing to jump in, but it seemed to
be out of the question.

I hope the consignment of books from Weber reached you. I was sorry to
hear that they had sent you an unbound copy of Hirt[436] by mistake. If you think
it worth while I shall send you another, and you can present that one to someone else. The cost of binding in Dublin would buy six bound copies here.

I have still to thank you for your quotation from Isidore of Seville. By the
way, I intend to follow a course of lectures on Vulgärlateinisch here. I hoped
that they would be an introduction to the mysteries of the libraries of Irish

427 Willibald Kirfel (1885-1964), Professor of Indian Philology in Bonn from 1922 to 1953. 428
Heinrich Hempel, Professor of German in Bonn until 1939. 429 With Prof. Rudolf Meissner
(1862-1948), Professor of Germanic and Nordic Philology in Bonn from 1913 to 1931. 430
"Pädagogische Strömungen im XX. Jahrhundert" (20th century trends in paedagogy) with Prof.
Kutzner. 431 With Professor P. Clemen. 432 Dr A. Schmitz taught a course in "analysing classical sonatas". 433 The university's PE lecturer Otto Landau lectured on the "Theory of Hiking,
Rowing and Swimming". Wandern, "hiking", was very much the fashion for young people at this
time in Germany, closely tied in with the Youth Movement. Myles dealt with this Movement in his
articles for the *Irish Statesman*. See Appendix. 434 "Time-table". 435 Hermann Georg Jacobi
(1850-1937), Prof. of Sanskrit and Comparative Philology, had already retired but continued to
give lectures in the summer semester of 1923 on "difficult Indian authors". 436 See Letter 61.

monasteries, but Thurneysen* does not seem to think so. I remember your saying you heard some lectures on *Middle* Latin, but that is probably more to the point. Have you any advice?

I am also attending Palaeography by one Schulte,[437] but he has a horrible voice, so I do not know how long I shall continue.

You held out hope that during the Easter holidays you might be able to look into my difficulties in connection with *Saltair na Rann*[438] and its offspring. Miss Mulchrone* has alarmed me by declaring that two other versions, or fragments, are contained in H. 2. 16. 844 and H. 2. 12. no. 9. If you chance to have kept a sheet which I enclosed, upon which I had collected my thoughts about the stemma, I should be glad to have it, when you write again. I had not the energy to make out two copies then, and I shrink before the small task of going through my notes again to rebuild it.

I am relieved to hear that you think I can qualify for the M.A. before I finish the work, as it may be well not to give too much time to it while I am here. You see, I am not yet blasé enough to smile contemptuously at degrees.

If you see Gerard Murphy,* I would be most thankful if you would give him my address. A sense of dignity forbids me to write to him again, even if I had time. I was threatened with legal proceedings some months ago, by the despairing printer of the *Reult*[439], and I forwarded the letter to Gerard; but he and the printer have remained silent ever since.

Commend me to Miss Wulff.* Why she or anybody else remains in Dublin, when they could be living here, is puzzling. But indeed with the French and the Africans in occupation, it is not so strange. One must try not to think of them.

Please give my love to Lloyd Jones.[440] I am still meaning to write to him, but I shall probably call on him instead, when I get home.

Delargy* has illtreated me too, but he has only to ask for forgiveness.

I finished collating my *LB*[441] transcript before leaving Berlin, and a long pause has followed. However, I shall soon commence to copy out the whole text of my transcript, extending the contractions, etc., and commence collecting rarer words for a glossary. That awful passage corresponding to the *Book of Numbers* will yield a few.

With best wishes,
Yours sincerely,
Myles Dillon.

My good will to Joseph O'Neill.* I was very glad to see a notice of his appointment.

---

437 Professor Aloys Schulte (1857-1941), Prof. of History, lectured on "Lateinische Paläographie". **438** "The Psalter of Quatrains", an Old Irish epic poem, composed in around AD 987, telling in verse the story of the Old Testament and the Life of Christ. See Letter 61. **439** See Letter 24. **440** J. Lloyd Jones, Lecturer in Welsh at U.C.D. **441** The *Lebor Brecc*, or "Speckled Book of Mac Egan", an Irish 14th cent. manuscript, containing mainly sacred material.

79

[Brian Dillon to Myles] [2 North Gt. George's St., Dublin], 5. 5. '23

Dear Myles,

I am moved at last to write to you. I waited till now in the hope that the books would arrive, but I have now despaired of them. Fortunately I was not dependent on them as I finally persuaded Browne and Nolan's to get me 2 books on German phonetics which fulfil my needs.

Nano's engagement is remarkable and very sudden. She only met Dr Smyth* about 2 months ago. Till then Norman Reddin* was in great favour, and indeed I was almost resigned to a wedding between them. But the acquaintance broke off suddenly and, I gather, sharply, and now she is wild excitement preparing to wed Smyth. I gather that the event is to take place on June 19th or near then. I have only met him for a moment, so I know little of him beyond that he is plain and small. He is only slightly taller than Nano. But I gather that he is a very worthy man, and he is making over £100 a year, which is remarkable for a young surgeon.

I was in the Mt.442 for 3 weeks round Easter and assisted in several Dramatic entertainments. I have forgotten whether I wrote to you since so I will not elaborate on it. We were raided twice while I was there, which seemed a pity.443

I am still fighting the battle of the guns, but am everywhere repulsed.

My chief object in writing this letter is to urge you to send 10/6, your subscription to the M.S.B.444 Society, either to John Sweetman or, if that is too much for you, to me.

I went to Clongowes last Sunday to see it and was very cordially entertained, but it seemed an unpleasant place. Shawn will be ordained almost at once.

Brian.

I urge you again to dispatch 10/6.

Jenny445 complains bitterly that you have only written once since you went away and only acknowledged the tie through Maria. It would be wise to write at once.

80

[Myles to John Dillon] Bonn, Schedestrasse 3, Friday, 11. v. '23

Many thanks for your long letter. I have been waiting for time and inspiration to reply, but I wait no longer, lest you should get anxious about the cheque.

---

442 I.e. Mount St. Benedict.   443 Fr Sweetman,* of course, was a notorious Republican sympathiser.   444 Mount St. Benedict.   445 The housemaid at 2 North Gt. George's St.

I rejoice to hear the news of Nano's wild performance. I hope, now that she has become a matrimonialist, she will assist her brethren to the higher life. Her flat will be a charming rendezvous for us, when lovesick. I only wish they had not come to the point so quickly, so that we could have been there to see.

I am enjoying Thurneysen's* lectures greatly. He lectures seven hours a week, and I attend all his classes. He is extremely kind, and invites us to his house to discuss work, and to arrange what we shall do. I am thinking of doing my doctorate in Comparative Philology, as a main feature, instead of in Celtic, if that is practicable, as it is hitherto an unknown study, almost, in Ireland, and Celtic proper is most easily perfected in Dublin.

We are going to visit the great Benedictine monastery near Coblenz, Maria Laach, at Whitsuntide, and I may go on up the Rhine from there to Heidelberg for a few days. A most friendly cleric here has promised to accompany us.

I enclose James's letters, which I have greatly enjoyed, and the cheque. It would be no harm to lodge money to my credit at once. The bank has as yet sent me no warning, nor any old cheques or account of my credit, but it will put them in good humour, and I have spent a good deal of money recently.

We are at present enduring a very unpleasant spell of cold weather, following a terrific thunderstorm some days ago. But it promises not to last.

You will have heard from me since you last wrote. I must beg forgiveness for this formless missive, but it is only an emergency letter.

I fear that George's Street will be for a short period rather a solitary dwelling. Perhaps you and Brian would set forth and visit the beautiful Rhineland for a few weeks. For travellers it is really unspoilt.

Much love to the family, and my special good will to Nano and to Shawn.

[PS] I sent the receipt to the University.

81

[John Dillon to Myles] Friday, 18 May, 1923

As far as I can recollect, I have not written to you since the 2nd of May. I have had a good deal of writing to do of late, and I was waiting to get your letter returning cheque. It takes quite a long time for letters to come from Bonn. Yours of 11 May with cheque enclosed arrived on Wed., 16th.

You are evidently becoming a true Gelehrter, because you sent back the cheque in precisely the condition in which it reached you. The object of sending it was of course to get your signature opposite the word "signed" on back of cheque. Please return it signed. I am sending a lodgement of £50 to your account.

I was delighted to have your account of Bonn. I felt sure you would fall in love with it—and of course when fine weather finally sets in its attractions will vastly increase. You will enjoy your excursion up the Rhine extremely, and by all means go on to Heidelberg. It is another fascinating German city. The French appear to me to have—like our own people—gone more or less mad. If they persevere on their present lines, they will plunge Europe in a series of bloody and ruinous wars, which will leave very little of the civilisation of Europe in existence.

We also have had a most shocking spell of weather here—cold as mid-winter, hail, snow and incessant storms. It looks a bit better today. Nano's affair goes on most prosperously. Everyone speaks in the *highest* terms of Dr Smyth,* and Nano, having abandoned all her previous principles, is in love with him frankly and avowedly. Congratulations pour in from all sides. I would feel this house sadly lonely, if I were to stay here all alone for the few weeks after the marriage, so I have made the following plan, which I hope to be able to carry out. I propose to go to London about the 15 June, stay there for a few days, then on to see Theo, and accompany him to a place in Switzerland where he proposes to try what is known as the sun cure. Then I think of taking you on my way back. What do you say to this unlooked for development on your antient parent's part? I should like to see Bonn and the Rhine again before I depart for another and let us hope a better world. The ... [*illegible*] I have of good in this old world—if the inhabitants could only abstain from behaving like lunatics—would scrap all aeroplanes and many other modern machines, and pass a rigorous law forbidding all scientific inventions for the future. I am afraid these are utopian aspirations.

I am glad you are getting on well with Thurneysen,* and your idea of Comparative Philology appears to me an excellent one. I have been thinking myself that there is a comparatively virgin field open for you in Ireland in that department of learning.

I forgot to tell you, it has been arranged by Father O'Reilly that Shawn is to carry out the marriage ceremony and Father Nicholas[446] to say the Nuptial Mass—Father O'Reilly superintending to see that all is correctly carried thro'.

Enclosed are from the letters from James. The man Kelly in his store called the Fair he is working in is a friend of Selfridge's,[447] and S. gave James a letter of introduction to Kelly. James' original destination was New York, but on his own suggestion it was changed to Chicago. He suggested that it would be an enormous advantage to him to be in a city where his cousin Willie[448] had a home, and I felt that he was quite right in this view. Young Insull is an Englishman whose father is a very wealthy and prominent man in Chicago,[449]

446 That is, his younger brother Henry (1856-1938), who became a Franciscan friar (and Provincial of the Order in Ireland from 1902-1914), and took this as his name in religion. 447 Gordon Selfridge, owner of Selfridge's in London. 448 William Dillon (1889-1959), son of William (1850-1935), John Dillon's older brother, who was head of the family in Chicago, and presided over the family law firm. 449 See Letter 75.

and to whom I got a letter introducing James from T.P.[450] Insull has been extrordinarily kind to James. James had also letters for Mrs O'Sullivan, and, as you will gather from enclosed letters, is moving in the highest circles of Chicago society. In his last letter, just received, he announces he is going to a fancy dress Ball dressed as a Cardinal. A very suitable get-up for James.

[PS] In my next letter I shall reply to you if I may about the Irish Texts Society.

You will have no difficulty in recognising the Rev. gentleman alluded to in Cosgrave's speech in enclosed cutting.[451]

82

[Theo Dillon to Myles] Institut François de Sales, Berck-plage, Pas de Calais, May 22, 1923

Dear Myles,

I would forgive you much, if much I had to forgive, for the last and fattest volume of the series.[452] It is a gem, transcending praise, and to my joy most easy to read—linguistically. Some day I hope, when the gods are kind, I will go and work in the midst of this world of wonderful physiologists. Meanwhile, you have heard that I am abandoning Calot definitely on the 22 June, and that Father is coming over to go with me to Leysin in Switzerland. He is obviously so over-joyed by the marriage that he finds some kind of a burst absolutely necessary. I feel no grief at the idea of leaving the Institut. A grey and unprofitable 9 months, only relieved by the fact that I had succeeded in making my room comfortable for working, and a similar process will take some time in Switzerland.

I don't know if Leysin is within week-end distance of Bonn or not, but I hope to see you before you go back to Dublin. There must be quite a lot we could say to each other after a year.

The marriage seems to be going on like a house on fire. I receive, as I suppose you do, enthusiastic letters from Nano from time to time, until, at last, my last small doubt as to the genuineness and lastingness of the passion has melted. Father wrote me three letters in as many days the other day, after a fortnight's silence, full of the virtues of Paddy Smith.*

Ralph [Barry]* was the first to send a present—correct as ever.

Shawn is either a priest or on the verge by now. Pat Sweetman[453] is to come here with Pott's Disease at the end of the month, which he contracted in the Free State Army!

Theo.

---

450 That is, T.P. O'Connor.* **451** The cutting is unfortunately lost and the reference must remain unclear. **452** The reference is to the *Zeitschrift für Biochemie*, as becomes apparent at the end of the letter. **453** Son of John Sweetman of Drumbaragh, M.P. He recovered, and later emigrated to Australia.

If and when you reply, will you tell me how many volumes you sent me in all. The reason I ask is that I received the 1st part of the Z. *Biochimie* for 1922 and the 2nd part for 1923, but the two intervening parts did not arrive. Theo.

83

[John Dillon to Myles] Wednesday, 23 May, 1923

I have been expecting a letter from you, but I suppose that you have gone up the Rhine, as foreshadowed in your last letter. If you did go on a Whitsuntide excursion I trust you have had better weather than we have had here recently. We have a second winter here for the last 3 weeks. It is struggling to clear up today, but still cold for May.

All goes well here. I think I mentioned in my last letter that Nano's marriage is fixed definitely for 12 June.

Enclosed is a cutting from M.G.[454] giving a most melancholy account of the condition of the students in Heidelberg.

Write soon and write copiously.

[PS] I have lodged £50 to your account.

84

[Myles to John Dillon] Hotel Holländischer Hof (Hotel de Hollande), Mainz, Thursday, 24. v. '23

I am wandering pleasantly through the Rhineland like Belloc on his way to Rome[455]—by land and river, sometimes on foot and oftener on something else.

Heneghan and I left Bonn on Saturday by steamer, to spend Whitsuntide at the old Benedictine Monastery of Laach. A friendly priest who had arranged the visit for us was to accompany us, but owing to trouble with the French he could not come, so we went alone. Our journey was adventurous, a horribly crowded slow steamer, with charming young wanderers on board who played Rhine music on fiddles and banjoes, and we arrived very late at Andernach, nine miles from the Abbey. A train goes from a field outside the town to a place within four miles. It cannot start from the station because the French have occupied it, so we had to walk out to this place, and stand in a queue outside an old railway coach which served as ticket office. While I was buried in the coach, the train started, and left us in the field, to wait for another, which was due at half past ten, and arrived at half past eleven. At twelve we reached Nieder Mindich

454 That is, the *Manchester Guardian.* 455 The reference is to Hilaire Belloc's travel book *The Path to Rome*. Engl. tr. London 1902.

and commenced to walk to the Abbey, which we found, after lighting many matches at signposts, at two in the morning. However, we were received with great hospitality, and had delightful days there, far away from hardship and hatred and the French. The Abbey owns a whole valley, and a wonderful lake. They have cattle and corn and everything they need, and we rejoiced in peace and plenty, and holiness. The ceremonies were more splendid than I have ever seen, and the church is perfect Romanesque.

On Tuesday we came on foot to Andernach, and boarded the express steamer to Coblenz. This was a much pleasanter voyage, and we found an excellent hotel. Yesterday afternoon I left Coblenz on foot at two o'clock for Boppard, hoping that the steamer would be some hours late, and that I might join it there. But it passed me about twenty minutes after I started, so I advanced in peace, resolved to try some other way, or stay the night wherever it found me. I hailed a motorcar at four o'clock, and a benevolent American lady took me up. She was paying a hasty visit, and was motoring from Köln nearly a hundred miles up the Rhine to see some friends, and she invited me to share the pleasure of the journey, so I passed the steamer triumphantly halfway. We had a glorious drive through the Rhine valleys, with vineyards on each side, and the castles of robber barons and archbishops of the Middle Ages overhead. At Bingen we parted most affectionately, and I had two hours wait for my steamer. I went to a beastly hotel, and met a most amusing old waiter. I have laughed since at his tone of voice when he told me that ten centners of coal cost two hundred and thirty thousand marks. He announced this in stupefaction, and laughed as one who had drunk much good wine, and then left me alone. Bingen is at present under martial law, and everyone must be indoors at nine o'clock. I walked through the town, and up to the Roman fortress, and returned to the pier just as my wicked steamer moved away, so I had to wait an hour and crawl on here in a slow boat, finishing by tram, because the boat only came to Biebrich.

Today it is wet and horrible. I think of walking to Wiesbaden, or possibly to Frankfurt, and then coming down the Rhine again to Bonn. I might stay here till tomorrow if it does not clear, but the hotel is dreary and not good, and crawling with French.

Heneghan* went back to Bonn from Coblenz yesterday. Our walk from Maria Lach to Andernach was one of the pleasantest parts of the journey. The country is rich and peaceful, and the villainies of the French cannot much disturb the country people. They have food in the fields around them, and their villages are free from the occupation, and they look perfectly happy.

I shall hope for a harvest of letters when I get back to Bonn. I could not arrange to have them sent after me. These are days of great preparation in George's Street. I am anxious to hear the date of Nano's wedding, and whether Shaun will assist at the function. What does Father Nicholas say to all this? I wrote to him after Christmas, but he did not answer.

85

[Myles to John Dillon] [*Postcard*, Cologne] Monday, [28 May 1923]

Many thanks for sending James' letters.

I returned yesterday, having had a glorious journey down the Rhine all day. I waited in Wiesbaden over Saturday as it was wet, but Sunday was delightful. I have got your two letters. It was ridiculous that I did not sign the cheque, but I shall do so and send it on. The news of Shaun and Nano is most welcome. I only wish I heard more of what is happening. I celebrated Shaun's ordination yesterday in the spirit, but I do not know whether this was right. I rejoice to hear that you are coming out here. If you go to Switzerland first, you might come back by Schaffhausen and see the Rhine falls, and sail down the river from wherever navigation starts.

86

[Myles to John Dillon] Bonn, Schedestrasse, 3, Tuesday, May 29th, '23

I sent you a card from Köln yesterday, as I had not time to write.

It is very good to hear that you are coming to Bonn. You will enjoy it greatly. This is a perfect university town, if it were not for the French, and you will be able to see the German university system at first hand. You can let me know when you are arriving and I shall arrange with the hotel. There are two excellent hotels here, and it would depend on when you arrive in Köln whether you should stay at a hotel there or not, assuming that you come that way. Bonn is only half an hour in an electric train. I hastened to Köln yesterday on hearing the date of Nano's wedding, to seek a permit from the English there to export something to her. It appears, however, to be quite hopeless. One requires two permits, one from the Germans, and one from the French, and each one damns the other. The English seem to play a very obscure role in the affair. He advised me to enquire further at the Consulate, which would be open next day at some hour, so I came home.

I had thought of sending her some Zeiss glasses, a field-glass and an opera-glass, for want of a better inspiration. I have also tried to order them from where they are made, but I am told that for export the price is reckoned in foreign exchange, and Zeiss now refuses to sell to private persons abroad.

Perhaps you could get the glasses in Dublin. The symbol of my residence in Germany will remain. Prism-field-glasses of 6-magnification are the best, I am told. There are more powerful ones, but they are accused of sacrificing clearness for magnitude. The opera-glasses you could choose. I imagine both could be obtained for a sum between £5–£10, which is not too much for so wonderful an occasion. I am sorry to be unable to do this myself, but it is not possible. If you have a better inspiration as to what I should give Nano, please act on it. I enclose the cheque, and James's two letters. He will have a great career, but I wonder whether he will suffer it to run in Ballaghaderreen. I can see him marrying prosperously in Chicago. However, his longing to assist in the undoing of the Irish Free State may call him home.

I should like some news of Shaun's ordination, or whether it has taken place.

[PS] I received a notification from the Bank that you had lodged £50 to my credit. Many thanks.

87

[John Dillon to Myles] Sat., 2nd June, 1923

Your delightful letter from Mainz, dated 24 May, arrived three days ago. I was extremely gratified to learn from it that you appreciate the Rhineland. I expected that you would. You have now seen far more of it, and of the people, than I. But from the few glimpses that I got in passing thro'[456] I have loved the Rhineland and the Rhinelanders all my life. I can heartily sympathise with your feelings about the French, but you had better be cautious about giving expression to them in your letters, as your letters may be opened and the results might be unpleasant.

I am looking forward with much satisfaction to spending some days with you in Bonn. When will you be free to come home? Your card from Cologne came yesterday and your letter from Bonn of 29 May, with cheque, duly signed, enclosed, came this morning.

I think the best plan in respect of the present is to concentrate on a really good and handsome opera glass. I have been making enquiries, but there are none of Zeiss in stock in any of the shops I have so far penetrated. I think I shall write to London and ask Aunt Kathleen to do the commission for me. I see very tempting ads of Zeiss glasses in the London papers. The idea is, I think, a very good one. Nano has been receiving a shower of very attractive presents, but so far no one has presented an opera glass.

I find I wrote to you last on 23 May, so I cannot have told you how the ordination went off. The ceremony was very impressive and really very beautiful. Everything went off admirably. We were all very nervous about Shawn's first Mass. That also happily was a complete success. The ordination took place in the Cathedral. There were about 50 ordained to various orders, and the ceremony lasted for two hours. Shawn's first Mass was said in St. Kevin's Chapel,

---

456 In 1900, John Dillon spent a few weeks recuperating in Bad Kissingen in Franconia.

and as the hour had been kept secret there was only a family party. Miss O'Farrelly* and her brother were the outsiders present.

The Mass was admirably said. I thought I never heard Mass more beautifully said. Shawn's voice was quite perfect, and his reading of the Mass was all that could be desired. After Mass Father John O'Reilly entertained all the company to a most gorgeous and elaborate breakfast. Your Uncle Theo came over from London for the ordination and 1st Mass, and was greatly pleased.

I shall write again soon.

[PS] Before investing in an opera glass I think I shall consult Nano. She might like something else much better. It now occurs to me that I have never seen her use an opera glass, as she is fortunate enough to have excellent sight.

Please sign enclosed Div. Warrant and return it to me.

Enclosed also a paper from the University, which came yesterday. You will probably prefer to vote in the University, so you had better sign enclosed and send it to the Registrar's Office as directed.

88

[Myles to John Dillon] [*Postcard*], Wednesday, [6 June 1923?]

Your letter with dividend certificate arrived. I am not sure whether you will be still in Dublin when this reaches you, so I shall not return the letter till I know where to find you. I much want to hear news of great events. Where has Nano gone to? Miss O'Farrelly* says that Brian is a lawyer. Can this mean that he has entered Con's office?[457] Is Shaun a chaplain somewhere, or resident in George's street?

I have delightful days here, though the amount there is to be known makes one hopeless. On Saturday I made a wonderful expedition up a valley of the Rhine, walking through vineyards, where the hills were so close that there was room only for the road and the river. I seem to have no time to write. Much love to Kensington Square, if you are already in London.

89

[John Dillon to Myles] 5 Morpeth Mansions, Victoria Street, London, S.W., [19 June 1923]

I was waiting to hear from you in response to my last letter before writing, but you have been very remiss in your correspondence.

457 Possibly a reference to C.P. Curran.*

I crossed yesterday, and am staying here with T.P. for a week, till Monday next, when I join Theo and go on to Paris and Switzerland with him. I was afraid you would not be sure to catch me with a letter in reply to this before I arrive. I will write you my address there as soon as I get it from Theo. Maria, Shawn and Brian are with Theo since Saturday. Enclosed is letter received from Maria this morning, which will interest you.

The wedding went off perfectly. Nano, on being consulted, rejected the opera glasses, but was very eager to have some table fittings, so your present took the form of a handsome silver dish, cost £5 - 8 - 0, which sum has been duly entered against you in the account I keep. On Saturday I had a letter from Nano from Paris giving a most cheerful and pleasant account of their proceedings so far, but she forgot to give me an address to which I could reply, so at this moment I do not know where to catch her with a letter.

Keep the warrant till you hear from me again, and write a decent long letter next time. I suppose you have declined Miss O'F[arrelly]'s* offer. It was a rather generous and tempting offer, but it would be foolish to break in upon your studies in Bonn. When do you expect to be free to go home for your holiday?

90

[Maria O'Reilly to Myles] 2 Nth. Gt. George's St., [Dublin], 24th June, 1923

My Beloved Myles,

I hope you got my card from Berck-Plage. I know you will be interested to hear about dear Theo. Well, Fr Shawn, Brian and I reached him after many trials on our journey, and found him looking the picture of health, but his knee is still as stiff as it was when he started the cure. It is wonderful how pleasant he is, and cheerful under his affliction, as it is to one who is so good and desirous to be useful to his fellow creatures, but the Almighty God has his own wise ways, and Please God this new place that he is going to on Monday, where your Father is to take him, will complete his cure. Everyone seemed to be most emphatic that he will be cured—I mean the people there who are an authority on the disease.[458]

Poor Pat Sweetman[459] is there 3 weeks and will be 2 years before he will be cured. He has got the trouble in his spine. He thinks himself he will be well in 6 months, but such is not the case. He will be dreadfully lonely for Theo. He is a nice poor fellow and has made a good many friends through Theo, who is most popular in the Institute. I ask you to pray for Theo's recovery. Every time he comes to your mind say a little prayer to remind our Lord to cure him. Thank God you are so healthy, and all the rest of the family.

458 See Letter 91. 459 See Letter 82.

Poor James is suffering his own share from the intense heat at present. We have no complaint of heat. It is quite the contrary here, and in Berck-plage I was perished with cold all the time I was there. I was sorry I could not remain till Monday but Brian had made engagements with his friend and could not remain, and I could never have made my journey home without him. He speaks French fluently, but Fr Shawn is worse than I am. I attempted to make myself understood on a few occasions. It's a pity he would not try and learn French.

Well, I told you all about Nano's marriage in my last letter. I had a P.C. from Lake Como from her the day I left Theo. She seems to be enjoying herself and will, as she is dreadfully in love with her husband. God keep her so, I constantly pray, as you know what it would mean were it otherwise. Theo was most amusing in his remarks regarding the union. He has a faint recollection of Dr Smyth's* appearance, but he was most grateful that he would not become the brother-in-law of Norman Reddin,* as there had been rumours that such might happen.

Poor Fr Shawn got into trouble with your Grandmother over the present she sent him for his ordination, it being an antique chalice which was supposed to be 200 years old. Well, when it came to Clonliffe, Fr Shawn showed it to the Dean who declared it was not sufficiently gilt, whereupon the Dean took it to have it gilt. The jeweller declared it too worn to have such done with it and would not undertake to gild it. The Dean declared it would be a sacrilege to use it and would not consecrate it, so when [Fr Shawn] went to see her Ladyship the night we arrived in London, leaving me in the Jermyn Court Hotel, he tried to explain why he did not use it saying his first Mass, she flew at him and gave him a very uncomfortable time, and then more he tried to pacify her the more angry she became, so he returned at 11.30 in a very agitated frame of mind. When he related the story to Theo, he thought it most unfortunate that Fr Shawn was so frank about the chalice and that he should have been more diplomatic in description, and given some other reason why he did not use it, but he got Fr Shawn to write and say he was remaining with him a few days, and asked her if he might call on his way back, so she wrote asking him to come, but not in a pressing tone. However, he started off before we left the Hotel, and he was to stay the night and go on to Downside[460] on Saturday. I don't know how he parted [from] her.

I was not asked to visit Kensington Square at all. I must be in the black books there still, and I really don't know for what, as I really think I don't deserve it. I never had the opportunity of behaving like Fr Shawn, to insult in that way even.[461]

---

460 Downside Abbey School, a Benedictine foundation in Somerset, where Shawn had been to school. Mount St. Benedict belonged to the Benedictines of Downside Abbey. It had been bought with money given to them by John Sweetman of Drumbaragh. **461** Possibly the truth was rather that Lady Mathew did not quite know how to treat Maria, who was officially just a servant, but in fact the surrogate mother of her grandchildren.

I am looking forward to see your dear face in the next month. Is it not July you are coming home?

The house is miserably lonely and I am all alone. Jenny is gone home, and Minnie out at Nan's, so I am having a long chat with you on this paper. I hope you will not be tired reading it. Did you hear Miss Marsh is dead? I forget if I told you. She died after an operation. It is well Nano is married, as she would miss her greatly. Imagine, Sarah was the only one sent a present to Nano. The staff behaved horribly mean. She got a lot of presents.

With my best love, I am

your loving Nurse,
M. O'Reilly.

91

[John Dillon to Myles] La Valerette, Leysin, Switzerland, Sunday, 30 June
[1923]

My dear Myles,

I have been expecting a letter from you for the last two days, but none has arrived so far. I propose to leave here on Wednesday morning, spend Wednesday night in Basle, and go on to Bonn on Thursday. I hope you will be able to get me decent accommodation in some good hotel, and you should *wire* the name of the hotel here immediately on receipt of this letter, if you have not already written, giving me an address. Up to Tuesday evening a wire will catch me here, and up to Wednesday night a wire would find me at the Grand Hotel Euler, Basle.

We arrived here on Thursday morning after a very wearisome night journey from Paris in a wagon-lit, a most infernal method of travel. This is an amazingly beautiful place, a mountain slope facing south-east, bounded by superb snowy mountains. The views are really glorious and the air most invigorating. After a few days' experience, I am quite clear that the change to this place has been for Theo an immense improvement on Berck Plage. The food here and the attendance are excellent—all that could be desired.

Yesterday Theo saw Dr Rollier,[462] the head man here, and was informed by him that he must make up his mind to remain under treatment for at least a year. For several months to come he will be kept strictly in bed. This is a hard fate. Nevertheless, Theo is in excellent spirits and accepts his sentence with perfect cheerfulness—and from what I have seen of this place, I am convinced that

462 Auguste Rollier (1874-1954), Swiss doctor and main proponent of heliotherapy (sun-cure) for tubercular illnesses. He built the large therapy centre at Leysin which Theo attended. His major works were *La cure du soleil* (1914) and *40 ans d'héliothérapie* (1944).

that it would not be possible to face such an ordeal under better conditions. The attendants and the nurse having special charge of Theo are most charming, pleasant people, and the Assistant Director in special charge of the Pension is a most agreeable, interesting man, who has already become a close friend of Theo's. In every respect the surroundings are all that could be wished for—very different from all the accounts I got of Berck Plage.

Don't fail to telegraph on receipt of this letter, giving me an address, if you have not already sent one. I shall probably wire from Basle, giving you the hour of my arrival in Bonn.

Your loving Father,
John Dillon.

92

[Harold Quinlan* to Myles] [Berlin] Schaperstr. 19, 5/7/'23

My Dear Dillon,

I was very glad to hear from you the other day. [...] Things are very pleasant here just now. Fr Boylan* has turned up and been enquiring for you. Langford is also here. Bewley[463] has retired to Dublin for good, Duane[464] being in his place here. McL[aughlin][465] is also in Dublin on holidays. Pokorny* is very angry with you for not writing to him. He has not lectured this term owing to an indisposition which he considered very serious. I expect to go home early in August. I would be glad to hear of your plans. Bewley went home via Hamburg and Southampton. Costs £5 1st Cl. on Cunard liner. I may go that way if nothing distracts me. Let me know if you feel like it as it is a very pleasant trip. Hope Theo is progressing well, and remember me to him. I am sorry you are not hear [*sic*] to come sailing during the week-ends at present during this warm weather. All here send you best wishes. [...] All best wishes.

Yours sincerely
Harold Quinlan

---

463 Charles Bewley (1890-1969), born in Dublin into a well-known Quaker family and educated at Winchester and Oxford. Called to the Bar in 1914. He joined the Irish diplomatic service and after returning from his posting in Germany (see Introduction for further details) he was appointed Irish Minister to the Vatican in 1929 and in 1933 was posted to Germany for a second time. His rather favourable attitude towards Nazism eventually led to his dismissal from the service in 1939. He settled in Italy and died there in 1969. **464** See Letter 41. **465** See Letter 25.

93

[John Dillon to Myles] The Bath Club, 34, Dover Street, [London],
Wednesday, 18 July [1923][466]

I had a most comfortable and prosperous journey. Got on board the Harwich
boat about 8.00. Had a most excellent dinner, then retired to a deck cabin and
an excellent bed, for which I had to pay £1 - 6 - 0, which so dislocated my
financial calculations that I had a narrow shave to get to London. I reached
London at 10.00 yesterday morning. Your Grandmother and Kathleen are quite
well, and were expecting me. Your Grandmother had written to that effect last
Tuesday, but I suppose the letter arrived after I left.

I shall be anxious to hear from you. No further bad effects of your accident,
I trust. Did you consult any doctor in Cologne? Do not forget to enquire about
... [*illegible*] of Wiesbaden. Did you dine with the Rev. Father in Cologne on
Monday evening?

I found a pile of letters awaiting me here, amongst them one from Nano at
last. In it she asked for your address, saying she wished to write to thank you for
your present. She will arrive in Leysin today or tomorrow and will doubtless
get the address from Theo. Remember [me] very kindly to Gräfin Beissel, and
to her sisters, and to other friends in Bonn. Nano will be in London probably by
the end of next week. You may possibly meet her there. What day do you propose to start from Bonn? I can strongly recommend the Antwerp route. You
can get a berth in a deck cabin containing four—very comfortable—for 11/0,
and the best plan is to remain on board the boat till 7.15, and come up to
London by the 10 minutes to 8—a splendid train, with five or six restaurant
cars, where one gets a most excellent breakfast.

Write soon. I expect to cross to Dublin on Saturday or Monday.

94

[Theo Dillon to Myles] La Valerette, July 22nd 1923

Dear Myles,

Your letter has just arrived and, as Paddy Smith* was here, I asked him
about your bothered ear. He urged me immediately to write to you and insist on
your going home, or at any rate taking a complete rest for the next fortnight, or
until the ear showed no further symptoms. I don't know if it is the result of the

---

466 Apart from the previous letter the interval of John Dillon's visit to the continent is unfortunately not recorded in the correspondence, for obvious reasons.

accident[467] but you said in your letter, written on last Thursday, that Father travelled "yesterday". Now, Father wrote to me from London on Tuesday, so that something is wrong somewhere.

I implore of you either to take Paddy Smith's* advice or to see a good doctor, as the results of neglect are sometimes very trying, and, if neglected, may last a long time.

Paddy is a much more interesting person than I at first thought. He has been, as you know, Major in the R.A.M.C.[468] and Surgical Specialist at Salonika, and he is thus completely emancipated from the very trying type of provincialism so common in Dublin circles. I have seen a good deal of him alone for the last few days (as Nano has had a slight gastric attack, which, by the way, is to be *kept a secret*) and I find him very sympathetic and of a robust intelligence. He is even more profoundly revolted than we are with the Free State, and seems to hold very much the same dark views on the general moral position as Father, collected from independent sources. I think you would like him, although of course he is at first, or rather seems, a very ordinary person. This, however, is by no means the case. On the contrary, he is the most independent minded person I have met in Dublin medical circles, and has one of those solid striking intellects, which are rather rare in Dublin, more English than Irish, generally speaking.

Nano is devoted, really devoted, and he of course worships her, literally, no other word would meet the case.

As you say, I owed you a letter since Berck-Plage, but the rush of transportation must be the excuse. I fully appreciated the "scorching" you administered in your last letter to Berck, though, like the gentleman who through [*sic*] his wife into the well, I still say "Saisson".[469] At any rate Gerard [Murphy]* suddenly wrote to me a strange letter beginning with a song of praise and thanksgiving for the great works of the Free State, and going on to tell me that his father had once more insisted that the marriage should be put off till Easter. If I told you all this in my last letter, you will forgive me. I enclose a letter from Brian which will amuse you.[470] I can hardly believe there is not some mistake about Ralph, as he wrote to me not long ago, referring with indignation to His Rev. manoeuvres to entrap him.[471]

I shall be naturally delighted to see you in October. German modern literature, of which I have read three novels, and a fantasy, is dull and difficult. Don't waste your time over it. I am going to fall back on the *Frankfurter Zeitung* and scientific works.

I suppose Father told you I would be here for at least a year, from what I hear of other cases, it will be a long year.

---

467 Unfortunately, we have no further details about this accident. **468** Royal Army Medical Corps. **469** Obviously some kind of in-joke. **470** This letter is lost. **471** Ralph had moved back to Mount St. Benedict.

I shall then speak German and French, and have forgotten my little medicine I ever knew.

My present idea, when finished with here, is to start again, without of course bothering about exams, and spend several years in various countries beginning with Physics and Chemistry and moving through Physiology and Biochemistry to X-rays. This, however, does not mean much to you.

If it interests you: I left Pat Sweetman[472] in good form, and have heard since that he is doing exceptionally well. With any luck, he will be cured before me. His complaint is always quicker than mine. Once more I implore you to take some steps. It would be a loss to learning if you became an idiot, and an expense to the family, which it could ill support.

Theo.

95

[Theo Dillon to Myles] La Valerette, Sept. 18, 1923

Dear Myles,

Your letter from Tourmakeady stirred me to the heart's core, unfortunately in the sense of a maudlin melancholy, which lasted for some half an hour, but, like all such emotions, yielded a sort of distorted voluptuousness. I imagine you must have enjoyed yourself profoundly after Germany and the French occupation. I hope you will make a dash to Aran before you leave Ireland. I should like to hear from you from the hob in Teach na Flaherty[473] (you see the effort of writing Flaherty in Irish even escapes me.) By the time this reaches you the Germans will probably have yielded to the French, and the Republicaine will have decided what they are going to do about it. It seems to me that the fate of the Free State is now clear. It may last for years, but there can be no question of eternity, and, though we shed no tears on its grave, business in Ballagh will probably be the worse. As you probably have gathered I spend a large part of my time reading newspapers, and ruminating on the perversity of nations—and the difficulty of establishing the truth about anything. One thing that emerges from reading journals of all nations is that the English are an amazing people. This may seem a very banal conclusion, but it translates a condition of mind far removed from the beautifully dogmatic scheme I used to develop on the growth of democracy. Contemporaneously with decency in England, I hear nothing from Ralph [Barry]*—nor indeed from Gerard [Murphy].* Did you, I wonder, get my last letter? It should have pursued you over the West.

472 See Letter 82. 473 Myles stayed with the Flahertys whenever he visited Inishmaan.

A silence has fallen upon Father. Whether he was overwhelmed by my last letter, which was, I admit, outrageously long, or whether he is ill again, or whether a letter has been lost, the fact remains that for ten days I have heard nothing from him.

I am plunged in Mathematics; having begun at the wrong side with the Calculus I have gradually worked backwards through solid geometry and conic sections to ordinary quadrature and find them very obscure.

P.S. You could ask Father, if you are near him, if he got my last letter, a long one, with a number of cuttings of his enclosed.

Year 2
October 1923–September 1924

INTRODUCTION

In Ireland, the autumn of 1923 was a period of relative calm and reconstruction, following on a period of turmoil and destruction. The Civil War was over. The elections of 27 August 1923 had brought electoral gains both for the Cumann na nGaedheal and for the republican side, but Sinn Féin refused to take their seats in the Dáil due to the required oath of allegiance to the British crown. Considerable tension persisted in the army, which was to eventuate in an abortive mutiny in March 1924. For John Dillon the mutiny was another sign that the present government would not last long. The year also saw the establishment of the Boundary Commission on Northern Ireland; its first meeting, however, was delayed due to the North's initial refusal to participate. For Myles Dillon the emergence of a national Irish educational system was of considerable interest; in this context the status of the Irish language was of particular importance to him. Myles was against the notion of compulsory Irish, as was his father; they were convinced that it would do nothing to promote the language.[1] We also sense in the letters (especially 105 and 125) how widespread a certain degree of admiration for Mussolini was in Ireland, John Dillon was no exception. He like many others feared that Communism was on the increase (Letter 131); in fact, with the election of Ramsey McDonald as Britain's first Labour Prime Minister he saw the Reds already on Ireland's doorstep. To many, Mussolini seemed to provide a safeguard in this respect.

In Germany, the crises continued until the very end of 1923 when finally some kind of stability was achieved. Upon the collapse of the Cuno government on 12 August, Gustav Stresemann had formed a broadly-based coalition government, and in a relatively short period—his "hundred days"—had turned the fortunes of the Weimar Republic around. He took office when the republic was at its lowest ebb politically and economically, and by the time his grand coalition collapsed in November, he had set it on the road to recovery. Recognising that the resources of the country were strained to breaking point by the policy of passive resistance, he called it off on 26 September, and announced Germany's willingness to resume reparations payments. The first problem was to halt the runaway inflation. Within three days he had estab-

---

1 It is highly likely that this position which was undoubtedly a minority view at the time, and an unpopular one at that, ultimately cost him the chair of Modern Irish in U.C.D. (as the successor of Douglas Hyde) when he applied for it in 1932.

lished a *Rentenbank* with power to issue a new currency, which he backed, in lieu of gold, by a mortgage put on all agricultural and industrial land. To oversee this operation, he appointed the astute banker Hjalmar Schacht, who pulled off something of an economic miracle. He issued a limited number of banknotes, and, when the first issue was quickly gobbled up, resolutely refused to issue any more. The Government curtailed expenditure, cut salaries, reduced the number of officials and government employees by 300,000, and increased taxation. This did the trick, though it was not accomplished without tensions, especially in Bavaria.

Nevertheless, there was still much to be alarmed at. Returning to his studies in Bonn at the beginning of November, after spending some time in Paris, and then with his brother Theo at his sanatorium in Leysin, Switzerland, Myles was not even sure that he would be able to get into the Rhineland, and his father, back in Dublin, was even less certain about the wisdom of his attempt.

The French authorities were giving active support to local separatists in the Rhineland in the hope of detaching the area from Germany and bringing it under French control. The separatists had actually very little local support, but they were liberally supplied with arms by the French, and were encouraged to proclaim a Rhineland Republic, which they eventually did in October. Small bands of separatists—many from outside the region and with police records— seized power in Aachen, Bonn, Trier, Wiesbaden and Mainz, and declared a Republic. A provisional government, headed by the separatist leaders, was set up at Koblenz. Britain protested vigorously, and refused to recognise autonomous governments set up in defiance of the Versailles Treaty. In fact the separatist regime never attracted more than negligible support, and collapsed by the end of the year. A similar regime in the Palatinate was encouraged by the local French general, but it collapsed in February 1924.

There were other internal political crises. The way the Weimar government dealt with them proved that it was far more concerned about perceived threats from the left than it was about right-wing extremism. Social Democrats in Saxony and Thuringia were greatly alarmed by events in Bavaria, where right-wing elements under von Kahr were planning a March on Berlin, on the model of Mussolini's recent March on Rome, and decided to ally themselves to the Communists. Communists were invited into the Land governments, and Red militias were formed. Stresemann, under pressure from Saxon industrialists to restore order, and anxious also to defuse right-wing militancy in Bavaria, sent the Reichswehr into both Länder at the end of October, deposed the elected governments, and declared a state of emergency. This was a move of doubtful legality, and it had serious repercussions for Stresemann's government: the Social Democratic ministers of his government resigned and Stresemann eventually fell by a vote of no confidence in the Reichstag on 23 November 1923. His government (and future governments as well) dealt much more leniently with right-wing extremism. When Adolf Hitler, then a relatively unknown political entity, and members of his party, the National Socialist Workers Party of Germany (NSDAP), staged a putsch in Munich on 8 November, it was put down the next day. But although Hitler himself was sentenced to five years' imprisonment he was released after serving only one year. He used this year to compose a book which was to become the bible of the "Nazi" movement he had founded: *Mein Kampf*.

"Is it not strange what power of resistance this tottering German republic possesses? The communist outbreak in Saxony, and Ludendorff in Bavaria have both collapsed, though no one is proud of Berlin," Myles comments on 10 November 1923 (Letter 105). Indeed there were few at this point who had reason to feel proud of the Government. Nevertheless things started to look up towards the beginning of 1924. Restoration of confidence was greatly helped by a solution to the problem of reparations, in the shape of the so-called "Dawes Plan" of early 1924. The French had overtly won a victory, but at considerable cost to themselves, and they were ready to make a deal. Britain seized the initiative, and appealed to the United States to take part in an international investigation into Germany's capacity to pay reparations. The Americans were enthusiastic, and put pressure on the French, with the result that in November the Reparations Commission, in response to a German request, agreed to set up two commissions of financial experts, one to deal with the problems posed by the flight of capital from Germany, the other, chaired by the American general, Charles Dawes, to consider ways and means of stabilising the German currency and balancing her budget. The latter committee met in Paris in January 1924, and published its report, the Dawes Plan, in April. After a change of government in France when the hardliner Poincaré was replaced by the more conciliatory left-wing premier Édouard Herriot, France also accepted the Dawes Plan.

From now on, John Dillon's side of the correspondence becomes more spotty, or more poorly preserved, but Myles' continued unabated. He came back to Dublin in July 1923 and returned to the Continent in mid-October. This time, he made his way first to Paris, and then to visit his brother Theo in Leysin, Switzerland, only reaching Bonn in early November 1923.

In Paris, he was able to enjoy the hospitality of a pair of sisters, Mabel and Mary Robinson (now Madame Duclaux),* who had made the acquaintance of John Dillon back in the 1880s in London, and who in consequence welcomed Myles warmly. In Bonn, Myles partook more than before of the cultural life of the city, no doubt aided by his infinitely better command of German. He was a frequent visitor to Cologne, where he became friendly with the British military chaplains Moloney and Coghlan, both Irishmen, and to Maria Laach, a Benedictine abbey near Coblenz. In Bonn University, Myles made the acquaintance of Wilhelm Dibelius,* Professor of English Philology, and an expert in things Irish.[2]

Dibelius also introduced him to a cousin of his, Prof. Franz Martin Dibelius who held a chair in the Dept. of Evangelical (Protestant) Theology in Heidelberg. It was there that Myles spent the summer semester of 1924 studying under the comparative philologist F.C.L. Bartholomae who had already retired at this point, and Heinrich Robert Zimmer, son of the famous Celticist Heinrich Zimmer, who was Professor of Indian Philology at Heidelberg. Judging by his letters, the time he spent in Heidelberg was perhaps the happiest he experienced during his three years in Germany. The year was also an important one for Myles because it saw his first attempts at journalism rewarded: the *Irish Statesman* printed five contributions of his which all dealt with the political and cultural situation in Germany. We reproduce them in the Appendix.

2 Dibelius had visited Ireland before the turn of the century, and had published several articles on Ireland in German periodicals. To gather his information he had corresponded with Douglas Hyde and the Sinn Féin leaders among others. During World War I Dibelius had particular responsibility for Ireland in the *Kriegspresseamt* (War Press Office). Dibelius was by no means the only scholar who supported the German propaganda machine by contributing tendentious anti-British articles, pamphlets and books on Ireland; Kuno Meyer, Pokorny and indeed Thurneysen also got themselves involved in the German propaganda efforts. For further details see Hünseler (1978), Kluge (1983) and especially Lerchenmüller (1996).

THE LETTERS

96

[Myles to John Dillon] Bailey's Hotel, London S.W.7, Friday, 12 Octo. '23

I have let it get too late to write you a decent letter tonight, as I must hasten to Kensington Square.

I have been having a very pleasant time, enjoying much of Grandmother's hospitality, and dined last night with Uncle Theo. Today I called on John McNeill,[3] who was in excellent form, and in a most peaceful mood. He led me out to have a cup of tea, and then went off to buy tobacco, his pipe being exhausted. Tomorrow I go to Oxford. I shall write again. Someone is waiting to write here now.

97

[Theo Dillon to Myles] La Vallerette, Leysin-Feydey, Suisse, Oct. 14, 1923

Dear Myles,

It is quite unnecessary to stop the night in Lausanne. Many people—relations, etc.—are continually coming here from Paris, and they all come straight through. I have asked a dame who arrived two days ago, and she tells me that the morning train leaves Paris—the Gare de Lyon—at 8 o'clock. You come straight through, and arrive here about 10 o'clock, having taken the Funiculaire—a kind of tramway—at Aigle, which crawls up here, to *Leysin-Feydey*. It is important to note that one does not get down at Leysin Village, which is the first station on the route, but rather, resisting the impulse to follow everyone else, one sits tight, and crawls up to Leysin-Feydey. There I will arrange to have a chariot waiting at the station for you, as the way here is complicated, and the nights are dark. The one point you will have to find out is whether you change at Lausanne or not. Some of the trains from Paris do not stop at Aigle, in which case you would be swept on heaven knows where. This information—as indeed all information—is better obtained at the Gare de Lyon. Cooks are unreliable.

You could if it was convenient bring me a book entitled *Electricité médicale, électrologie et radiologie*, by H. Guillemot. The most likely shop is Masson et

3 Eoin [or: John] MacNeill (1867-1945), then Minister for Education in Cosgrave's cabinet, headed the Irish delegation to the Imperial Conference of 1923. See also Letter 98.

Cie, 120 Boulevard St. Germain—which is not far, I imagine, from your hotel. There is also a book published by Masson et Cie, but I am unfortunately sure neither of the author's name nor of the name of the book. At a hazard—if I were enquiring myself—I should ask for *Le Foie*, by Aulard—but this is quite probably imaginary.[4] What I know is that it was published within the last year by Masson, deals with diseases and function of the liver, and it now occurs to me that by boldly marching into the shop and demanding their latest list of medical works (ouvrages médicaux) you would probably be able to spot the real name yourself. In any case, I would easily run it to earth if you brought the list on here. If you bring one of these books as an offering, and if you by a happy chance hit upon the other, I will reimburse you.

I feel that I have a great deal to say to you, which will take a full week. Therefore I urge you to stay no night in Lausanne on your way here. You could see it on your way back by leaving here a few hours earlier. I will brew you a cup of tea, which with bread, butter, jam—and perhaps an egg or two—is what I imagine you would fancy on your arrival.

Wire me the morning of your coming, or, if you rely on a letter, remember to post it two days before. The posts here are most irregular.

Till we meet,
Theo.

P.S. Could you perhaps look in at the English book shop, and buy me the *Quarterly Review* for October. There is an article by Caillaux[5] which will interest you and me.

98

[Myles to John Dillon] Balliol College, Oxford, 15. x. '23

Dear Father

I came up here on Saturday and have had a most interesting and pleasant time. Shortly after I arrived, Martin Hemple, accompanied by Osmonde Esmonde,[6] came into Conor's[7] rooms, and we dined together. Esmonde was

4 It was not: François Victor Alphonse Aulard, *Le Foie* was published by Masson in 1922. 5 Joseph Marie Auguste Caillaux (1863-1944), French politician, specialising in finance. After a distinguished parliamentary career, he fell under suspicion of having plotted for an early peace with Germany in 1915. He was eventually brought to trial in 1920, and, exonerated of most charges, was condemned to a spell in prison, which, however, he never actually served. He turned to writing at this time, and had just produced a book *Whither France? Whither Europe?* A full amnesty was granted him in 1924, and in 1925 Painlevé invited him back into government, as the one man who could restore France's finances to order, but his remedies were too radical, and he was sacked in October, retiring to the Senate. 6 Osmund Thomas Grattan Esmonde (1896-1936), delegate of Dáil Éireann to U.S.A., Canada and Australia in 1920-1; Cumann na nGaedheal T.D. for Wexford

interesting on the personnel of the government, and their disputes. He said that O'Higgins actually resigned last week as a protest against Mulcahy and his army[8]—and his uncle[9] said that he would leave the Viceregal if O'Higgins went. This crisis was dealt with, but apparently the feeling is very bad. Cosgrave is with Mulcahy, and Desmond Fitzgerald,[10] I think, with O'Higgins. Esmonde is in London for the Imperial Conference,[11] and is going down again tomorrow.

We visited the colleges yesterday morning, and many of them were delightful. The Bodleian was closed, but I hope to see it today. I have not yet met Charles,[12] who has not been easy to find. He did not know what day I was coming up, and has not put in an appearance. However, Conor has very kindly invited him to breakfast today. Martindale[13] is at a Catholic congress at Reading, so I shall not see him either this time. The famous Urquhart of Balliol I have only seen.

I must go back to London this afternoon as Kathleen has got tickets for *Hassan*[14] tonight. I think I told you that we paid a delightful visit to the National Gallery and I went myself to see the Wallace Collection,[15] and much enjoyed it. Tomorrow evening I am spending with Uncle Theo, and on Wednesday I hope to go to Paris. I shall write to Miss Robinson* before I leave. I called on Robin Flower* at the museum on Friday, and was well received. He very kindly promised to try to dispose of the books I was asked to sell, so there is hope.

Anna[16] gave me lunch on Saturday, and she is full of courage and wonderfully calm. Toby of that family is now quite well again, and she says doing well at the Bar.[17]

I shall write from Paris.

from 1923 to 1936. Succeeded as twelfth baronet, 1935. 7 Presumably, Conor Carrigan, a school friend of Myles Dillon. 8 Tension was certainly high between O'Higgins and Mulcahy towards the end of 1923, but we can find no other evidence of his actual threat of resignation. 9 That is, the Governor-General, T.M. Healy. 10 Desmond Fitzgerald (1888-1947) had served in the Irish Volunteers and had been involved in the Rising. He joined the pro-Treaty side and was appointed Minister for Foreign Affairs in 1922. He remained in Cosgrave's cabinet until 1932, serving as Minister for Defence from 1927 to 1932. His son was Garret Fitzgerald, Taoiseach 1981-2 and 1982-7. 11 Imperial Conferences took place every few years and provided a forum in which to discuss matters of common concern to Britain and the empire countries. The Irish Free State tried to use this particular conference, which lasted from 1 October to 8 November 1923, to assert its new found independence. 12 That is, his cousin, Charles Mathew. 13 Cyril Charles Martindale (1879-1963), English priest and scholar, one of the most famous English Jesuits of the 20th century. Between 1916 and 1927 he was lecturing in Classics at Oxford University. In later years he became a very prolific writer and broadcaster on religious matters, publishing over 80 books. He also became involved in the Roman Catholic international university movement. 14 A play by James Elroy Flecker (1884-1915). Written in 1913/14, it was first produced to high acclaim in 1923, with ballets by Fokine and music by Delius. 15 The invaluable collection of art works collected by Sir Richard Wallace (1818-1890) had been bequeathed to the English nation after his death. It was later located in Hertford House. 16 Anna Mathew, widow of his Uncle Charles. 17 Later Sir Theobald Mathew, Director of Public Prosecutions from 1944-1964.

99

[John Dillon to Myles] 2 North Great George's St., Dublin, Tuesday, 16 Oct.,
1923

Your short note written on Friday arrived here yesterday morning, and as I
understood you were not leaving for Paris till Thursday I put off answering it,
hoping for a decent letter today. This morning came your very satisfactory and
most interesting letter from Oxford. I hope you did explore the Bodleian. It is
one of the most wonderful and ... [*illegible*] libraries in the world, and if I
remember rightly there are a considerable number of old Irish mss. in it.

What you tell me of the situation in the Government is *extremely* interesting.
I had heard some rumours of what was going [on], but am glad to have authen-
tic details. Things are, I believe, moving pretty rapidly towards a crash in this
country. What will follow the crash I am quite unable to predict.

No, you did not tell me about the National Gallery or the Wallace
Collection. I am glad to hear that you visited, and enjoyed, them! London is
truly a wonderful city. It is full of things worth seeing and studying. I shall be
very curious to hear your impressions of *Hassan*. It was a great achievement of
Kathleen to secure seats. I was very glad to hear your good news of poor
Anna. It is a comfort to hear that Toby is recovered and doing well at the
Bar.

Brian had a very pleasant letter from his grandmother, thanking him for his
pheasant, and saying she and K. were enjoying your visit very much. Very
cheerful letters continue to arrive from Theobald. He is looking forward eagerly to your visit.

Read enclosed report of coroner's inquest on Lemass.[18] It is ghastly reading.
The Republicans are evidently resolved to make this case a big propaganda case,
and no wonder. It is an awful exposure of Government methods.

I am wiring you today asking whether you are starting tomorrow, and if you
are what your address in Paris will be. I do not know whether you have stuck to
the Hotel de l'Arcade. I hope you will write me *full* accounts of all your adventures in Paris.

[PS] Did you read Garvin[19] in last Sunday's *Observer*? It is really a very full
and powerful statement of the case against France. Germany seems to be in an

18 This is preserved, from the *Irish Times* of 16 October. It does indeed make appalling reading.
Noel Lemass, brother of Sean, had actually been abducted and murdered on 3 July, so his body was
badly decomposed when discovered. There was evidence, however, of torture, and certain members
of the Free State Army seemed to be involved in intimidation of witnesses. A Capt. J. Murry was
mentioned as the man who had shot Lemass. 19 This is James Louis Garvin (1868-1947), editor of
The Observer. The son of an Irish immigrant, Garvin became a journalist. In his articles written for
the *Eastern Morning News* (Hull) he defended the Home Rule movement. He also contributed to

appalling condition, and, judging from newspaper reports, I can see no light, or hope of improvement.

As I have got no wire from you up to this time, 3 o'c, I am sending this letter to Paris.

Your loving Father,
John Dillon

Enclosed cutting from Morning Post will amuse you, if you have not seen it already.[20]

100

[John Dillon to Myles] Monday, 18 Oct. [1923]

Your telegram arrived yesterday. I had posted my letter on Tuesday to the Hotel de l'Arcade, so it ought to arrive in Paris with you. I shall expect a long letter from Paris giving full details of all your doings. I wonder whether you will see Franklin Bouillon. I am very curious to learn where he stands on the Ruhr question, and what are the present relations between him and Poincaré.

You will see that things seem to be quite hopeless in Germany—rapidly going from bad to worse. To me it seems that the French will find their victory in the Ruhr a very Pyrrhic affair. You might send me anything striking you see in the Paris press.

While in Paris, invest in the *Souvenirs d'Enfance et de Jeunesse*.[21] You will find it one of the most fascinating books you have ever read.

Enclosed came this morning.[22] Here all goes on as usual. All the family are in good health.

[PS] You and Theo will have very keen discussions on Franco-German questions when you meet. He is still a good bit infected with pro-French atmosphere.

101

[Myles to John Dillon] La Vallerette, Leysin Feydey, Suisse, Thursday,
23 x '23

I had a delightful journey from Paris yesterday. I wish I could tell of the wonderful colour of trees and fields at this time of year. It makes me unhappy to

United Ireland. After World War I he was one of the most outspoken critics of Poincaré whom he dubbed, "Kaiser of the peace". 20 This has not survived. 21 This is the French translation of a book John Dillon refers to again later in this correspondence: G.M.C. Brandes, *Recollections of My Childhood and Youth*. London: Heinemann 1906 (Danish orig. 1905); see Letter 153. 22 A note from Stephen Gwynn in London, asking Dillon to lunch, which obviously came too late.

see so much beauty and feel that one cannot enjoy it enough, and then it is gone.

I had pleasant days in Paris since I last wrote—the Louvre, Madame Duclaux's* intellectual tea, the Opera, and great kindness from Mabel Robinson.* She and Madame Duclaux send you messages of love.

I found Mlle. Tery[23] only the day before I left, which I much regret. She lives in the Quartier Latin garret of which one has read, and in which I had begun to disbelieve. I breakfasted with her on Tuesday and met her again at night.

Theo is looking very well and in excellent spirits. He has a pleasant life here, and it is a Land of Wonder. I managed to get through all my impedimenta safely, and am now unloading gifts upon him. I shall stay till next Wednesday, and then return to Bonn.

This is brief, but I have not yet written to Kensington Square since I left, and there are letters to be written to Bonn also.

Much love to the family.

[PS] Franklin Bouillon never manifested himself. The *Echo de Paris* are to send you the papers.

102

[Myles to John Dillon] La Valerette, Tuesday, 30. x. '23

Many thanks for your interesting letter, and for the cuttings. I read the Magennis-O'F.[24] controversy, and Philips' letter, with much interest. I had heard something about the meeting to select a candidate for the University, to which Miss O'F. darkly refers. Magennis' statement about the respective grants to the Universities was bold, but he is too cute, I would have thought, to tell a straight lie. There must be some obscurity. Allison Philips is not a very acceptable person. It is perverse of him to write anything about Irish history, because he is violently prejudiced, but he got the better of the archbishop all the same.[25]

---

23 Simone Téry, French author of two books on Ireland, *En Irlande. De la guerre d'indépendance à la guerre civile (1914-1923)*, Paris: Flammarion, 1923, and *L'île des bardes*. *"Notes sur la littérature irlandaise contemporaine*, Paris: Flammarion, 1925. The latter was dedicated to Æ. 24 William Magennis (1869-1946), Professor of Metaphysics in U.C.D. from 1909 to 1941; T.D. for the National University, 1922-7; Senator from 1938 to his death. The controversy with Miss O'Farrelly most probably concerned an internal U.C.D. issue debated at Governing Body. 25 Walter Allison Phillips (1864-1950), historian, appointed to the Lecky chair of Modern History in Trinity College Dublin in 1914. He wrote *The Revolution in Ireland 1906-1923* (London: Longmans and Greene, 1923) in which he was highly critical of Sinn Féin. The letter in question has not survived and could not be identified.

We are having delightful weather here. It is as hot as summer, and I wear only flannels and a cotton jacket. This morning the sun was hardly bearable. But as soon as it goes down, it becomes quite cold. We have been living in a wonderful cloudworld, often above the clouds, sometimes below them, and yesterday unfortunately they crept up the mountains and surrounded us.

Theo is in splendid form. He is now very reasonable about the Franco-German question which we discuss at length, but he knows a great deal about it and I very little, so I do not come well out of it.

Your wire came yesterday, and the letter came almost immediately afterwards.[26] From here the position in the Rhineland does not look so dangerous, and it would be a great misfortune to abandon my work with Thurneysen.* I think the alternative would have to be Berlin for the present rather than Paris. I have taken counsel with Theo and decided to advance as far as Strasbourg and see how things are. Quite possibly, I shall arrive in Bonn to find it absolutely quiet. This has been the most wicked and I believe the most foolish thing the French have done.[27] The French papers have been amazing on the subject. Sometimes they have manifested their neutrality in the affair by arresting or disarming the German police where they opposed the Separatists. You will have seen an article in *The Times* from Crefeld, describing their personnel and their remarkable leader.[28] I shall wire from Bonn as soon as I arrive if the wires are in order. Else I shall get a letter over Cologne.

A feeble letter from me here will have reached you by now. It was written in a hurry. Theo expects to hear from you.

I have had a most pleasant time here. It could not be pleasanter. Everyone is delightful, and the country wonderful. As a teaparty is now in progress on the gallery I must close this and join it.

103

[Myles to John Dillon] Hotel Terminus, Place de la Gare, 10-14 rue Kuss, Strasbourg, All Saints', 1. xi. '23

The journey from Leysin has been pleasant and mildly adventurous. Switzerland is an ideal country to travel in. Splendid trains, excellent food, and a delightful people. We reached Basel at eleven o'clock, and the Strasbourg train did not start till a quarter past twelve, so I had an hour's wait in the station. A group of

26 This letter is unfortunately lost, as are all further letters from John Dillon until 28 April 1924.
27 That is, encourage the establishment of a separatist regime in the Rhineland. See Introduction.
28 The leader of the separatists was a man called Matthes. He posted up proclamations announcing the Rhine Republic and sent a note to the Inter-Allied High Commission informing them that a Provisional Government had been constituted and negotiations with the occupation authorities would start at once. Matthes was certainly not lacking in self confidence.

Italians, on their way to rebuild France, made it amusing. They were wild-looking fellows, and one of them played on a giant melodeon which made as much noise as an American organ. I arrived here at two o'clock this morning, and should have left at eight-thirty to reach Bonn today, but that was too much for me, so I must remain here till tomorrow morning. I could not get past Mainz tonight. I am told everything is quiet in Bonn, and the trains are running regularly.

This is a pleasing city, and I rejoiced in the cathedral. I went there this morning to find high mass just at an end and a bishop in cloth of gold, crozier in hand, ascending the pulpit. He preached in French for half an hour, after which I was able to hear mass. Why does one expect to find Catholicism dead in this part of the world? The church was filled with men and women, young and old. However, this is more Germany than France.[29]

I left Theo in very good form, and have half-promised to go down to Leysin for Christmas, that is in eight weeks time. When I left yesterday afternoon, it was mid-summer, hot sun, and delightful air and light on the mountains. Here it is cold and foggy, so that I can hardly see the houses.

Miss Robinson* lent me a fascinating work of Madame Duclaux's* on French Writers of the Twentieth Century which Grandmother had recommended to me. If you have not got it you would do well to get it. I think you will like it greatly. The publisher is Collins (1919)—*Twentieth Century French Writers*.

I expect to find Bonn quiet and despairing. You will have seen a statement published here in the Echo de Paris that the English refuse to recognise the Separatists and will arrest and imprison any who appear in Cologne. The Times correspondent is very good. Meanwhile, Theo has been lecturing me with great effect on the French side of the case. He is now less French than when you saw him, I imagine, as he reads a German Swiss paper, and speaks German a great part of the day. I have resolved to seek out politically-minded Germans when I return and hear what they have to say. Theo joins in the outcry against Stinnes and the industrialists.[30] They have sent money to Switzerland and America which should have been paid to the workers, and so on. Certainly the statement that Germany bought more from America than England last year is puzzling, if one believes it. The *Temps* now accuses the German government of abolishing the coal tax and all export duties, so as to appear bankrupt before the commission of experts.[31] I think of taking a French newspaper when I get back to Bonn, but I

---

29 Strasbourg had been captured by Germany in 1871, and only returned to French control in 1918. 30 Hugo Stinnes (1870-1924), prominent industrialist, who currently presided over a consortium which controlled about 20 per cent of German industrial potential, its interests ranging from iron and steel to timber, shipping and newspapers. He joined together with the Thyssen, Phoenix and Otto Wolff groups to found the *Vereinigte Stahlwerke*. He was a rabid German nationalist, profiteer and speculator, who provoked great ill-feeling among his less fortunate or astute fellow-countrymen. 31 I.e. the Reparations Commission. 32 This is an apposite remark to direct to

am nervous of newspapers. If you take them, you have to read them.[32] Did you see Mussolini's speech at Milan?[33] He has apparently forgotten that this is 1923. It read like an imitation of Caesar's speeches to the troops in the war against Gaul. One begins to wish him a short life in public affairs.

My short stay in France has rather reconciled me to the French. Miss Robinson assures me that the ordinary Frenchman who has served in the war is not at all violent against the Germans. I think she said the majority of her friends are opposed to the Ruhr adventure. She told me a strange story about the feeling towards prisoners during the war. She was passing a barracks and found a crowd of women in great excitement who told her that "Boche" prisoners were coming that way, and that they would tear them to pieces, and tear their eyes out. She waited with the idea that she would try to interfere if anything happened, and soon about thirty weary and rather timid-looking men were marched up to the barracks. When they came, the women became silent, and some of them began to cry.

I shall write from Bonn. Much love to everyone. I got Maria's letter and will write to her soon. Theo had a letter from Nano in which she said that His Reverence is ill again.[34] Please let me know whether it is serious.

[PS] I have tried to hear something of the feeling here towards the French, but it is a delicate subject. One man said they were accustomed to changes, and just went on working. He admitted that the feeling was mostly German. I would say the language is much more German than French in this country.

104

[Myles to John Dillon] Bonn, Schedestrasse 3, bei Beissel, Thursday, 8. xi. '23

Theo forwarded your last letter from Leysin. You will have had two from me since you wrote, one from Leysin and one from Strasbourg.

I arrived here last Friday to find things peaceful, and they have remained so since. I think the Separatist performance is, morally speaking, at an end.[35] The only incident since I came was the arrival of a party of warriors who had been expelled by the Belgians from Aachen.[36] They departed the next day, and I read

his father, who took six newspapers every day, and often did not read them. **33** In this speech to celebrate the first anniversary of the March on Rome, Mussolini defended the invasion of Corfu and criticised the League of Nations. Italy had been forced to withdraw one month after the invasion, but Mussolini maintained, the incident had proved to the world that the Italians were ready to take decisive action: "If it had been necessary to march, they [the Italian people] would undoubtedly have done so" (*IT*, 29 October 1923). **34** Perhaps a reference to his uncle, Fr Nicholas, or to Fr Sweetman.* **35** Myles may have been right on the moral side, but politically or militarily the separatists were by no means beaten yet, as he would come to realize. **36** Separatists had taken the City Hall in Aachen, but were subsequently expelled by Belgian troops. 2000 separatists passed

in the *Times* yesterday that they had been mysteriously disarmed by the French before they went. I did not see them at all. The position here is that their flag still flies over the Rathaus, apparently under French protection. French soldiers were in the Rathaus the last time I passed by, and they have cleared two rooms in the building for the Separatists. The civil servants continue their work, as do the police, under the old regime. It seems likely that the affair will come to a quiet end, but you will have more general news than I have.

I was in Köln yesterday, buying food, which has become rather a difficulty here for the unwary, and called on Father Moloney[37] and Father Coghlan. They send you greetings.

The term has commenced here, and I am full of great purpose, with little hope of achievement. German is still a very foreign language to me, but I shall go peacefully on, and hope for the best. Thurneysen* having retired, there are no lectures on comparative philology this semester, which is a drawback, but he is reading Welsh with us two hours a week. Sanskrit,[38] and six hours a week with a great Romance philologist, Meyer-Lübke,[39] who is lecturing on the history of the French language, will probably complete my programme. Norse lectures were promised, but no students appear to have turned up for them. There are three of us anxious to hear them, and I am calling on the learned professor today.[40] The philology of Latin and Greek I propose to work on myself, but I have had this purpose for long, and made little progress. Christmas will be soon upon us, and I am strengthening in my resolve to visit Theo for a while. Is Brian inclined to come out? I believe we shall have a chance of skating as well as skiing and sleighing, which I am glad of, because it will be pleasant to start unobtrusively. I think I told you that I had planned to have a lesson from a Swede at the Ice Palace in the Champs Elysées, but it fell through.

Tomorrow I am invited to lunch by her ladyship, a deer having been killed on the preserve, which permits her to issue invitations. She has enquired affectionately for you and dwelt with smiles in happy memory on the wonderful evening spent in your company in the Königshof Hotel.[41]

I was with Thurneysen* on Monday and he also asked kindly for you.

I have had no letters since I arrived, except yours, forwarded by Theo, but I live in hope. With love to everyone.

through Bonn after the event. The Bonn newspaper *Generalanzeiger* reported that the British had put pressure on the Belgian government to deal decisively with the separatists (*G*, 3 November 1923). **37** Fr Moloney was the Senior Chaplain to the British Forces. He was transferred back to Britain in April 1924. See Letter 122. **38** With Prof. Willibald Kirfel; see Letter 78. **39** Wilhelm Meyer-Lübke (1861-1936), born in Zurich, Switzerland, Professor of Romance Philology in Bonn from 1915 to 1925. **40** This was Prof. Rudolf Meissner (1862-1948), Professor of Germanic and Nordic Philology in Bonn between 1913 and 1931. **41** The original "Grandhotel Royal—Hotel Königshof", built in 1871, was Bonn's most expensive hotel. It lost some of its exclusivity during the immediate post-war period, due to the fact that the European nobility who used to frequent the

105

[Myles to John Dillon] Saturday [10 November 1923].

Your letter arrived just after I had written. I enclose the cheque signed. I sent a cheque for £5 conferring fee, with the card which you sent to me in Switzerland, to the University, on the assumption that you had paid the fee. It will have arrived a day or two later, but I explained to them that this was unavoidable. If you had already paid the fee, I daresay they will return one of the cheques. Did you perhaps notice whether my name appeared amongst the list of degrees conferred?

We have splendid weather here, but very cold. The republic[42] has made no further sign of its existence. Is it not strange what power of resistance this tottering German republic possesses? The communist outbreak in Saxony,[43] and Ludendorff in Bavaria,[44] have both collapsed, though no one is proud of Berlin.

Here I get no nearer understanding the situation. Most people I know are royalist, and would like to have seen Ludendorff take Berlin. The Sanscrit professor Kirfel rejoices at his failure, being of socialist tendencies. I have met an interesting man called Dibelius,* Prof. of English, whose book on England was favourably reviewed in the *Times Supplement* some months ago. He is professor of English here, and is lecturing at present on Ireland as a British problem. His point of view is very interesting, and he seems to understand the question.

I shall write when there is news.

[PS] *Saturday Evening*: O'Toole's book[45] has just arrived, Many thanks.

[...] What you say about Mussolini is not complimentary to Democracy.[46] I would not mind that, because I suppose no one could claim that Democracy is at all times the best, or even the right system. But Mussolini in his Milan utterances rather lacked the dignity and wisdom fitting a dictator.[47]

I have met the curate to whom I sent Shaun's mass offerings, and he sent him many thanks. I shall ask him to write a statement that he has said the masses the next time I see him.

hotel until 1918, tended to stay away from a Germany, which was now a republic. The imposing building on the Koblenzer Straße (now Adenauer Allee) was completely destroyed during an air raid on 18 October 1944. John Dillon had stayed in the hotel during his visit to Bonn in July 1923. **42** That is, the separatist republic of the Rhineland. **43** The Social Democratic government of Saxony, alarmed at developments in Bavaria, allied itself with the Communists, giving them seats in the Land government. Red militias were set up. In response, Chancellor Stresemann, at the end of October, ordered the Reichswehr into Saxony, and deposed the government. See also Introduction. **44** This was the attempted putsch staged by Hitler in Munich on 8 November, which was backed by Ludendorff. It was suppressed the next day. **45** Éamonn Ó Tuathail, *Rainn agus amhráin. Cnuasacht rann agus amhrán ó Chonndae na Midhe, ó Chonndae Lughmhaidh agus ó Chonndae Ardmacha*. Baile Átha Cliath: Brún agus Ó Nóláin 1923. The book contained, as the title says, folk songs from Cos. Meath, Louth and Armagh. **46** John Dillon, like many another at this time,was inclined to look favourably on Mussolini, as licking the Italians into shape. **47** See Letter 103.

106

[Myles to John Dillon] Friday, 23. xi. '23

The certificate[48] arrived safely, and also your letter of the 16th. Correspondence from George's Street has fallen rather short of late, and I am beginning to feel hostile to the postmen.

I sent a card to Nevinson,[49] addressed on chance to the Dom Hotel, and to my great delight received a very friendly answer from him, in which he has promised to come out here, but he has not yet appeared.

Dibelius* is quite an interesting man, and very kind. He invited me to tea the other day, and we had a long discussion of German and Irish politics. One of the questions he asked me was about the case against Dublin Castle adminis-tration from the point of view of ordinary efficiency. I found myself with little to say. I should think that the objections could only be put in a more general way by an unlearned critic, that is that Dublin Castle was the people's enemy instead of being its government, but I remember a dictum—was it of Lloyd George at the introduction of the partition bill in the House of Commons?—about the whole system, which admitted its complete inefficiency. I wonder whether you could find me the reference, or any other evidence which I could give Dibelius.* He told me too that Casement[50] had told him, as showing the true feeling of Ireland, and that all Ireland would join in the 1916 rising, that Redmond had once said to him privately, "I have nothing against an Irish Republic". This shows how little Casement knew about the Irish. I told Dibelius I should have expected if Redmond ever said such a thing he would have said it publicly, with the necessary qualifications, but that I hardly believed he would have said it pri-vately to Casement or to anyone else, because it was not his real feeling.

A number of us are starting Old Norse here next week, and we are to read the Gisla Saga. Perhaps you could let me have a translation of it. I think I have seen one in the drawingroom, but if that is a treasure, please order me one. If I make another petition, I should like to become a subscriber to Æ's* paper.[51] I have not got the business address nor the subscription rates, but perhaps you might find them out, if you think of it, and debit me in your book.

48 Myles had been awarded an MA by University College Dublin. 49 Henry Woodd Nevinson (1856-1941), English essayist, philanthropist and journalist. He studied German literature during two sojourns in Jena in the early 1880s and published biographies on Herder (1884), Schiller (1889) and Goethe (1931). As a foreign reporter for the *Daily Chronicle* and the *Manchester Guardian* he served as a war correspondent 1914-1918 and later witnessed the Black and Tans outrages in Ireland. He obtained a D.Litt. from Trinity College Dublin in 1936. In later years he joined the British Labour Party. 50 Sir Roger Casement (1864-1916), who was, of course, in Germany from November 1914 to April 1916, trying to organise an "Irish Brigade". On Dibelius' involvement in the German propaganda efforts during World War I, see Introduction. 51 *Irish Statesman.* The first number had appeared on 15 September 1923.

We enjoy absolute peace here, though there have been horrible conflicts between Separatists and country people elsewhere. The fact that the country people arose and slew 113 of these unfortunate people in one place[52] is enough to show what madness the thing is. However, I should think it is nearly over. I have never seen a Separatist in Bonn.

I am greatly pleased because I have bought a splendid bicycle, and propose to travel all over the country. On Sunday fortnight I hope to visit Maria Laach again.[53]

I wrote a rather fevered letter to Brian, exhorting him to come out and visit Theo at Christmas. I wonder will it have any effect. I shall be there probably the week after Christmas week, as I am going first to Munich. If Brian comes, he will be able to bring me out a collection of notes on Welsh and Old Irish which I did not think of bringing with me, and without which I could badly prepare my doctorate. Sending them through the post might be awkward, because they are bulky. However, someone else will possibly be coming after Christmas, if he is not inclined. I exhorted him to resolve to spend some time here or in Paris before he departs into the world of deeds and deaths and affidavits, and I hope it will somehow be practicable. It makes so much difference to make the acquaintance of German—or I should think French—university life, that it is a great mistake not to do it, if possible.

Do not be alarmed about the troubles here, as far as personal safety is concerned. In Bonn it is very unlikely that there will be any disturbance, as there is no industrial population, and otherwise the trouble is generally in small towns and in the country. Even when anything does happen, it is usually slight in comparison with many of our adventures at home. At any rate, silence from me will always be a good sign. If there is any sensation I shall wire.

Did you see that Yeats has got the Nobel Prize?[54] Maria—on an unpardonable postcard after nearly a month's silence—says that Nano has sprained her ankle. I hope that this is not bad. Give her my love.

Please write at length when you have time.

[PS] A most welcome letter from Maria has just come, in which there is news of James' love and Nano's recovery. Brian's dance is tonight. I wonder will he dance. I lament twice a week that I cannot dance, and yet I do not believe I shall ever learn.

---

52 This is based on an article in the *Generalanzeiger* of 22 November 1923. Fighting between separatist units and local militias in the Siebengebirge area continued unabated and claimed at least 113 lives. In the militias communists and right wing extremists fought side by side—for the last time.
53 See Letter 84. 54 This was awarded on 14 November 1923 and presented in Stockholm on 10 December.

107
[Myles to John Dillon] 14. xii. '23

Your letter has been a great pleasure. It is splendid that you have quite recovered the chill. Here I find the climate delightful, because though the cold is considerable it hardly ever rains, which is a great relief from the familiar Dublin winter.

Nevinson[55] came out to see me, with great kindness, for he was going to London the same night, and could only stay an hour. But he was in charming humour. Of his news from the Ruhr you will know more than I, because you have seen his articles.

Three copies of the *Statesman*[56] have arrived, including one forwarded by you. I enjoy it because it is not a newspaper, and there is a good deal of interest. Æ's* leading article I never got through, but his reviews are pleasant, and Joseph O'Neill's* articles defending Irish are worth reading. It is possible that "Seosamh O Néill" concealed his identity from you.

I wrote to Theo suggesting that I should put off my visit till Easter, and he has replied agreeing, but with my usual perversity I at once began to feel inclined to go now. And your letter is an encouragement, I had hesitated before the journey, which is as long in point of time as that to Dublin, and the expense, but that would be the same at Easter. The state of my fortune is not without cause for alarm. My days in London and Paris and Leysin must have cost a good deal, and living here has now become a nightmare, as my letter to Maria will have told you. At any rate, I have spent since September about £80, which is quite out of proportion to my resources. My bicycle and dentist's bill, Sheridan[57] having overlooked something when I was with him in October, added to the rest. Perhaps you might consider a small grant in aid at the end of the year to make my balance look more creditable. I hardly think I shall be bankrupt in August, but I do not expect to have finished my thesis before next Winter, and I should like to go to Meillet[58] in Paris after that if possible.

I shall bring the copies of the *Statesman* to Dibelius.* He was in Ireland about twenty years ago, I think, but I do not know whom he saw. He gave a good account of the Land War, though quite general. But it was an exciting story. Some details, as for instance that Parnell was the founder of the Land

55 See previous letter (106). 56 *Irish Statesman* was edited by Æ from 1923 to 1930. Myles eventually contributed a number of articles and reviews to it. See Appendix. 57 Myles' dentist in Dublin? 58 Antoine Meillet (1866-1936) was one of the most influential linguists of his time who used the comparative method with the utmost precision. In 1903, he published his seminal work *Introduction à l'étude comparative des langues indo-européennes*. Meillet became Professor of Comparative Philology at the Collège de France in 1906. When Myles eventually went to Paris in 1925, Meillet became one of his teachers.

League, were at fault.[59] But now he has moved from Ireland to India, and I have forbidden myself the luxury of hearing him.

Many thanks for your generous present, and for the money for the students. I have a penurious friend in Berlin to whom I shall send some, and the rest can be disposed of in many ways. I am sure the Welsh and Irish notes can be sent out, as you say. I shall write to Brian with a statement of what I want. It is silly to have left them behind, but he must not be stern. There are four small volumes of a series on Modern Irish Syntax by Father Gerard O'Nolan[60] which are also in the drawer, and which I shall want too. I will write to him soon. By the way, I put back the key in the middle drawer of your desk before leaving. The Icelandic is pleasant. The man here is very good and an attractive old fellow with splendid hair.[61] We have only had two sessions so far, but after Christmas it will be better.

The election result is extremely interesting.[62] Was it absolutely necessary for Baldwin to declare an election before introducing protection, or was he merely anxious to clear the issue?[63]

I shall probably stay here and work over Christmas and then possibly go to Theo. Lectures recommence here on the 8th. I should be glad to have advice from you about this. Please write again as soon as you can. I envy Brian his shooting. I dreamt last night that I was out myself, and shot a strange sea bird.

Much love to the family,

108

[Myles to John Dillon] Wednesday, 9. i. '24

My travels are over, and I am again in the way of writing letters. I only hope my visit to Theo was nearly as pleasant for him as it was for me. We had the most perfect weather, and the country is completely snowed up, so I skied almost every day, finishing on Sunday by a tour with Theo's Lehrerin[64] to Diablerets,

---

59 The real founder of the Land League was Michael Davitt, assisted by John Dillon and others. Parnell was initially cool towards it, but came in behind it when it proved a success. **60** Gerard O'Nolan, *Studies in Modern Irish.* 3 vols. Dublin 1919-1921 and *Introduction to Modern Irish: a handbook for beginners.* Dublin 1921. **61** Prof Meissner; see Letter 104. **62** That is, the British General Election result. Stanley Baldwin, who had succeeded Bonar Law as Conservative Prime Minister on 21 May, called a General Election for 6 December 1923, mainly because he wished to revert from free trade to protectionism. The decision proved unfortunate, and resulted in considerable Conservative losses and in the country's first Labour government, under Ramsay MacDonald. This, however, did not come to fruition till 22 January 1924. **63** Bonar Law had actually given an election pledge that there would be no change from the previous Liberal policy of Free Trade, so this was certainly the honourable thing for Baldwin to do. **64** That is, his lady teacher (of German), Frl. Tempelmann.

which is a minor St. Moritz about ten miles from Leysin. We went on skis to the village of Sepey, about three miles, and from there by train to Diablerets. Then we wandered up a valley on our skis, and skimmed down. I confess my progress was less regular than Fräulein Tempelmann's, but I was very proud of managing the expedition at all. The light on the snow mountains and in the sky at sunset was too wonderful for me to try to describe it, but every evening at Leysin we had something almost as glorious.

I left Leysin unwillingly on Monday night, and, as it turned out to be cheaper, and probably less fraught with complication, I resolved to travel by night to Paris, spend the day there, and come on here the next night—rather an arduous programme, but economical of hotel bills. I arrived in Paris, having travelled for hours through a country under water, with boats floating down the streets of villages, to find fog and rain and no taxis to be had for gold. However, I ultimately reached the hotel, and, having removed the signs of travel, presented myself at Mabel Robinson's* flat. She had prepared an excellent lunch, and had large quantities of chocolates which people give her at Christmas though she does not eat them, so I began to find Paris delightful.

After lunch Madame Duclaux* appeared and asked me to come to her for dinner, to partake of a haunch of venison sent to her by the Baroness de Rothschild. I accepted this gracious invitation, and Mabel Robinson then led me out to the Musée Rodin. The dinner was pleasant, the two other strangers were an uninteresting Madame Darmstadter,[65] sister-in-law of Madame Duclaux,* and another very attractive young wife, but I had soon to leave, in the middle of the chocolates, which appeared here too in plenty, as my train started before ten. Both Miss Robinson and her sister spoke often of you.

The train crawled from Paris to Cologne, arriving after twelve o'clock today, I think, and there had apparently been no saloon car, but I am none the worse of the adventure. The journey from Paris to Cologne cost about 11/1d.

A short article of mine appeared in the *Irish Statesman* of the 5th of January.[66] It is not ambitious, but I would be glad of your opinion of it. I promised Kathleen to have a copy sent to her if it were published. Perhaps you could order her one. I asked Æ to omit my name, so it appears under the initials O.I.

Your letter reached me at Leysin, and gave me the consolation I required in a moment of doubt about my finances. The avalanches at Leysin were not near La Valerette, and did little harm. At Diablerets two people were killed, and sixteen huts or more were buried. I saw the place, and the remains of two of the lower houses were visible.

Maria's letter also found me there, as also the Hazeline Snow she sent, and I rejoice to say that the coffee arrived here yesterday, having been posted on

65 A sister of the historian James Darmesteter, to whom Mary Robinson* had been married before Emile Duclaux. 66 See Appendix.

December 14th. The tea, chocolate biscuits, and Gräfin Beissel's coffee have still to come, but I quite expect them to arrive. The special treatment given to Liebesgaben[67] causes delay. Please give her my thanks for a calendar which came before I went away, but I forgot, as usual, to mention it to her. I am glad that she was able to send Peg her parcel.

I found a very kind letter from Dr Bergin* awaiting me this afternoon, which has recalled me to a more sombre mood. Things look different when one is commencing them.

[PS] Fathers Moloney and Coghlan[68] enquire affectionately for you.

Please tell me about the Boundary Commission.[69] Have some steps been taken? Kathleen Sullivan,[70] who writes to Mabel Robinson,* has got some post in the Boundary Commission Office.

Thurs. Gräfin Beissel's parcel came this morning.

109

[Myles to John Dillon] Bonn, Schedestrasse 3, bei Gräfin Beissel, Tuesday,
29. i. '24

Your second letter has just arrived. I have been very remiss for some time, and have been resolving every day to write, but the weeks pass here like days, and my thesis would need more time than I have for it.

Many thanks for the cuttings. I shall return them in my next letter. The Youth Movement here is a very interesting one, and to my mind [a] most typically German development.[71] Very sound in most of its doctrine, but to our feeling much too sentimental and naive. In Germany things take on a form which becomes a standard, so that in breaking with one tradition they immediately tie themselves to another. Dibelius,* speaking of this movement, used it as a proof of the strong individuality in Germany, and made the rather acute observation that the standard of good conduct in England is to do what other people do, to be normal, while here the great longing is to do what nobody else is doing.

---

67 Presents. 68 See above, Letter 104. 69 The Anglo-Irish Treaty of December 1921 provided for the setting up of a Boundary Commission to determine the boundaries of Northern Ireland. Its first meeting was delayed by the North's refusal to participate in the negotiations. It eventually took place in London on 6 November 1924. 70 Daughter of A. M. Sullivan; see Letter 35. 71 The youth movement (*Jugendbewegung*) in the Weimar Republic was a largely middle-class neo-Romantic reform movement which criticized the intellectualism, materialism and utilitarianism it perceived in society. Against the anonymity, impersonality and machine culture of the period it posited the creation of a new vitality in individuals and a love of nature (Laqueur 1974, p. 86). In its idealism and love of country, community and fatherland it paved the way for right-wing ideologies like National Socialism.

Some of the Wandervogel,[72] he tells me, simply decline to do anything: "eine Bewegung gegen irgendetwas werden",[73] said he.

The Movement has developed in every direction, and since the war many new associations have been formed, and the Catholic clergy have become active organisers. Coming home from an expedition into the Siebengebirge last Sunday, I met a crowd of little boys marching through the street, singing rather feebly, dominated by a strange black figure which walked in their midst shouting out the Wanderlieden[74] [*sic*]. My companion told me these were the "Quickborne",[75] led by a well-known Jesuit enthusiast.

I read Yeats' lecture with much pleasure.[76] The article on Hebrew seemed familiar, and then I remembered that I was in Switzerland with Theo when it appeared. However, I shall be glad to read it again.

Theo has written twice in the last week, and his letters are more than cheerful. St. Francis and Goethe are his inspiration.

I continue Icelandic with the charming professor.[77] The last night of the lecture (which is held in his house) we had been to a Schubert concert, and he opened the evening's entertainment by singing something composed by himself, in a pleasant baritone voice. He has a charming wife who makes wonderful wax models, amongst other accomplishments. Tomorrow night I intend to go early in the hope of hearing some more songs.

About the dictionary, I doubt if it is worth sending it, as we have only four weeks more of this term, and I have the use of two very insufficient dictionaries in the Library. But I await impatiently the arrival of the translation. It is an interesting tale. I wish I knew a little more about Iceland, and how far one may see resemblances to our own past. At one time it was boasted that the Norse learned the saga form itself from the Irish, but apart from that there are interesting features in common.

I am reading Shaw's *Back to Methuselah* with great delight.[78] I have not laughed so much for months. Someone told me that for the excellent but almost unpardonable scene between Asquith and Lloyd George, it was forbidden to show any resemblance on the stage at the Manchester performance.

72 The *Wandervogel* was an integral part of the movement described in the previous note. It was the first organised group of the Youth Movement, founded by K. Fischer (1881-1956) in 1896. Originally dedicated to a love of nature and physical exercise in the form of hiking, parts of the organisation took a more spiritual and general culture-political turn in 1907 under H. Breuer. Besides hiking, the activities of the *Wandervogel* groups, numbering about 30,000 all over Germany in 1929, included the performance of folk songs, folk drama and folk dances. In their earthy pursuits the groups rivalled the Hitler Youth after the Nazis had gained power, and Hitler dissolved the *Wandervogel* in 1933. 73 "A movement against becoming anything at all". 74 Wanderlieder: "hiking songs". 75 The *Quickborn*, founded in 1909, was a Catholic Youth Organisation, strongly influenced by R. Guardini's ideas. It was dissolved in 1939 and refounded in 1946. 76 Presumably his speech accepting the Nobel Prize. 77 Prof. Rudolf Meissner; see Letter 104. 78 This was published in 1921. First produced in New York on 27 February 1922; the first British production

I intend to spend the Summer term in Berlin, to take advantage of the Celtic library there. It will be hot in July, and ugly too, but I hope to enjoy it more because I know my way about better now, and I know some people there. There will be plenty to do outside my work if I have time for it. I shall go up at the end of the month to see about digs, and then return here till May. May, June and July I shall spend in Berlin, and then come back to Bonn to finish my thesis.

We have had one or two gloomy days, but today is again delightful.

My love to the household.

110

[Myles to Brian Dillon] Bonn, Schedestrasse 3, Wednesday, 6. ii. '24

Dear Brian,

Your letter arrived this evening. I shall write to Arthur [Cox]* without delay. Father did not mention the matter, but I suppose he approves. The simplest plan will be for me to withdraw, and leave the lady undisturbed.[79]

You can be of great help to me if you will, by sending me some books and notes from the bottom drawer in my room, which have unexpectedly become very necessary. The books are four small volumes (I think there are four) called *Studies in Modern Irish* by Father Gerard O'Nolan,[80] and I believe they are in the drawer, towards the front, and ought to be easily found. [...] Books can be sent without difficulty, but please do not let them be wrapped in thin paper, or they will suffer severely. The notes will not be so convenient, but Father will have some plans for packing them. It will be best to send them by book post with "Private Matter" on them. Should there be any trouble about Customs, Father Moloney has suggested to me that anything sent out from Dublin should be addressed to him: Rev. Lieut. Col. Moloney, Senior Chaplain, G.H.D., Cologne. It can then be sent for Ireland postal rates, as Mrs Wilson will know. I do not like to ask you to do this, but you will earn many thanks.

Shaun's letter enclosing mass offerings arrived today. Please give him my thanks. I will send him the acknowledgement he requires.

I hope you will take kindlier to the law than I did,[81] and thereby guard the family fortune. If you thrive, I shall give you charge of my affairs, if I have any.

With much love,
Myles.

was at the Birmingham Repertory Theatre on 9 October 1923. **79** This sounds interesting, but the reference remains unfortunately quite obscure. **80** See Letter 107. **81** Myles had served about six months in the solicitors' firm of Arthur Cox* (whose father, Sir Michael Cox, had been the family doctor), but it did not appeal to him at all. He retained, however, an affection for Arthur Cox, who remained the family solicitor until his retirement.

III

[Myles to John Dillon] Bonn, Schedestrasse 3, Monday, 11 February 1924

Thank you for the letter and the cuttings. I am keeping them for the moment, as I should like to hear the opinions of some people here on them. [...]

I am considering various possibilities for the Summer Semester. I must go to Berlin for some time, on account of the books there, but my pressing need is some philology, as Thurneysen* has retired from his chair here (and reads only Celtic, privately), and no one has been appointed to succeed him. There is a very good man in Jena,[82] and alternatively I might go to Freiburg. There the lector in English is a friend from Dublin, Prionnseas O'Sullivan,[83] and one would not be quite alone, and I would be less than a day's journey from Theo, which is a consideration. If I decide on either of these latter plans, I shall spend the Easter vacation in Berlin collecting material, and get away before the heat comes. I have written to Jena and Freiburg for their programmes, as well as to Berlin.

My thesis is still struggling for existence. I am living in hope that some light will show itself after a time. Thurneysen went through what I had to show him on Friday afternoon, and was very kind. His charming daughter who gave you tea, and then disappeared, has just become engaged, and the household is rejoicing.

I am writing to Arthur [Cox]* about the apprenticeship. In my letter to Brian I told him the books and notes I want. I hope it will be possible to send them without too much trouble.

Dibelius* lectured publicly here the other night on "Politik", to a great crowd of people. He appealed to those of the students who had turned away in disgust from politics in the new Republic to return. It was an interesting lecture, but delivered under difficulties.[84]

There may be a letter from me in this week's *Statesman*.[85] I must say I think Æ will do good with his paper. For the first time I have begun to read some of his political articles, criticisms of the Dáil, and particularly his summing-up of recent Irish history, with approval. He made a most unfortunate attack on a cynical farmer the other day, when T.P. Gill rose to defend.[86]

82 This probably refers to Albert Debrunner (1884-1958), Prof. of Comparative Philology and Sanskrit, who came to Jena in 1924. 83 Proineas Ó Súilleabháin completed his doctorate in Freiburg in September 1924 and, after returning to Ireland, became an Inspector in the Technical Branch of the Dept. of Education. He gained some notoriety in the 1930s for his outspoken support of the Nazi regime. He became involved in organizing trips to Germany, and published favourable accounts afterwards. For further details see Fischer 1996, vol. II, pp. 33ff. 84 As becomes plain from the next letter, this refers to difficulties from the French authorities, not the audience. 85 See Appendix. 86 In an article which appeared in the *Irish Statesman* on 5 January 1924 Æ had launched a vicious attack on the Farmers' Party, arguing that they did not have the intellectual

Kensington Square sends me the *Times Supplement* every week, and it is a feast of enjoyment. I wonder whether you saw in the number for January 17th an article on Montaigne, written to introduce a new edition of his *Essays* by the Navarre Society. I am hoping that you will have added it to the library when I get home. I often try to feel glad that there is still so much to read, but it is really miserable to know so little, and there's no danger of one's ever getting to the end.

Please tell Shaun I shall write. I have given the offerings to the cleric, and he was most grateful.

[PS] Let me know when this arrives, as I am not bothering to register it.

112

[Myles to John Dillon] Thursday, 21. ii. '24

Your letter arrived on Monday, just as I was starting for Cologne. I was going to a dentist whom her ladyship had specially recommended, and he proved a most charming person. For the first time I really enjoyed a dentist visit. After lunch I went to see a great oriental collection, with the most delightful Japanese paintings on silk, and Chinese and Japanese work of all kinds. We drove past the museum on our memorable tour, but I had not heard of it at the time. I took tea with Father Coghlan, and to my great satisfaction found all three parcels of notes in Father Moloney's office. The Rev. Lieut. Col. is in Rome on leave. Many thanks for sending the notes and books so safely. Father Coghlan insisted on my dining with him, as a result of which I arrived breathless and very late at the theatre to see a very good performance of Molière. The house was crowded, but I had engaged quite a good seat for one and sixpence. Why is it that in this country every city has a repertory theatre where Shakespeare and Schiller, Goethe, and the French and Spanish plays, and of course Shaw and Wilde, are constantly produced, while in England or Ireland it is almost unknown? This week in Bonn there are two Shaw performances, and tonight *King Lear*. Albeit I never go to the theatre here, though I hardly know why.

capacity to develop a proper agricultural policy for Ireland. Interestingly enough, Deputy C. Hogan of the Farmers' Party did not defend his party against Æ's criticism but rather chose to launch a counter-attack against Irish intellectuals: he stated that most of the calamities in recent Irish history had been due to "the evils they [the intellectuals] had wrought [...] by almost effacing our culture and extinguishing our prosperity" (*IS*, 12 January 1924). This was grist to Æ's mill who obviously enjoyed a good argument and quite justifiably criticised Hogan's "glorification of stupidity and ignorance" (*IS*, 12 January 1924). T.P. Gill argued in Hogan's defence that intellectuals are often enough influenced by Communist ideas of the "insane Russians" (*IS*, 26 January 1924), which smacks very much of the ideological strategy the Nazis were to employ in the early 1030s in order to denigrate Weimar culture. Anti-communism was, of course, rampant in Ireland from the beginning of the century onwards.

I am still in doubt as to where fate will lead me in the Summer, none of the Universities having yet sent their programmes.

The change here is noticeable, though I am told that many now realise for the first time how poor they really are. There was a good speech by the foreign minister, I think in Duisburg, in the *Kölnische Zeitung* on Monday,[87] which I thought of sending you, but I daresay you saw a report of it. Still, it is puzzling to see so much luxury in spite of adversity. Father Coghlan told me he gave a dinner to friends on Sunday night at 25/- a head, and the restaurant was crowded with Germans, some of them eating much more expensively. If one goes into a restaurant or café here or in Cologne it is usually the same, and now that the exchange is fixed, one can't explain it as recklessness. I presume these are business people. It would be interesting to know what the income tax is in Germany. It may be a mistake to tax industry, but the incomes should be taxed. This would not affect my friends at all, as they have long ceased to have any income, and live by selling their shares, which others are glad to buy, and wait for the good days coming.

When I spoke of Dibelius* being under difficulties I only meant the presence of the French. He was already once rumoured to have been expelled, but up to now they have not touched the University. The seizing of people's houses continues. Two or three large houses were taken recently.

It is a pity that Brian is going into the office at this stage, but as the apprenticeship lasts him for four years, it might be disheartening to start much later. But perhaps when James is established in Ireland, and if I ever get to Paris, his heart will be turned, and he may join me for a few months. Arthur [Cox]* would certainly make no difficulty. I sometimes long to be in Paris already. I think the friendship of Miss Robinson* and Madame Duclaux* will make living there a great pleasure.

I am reading Carlyle, a splendid critic.

Much love to everyone. Please write when you have time. Is there any news of James? I have heard nothing from Kensington Square since Christmas, but I wrote to Kathleen a few days ago, and am in hope. They send the *Literary Supplement* very faithfully.

[PS] The text I meant is a small green paper-covered book called *Pedair Ceinc y Mabinogi*,[88] and the interior bears the marks of study in many places. If you can identify this one I should be glad to have it. If not, perhaps Brian would buy them all again and secure them against the cat or whatever the mysterious book-devourer may be.

87 Stresemann actually spoke in Elberfeld, where he argued for a careful and pragmatic approach in foreign policy including negotiations with France and the Allies, instead of the loud-mouthed absolutist demands from right-wing extremists (*KZ*, 18 February 1924). 88 This was probably the edition by J.G. Evans, published in Oxford in 1905.

113

[Æ (George Russell)* to Myles] The Irish Statesman, 84 Merrion Square,
Dublin, February 26, 1924

Dear Miles,
   Many thanks for your letter and the note on life in Germany which will get
in next week, I hope.[89] I am always glad to have anything that throws any light
on conditions in Europe. You need not be puzzled at a time of adversity in
seeing so much luxury among Germans. In every country, even the poorest,
there is one class which controls wealth, and they can always manage to have a
good time. They float on the top of the national life the way a boat floats on the
tide; the tide may rise or fall but the boat is always on top. I saw the articles by
John Eglinton[90] and Padraic Colum[91] in the *Dial*. I was thinking of writing something about John Eglinton and his views on Irish literature, but he is perfectly
hopeless, and he is more concerned about shaping a nice sentence than getting at
the truth. He has left Ireland and is now living in Wales. He is a very nice
fellow personally, and a great friend of mine, but anybody more hopelessly at sea
when he talks about Ireland I do not know.

Yours sincerely,
Æ.

114

[Myles to John Dillon] Bonn, Schedestrasse 3, Saturday, 1. iii. '24

Your letter came on Monday, shortly before I left for Köln. Father Coghlan
had kindly got me a seat at the opera, and as I arrived only half an hour before
the show commenced I could not order the Eau de Cologne. I shall do it the
next time I am there. The opera was excellent, a very good performance of the
Meistersinger, which lasted over five hours, but I did not find it too long. The
reverend warriors gave me supper afterwards, and plied me with bottles of beer,
and as my train did not leave Köln till twenty to two, Fr Moloney insisted on
my coming to his dwelling to share a large bottle of champagne. Following the
beer, this proved very unwholesome, but I arrived home safely. He interviewed
the Pope while in Rome, and also Father Butler.[92]

89 It was published on 15 March 1924. See Appendix. **90** Pen-name of W.K. Magee (1868-1961),
literary critic and essayist. He retired to Wales, and then England, declining to live under the Free
State government. He actually wrote a *Memoir of Æ* in 1937. **91** Padraic Colum (1881-1972), poet
and dramatist, close friend of Æ's.* Had emigrated with his wife Mary to America in 1915, and
was lecturing in the English Department of Columbia University. **92** Possibly Dom Cuthbert
Butler (1858-1934), Abbot of the Benedictine monastery of Downside until 1922. Shawn Dillon had
been at school in Downside and Mount St. Benedict was owned by the Bendictines of Downside.

The Welsh dictionary and the Gisli translation arrived, for which much thanks. It seems to be a simpler affair than I thought, but I am most grateful for the various parcels.

The programmes for Göttingen and Freiburg have come, and unfortunately do not contain what I want, but a few days ago, under a happy inspiration from Kathleen, I wrote to Frau Dr Fischer in Heidelberg, with whom Theo and I intended to stay two years ago, and she has sent me the programme from there which is much more promising. I shall send you a copy with the lectures marked which interest me. It contains also a list of professors, ordinary and honorary, and dozents, which will give you an idea of the German plan, and also an analysis of students and faculties. I only await now the Berlin programme, which I am almost hoping will not be tempting. Then I shall start for Berlin and remain there till May, and spend the Summer at Heidelberg, and swim in the Neckar. If Frau Fischer can put me up, it will be very happy, and I shall not be very far from my mentor here, when I want help with my work.

I had a very pleasant letter from Maria this morning, with lots of news. I have not heard from Theo for some time, but she tells me the doctors have reported well of him.

I hope you will not disapprove of my performance in the *Statesman* which is due to appear this week.[93] It occurred to me that one sentence about the professions in Ireland may be rather impertinent, but I hope this is only a nervous feeling.

We have holidays now, so I am living peacefully. We are emerging into delightful spring weather, but in spite of glorious sunshine it is still very cold. Maria says you may go to Wexford tomorrow. Please let me have an account of the proceedings there. I was with Thurneysen* on Thursday and he asked kindly for you and for Nano. Though he only knows her photograph he often enquires for her.

Tonight, for the second time since I came, I am going to the theatre here, to see a play of Hauptmann.[94] With love to everyone,

[PS] I hope all signs of your cold have vanished. I shall be expecting a letter. Love M.

115

[Myles to John Dillon] Saint Patrick's Day, 1924.

It is late at night, but I am in heavy debt as regards letters to George's Street, and tomorrow will be a day of upheaval. I hope to get away on Wednesday, and am going first for a few days to Heidelberg. From there I shall go on to Jena to

93 It was delayed and appeared on 15 March 1924. See Appendix. 94 See Letter 8.

see what the prospect there is, and then to Berlin. Weimar appears to be on the way, and I hope to spend a day there too.

I enjoyed your letter greatly, and the one from James which you enclosed. The papers came too, and I read with great interest of the excellent meeting in Wexford. It is splendid that you were able to go, and that it was such a success. The other news from Ireland is depressing. It shows again how far behind we are, but it is probably to the good that such things manifest themselves.[95] If you see Æ's* articles you will find sometimes a rather wholesome disillusionment.

I had been in Köln on Friday and found some letters from you and Brian awaiting me. The Eau de Cologne should arrive soon. There was a difficulty about having it sent from the shop, owing to the French demand for a special tax and special permission to export, so Father Coghlan undertook to have it sent by the military post. The price was 8/- a bottle, so my supply of German money only allowed two, and the lady said you could probably get it cheaper in England or Ireland. She gave me the address of the wholesale man in London, who will either supply you or say what shops in Dublin or London keep the stuff: Blackaller and Pleasance, 9 Laurence Pountney Hill, Cannon Street, London EC 4.

On Saturday I cycled to Maria Laach, and was at some delightful ceremonies there. They have the privilege to say the Missa Recitata, at which the priest faces the congregation, and they make the responses and repeat aloud the Credo and other parts of the Mass. One had to get up before six o'clock to be there, but I confess I was very glad to do it. The least pleasant part of the adventure was the horrible dust of the road. Dozens of motors passed as I toiled there and back, and I felt like an old mudguard when I arrived home last night.

Please tell Brian I will write as soon as my wits are about me. I was very glad to have his letter. Maria's shamrock was here when I returned, so I was able to honour the day. I owe her two letters, and am in haste to write to her too. In Heidelberg my address will be Gaisbergerstrasse 19, bei Fischer (till next Wednesday) and in Berlin, Karlstrasse 31, Pension Utke.

Thurneysen* sends you greetings. He has been very kind in enduring my visitations. I took my leave of him on Friday, when we all went to congratulate him on his birthday.

Please give me news of Nano when you write. I hope she is well and happy. I look forward with pleasure to the dignity of being an uncle. I am afraid this is a confused letter, but if so it fairly reflects my state of mind.

[PS] I have just been sent two catalogues from Neale, which I daresay you will have seen too. There is a good deal of interest in them. The enclosed cheque is for Brian, in answer to his letter. I wonder if he ever sent off my parcel to Inis Meadhoin last Autumn. He ordered tobacco and other things, and he was to

95 It is not clear what the reference is here.

pay for them next day and have them sent. But I never heard whether they arrived. M.

A girl who had borrowed the Verzeichnis[96] from me has forwarded it to you. On page 12 you will find most of my special subjects. Bartholomae,[97] Bergstrasser,[98] and Zimmer[99] are the people I shall hear. M.

116

[Myles to John Dillon] Berlin N.W.6., Karlstrasse 31, Pension Utke, Sunday, 30. iii. '24

Your letter came this morning, and was most welcome. You will have seen from mine to Brian that your communication to Heidelberg found me still there. I had a most enjoyable time there, and went on afterwards to Würzburg, Weimar and Jena, all of which was interesting. I called on the professor in Jena[100] who is a pupil and friend of Thurneysen* and whom I hope some day to hear, but I had already arranged to go to Heidelberg for the Summer. Between Bonn and Heidelberg I had an afternoon in Frankfurt, where the memory of Goethe is the chief attraction.[101] So many charming cities make one envy the people who possess them, and everywhere the change to comparative comfort was evident. Berlin too is a very changed place since I was here a year ago, and a much pleasanter place to live in. As I almost expected, I no longer find it horrible, and am only at a loss to decide what to visit first, and how to do my work and not do it at the same time. My stay here will be frightfully expensive, and this has caused me much distress of mind for a few days, but now I have become resigned, and resolved to spend while I have something to spend.

I am not sure whether it will be right to apply now for an extension of my studentship when I have no special recommendation except that I have no hope of finishing my thesis within the time. I had an idea of trying to live somehow or other until I had finished the doctorate in Germany and then appealing for a special grant to do further work in Paris under Meillet.[102] That would be a more reasonable request, and I would have justified my existence for the last two

---

96 That is, the (Heidelberg University) catalogue. 97 Friedrich Christian Bartholomae (1855-1925), Professor of Comparative Philology and Sanskrit in Heidelberg from 1909 to 1924. See Letter 124. 98 Gotthelf Bergsträsser (1886-1933), Professor of Oriental Philology in Heidelberg from 1923 to 1926. 99 Heinrich Robert Zimmer (1890-1943), son of the great German Celtic scholar Heinrich Zimmer (1851-1920); Professor of Indian Philology in Heidelberg from 1922 to 1938. In 1928, Zimmer married Christiane Anna von Hofmannsthal, daughter of the Austrian writer Hugo von Hofmannsthal. In 1938, he was expelled from his university post by the Nazis under the racial purity laws; he emigrated to Oxford and subsequently to New York, where he died in 1943. 100 See Letter 111. 101 Goethe was born in Frankfurt in 1749, and lived there till 1765. 102 See Letter 107.

years, but this would mean waiting to apply until next Christmas. If you think it wise I could write to Coffey* and ask his opinion, or perhaps if you see him you could hear what he thinks.

I have been reading for the first time Thurneysen's really admirable book on the Irish saga literature which appeared two years ago.[103] There is a paper-bound copy amongst my books in the back drawingroom, and if you ever feel inclined to look through it I think you will find many charming things in it. The first part is mainly technical, except for a section on "Land und Leute", which is a good summary of what is known of early Ireland, but in the second part he analyses and tells the story of each of the sagas. As few people in Ireland have bothered their heads about them, and the great majority are published only in French and German journals, this book is the only introduction to them. I wish someone would translate it. In ten years, if no one has done it, I will do it myself.[104] He has planned two further sections which would complete the Irish literature of the older manuscripts, but for this he would have to come to Ireland again, and many things make this unlikely.[105] If there ever was question of his coming, would it be possible that you could offer him hospitality for a few weeks? It occurred to me that in George's Street now he would find very pleas-ant accommodation, and he would probably be an unobtrusive guest, as he would be working all the time.

I think I mentioned in Brian's letter that I made the acquaintance in Heidelberg of a very attractive American female who has lived there for five years.[106] She took me to tea to the house of a singer who gave us music and hospitality in plenty.

I spend hours arranging to go to the theatre and operas here, though they will cost a good deal. But O'Brien,* a fellow student, has just got married to a very pretty and pleasant girl who plays at a theatre here, and she has promised to get me free tickets whenever I want to go. I hoped to see *Faust* for the first time on Tuesday.

Give my love to Nano. I am often thinking of her, and am expecting joyful news every day.

If this finds you still in Dublin, please tell Maria that I got her letter this morning. The chocolates she sent had not arrived when I left Bonn, but this is not at all strange, as Liebesgaben[107] take over a month to come. They will be safely kept till I return, and I shall have a month's enjoyment in anticipation.

Salutations to Fr Shaun and Brian.

---

103 *Die irische Helden- und Königsage bis zum siebzehnten Jahrhundert.* Halle (Saale) 1921. **104** He did not fulfil this promise, but he did later partially fill the gap by publishing his own account of at least some of the sagas, in *The Cycles of the Kings* (Oxford, 1946; reissued, Dublin 1994), and in *Early Irish Literature* (Chicago, 1948; reissued, Dublin 1994). **105** Thurneysen* did eventually come to Ireland again in 1929. **106** Joan Marie Egls, see Letter 137. **107** Presents.

117

[Myles to John Dillon] [*Postcard*] Berlin, Thursday, [17 April 1924]

Many thanks for your letter and the *Freeman*, which I read with great enjoyment. I sometimes say things I regret when I say anything about the Irish government, so I say nothing. It is splendid that the perverse old ladies[108] have at
last made way. I was wondering what would be done if they refused. It is well to
bear in mind with Coffey* that his advice is nearly always wrong in our experience.[109] However, it has to be asked for. It would be interesting to know whether
anyone is expected to enter for the Celtic Studies studentship this year. It may
be that it goes free.

I am sorry and glad to be leaving here. It has been much pleasanter than
before, and I have been to some very good plays and concerts. On Saturday I go
to Minden,[110] where I shall stay till Sunday night or Monday, and then go on to
Bonn. Probably on Monday or Tuesday week I shall depart for Heidelberg.

[PS] *Independent* has just come. Many thanks. M.

118

[Brian Dillon to Myles] [2 Nth Gt Georges St., Dublin] 18.4.24

Dear Myles
I have just returned from one of my periodic visits to Mount St. Benedict.
Father Davies of Downside gave a retreat there and the Old Boys were invited
to attend. Some of us went down and on the whole it was very pleasant. The
retreat lasted only from Thursday night to the Sunday morning but I arrived a
couple of days early and left a few days late.

Jenny has actually left and the house is completely disorganized. Fortunately
Minny arrived on Wednesday last (the day Jenny left) so she is keeping Maria
company. [...] Our nephew appears to be very pleasant. Did I tell you that Kane
Smith[111] spent six weeks in Downside as a postulant and then came home? His
Reverence[112] is speechless with rage.

George[113] sits daily in the Law Library getting no work and is apparently
quite unmoved. He tells me that Ralph does get a little down the country.

James it appears will be upon us almost immediately. Our revered parent
declares that he will insist on him staying behind the counter in Ballaghadereen

108 Unfortunately this very interesting remark remains obscure. 109 This would be in reference to
applying for further support from the College. See previous letter. 110 To visit his cousin Toby
Mathew. 111 A school friend. 112 Fr John Francis Sweetman.* 113 George Kenny, a school
friend.

from 9.30 to 7 pm each day except for a month's holiday in the year, but of course that will come to nothing.

Shawn is still here but I imagine he will hardly stay much longer as priests are dying off with the most amazing rapidity.

I do not think that I will return to Con's[114] office but one can't be sure. My present plan is to move to the King's Inns. I have got leave to read in the King's Inns library and I find it very pleasant. Gavan-Duffy,[115] a strange man called Macnamara (who is a student of Irish and Philology and has published a book on place names), another youth and myself are the only occupants and there we sit in great comfort surrounded by what appears to be an excellent library. The University is as dreary as ever and Mount St Benedict slightly more so than the last time I was there. They have only 35 boys now.

Everybody prophecies amazing political developments but things seem to go on much as before.

Brian.

119

[Myles to John Dillon] Bonn, Schedestrasse 3, bei Gräfin Beissel, Friday, 25. iv. '24

Your letter has just arrived. I came back on Tuesday and have been rejoicing in the comfort and kindness of this house. My return was celebrated by an excellent cake, made by the major domo, which I am still enjoying. Please tell Maria that the biscuits arrived yesterday and are most welcome. They must have been nearly two months on the way.

I shall commence with dreary finance so as to get it over. My bankbook records that last September I had a balance of £101.8.9, and since then I have evidence of drafts on my account amounting to £168.17.8. I do not know how much you have lodged to my credit since, but you will from this letter be able to arrive at my present condition. If you had lodged nothing, I should now have a debit of £67.9.5. This will be a more expensive year than last year, but considering the changed conditions and my two journeys to Switzerland it was to be expected. I am sorry to hear that the family fortunes are threatened. However, most of us, if we had to put to sea, would probably float somehow.[116]

114 Constantine Curran.* 115 George Gavan Duffy (1882-1951), lawyer, son of Charles Gavan Duffy. Qualified as solicitor in England in 1907 and defended Roger Casement in 1916. Called to the Irish Bar in 1917, elected Sinn Féin M.P. for South Co. Dublin in 1918. Member of the Treaty negotiation team, afterwards pro-Treaty; first Free State Minister for Foreign Affairs, resigned 1922. Senior Counsel 1929, High Court Judge 1936 and President of the High Court in 1946. 116 Business will have been somewhat depressed in the shop in Ballaghadereen, in accordance with the generally depressed state of the economy. What exactly Myles means by "most of us" being

I left Bonn while it was still Winter, and have come back into the most glorious Spring. Everything is green, and there is the most delicious warm air. I am sitting before the open glass door of my room, over the garden. If Tir na n-Og was like Bonn in Spring one almost wonders at Oisin ever wanting to leave it. Last night I heard the nightingales for the first time this year. Soon after twelve o'clock one commenced, and I ran from bed and went out onto the balcony to hear her. Later, at two o'clock, I awoke to hear a perfect choir, and at five, when the other birds had begun, I could still hear their wonderful music amongst them. However, it spoils the charm to describe it. Now the nightingales have gone to bed, and the thrushes and finches and blackbirds, and whatever else they are, hold the field.

I shall stay here until the end of next week anyway, probably Saturday or Sunday. I imagine the term in Heidelberg will commence on the Monday. A card came from the University admitting me to lectures, and another from Mrs Fischer, who has kindly found me lodgings. Heidelberg will be pleasant, but I do not like to leave Bonn. My work is behaving itself fairly well. I have not seen Thurneysen since I came back, but I am going to him this afternoon, and shall convey your greetings.

The news of Nano and my nephew is splendid.[117] I did not know that he could emerge into society at so early an age.

There may have been something from me in the *Statesman* last Saturday.[118] Owing to my wanderings my copy is gone somewhere else, and I have not heard from Æ. I must say I find the paper often very good, and, whatever its merit or demerit, it represents the best that the best modern Irish writers can do.[119]

By the way, have the University cheques all been sent in up to date? There should have been three since I left, not counting the one now due. I have not kept any count of them, but one of the girls here told me one of hers after Christmas was not sent till she wrote demanding it.

The *Supplement* which Kensington Square always sends me gives a review of a book of Herbert Fischer, *The Common Weal* [sic],[120] which I am thinking of ordering. I see too that Hugh Law has partly written a book on Ireland.[121] I am reading Lessing's and Nietzsche's letters with great enjoyment. Letters are for me a charming form of reading.

If you write before long you can still send the letter here.

[PS] Gräfin Beissel enquires for you constantly. I deliver this to serve for many messages.

able to float is not clear. James, Nano and Shawn, perhaps; but not himself, Theo, or Brian, surely.
117 Nicholas Smyth was born on 1 April 1924. 118 His next contribution appeared on 10 May 1924. See Appendix. 119 Among those writing for the *Statesman* at this time were Yeats, O'Casey, Rolleston, Francis Stuart (whom the Dillons would not have approved of), Padraic Colum and many others. 120 Herbert Fischer's book was published by the Clarendon Press, Oxford in 1924. 121 Robert H. Murray and Hugh Law, *Ireland*. London: Hodder & Stoughton 1924.

120

[Myles to John Dillon] [*Postcard*], Bonn, Saturday [26 April 1924]

[...]

Brian's letter came today. Many thanks.

I forgot to mention my visit to Toby in my letter. He was in excellent form. During his stay in Leipzig he was informed by an authority that he had a promising baritone voice, and he now sings Schubert, Brahms and Grieg, but very badly, as he had no time to train while he was there. He has been earning large sums of money for lessons in English and even in Spanish (which he is learning himself).

I visited a charming palace of the old Archbishops of Cologne, who were also Kurfürsten of Bonn, at Brühl the other day. It is melancholy to see these wonderful houses turned into rather monotonous museums. The Schloss in Berlin,[122] by the way, has now been added to the number, and I went through it for 6d. when I was there.

The Königshofterrasse is open and I sat there over an ice last night till after 11 o'clock. Is it not possible that you will make another expedition this Summer? Heidelberg would delight you perhaps more than Bonn.

121

[John Dillon to Myles] Monday, 28 April 1924

Your letter of 25th came this morning. I can most thoroughly and heartily appreciate your keen enjoyment in getting back to your comfortable room and your very kind hostess, and I almost envy you sitting listening to nightingales and other song birds. You are quite right. Bonn is a very fascinating place, and I knew it would be rather a wrench for you to leave it. However, you will find Heidelberg a delightful abode, and full of interest.

Coffey* was here last night, and I discussed your case fully with him. He advises that you should make an application at any early date for an extension of your scholarship for a year. There are to be meetings of the Senate in May and in July. He thinks that it would be best if you could mention some historical subject which you were engaged in investigating, as he says all extensions given so far have been on this ground. But if you cannot think of any historical subject, you can tax your ingenuity to devise some other desirable subject of investigation. As soon as you let me know that you have sent in the application, I shall do what I can to promote it.

122 The Berlin City Palace (*Stadtschloß*) was destroyed during World War II.

I spoke to Coffey also about Thurneysen.* He was enthusiastically in favour of T.'s being brought over by the Irish Govt., and promised to approach old MacNeill[123] on the subject.

I agree with your taste for letters. There is barely any other form of literature which I enjoy so much as good letters. I have lately been reading some very interesting collections.

We are all going on as usual here. The weather has turned cold and wet, to the immense relief of all farmers, as we have had an unprecedented spell of warm, dry weather. Nano—in great spirits—and Smyth* dined here yesterday. Nicholas was to have visited us, but the day was too wet.

I hope you will arrange to spend some weeks with us in the autumn. When may we expect to see you? I have lodged £50 since Christmas, so you must be overdrawn £17. 9 . 5. I shall lodge £30 this week, and that will keep you going for the moment. All the scholarship cheques up to Jan. last have come, but there is one due 1st April which has not yet come. If it does not arrive in the course of the next few days, I shall call at the University and enquire about it. And I suppose I may forge your signature and lodge it, without the delay of sending it to you for signature. As soon as I get the cheque, I shall lodge a further £20 to your credit. There will be £25 interest in War Stock coming to you on 1st June. This I shall lodge as soon as I get it. Then on 1st July there will be another scholarship cheque of £50, so that your financial position is quite sound for many months ahead.

I have been reading an extremely interesting review in the *Times Lit. Supplement* of 17 Jan. '24, of a book by F.M.W. Foerster on the German Youth Movement.[124] Foerster is a professor of Philosophie and Pädagogik in the University of Munich. The book is published by Rotapfel-Verlag, [*illegible*] Zürich, München and Leipzig. Also an interesting article based largely on this book in the *Hibbert Journal* by a man named Meyrick Booth.[125] There must be a lot of literature in Germany on this subject, and you would have a fine opportunity of studying it in a place like Heidelberg. It would, I think, be a most interesting study, and you might write a series of most interesting papers for Æ's* Journal.[126] I don't often read that Journal, tho' I have subscribed to it for 3 months. But judging it from the *political* standpoint, it seems to be singularly futile. Of course, I can quite understand your liking it, as there is often good writing on other subjects.

---

123 Eoin MacNeill (1867-1945), currently Minister of Education (until 1926). He had been Professor of Early Irish History at U.C.D. from the foundation of the College in 1908 until 1922. He was also at this time the Free State representative on the ill-fated Boundary Commission, which would be taking up much of his attention. 124 Friedrich Wilhelm Förster, *Jugendseele, Jugendbewegung, Jugendziel*. Zürich: Rotapfel Verlag 1923-4. 125 Meyrick Booth had translated another one of Förster's books (*Marriage and the Sex Problem*) in 1912. Other books from his pen prove that he was an expert in things German. 126 Myles did touch on this subject in his next contribution to the *Irish Statesman*, which was published on 31 May 1924. See Appendix and also Letter 109.

I had a most pleasant letter from Theo on Saturday.

We are involved in a new political crisis, over the boundary question this time.[127] But I have got so used to political crises that it would feel quite strange if we were without one.

[PS] Coffey* said that your application for extension of scholarship should of course be accompanied by a letter of recommendation from Thurneysen.*

Don't forget to send me your Heidelberg address.

122

[Myles to John Dillon] [*Postcard*] Heidelberg, Karl Ludwigstr. 6, bei Fräulein Knecht, Sunday [4 May 1924]

Many thanks for your letter. Came down here yesterday and have found myself comfortably lodged through the kindness of the Fischers. Thurneysen gave me a letter and I shall write to the University in the next few days. I suppose the letter should be addressed to the Secretary at Merrion Square. Heidelberg is at its best, but I have not yet got rid of loneliness, and the melancholy letters of Lessing, which I am still reading, do not give much consolation. He seems to have been a most unhappy man, almost all his life, if his letters are fair evidence.[128] But Nietzsche and Goethe, I think, were, in this, much the same. Who defined the purpose of life as the pursuit of happiness?[129]

My address is above. I thought I had given it in my letter.[130] Is there any chance of your coming out during the Summer? You would be very comfortable here. By the way, Prof. Dibelius* has introduced me to a cousin of his who is professor here, and one of the chiefs of a society for music and art.[131] I have not called on him yet, but I am hoping to be kindly received. I owe Fr Shaun many apologies for the misdemeanour of Kaplan Mauss,[132] but I spoke to him on Friday. He has said all the masses long ago, but had forgotten to write to Shaun. He promised to write in the next few days. I shall let you know when I have written to the University. Father Moloney has been promoted Colonel and transferred to Aldershot, the best place in the army.

Love to everyone,

---

127 This was not the main crisis, which did not blow up until November 1925.   128 Gotthold Ephraim Lessing (1729–81) was indeed a man of many sorrows, some of which, appropriately to Myles' current preoccupations, were financial.   129 Aristotle, in the *Nicomachean Ethics*.   130 He had not, in fact.   131 Franz Martin Dibelius (1883–1947) who was Prof. of Biblical Exegesis and Criticism in the Protestant Theological Faculty in Heidelberg from 1915 to 1947.   132 This is the clergyman who was commissioned to say masses.

123

[Myles to John Dillon] Heidelberg, Tuesday, 13. v. '24

Many thanks for your letter. The Fischers very kindly found me a most satisfactory lodging here, and I am now at peace. My correspondence rather failed
since I left Bonn, as I was somehow in no humour to write, and badly able to
enjoy Heidelberg. That is gone, and I find myself passing shamelessly from one
enthusiasm to another. Not to have been at Heidelberg would have been so
wrong that I don't like to think of it. There is every sort of charm, and irre-
sistible romance, and one is finally rid of Prussia. In Bonn the only traces of
Berlin were perhaps in the police and public offices. Here it is entirely delightful, and the university and the town are much smaller, so that one sees people
continually. On Saturday night the castle was illuminated, and also the old
bridge into the town, and fireworks were sent up. This function occurs period-
ically in honour of one or other society which visits the town. Perhaps it is a
little wicked, and crowds come from near and far in trains and motor cars, but
it is really a wonderful sight. I climbed the mountain across the Neckar with two
companions and sat in the wood to see the show. And I must say the lighted
canoes filled with singers, and bands playing on the banks of the Neckar, were
delightfully festive.

The elderly philologian[133] here is more than kind and reads two hours a week
for me alone, which is a feast of information. Besides, he is lecturing three times
a week in comparative grammar. The Sanskrit man[134] is a son of Heinrich
Zimmer, whose library is in the College, and he is a pleasant fellow. For the
rest, I am for the moment hearing a good many other lectures on Goethe and
Schopenhauer, and Rembrandt, and 17th century literature. These are tempta-
tions which it is hard to resist at the start.

We had elections here on Sunday week,[135] but it was a quiet affair. The
result was as expected. By the way, are you still inclined to favour Mussolini?
He appears to be vexed with the pope,[136] but his plan of sending out punitive
expeditions is even more naive than the I.R.A. I saw with much satisfaction an
interview by Don Sturzo[137] in the *M[anchester] G[uardian]* some time ago which
dealt rather well with Fascism.

133 Friedrich Christian Bartholomae, who had retired at the end of the previous semester. See
Letter 115. 134 Heinrich Robert Zimmer; see Letter 115. 135 The Reichstag elections of 4 May
1924 resulted in massive losses for the government parties and the SPD whose vacillation between
sharing in government and acting as opposition did not impress voters. It was the extreme parties
who gained votes, the German National People's Party (DNVP) and the Deutschvölkische
Freiheitspartei which included the National Socialists on the right, and the Communists (KPD) on
the left. Only the catholic Centre Party, the party of Chancellor Wilhelm Marx, remained more or
less intact. 136 Pius XI was generally inclined to favour Mussolini. 137 Don Luigi Sturzo (1871-
1959), a Catholic priest, who was leader of the Catholic party, the Partito Popolare Italiano (ances-

Thanks for lodging the money. The Bank sent me a notice the other day of the lodgement. The treasure which I sent to the *Statesman* from Berlin was published last week (May 10th), so you may have seen it. I had a cheerful letter from Theo today in which he spoke his approval.

I am glad to say that my plans for the holidays have changed. Dublin is the best place in which to prepare any Celtic work, because all the books and most of the MSS are there. Accordingly I shall go home early in August and stay till October. When is James due to return?

Please do not dismiss the idea of visiting Heidelberg without consideration. It is so delightful, and the university life here so much nearer the ideal, you would enjoy it greatly.

I have not yet copied out my application to the University, but I have long had it ready, and have got a letter from Thurneysen.

[PS] I have forgotten how I stand with regard to Maria. Please tell her that I shall expect to hear from her next.

Æ* is in one of his best moods in the *Statesman* on "Literature and Life", signed "Querist".[138]

The Baden people are at least as charming as the Rhinelanders. I have never met more friendliness and easiness of temper than here. And the Fischers have found me a delightful landlady. She bakes me cakes and makes marmalade, and tonight invited me to an excellent supper of omelette and rolls. Heidelberg, being entirely a university town, is planned for students and, while high life is very expensive, the cheap restaurants are incredible. I dine every day for nine pence, and get very good meat and vegetables and soup. The other day I found myself for the first time in the Mensa Academica, and it made a strange impression. Our dinner cost 30 Pfennig (in normal times = threepence), and there were hundreds of well and ill dressed students at the tables. Each took a plate and filled it with soup. This over, one laid the spoon on the table, and advanced, plate in hand, to a counter, where a lady stood over a cauldron ladling the pottage. The plate was filled and a sausage forked into the middle, and off we went. And the food was really good, and tasted tolerably well. Would any other country do this? English or Irish students would not dream of staying in a university under such conditions. But here, if a man wants to study, he studies, food or no food, and the University makes a fight for his life by giving him dinner for 30 Pfennig.

tor of the post-war Christian Democrats), and a firm opponent of Mussolini. He was forced to resign as leader shortly after this by the Pope, who did not wish to antagonise Mussolini. **138** In the article in question entitled "The antecedents of history", Æ argues that nationality and the nation are constituted first and foremost by "a collective imagination held with intensity, an identity of culture or consciousness". It is not race, language or religious denomination which define a nation but an imagination common to its members. This idea of a nation as an intellectual construct obviously appealed to Myles (*IS*, 10 May 1924).

124

[Theo Dillon to Myles] La Valerette, Leysin-Feydey, Suisse, Saturday,
[late May 1924]

Your letter arrived this morning with this week's *Irish Statesman* hot on its
heels. I don't know which I liked best, your letter or O.I.,[139] but the latter was
very pleasing. Do you mind if I say that had I not known O.I., I should have
died of spleen at the idea of someone using Marcel Proust and Renan so aptly in
an article on German Weltanschauung. As it is, I merely sigh and recognize that
you have the faculty of getting nearer to the soul of things, while I must be
content to fumble analytically with their component parts. This is not a compliment, but a genuine attempt to say what I have long felt. (Here I must proceed
in pencil.) O.I.'s style becomes more limpid, what can I say more except that I
find it really soothing to read, and the choice of words most excellent. This is all
the more poignant, as I have spent the day in an agony approximating to the
pangs of childbirth (I ache all over) producing an article on Leysin, which I
have sent to the N.S.[140] in the hope of boosting Cappagh.[141] It is now gone and
I am glad to be rid of it: it is a poor toothless rickety production with no grace
or distinction.

I wish you would continue to collect the names of German books. As you
know I am lost for the want of just such a guiding line. Your announcement of
the rich literature rather took my breath away. It is certainly amazingly difficult
to hear anything about it.

More tomorrow. I cannot tolerate this pencil.

[*Continued in ink.*] I have just got the current number of *La Nouvelle Revue
Française*—the monthly of the young literary group in France.[142] Perhaps it
would interest you to see it—if so I shall send it on when I have finished it.
Like all such periodicals one feels despairing at the quantities of stuff one should
read to keep abreast with the times. By the way, is there no such periodical in
Germany, the home of periodicals, which might salve our consciences without
making too great demands on our time?

I got a long and friendly letter from Gerard the other day, set out in the
purest and most idiomatic Munster Irish, which rather intimidated me, but,
with a little effort, the sense, which was excellent, emerged. I am torn between
the desire to revive my Irish, and a strange wish to learn Russian, which Hugo
advertises as at last simplified in two volumes. The wisest, perhaps, would be to

---

139 The article in question appeared on 10 May 1924; see Appendix. **140** *New Statesman.* **141** A
rather obscure remark. **142** *La nouvelle revue française*, founded in 1909, soon came to symbolize
contemporary trends in French literature, art and thought. It encouraged new writers and launched
the careers of Rolland, Giraudoux and many others. The driving force behind the journal was
André Gide.

do neither, but to devote the year which I must still remain, to consolidating my German and Italian. The worst of it is, I never was much good at consolidating my knowledge of any language; it begins to bore me at that stage.

Gerard, by the way, spoke a good deal of philosophy, comparing Plato and St Paul, anent a discussion on Time and Eternity with Eimar O'Duffy,* who, it appears, has reverted to paganism under the tutelage of Bernard Shaw in *Back to Methuselah*,[143] and James Anthony Meagher, whom he met for the first time, and was duly taken in, I imagine, by his specious solemnity.

From Ralph [Barry]* I have not heard, but Brian tells me he has settled down in the Four Courts, attended by the inevitable George.

As far as I can gather from father, Duff[144] closed another half-year without any profits at all, on which he makes the characteristic comment that he will have to "take steps to reduce the staff". By the time the steps have been taken and the reduction of the staff falls due, the crisis will be over and a new era of prosperity will have opened.

I shall try to send you *In the Key of Blue*[145] tomorrow, it is well worth reading. What are your plans after the Doctoral examination, or have you given up the idea of Paris? I gather the exam. has been postponed to next Christmas. Have you secured your extension for another year?

Theo

[...]

125

[Myles to Osborn Bergin*] Heidelberg, Karl Ludwigstraße 6 II, Frl. Knecht,
20. v. '24

Dear Sir,

I have migrated to Heidelberg this semester, and have on the whole been fortunate in the lectures. Bartholomae[146] is reading an "Einführung in die Vergleichende Grammatik"[147], which is so far very elementary, but before he finishes I daresay we will have got at least a good idea of the outlines, and of the length and breadth of the matter. He is giving me two hours alone on the Greek inscriptions, which he makes a basis for detailed comparative grammar. Up to now we have read, I think, five words. One Bergsträßer,[148] whom Thurneysen* rather recommended, is lecturing on Allgemeine Sprachwissenschaft,[149] and that is a much more ambitious affair. He leaves me stranded when he talks of Aphasie,[150] and even a little bewildered by the distinction between unanschauliches Bewusstsein of abstractions and different (schauliches) Bewusstsein of

---

143 See Letter 109. 144 I.e. the family shop Monica Duff's. 145 John Addington Symonds, *In the Key of Blue and Other Prose Essays*. London, New York 1893. 146 See Letter 115. 147 Introduction to comparative grammar. 148 See Letter 115. 149 General linguistics. 150 Aphasia, loss of language.

particular objects, and the consequently stronger bond in the latter between Wortklang and Bedeutungsvorstellung.[151] He has not the gift of simplicity, in which he is the reverse of the venerable Bartholomae, but I hope to get something out of it. The Sanskrit man is a son of Heinrich Zimmer,[152] and a very lively character. He is now trying to buy O'Brien's* boat, and we are to have it transported from Berlin and sail on the Neckar. We are reading Bhâsa's Urubhangam, and more Mahâbhârata. I return even now from over three hours of it on end.

Heidelberg perhaps you know. It is a most delightful place, and it is so hot at present that one is more inclined to sit in the Neckar than trace roots in Kielhorn.[153] I try to do both. My thesis is gradually explaining itself and I am not quite as destitute of books here as I thought, as the *Zeitschrift*,[154] *Revue Celtique*, Meyer's *Contributions*[155] and a few other books are in the library, probably a relic of Osthoff's[156] time—Bartholomae makes no claim to knowledge of Keltic. But I shall go home to the Academy in August.

I have applied to the Senate for an extension of my studentship, as I shall not be able to take the exam. before Christmas, and I should not like to finish without having some time in Paris. During the holidays I was in Berlin and saw a lot of O'Brien and his wife. She is a charming girl, very pretty and fervent and I think she will change O'Brien a good deal.

By the way, Thurneysen* at the head of some Americans is about to continue Hessen's planned shorter dictionary of Old Irish, so at last there is hope.[157] A Festschrift to Streitberg entitled *Aufgabe u. Stand der Sprachwissenschaft*,[158] and another to Wackernagel[159] (to which Thurneysen* contributed) have appeared lately, but I have mended my ways as regards buying books now.

Please write when you have time. I sometimes hear from Æ.* He has baptised me a journalist to my great pleasure.

With all good wishes

Yours sincerely
Myles Dillon.

151 It is argued here that there is a stronger bond between phonetic form and meaning in words denoting concrete objects than in words denoting abstract concepts, a discussion very much en vogue during these early years of general linguistics as distinct from comparative (Indo-European) linguistics. **152** See Letter 115. **153** Kielhorn is a part of Heidelberg. **154** *Zeitschrift für celtische Philologie*. **155** *Contributions to Irish Lexicography* (Halle 1906). **156** Hermann Osthoff (1847-1909) was one of the foremost Indo-European scholars of his time. He was professor in Heidelberg since 1877 and co-founded the "Young Grammarians" school which dominated the subject of Indo-European Philology for decades. **157** The first fascicles of *Hessen's Irish Lexicon. A Concise Dictionary of Early Irish* did not appear until 1933. The editors were Seamus Caomhánach of University College Cork, Rudolf Hertz of Bonn and the American Vernam Hull. Gustav Lehmacher S.J., who instigated the "Lehmacher controversy" (see Letter 61), was the fourth collaborator. **158** Wilhelm Streitberg (1864-1925) was Professor of Indo-European Philology in Freiburg (Switzerland), Münster, Munich and Leipzig. The *Festschrift* was edited by former colleagues in Leipzig and appeared in 1924. **159** Jakob Wackernagel (1853-1938), a Greek scholar of high repute, was Professor in Basle and

126

[John Dillon to Myles] Thursday, 22 May 1924

I appear not to have written to you since 8 May,[160] which is rather disgraceful. The explanation is that I have had rather a busy and troubled time. I forget whether I told you in my last letter that at last my house was evacuated and handed over to me just a fortnight ago, with the result that I had to make arrangements for a valuation of damages, and had to go to Ballaghaderreen last week. The house is in a deplorable state. It made me sad to go thro' it. I could hardly recognise it. However, on detailed inspection, I came to the conclusion that with the aid of Farrell[161] I should be able to put it in habitable condition at a rather less cost than I had been led to expect. I have got a Dublin valuer to assess the damage, but what chance I have of getting money from the Government remains uncertain.

Just as I was about to start for Ballaghaderreen last Tuesday, Father Nicholas[162] walked in unexpectedly, so I put off my departure and had a very pleasant family dinner party on Wednesday. Father Nicholas was looking extremely well. He staid on till Friday, and dined with Smyth[163] on Thursday, and gave a solemn Franciscan blessing to his namesake.[164]

On Friday in Ballaghaderreen I received two letters from your Uncle William,[165] written from an hospital in Denver, in which he was lying waiting for a very serious operation, so you may imagine I was not in a happy frame of mind when I arrived home on Saturday. However, no news under the circumstances was good news, and as there was no news I immediately despatched a cable, and on Sunday morning, to my great relief, received a cable from James, who is out in Colorado, "Doing splendidly". This morning I received a letter from your cousin Willie,[166] written from the Hospital on 8 May, three days after the operation, telling me that the Doctors were very satisfied with the result of the operation, and that his father was doing well, and as the cable was sent ten days after date of Willie's letter, I may assume that your uncle is now quite out of danger, and will soon be quite recovered.

Göttingen. The *Festschrift* on the occasion of his 70th birthday appeared in Göttingen in 1923. **160** This letter is lost. **161** Presumably a local builder or handyman. **162** That is to say, his brother Henry (1856-1938), who was a Franciscan monk, and who had actually held the position of Provincial of the Order from 1902 to 1914. He was a man of strong views on most subjects. **163** P.J. Smyth seems to have been called simply "Smyth" in the family from the outset. Certainly his wife always later referred to him thus. It is unlikely, however, that any disrespect was intended. **164** I.e. young Nicholas Smyth. **165** William Dillon (1850-1935), emigrated to Colorado in 1883, and set up as a lawyer in Castle Rock, Colo., subsequently moving to Chicago, where he founded the law firm of Concannon, Dillon, which still flourishes. He had been active politically, with John Dillon, before he left, and always retained a vivid interest in Irish affairs. He wrote, among other things, a *Life of John Mitchell* (London, 1888). **166** William Henry Dillon (1889-1959).

Your post card, and your letter of 13 May, came in due course, and were read with very great interest. I have written to Coffey* to say that you are sending in your application and asking him to do what he can to support it in the Senate. I am not at all surprised at your enthusiasm for Heidelberg. I saw it only once,[167] for a day or two, and under very unfavourable circumstances, for I was in a very seedy condition, yet I have always had a most agreeable impression of it. All that you tell me of the life and of the people there interested me exceedingly, as also what you say about your studies. It is really wonderful that the Philologer [sic] should give you two hours private teaching. Is that a usual proceeding, or are you specially favoured? The lectures on German writers must be extremely interesting. I think you are quite right *not* to resist the temptation.

You ask me whether I am still inclined to favour Mussolini. Some of Mussolini's speeches have been outrageous, and some of the proceedings of his fascisti detestable.[168] Still, I think if I were an Italian I would be a supporter of his, for one reason, that he saved Italy from the tyranny of the Communists, and that things had been allowed by all previous governments in Italy to drift into such a condition that nothing but such violent methods as Mussolini used could have rescued the country from the abominable tyranny of the Reds. If we had had a Mussolini in Ireland when the S.F.'s began to enforce revolver rule, Ireland would now be a civilised country, and prosperous, instead of being what it is, a semi-savage community, on the verge of bankruptcy.[169]

I read your Berlin letter in the *Statesman* of 10 May with much interest and approval. It is the best you have done yet. The previous ones I thought rather too bald and brief. I hope you will continue to send letters, and I am very much gratified indeed to hear your change in plans, and that we are to have you at home for August and September. I shall have a regular family gathering in Aug. James is due to arrive about the 20 June, and Lucy Ratcliffe (Mrs Clark)[170] and her husband are coming to Dublin for the Horse Show and I have asked them to stay here, so the old house will be crowded again.

Business is shockingly bad, and we are all on the verge of bankruptcy.[171] However, if I can manage to keep afloat for a couple of years times may mend.

167 This was probably during his visit to Bad Kissingen for health reasons in 1899. The Franconian spa of Bad Kissingen is about 80 miles NE of Heidelberg. 168 The Fascist *squadristi* were rampant at this time, trying to stir up revolution and intimidate the opposition, particularly the Socialists. Mussolini, to be fair to him, was concerned to control them. 169 This shows John Dillon in a most interesting and disturbing state of mind, but his reasoning here is unclear. From what quarter would the "Mussolini" have emerged? Surely not from the moribund Irish Party? The nearest thing to a potential Mussolini at the relevant point in history was probably Michael Collins, the arch-proponent of "revolver rule", and he would hardly have approved of him. 170 This would be a sister-in-law of William Dillon, who had married a Miss Elizabeth Ratcliffe of Castle Rock, Colo. 171 The Irish economy was indeed in a sorry state at this time. There had been an economic depression since mid-1923. Farmers, who would be the chief customers of "Monica Duff's", suffered doubly as agricultural prices fell, and bad weather reduced output. Cf. Cullen

Your scholarship cheque has not turned up yet. I shall enquire about it tomorrow. It came before this date last year. I shall send in your War Stock dividend when it comes on 1st June, and you can lodge it to your account yourself.

I shall read Æ* on Literature and Life. Æ is all very well on literature, but on *life*, and when he touches politics, he becomes utterly impractical and preposterous. By the way, your friend Stephens[172] had a most objectionable piece of writing, about Connolly, Arthur Griffith and Co., in the *New Leader* a few weeks ago. I am afraid I have little patience with these men. They have done a very great deal of mischief, and are quite incapable of doing *any* good, so far as public affairs are concerned.[173] Ne Sutor ultra Crepidam[174]—I do not know whether the last word is correctly spelled.

Going back to Mussolini, the punitive expeditions were of course monstrous.[175] I did not see Don Sturzo's interview. I must have missed that copy of the *Guardian*. How did you see it? Have you got the date?

I have not heard from your Grandmother or Aunt K[athleen] for a long time, and am a little uneasy about them. Does Aunt K. ever write to you? Nicholas and his mother are both flourishing. He was in to see me yesterday.

127

[John Dillon to Myles] 26 May, 1924

Coffey* called here on Friday to tell me the fate of your application in the Senate. It was successful. When the application came up, so he told me, no one said anything, so he said that he thought the application a fair and reasonable one, and moved that the studentship be extended for half a year. He said he was afraid that if he moved the whole year there might be opposition. His proposal passed nem. con., and he says he is quite confident that when the time comes the extension will be continued for the whole year. This is very satisfactory. You may make your arrangements for a year in Paris without anxiety.[176]

What date does your term end? You are a good deal nearer to Theo than you were at Bonn. It would be a charitable act to spend a few days with him on your way home. I am afraid that Miss Robinson* will be out of Paris when you are passing thro', or I would advise you spend a couple of days there. However,

---

1972, p. 172. **172** James Stephens (1880-1950), poet and storyteller. Myles got to know him through Padraic Colum, with whom he remained friendly throughout his life. **173** This presumably refers to Stephens and Æ, rather than the deceased Connolly and Griffith. **174** "Let the cobbler not stray from his last". **175** This probably refers to the landing of Mussolini's army on Corfu. See Letter 103. **176** Eyebrows may well be raised at this piece of business, and the fact that the President should hurry round to John Dillon to give him the good news, but it should be borne in mind that President Coffey was largely indebted to him for his position, and was duly grateful. Which is not to say, of course, that Myles' application was not "fair and reasonable".

it will probably be intolerably hot in August. Later on, I am sure, Miss Robinson will be a very valuable aid in finding comfortable and decent lodgings.

Enclosed is an article from the *Observer* of yesterday. It states the views I hold about Fascismo with great clearness and force.

What kind of weather are you getting in Heidelberg? Here it has been very showery for the last week.

128

[Myles to John Dillon] Heidelberg, Karl Ludwigstrasse 6, 2. vi. '24.

I have to thank you for two letters, and for the *Observer* cutting, which I read. I daresay Fascismo has a lot to say for itself, but its excesses, as I suppose is usual, have lasted beyond the cause which provoked them, and surely Mussolini is a demagogue. Don Sturzo was very prudent and satisfactory. The *Weekly*, which I get, published his interview before I went to Berlin, probably early in March, but I have not got the date. I preserved it to send it to you, and then it vanished.

It is pleasant that the University has been so generous. I hope that I shall not disgrace myself, having asked them for an extension. I shall write to Coffey to thank him. Whether I should not write some acknowledgement to the Senate also is a question.

Life here continues to be delightful. Somehow the Heidelberg air makes friends for one, and I know more people here now than I ever did in Bonn.

Whitsuntide holidays commence at the end of the week, and I am going up the Neckar valley or into the Schwarzwald for three days, and then to Bonn to see Thurneysen*, and gather some belongings. I hope to be able to clear myself there, so that I can go straight from here to Leysin and from there home, and this involves packing books and fetching some that I want here and so on.

It is splendid that the house is at least cleared. I had almost given up hope of living there again. I shall be glad to hear that you extort an enormous sum from the Government in reparation.

By the way, Garvin's[177] sermon in the *Observer* seemed to amount to championing Winston Churchill. Is it possible that he has won Garvin's heart? I met

177 The distinguished journalist, now editor of the *Observer*, J.L. Garvin, who had always been a friend of Ireland, and of the Irish Party (see Letter 99). Garvin had actually been a friend and supporter of Churchill for many years, while he was a Liberal, though it is interesting that he is still supporting him at this stage, when Churchill is in the process of insinuating himself back into the Conservative Party. Churchill was out of parliament at the moment, but soon to return, as a Conservative, in the General Election of November.

an unattractive Dominican in Cologne one night who was heart and soul for Churchill, and was especially touched because C. had interviewed him in his bedroom one morning as deputations were in all the other rooms.

Theo remains silent. Thanks for sending his letter on Leysin. It was good that the *Independent* gave it a leaderette.[178] He sent me an interesting book on S. Francis the other day, which I am now wading through, but not a word with it. Kathleen and Grandmother have been in Rye, whence I had a loving postcard from Kathleen and a promise of more, but since then nothing has happened. They send me the *Supplement* every week, to my great joy.

In about ten weeks I shall be home, and between this and then there is a lot to be done. I look forward to renewing acquaintaince with James and to meeting my nephew.

Maria's silence gives me an uneasy feeling that I am guilty of some omission or commission which causes it.

I shall write when inspiration comes.

[PS] You may have seen another performance of mine in the last *Statesman*, but I hardly expect you to approve of it.[179]

129

[John Dillon to Myles] Monday, 2 June 1924

What has become of you? I have been looking out for a letter for some days.

Enclosed is your dividend warrant. Sign it, and send it to the Manager, Nat. Bank, Charing Cross, with note requesting him to place enclosed £25 to your credit.

I hope you are continuing to enjoy Heidelberg, and that you are getting better weather than we are getting here. Last week we had some lovely summer days, but yesterday the floodgates opened and it rained steadily for almost 24 hours on end.

I am sending you a copy of this day's *Independent*, which is full of lively and interesting news.[180] Apart from what you will see in it, there is little news here. Things are going from bad to worse, and I think the days of the present

178 His letter appeared in the *Irish Independent* on 28 May 1924 under the headline "Sun cure at Leysin. Wonderful results in tubercular cases". The leader writer commented: "T.W.T. Dillon's admirable and instructive letter [...] demonstrates the efficacy of the sun cure. [...] It is incumbent upon the nation to come to the rescue of the child sufferers." The same letter appeared in the *Irish Times* of the same day. 179 This appeared in the issue of 31 May 1924 (see Appendix). Perhaps Myles is referring to his remark about the Republicans as heroes. 180 The paper contained articles on a major strike in Derry, on the lack of progress in the boundary discussions and on a strike threat at Irish Railways.

Government of the Free State will be short.[181] What will follow, Heaven knows. I wonder how his fellow bishops feel this morning after reading the Bishop of Clonfert's speech.[182]

Write and tell me all particulars of how you are getting on in Heidelberg. Nano and Nicholas continue to flourish. I never saw Nano looking better. James has arrived in New York, and is to sail on the 10th.

130

[Myles to John Dillon] Heidelberg, Karl Ludwigstrasse 6, Monday, 9. vi. '24

Dear Father,

Many thanks for sending the warrant. I have forwarded it to the bank. The paper and the cutting with the Senate committee's report[183] came too. The new bishop is rather a thrill.[184] Not the least remarkable of his precepts was that we should use the Irish language as a barrier against the wicked knowledge of the world which might reach our island from outside. What sort of an opinion have such reverend men got of the intelligence of the Irish?[185]

I am leaving for Bonn tonight for a week, to see Thurneysen* and her ladyship. I shall probably take the exam. here after all, as the lectures are better and learned men kinder than in Bonn, but Thurneysen will have to approve my thesis, as the man here knows no Celtic.

It is not easy to leave Heidelberg at present. There is always something happening, but Whitsuntide has been a climax. The town is decorated with flags, a Bavarian military band has come, and yesterday there was a procession of Bavarians with banners through the streets. Last night the castle was illuminated and the fireworks were perhaps more festive than before. On Tuesday sixty canoes are to come down between the two bridges in celebration of some other festivity and the Bavarians are to give another concert. Old gentlemen who have returned to drink to the memory of their youth are marching about in the caps and ribbons of their Studentencorporationen.[186]

---

181 He was quite wrong about this, though in the aftermath of the Army Mutiny this might have seemed plausible. 182 Among other things the Bishop, Dr Dignan, said that he expected the Republicans to be in power soon. 183 This was probably the Senate Committee on Irish Learning whose brief it had been "to prepare for recommendations to the Government a scheme that would promote the editing of old Irish manuscripts and the scientific investigation of living dialects". It had just submitted its report which recommended that an annual sum of £5,000 should be earmarked for the purpose. This would seem modest enough (*IT*, 3 June 1924). 184 That is, the Bishop of Clonfert. See previous letter. 185 It is worth quoting Dr Dignan here. He wished "to stem the wave of paganism and materialism and sin that now swept the world by erecting around their [i.e. the Irish] coasts the barrier of the language" (*II*, 2 June 1924). Certainly an interesting insight into Irish language politics—and into the reasons why the rescue operations for the Irish language failed. 186 Many of these student fraternities, or *Burschenschaften*, had their origin in the

Life in Heidelberg is really a sort of dance, but fortunately for those who cannot dance wisdom is not neglected in the University. My faltering steps have been stilled for the moment, as I cut my foot slightly bathing on Saturday, but it is nearly all right again. I shall arrive in Mainz tomorrow afternoon at six and sail down the Rhine to Bonn.

James should be starting from New York tomorrow. It will be amusing to meet him again. In eight weeks I shall be nearly home.

131

[John Dillon to Myles] 9 June 1924

Your letter of 2 June came on Thursday last, to my great satisfaction. I had been wondering what had become of you.

Garvin[187] is a very erratic person, but at times quite brilliant. And the truth is that the Communists are making progress in Great Britain, and becoming a very serious and menacing phenomenon. I have no doubt that they will succeed in splitting the Labour Party and pulling down MacDonald's Government.[188]

I am rejoiced to hear that Heidelberg has turned out so well. You will enjoy your Whitsuntide holiday immensely, I feel confident. I hope you have selected the Schwarzwald, and that you will write me a full account of your adventure. For many years I planned a tour in the Schwarzwald, but it never came off. And of course if one could not speak German three fourths of the pleasure would be lost.

I am very glad you have decided to visit Theo on your way home, all the more as I can't go out to see him this Autumn, as I had intended. I need not say you will be very welcome home. I have not yet commenced operations on the house, as the valuer has advised that it should not be touched till his report has been sent in, and the Government has had an opportunity of sending an Inspector to check his valuation, if they desire to do so. Next week I hope to be

early 19th century when they fuelled German nationalism in the fight against Napoleon. In the course of the next hundred years they retained their nationalist outlook, but what was progressive during the first years of their existence became increasingly reactionary and conservative. During Myles' days they would not have counted among the friends of the Weimar Republic, however colourful their celebrations may have been (and still are). The Old Boys' (*Alte Herren*) network ensured that the members of the *Studentencorporationen* often found it easier to gain influential positions in business, industry or administration. 187 See Letters 99 and 128. 188 This was actually to accord far too much importance to the Communist threat, but this is to some extent excusable. Only two Communists had been elected to parliament in the last election, but there had been, admittedly, many militant and apocalyptic utterances by left-wing Socialists in the aftermath of Labour's coming to power, and there had been a considerable element of "red scare" in the journals that John Dillon would be reading, culminating in the "Zinoviev Letter" just before the general election in October. See also Letter 139.

able to begin operations, and I hope to have the house fixed up in about a month. The prospect of compensation is, I fear, by no means rosy.

I have heard nothing from your Grandmother or Kathleen for a long time. I sent Kathleen Theo's letter, hoping to elicit some communication, but so far there has been no response. I was glad to learn from your letter that they were out of town. I had been even fearing they were ill.

Jim sails tomorrow and I expect him to arrive about Thursday week. He saw your uncle in Denver hospital before he left for Chicago. Your uncle was recovering very well from the effects of the operation, and promised to consider favourably a warm invitation extended by James to visit Ireland with your Aunt Lizzy next autumn, so we may have a very large family gathering.

I am sending you a copy of this day's *Independent*, as there is a good deal of interesting news in it. The air here is thick with rumours. The Govt. is, I think, on its last legs, but what combination is to take its place no one knows.

I read your last communication in the *Statesman*,[189] and liked it. You are steadily improving as a writer. I hope to see something very good as a result of your Whitsuntide wanderings. Paragraph (2) in the front page of the *Irish Statesman* of 7 June expresses fairly well the spirit of Æ and Co, which enrages me and proves them to be utterly rotten as political guides.[190] A nice result they produced with their "new theory of an Irish civilisation different in character from that of the generation that preceded them."

Write soon.

132

[John Dillon to Myles] Monday, 16 June 1924.

Your letter arrived on Friday morning, to my great satisfaction, as I had been wondering what had become of you. I am pleased you took notice of the obscurantist declamation of the Bishop of Clonfert. It is the expression of a spirit which has been, and still is, very rampant in Ireland, and threatens to do enormous mischief. The reports on the new education programme which I sent you a few days ago bear on the same subject,[191] as does also letter enclosed from today's

189 See Appendix. 190 The article associated the movement under John Redmond with old ideas which had to be overcome, listing Arthur Griffith, Horace Plunkett and James Connolly among those representing the new Ireland; none of them John Dillon would have approved of. Æ also pointed out that the Republicans did not present as clear an alternative to the present government as the "new Irish movement" of writers and intellectuals had done in their time. 191 A Department of Education had been set up on 1 June, 1924, and later that month the Intermediate Education (Amendment) Act was passed. Among its provisions was one, designed to encourage the use of Irish, which created three grades of school, A, B (which became subdivided into B1 and B2), and C. Irish was to be the official language in Grade A schools, and all languages were to be taught through the medium of Irish. Irish was to be the official language also in Grade B

Freeman.[192] All this bullying and compulsion will end badly for the Irish language.

I suppose you will be back in Heidelberg by this. From your letter I assume you gave up your proposed visit to the Black Forest. I enjoyed very much your account of life in Heidelberg, and regret very much that it is not possible for me to join you there for a week or a fortnight.

You asked in a previous letter whether you should write to the university authorities to thank them for extending your scholarship. That I think would depend on whether you received any official communication from the authorities. If you did, you should of course acknowledge, and thank them.

I hope your foot is quite well. Cuts on one's foot are apt to be very troublesome, if not carefully attended to immediately.

I have had no further news from James, except that he was to sail on the Pittsburgh on Tuesday, 10 June. I expect him to arrive on Thursday or Friday this week.

I sent you some newspapers last week, as the political situation here has again become very critical and interesting.[193]

I have not yet been able to commence operations on the house in Ballaghaderreen, waiting for the report of my valuer.

[PS] I had a pleasant letter from Aunt Kathleen—at last—on Saturday, telling me that your Grandmother and she herself were better.

133

[Myles to John Dillon] Heidelberg, Karl Ludwigstrasse 6, bei Frl. Knecht, Tuesday, 17. vi. '24

This will be brief, as I have just returned from Bonn and find myself surrounded by unaccomplished tasks and newspapers to read. Besides, as you will observe, my hand is partially incapacitated from carrying luggage yesterday. Our planned expedition did not come off as my companion was penniless, and we both found muscles uninclined at the moment on account of work to be done. However, the Schwarzwald will still be there when I have time to visit it.

I had a pleasant week in Bonn, and enjoyed great hospitality from her ladyship. I travelled from Mainz on the steamer, and had delightful weather, but as I had to

schools, and some subjects were to be taught through Irish. In Grade C schools Irish was just taught as a school subject. There was an extra grant of 25 per cent made to Grade A schools, and Grade B schools got an extra financial incentive, depending on the proportion of subjects taught through Irish. 192 In this letter "Submerged" criticised the enforced Gaelicisation of the educational programme and of the teachers' organisations. 193 At the time, the Boundary Commission and the Army Inquiry Committee which investigated the army mutiny and the Government's handling of it provided new dangers for the latter.

leave at midnight and sleep on a bench in Darmstadt for three hours waiting for a connection with the abominable French régie, I was rather sleepy on the way. The return was more rational. A very decent express left Bonn at four, and I arrived here at 10.30 last night, but the French lost my bicycle on the way, and as there is no through travelling between the *régie* and Germany I shall apparently have to journey to Ludwigshafen to recover it during the week. One requires a special licence to cross the bridge to Mannheim or one must pay a tax, so I may have difficulty. You will see that travelling in the Rhineland at present is bedlam.

Heidelberg is in its best humour, and I found some friendly messages and invitations awaiting me last night. The term will be over in six weeks, which almost makes me despair. However, here everyone is optimistic, and one gets the feeling that German Wissenschaft is not so unattainable after all.

I am glad that my last article was approved of. There should be one this week, no longer on German life, but arising out of my work—and partly out of my ignorance—but it pleased me.[194] I will be glad to hear what you think of it. It turns out that the Irish saga which I so much enjoyed has been given by Lady Gregory in *Gods and Fighting Men*,[195] which I am ashamed to say I never read through, though I have given it to other people more than once.

Kathleen promised to write some weeks ago—on a postcard—but since then I have heard nothing. She was evidently delighted with Rye, but I should think the new sorrow in Aunt Anna's household troubled Kensington Square a good deal.[196]

There is lots of interesting news in the world. Herriot[197] ought to bring a change for Germany. If what you say of English Communism is true, perhaps Churchill will make his political future yet.[198]

Thurneysen* enquired affectionately for you and for Nano, and Gräfin Beissel and her sister sent messages of esteem. They had hoped to meet you again this summer.

Please tell Maria I shall besiege her with cablegrams if she refuses to write much longer.

I had thought James would have got home in 6 or 7 days from New York. Give him my love when he arrives. Perhaps he would write and reveal the new philosophy he has evolved in Chicago.

I was pleased by a sentence in Æ's* article on Yeats' essays, quoting Plato, who said that if there were Gods, they certainly did not philosophise.[199] The

194 This did not appear. **195** First published in 1904. **196** The reference is not clear, unless it still relates back to Charles Mathew's death. **197** Édouard Herriot (1872-1957), French statesman and man of letters, long-time leader of the Radical Party. Herriot had just become premier of France as the leader of a left-wing coalition of Radicals and Socialists. While Poincaré had largely steered an anti-German course, Herriot proved far more conciliatory, as Myles predicted. Under his premiership France accepted the Dawes Plan and agreed to evacuate the Ruhr. His cabinet fell in April 1925 because of its controversial financial policies. **198** Churchill in fact returned to parliament, as a Conservative, in the election of October 1924, and became Chancellor of the Exchequer in Baldwin's government. **199** This appeared in the *Irish Statesman* of 7 June 1924, pp. 397-8.

Germans could learn a lot from that. I seldom read Æ's politics, because I like him very much. Perhaps the reason why they are so provoking is that he does not really believe what he says. Æ was certainly never a Sinn Feiner. I can imagine his feeling it very banal that I should use the word in connection with him. He probably has the right to exemption from these parties, but he does not remain quite outside the controversial territory. His friends, and Yeats too, are apparently in a rather feeble frame of mind with regard to this government, but Yeats confines himself to remarks in the drawing-room, and is ennobling his promise for the future by planning an Irish fascism, which will be combined with a new Irish aristocracy of the intellect.[200] I had a letter from Susan Mitchell,[201] acknowledging my last article, and she was also pleased with the mediocrity of the present crowd. There was no mention of the approaching downfall of the government of which you speak.

Many thanks for the papers and cuttings. I have not read them all yet. The moderation of the *Irish Times* on the language question is still too moderate for me,[202] I am glad to say, as I sometimes fear that one gets too wise looking at Ireland from here.

134

[Myles to John Dillon] Sunday, 13. vii. '24

I owe you a letter for a long time, but Shaun and James could have proved that I am still alive. The semester is very nearly over, and I am glad because of the excitement and pleasure of going home, and sorry because it has been the most interesting time I have had in Germany. Only after a few terms does one begin to enjoy what is to be enjoyed, and besides Heidelberg is an enchanted city. I wish I had come here years ago, instead of last May.

Fortunately for my exam.,[203] an excellent man is coming to Bonn next term to succeed Thurneysen,[204] so I shall go back there for the Winter and endeavour to finish after Christmas. If he had not come, I intended to remain here, and gather together enough English to take it for the exam., but this has been spared.

My time here has been made so pleasant through knowing the Fischers.[205] A relative of Mrs Fischer's, who has lived in Germany nearly all her life, has intro-

---

200 After the Civil War and during his years in the Seanad, Yeats did indeed voice his admiration for fascist Italy quite openly (Freyer 1981, pp. 94ff). **201** Susan Langstaff Mitchell (1888-1926), journalist and poet. At the time she was Æ's assistant editor of *The Irish Statesman*. **202** In a leader of 3 June 1924, the *Irish Times* wholeheartedly endorsed the finding of a committee which recommended a scheme to support scholarly research into the Irish language (see Letter 130). This, the leader writer argued, was something completely different from using the Irish language "as an instrument of political and economic theory", which, of course, the *Irish Times* did not approve of. **203** This would be the doctorate. **204** Ferdinand Sommer (1875-1962), Prof. of Comparative Philology in Bonn from 1924 to 1926. Sommer, however, was not a specialist in Celtic Philology. **205** See Letter 114.

duced me to pleasant people. She asked me to go to Bayreuth with her in August, but it would cost a great deal, and I have hardly time.

We are having glorious weather here, so hot it is hardly to be believed, and the Neckar is crowded all day.

I think I told you of my Polish friend who is living on the edge of existence, and refuses to accept more than a minimum for his work.[206] He lent me Romain Rolland's[207] book on Gandhi, which I read with joy. It has been translated, and everyone here seems to be reading it. I wonder whether it has appeared in England yet. Rolland is too cynical over the war and the allies to be fair in his study, but the picture of India, so infinitely superior to England in religion and mind, being treated as they were, and their strange retaliations, is consoling when one is living in a heathen country. It would do good to the self-satisfaction of our patriots.

I expect to leave here in the first week of August, and now that I am returning to Bonn, I shall probably bring my books and things there first. I may stay a day or two in London to see the Exhibition,[208] but by the 12th or 14th of August I will be home.

I begin to suspect that the *Statesman* has changed its mind, and given my article to the lethal waste paper basket. I shall break off all relations with them until they explain themselves.

I am buried in work which does not get itself done. Ask James to write. I hope to hear from you when you have time. What news of Ballagh? Love to everyone.

135

[Oliver Edwards[209] to Myles] Wien, Thursday evening, 17 July, 1924 A.D., (54 Waterville Av., Belfast.)

Dear Myles Dillon,

I am annoyed, very annoyed. Not with you, but with me. I meant to leave Wien this evening by the 10.40, but I have too many possessions and couldn't get my bags packed in time. *Was man nicht nützt ist eine schwere Last.*[210] I had a ticket for the theatre and my only salvation was to get the bags into the cloak-

206 No, unless he is the companion who was too poor to undertake the journey into the Schwarzwald. See Letter 133. **207** Romain Rolland (1866-1944), French man of letters, philosopher of art, and author of many critical and historical works. He had become very unpopular in France by reason of a series of articles published in Switzerland in the autumn of 1914 (and subsequently in book form as *Au-dessus de la melée*) profoundly critical of the war. He was given the Nobel Prize for literature in 1915. His book *Mahatma Gandhi* had just been published. It contained an impassioned defence of the Indian leader. **208** It is unclear which exhibition Myles is referring to here. **209** According to the University of Bonn's annual report Edwards studied in Bonn in 1923; for the academic year 1923/24, the report also records book donations to the library of Prof. Dibelius' English Dept. by both Edwards and Myles Dillon. **210** What one doesn't use is a heavy burden.

room and rush to the station as soon as the Spiel was aus.[211] I had eigentlich[212] stayed on till today to see Tchekhov's *Heiratsantrag*,[213] which as I saw it in München two years ago was the funniest thing ever played. Here it was comparatively tame, altho' given by the famed Reinhardt,[214] and that hasn't improved my humour. At seven o'clock I gave the bags up as a bad job and rushed off to the theatre.

Green[215] left Wien this afternoon for a place called Fronleiten in the Austrian province of Steiermark. He consulted a couple of doctors here—one of them I know already personally, he is a delightful fellow—and they decided the source of his trouble is in the lungs—more especially the left lung—the top is too narrow. After three months' Liegekur[216] the best hopes are held out to him. In that case he means to spend the winter in Wien—if not better, he may go to Italy instead. He took six lessons with an Italianess lately and they, tho' nominally an hour each, got longer and longer.

Thanks for the *Statesman* address. I sent the editor today something about the Schottenstift in Wien founded by Irish monks in the middle of the twelfth century.[217] They got chucked out in 1418 for bad behaviour. Write at once into your address book: Dr Anselm Weissenhofer, Schottenstift, Schottenhof, Wien I. When you come here, go to him and mention Green and me. He is a Benedictine—the monastery is Benedictine—and you will like him very much. I almost wish Æ* would send back the article, as I'm dissatisfied with some of it, of course—I sent it off in such a hurry, for one thing. However, I expect it will be waiting for me in Belfast next Wednesday: "The editor thanks ... and regrets...".

Green heard from McKie and wrote to him.

You say kein Wort of my friend Strachan in Birmingham. If you didn't hear from him. My or his letter must have gone astray.

I arrive in Bonn Saturday evening and hope to discover Kronsbein's address.

Write to me *as soon* as you get home, or before. I hope to be in Dublin a day or two this summer: my brother Brian, and a sister you met in Bonn sehr flüchtig,[218] are going there next week for two months' midwifery at something called "the Rotunda"—I suppose it's a hospital—and I may visit them.

Yes, v. Buol was in Tübingen. He is now vanished from the earth's face. I haven't seen him for a long time.

The best bit in my story of the Schottenstift was translated by Green from the life of Marian, a north of Ireland monk who dwelt at Regensburg in the eleventh century. It is a legend that tells how on a certain night he was writing

211 "as soon as the play was over". 212 "originally". 213 That is, *The Marriage Proposal*, a one-act play by Anton Tchekhov (1860-1904), first produced in 1890. 214 Max Reinhardt (1873-1943), Austrian theatrical producer and one of the formost theatre directors of the Weimar Republic. He was working in Berlin for most the 1920s. 215 The names mentioned in this letter are obviously those of friends and fellow students. It proved impossible to identify them. 216 Bed rest, lit. "lying-down cure". 217 It does not appear to have been published. 218 "very briefly".

a holy book according to his custom, and by the negligence of a servant no light was brought when darkness came on. But he continued to write without the aid of any natural light. For the mercy of God caused three fingers of his left hand to burn and shine in the fashion of three candles.

I hope this isn't a commonplace of Irish mysticism. I quote from memory, and have probably spoilt it a bit.

Your turn to write me a letter now. Then I'll send you your four pounds of flesh.

Yours truly,
Oliver Edwards.

136

[Myles to John Dillon] Heidelberg, Karl Ludwigstrasse 6, Thursday evening,
24. vii. '24

Your letter[219] was very welcome, and also the enclosures, one of which was from the *Statesman*, sending a generous cheque for my last accepted contributions, so I am feeling kind towards them.

Lectures are stopping already, and I expect to leave here on Wednesday, and I confess that it makes me a little miserable. Heidelberg is *en fête* for the end of the term, the streets are lined with flags, and everyone is in good humour. And I am getting invitations to last visits. I hope I am much wiser than when I came here, but the end of term always leaves me feeling a beginner. I went for the first time this morning to hear a well-known philosopher[220] here lecture, and was delighted and despairing at the end. He is a specially amiable man, who has no special cause of his own, but interprets everyone, and this morning he spoke of Leibnitz, Pascal, Bésle,[221] Montaigne, Spinoza, Descartes in the pleasantest way. But if he had asked me more than the names of any one of them I should have been silent. One feels that if one had the opportunity of the youths who come out of school to universities like these one would break records, but that is a foolish consolation. I cannot help blaming the organisation of the Church in Ireland for part of our ignorance, and it is a horrible fact if it is true. The divines are pleased if the people obey the commandments, whether they know why they are obeying them or not, and yet anyone would admit that it is better to do good because it is good than because you will be read from the altar or go to hell if you don't. It is the same fanaticism for the letter instead of the spirit which makes people insist on Irish words without regard to Irish men-

219 Unfortunately lost. The next surviving letter from John Dillon is dated 18 November 1924.
220 This was Count Hermann Keyserling, as Myles reveals in Letter 176. 221 That is to say, Pierre Bayle (1647-1706).

tality, as if it really much mattered whether we spoke Irish or Tungusish so long as we possessed our own tradition. I hope this does not seem irreverent, which would be the reverse of what I mean, but I think it is fair.

The *Frankfurter Zeitung* has been publishing very well informed articles on Ireland, two of which I enclose. The second is the more interesting, though it contains nothing that is not familiar in Dublin, but the soundness and complete neutrality of it pleased me.

In spite of my devotion to Heidelberg, I am glad to return to Bonn in the Winter, firstly because of my delightful room there—my dwelling here has been the only misfortune[222]—and because an excellent professor of philology[223] has been called to succeed Thurneysen,* so that I shall have all my subjects together there for the exam. I hope to be finished in March, and then I shall be free. When I should go to Paris will be a question. I am told that there is nothing done there in the Summer, but I still have a lot of French to learn, so I shall go some time ahead. By the way, I had a letter from Mabel Robinson* the other day asking when I was coming and offering to find me rooms.

A magazine here has published letters from the Bolshevist archives which prove—apparently beyond denial—that Russia, at the suggestion of Poincaré himself, spent 3 million francs on bribing the French press before the war. Poincaré, in a conversation with the Ambassador, says that Caillaux, Herriot, Painlevé and others will make difficulties, especially if the war should arise out of a Balkan dispute, and it should be brought about otherwise. The Russian Ambassador reports that Henry Wilson[224] has been in Paris in connection with the plans, and so on, and these reports are dated 1912.[225]

In spite of my affection for Germany I need hardly say that I rejoice at getting home. I do not think I could ever live in Germany without an interval. I shall go to Bonn on Wednesday, and on Thursday or Friday to London, so that I should be home by Monday week, but I shall let you hear on the way. If you have time to write, a letter will find me in Bonn until Thursday.

[PS] The first of the two articles has been taken from me, but enclosed is the better one.

222 This seems to have gone somewhat sour on him. Cf. Letters 122-123, where he is delighted both with his lodgings and with the service provided by his landlady, Frl. Knecht. It will become clearer later that it was largely the food, or the lack of it, which contributed to his discomfort. 223 Ferdinand Sommer; see Letter 134. 224 Sir Henry Hughes Wilson (1864-1922), British army officer. Born in Edgeworthtown, Co. Longford, Wilson rose to the position of Asst. Chief of Staff of the British Army and was chief liaison officer with the French Supreme Command during World War I. After the war he disagreed with the British Government's Irish policies and resigned from the Army. He was elected MP for North Down in 1922 but soon afterwards he was assassinated in London by members of the I.R.A. 225 This is a most interesting little scandal, which would be of great interest to a German public. Poincaré in 1912 was still premier (he was elected President in January 1913), in succession to Caillaux. Édouard Herriot was the Radical leader, who had just become premier as a result of the 1924 elections. Paul Painlevé was another prominent Radical.

137

[Joan Marie Egls[226] to Myles] Bunsenstrasse 8, Heidelberg, August 26, 1924

Dear Mr Dillon,

Your letter sent me into a perfect gale of laughter! How I did enjoy it! And, of course, you *knew* I would take it to Lolo Bach, and let her enjoy it also; so that is just what I did; and she begs me to enclose a note from her.[227]

I am sorry to hear that you have been ill, a thing of the past, I hope, by now: so that you can enjoy your holidays, and the pleasant journey to Switzerland, Paris, etc. later.

My plans do not extend very far into the future. I take the pleasant things that offer, and drift, more or less, waiting to see how the world will settle present difficulties; as usual here there are as many opinions as minds, and one wonders what the outcome will be. I wonder if the French have anything up their sleeve?

For the immediate future, I am expecting an English friend next week. She will remain through September and then wants me to go to Venice with her, which I shall be delighted to do. Why not come *there* instead of Paris, as you already know the latter?

Venezia, the unique, there is nothing like this Queen of the Adriatic; we will be in the *Casa Petrarca* and revel in art and romance. After that *more* Italy, or perhaps Vienna; have not yet decided.

We *quite depend* upon having you here with us next Spring and Summer, and will make it as pleasant as possible for you, so arrange your plans accordingly.

Frau Dr Fischer sends best wishes, and had hoped for a letter. Helma is visiting my friends in the country, and has a gentle horse, no doubt, and not a "männliches Pferd".[228] She would surely send a message, were she here; but I believe that she has written you a letter which will contain all her news.

Do let me hear from you again. This address will always reach me. I shall be interested to hear of your examination.

Yours very sincerely,
Joan Marie Egls.

---

226 This is almost certainly the "very attractive American girl" referred to casually in letter 116 above. Plainly Myles did not tell his father everything. **227** Two notes in German from this girl are enclosed. They indicate a high degree of familiarity but fewer romantic details than one might hope for. **228** "male horse".

Year 3
October 1924–September 1925

INTRODUCTION

After a few months at home, in Dublin and Ballaghaderreen, Myles Dillon set out again for Germany in October, to complete his work for the doctorate. As usual, he travelled *via* London and Paris, visiting, in London, his Mathew cousins, and, in Paris, Mabel Robinson* and her sister, Madame Duclaux*. By the beginning of November he was back in Bonn, determined to finish off his thesis before the spring. He was by now thoroughly comfortable in Germany, and a confirmed, if critical, Germanophile.

Germany at this stage was well on the way of economic recovery. The years which were to be called "The Golden Twenties" were about to begin. Certainly the year marked a noticeable stabilisation of the political situation in Germany; in July 1925, French troops finally started to leave the Ruhrgebiet. However, the election of Field Marshal Paul von Hindenburg in April 1925 did not augur well for the future of the Republic. It marked a step back for the democratic process and pointed backwards to the authoritarian structures of the *Kaiserreich* rather than forward to a system of modern parliamentary democracy. Myles supported the candidate of the Weimar coalition (the SPD was in opposition since the end of 1923, but in the second poll of the Presidential Elections the party had joined forces with the Centre Party and the Democratic Party), Wilhelm Marx, against the dream candidate of all conservative and anti-democratic forces, Paul von Hindenburg. Hindenburg, who had only agreed to stand two weeks before the final election date, was elected on 26 April 1925. The catholic Rhineland of course supported the Centre Party candidate Marx. In Cologne, he received twice as many votes as Hindenburg. Despite his misgivings, Myles like his father did not fear that Hindenburg's election would lead to a major change in German foreign policy, as indeed it didn't—until 1929, when the Wall Street crash heralded political changes of global proportions. From 16 to 27 May 1925, the Rhineland celebrated a millenium: for a thousand years the Rhineland had been part of the German Reich. Understandably, the celebrations were suffused with national and local patriotic fervour and, hardly surprisingly, they gained additional political significance due to the continued presence of the French occupying forces in the area. Myles became more and more part of German life and managed to get new insights into the family life of ordinary people. Now well at home in the German language, his letters offer interesting views on the German national character, in particular, the ways of the (educated) middle classes, whose "wretched formality" he finds increasingly irritating.

At Bonn University, Myles was asked to deliver a series of lectures on the Celtic Renaissance, which as far as we can tell went down very well. Myles discovered the "special virtue of a German audience, that they are never indifferent or unreceptive", which may indicate that his lectures were followed by lively discussions among the 130-strong audience. More importantly, however, Myles passed his *Doktorprüfung*; he passed his oral exam with flying colours (his fear of Prof. Sommer proved to be unfounded), while his written thesis needed some last minute changes before Thurneysen* deemed it ready for publication. Myles worked on these last changes when he had already settled in Paris, where he was to spend the next two years. His thesis, entitled *Nominal Predicates in Irish*, finally appeared in 1928.

Ireland also entered a phase of relative stability, but there were changes too, though this time of a more peaceful nature. The language question and the role of universities in the new state occupy considerable space in the correspondence. For Dom John Francis Sweetman and his experimental school Mount St. Benedict in Gorey, Co. Wexford, which three Dillon boys had attended, the year marked the end of the road. Dom Sweetman's closeness to republican ideals finally lead to the closure of the school by the local bishop, a development which Myles and even more so Brian very much regretted. We also hear of the Gaeltacht Commission which was appointed in January 1925 to examine how the economic base for the survival of the Irish language in the West could be improved. The Boundary Commission started its work, the *Freeman's Journal* finished its: the paper with which John Dillon had such a close connection throughout his life finally folded on 19 December 1924. Douglas Hyde and other political friends of John Dillon's lost their senate seats in the elections of September 1925. There was no end to the disillusionment which Dillon had been experiencing since 1918. The debate concerning the Shannon Scheme which was to be executed by the German firm Siemens-Schuckert and would propel Ireland into the modern technological era, did not elicit any comment from John Dillon. He was now 73, and perhaps understandably, his interest in the future was waning. Quelling the strike at Monica Duff's in Ballaghaderrin gave him a last lease of life and he threw himself into the struggle with the unions with all the strength left to him, but increasingly he came to rely on his son James, who had returned from America and had taken over the management of the family business in Ballaghaderrin. In the summer he went on an extended holiday to the Italian lakes, collecting his sons Myles and Theo on the way. It was to be John Dillon's last visit to the Continent. He died two years later on 4 August 1927.

138

[Myles to John Dillon] Bailey's Hotel, London S.W.7, Friday, 7. x. '24

I had a pleasant journey, and have been well received by my relatives. I went to a play last night, and lunched and took tea at Kensington Square and Cornwall Gardens. Grandmother has a slight cold and did not appear, but she is to be well tomorrow.

It was well that I wired, as the place was packed, and only a more expensive room available.

Tonight I am going to another show which has been recommended, and tomorrow I shall probably make a pilgrimage to T.P.[1] I shall probably go to Paris on Monday.

[PS] Maria will remember to send my fresh clothes as soon as possible.

130

[Myles to John Dillon] Grand Hotel Doré, Boulevard Montmartre, Paris,
Wednesday, 22. x. '24

I came over last night, and found quite a decent hotel in this wild and pleasant part of Paris.[2] I have spent the morning wandering to the Sacré Coeur and back—a wonderful view of Paris from the church, and the walk was amusing. I lunched well at some obscure place in the Boulevard Rouchefoucaud,[3] and had a little too much wine, and now I am going forth to explore the Marais,[4] which Lucas[5] recommends.

I am lunching with Miss Robinson* tomorrow and taking tea with a Celt named Goblet[6] on Friday, and for the rest I must wander alone. But this is a

1 I.e. T.P. O'Connor.* 2 The hotel was situated at 3, Blvd. Montmartre. 3 He probably means the Boulevard Rochechouard, which runs below Sacré Coeur. 4 The Marais, originally built on a stretch of marshy land, through which a tributary of the Seine used to flow, was at this time rather dilapidated, but still charming. Chief features are the Hotel de Ville, the Carnavalet Museum, and the Places des Vosges. 5 Edward Verrall Lucas (1865-1938), English man of letters. His very popular travel book *A Wanderer in Paris* was first published in 1909 (London: Methuen) and had reached the 21st edition by 1924. 6 Louis Jean Jacques Goblet (1881-1955), well known French

great improvement on the Rue de l'Arcade—surrounded by cafés, which are merry till one o'clock.

Nevinson[7] very kindly introduced me to the 1917 club, of which he is President, on Monday, and I met Brailsford,[8] Clifford Allen,[9] and some others, including a son of MacDonald.[10] They were mostly not optimistic about the election result,[11] and seemed sorry that MacDonald had not succeeded in raising some more creditable election issue,[12] but Clifford Allen prophesied 50 new seats. Nevinson was delightful, and invited me to join the club.

I expect to go on to Theo on Saturday, and shall send a letter from there. Yours,[13] enclosing Theo's card, reached me in London.

[PS] Maria's parcel arrived safely. Many thanks. M.

140

[Myles to John Dillon] Grand Hotel Doré, Friday, 25. x. '24

Mabel Robinson* gave me your letter tonight. I have been staying at this hotel, but I seem to have told you that already from here. I have enjoyed the last few days very much. Wednesday I spent wandering about, guidebook in hand, having made an early pilgrimage to the Sacré Coeur church, and at night I feasted on horrors at the Grand Guignol.[14] Yesterday Mabel Robinson entertained me half the day, part of the time at the circus. The morning was splendid, and I marched up the Champs Elysées, to find 100 Americans clustered round the

political and economic geographer. He published under the name Yann-Morvran Goblet and was a particular authority on Ireland. Among his books on the subject were *L'Irlande dans la crise universelle* (1918) and his doctoral thesis of 1930 on Sir William Petty's geography of Ireland. 7 See Letter 106. 8 Henry Noel Brailsford (1873-1958), distinguished British journalist and authority on Germany, socialist theorist. Educated at Oxford and Berlin, he travelled Europe after World War I and became one of the most outspoken critics of the Versailles Treaty. Between 1922 and 1926 he edited the *New Leader*, whose writing staff at the time included Shaw, H.G. Wells and E.M. Forster. His book *Socialism for To-day* was published in 1925. 9 Reginald Clifford Allen, Baron Allen of Hurtwood (1889-1939), British Labour politician. Opposed conscription during World War I, later supported the League of Nations. From 1922 to 1926 he was chairman and treasurer of the Independent Labour Party and editor of the *New Leader*, its official weekly journal. Raised to peerage in 1932. 10 That is to say Ramsay MacDonald, then Prime Minister. This would have been Malcolm MacDonald, M.P. 11 That is to say, the General Election coming up on 29 October 1924. Their fears were well founded: the Conservatives gained considerably, while Labour lost 40 seats. See Letter 141. 12 MacDonald claimed that the opposition wanted to get rid of the Labour government because it had been a success and had not "made a mess of things" as previous governments had. The opposition employed "Red scare" tactics which included forged documents and unsubstantiated allegations, which in the end ensured victory. 13 Not extant. 14 A theatre in Montmârtre, founded in 1895 and specialising[14] short plays of violence, horror, and sadism.

eternal fire under the Arc de Triomphe, and on to the Bois de Boulogne. I went to the Opera in the evening, and heard a rather unsatisfactory performance of *Siegfried*.[15]

Today I did more that was pleasant, and took tea with a man named Goblet[16] whom I had met in Dublin (he was once entertained by P.J. Boland[17] at the House, and met you), and dinner with Madame Duclaux,* who was as nice as ever.

I am starting for Theo tomorrow morning, and should arrive there at nine o'clock.

141

[Myles to John Dillon] Bonn a/ Rh., Schedestrasse 3, 3. xi. '24

Europe is gradually becoming smaller. I finished my wandering yesterday morning, arriving here on a tram in torrents of rain, but without having lost anything. The journey from Leysin was simple enough this time except for the last ten miles. The Basel-Köln train passes east of Bonn, and as it seemed doubtful whether I could get a connection at Frankfurt I came on to the nearest station and got on the tram. It was raining like the devils and as I had to drag my luggage from tram to tram in order to reach the house, it was rather an adventure, but it went well.

Theo was looking better than I had seen him since he came to Leysin, and is in very good spirits. He wears a short French beard, which is now quite respectable, and I thought rather becoming. I got there on Sunday, having spent a night at Montreux, and stayed till Saturday morning. He has given me a book on Kant, and another by Newman,[18] for the good of my soul, and I was able to bring him a large parcel of books from Miss Robinson, probably of less spiritual value. I daresay I told you of my visit to Madame Duclaux. They were both very kind. By the way, we spoke of *Juno and the Paycock* and its author,[19] and I should like to have those plays sent to Miss Robinson as soon as they appear. I think someone told me they were to be published soon.[20] Perhaps you would send her a copy.

I arrived just in time for the first lectures here. The new philologian[21] commenced this morning, and I heard the end of his lecture. I met him this after-

---

15 Opera by Richard Wagner. 16 See previous letter (139). 17 Former member of the Irish Parliamentary Party. 18 *The Grammar of Assent.* See Letter 144. 19 Sean O'Casey was now approaching the height of his popularity. He had just produced *Juno* in the Abbey, following on *The Shadow of a Gunman* in 1923. *The Plough and the Stars* would be premièred in 1926. 20 Both *Juno and the Paycock* and *The Shadow of a Gunman* were published in 1925. 21 Ferdinand Sommer, see Letter 134.

noon at Thurneysen's* house, and he seemed friendly and wise. If he is satisfied with my ignorance, I hope to take the exam at Easter.

M. Joseph Bedier[22] has written a delightful version of the *Tristan and Iseult* saga which I found in Paris, and Madame Duclaux spoke of it with enthusiasm when I told her. I have since read it with joy. It is called *Le Roman de Tristan et Iseult*, par Joseph Bedier: Piazza: Paris, 1924. The French bookshop would probably have it, and as you see it costs very little.

Talking of money, I have none. The twenty-five pounds is gone, and I am writing to the Bank for more, but it would be well to make a lodgement at once. Did the last lodgement by you leave us clear, or do you owe me something still?

My old life here is returning quickly, though it always seems unreal to be so transplanted. Yesterday I was forlorn and uncomfortable and alone, but I shall be working from now on. Much love to all the household.

[PS] Please do not forget the Bank.

I suppose the English elections surprised even you.[23] Fate seems to be angry with the Liberals. They are not worth much to anybody now. But isn't it strange that such big changes can come in spite of the proportion of votes?[24] The Labour people gained nearly as many votes as the Tories, polling nearly a million more than last time, and yet they lost fifty seats, and the other fellows gained nearly 200. I think the result may affect the elections here to some extent.[25] Had no one a chance in Northern Ireland?[26] It looks on the voting as if even a Nationalist could not have won, but was it really better not to try? Did the priests accept the republican candidates? Ireland can hardly benefit from any more humiliation, as she is humiliated already.

Please tell Maria that I found the missing shirt here on my return.

142

[Myles to John Dillon] [*Postcard*] Bonn, 12. xi. '24

Many thanks for your letter, enclosing cheque and cuttings wh. interested me. The one thing about the *Irish Times* criticism and other criticism of the new

22 Joseph Bedier (1864-1938), Prof. of Mediaeval French Literature at the Collège de France and member of the Académie Française since 1920. His edition of *Tristan et Iseult* was first published in 1900. 23 The General Election of October 29, which swept the Conservatives back into power with 419 seats, actually fell harder on the Liberals, who lost 100 seats, than on Labour (despite the "Zinoviev Letter", a forged document which claimed to prove links between the Labour Party and Russian Communists), who lost 40 overall. This was the decisive blow to the Liberal Party as a significant force in British politics. 24 Not in the British "first past the post" system, it isn't. 25 German elections were to be held on 7 December 1924. 26 That is, no one from the old Irish Parliamentary Party. In fact, all seats went to the Unionists in Northern Ireland.

educational plan[27] (including what I used to say myself) is that it does not apply. My first real information about the effect of it was from the Rector of Clongowes,[28] who told me that he found it much better than the previous one, and that, as regards Irish, it did not spoil his work at all. The fact is that while theoretically schools are divided into three classes, really all the schools have chosen class (c), where Irish is simply one of the subjects taught. The class (a), where Irish is the medium of teaching contains, I believe, two convent schools, and it remains to be seen what will happen to them.[29] At any rate, this class (a) merely amounts to giving a special bounty to schools who can really teach all subjects through Irish, and God knows they deserve it.

I had written just before your letter came, hence this postcard. My work is interesting and I am enjoying life, but I shall have to labour at the thesis. Love to James. He owes me a letter, and I should like to hear of Ballagh.

143

[John Dillon to Myles] 2 North George's St., Dublin, 18 November 1924

Your post card reached me here this morning. The marvel is that it ever reached me, in view of the nature of the address.[30] I returned here on Saturday evening, after spending ten days in Ballaghaderreen very pleasantly, enjoying every day the pleasant aspect of the renovated house. I came away from Ballagh in much better spirits than the frame of mind in which I went there. The accounts for the year, though not brilliant, turned out a good deal better than I had expected.

I shall give your message to James. He appears to be settling down to his task in Ballaghaderreen, and all appears to be going smoothly there. I have decided to put off my departure till after Christmas, and I now think that the arrangement will be to have Maria, Brian and Shaun in the house, and not to lock up the house. I propose to return to Ballaghaderreen on 15 Jan. and reside there till this time next year, when I hope to return to Dublin and start this house as a going concern again.

We are in the throes of an election here. This is the polling day in Dublin and in Mayo, and if one judges from the newspaper reports the Government

27 To be found in the *Irish Times* of 5 November 1924. Hardly surprising, the *Irish Times* was particularly concerned about the effects the new regulations would have on the Protestant community and on Protestant schools, none of which would fall into the favoured category A. Despite its obvious bias, the *Irish Times* had a point when it commented: "The history of government furnishes no proof that compulsion can breed affection or even good-will: all its illustrations are to the contrary." See also Letter 132. 28 The Very Rev. John C. Joy S.J., M.A. 29 Myles was quite correct in stating that only two schools opted initially for class A (and 17 for class B), but the proportion gradually grew. In 1956, 17 per cent of all schools were class A schools. 30 Myles had addressed the postcard, in Irish, to Ballaghaderreen.

men are going to win,[31] but of course all the newspapers are violently supporting the Government. In Mayo the priests are working for all they are worth for the Government, and, altho' their influence has nearly disappeared, they may succeed in frightening a number of people as to the results of a defeat of the Government, and so getting them to come out and vote.[32]

You do not make any allusion in your post card to my enquiry about Prof. Jones' Welsh book, the title of which I think I sent you. He has been pressing for it, this Delargy*. Nor do you reply to my enquiry about the secret papers of Admiral Torpitz [*sic*].[33]

Yes, the world is becoming very small, disgustingly small, specially to one who loves the old books of travel and adventure in distant unexplored lands.[34] Matters will become much worse when the new aerial services are in full working order.

Theo gave me rather a depressing account of your appearance. He said you had a bad cold and looked badly. You ought to be more generous about your feeding. I have no doubt you injured your health by starving yourself while at Heidelberg. Now that you are back at Bonn, where you are more at home, you should take the trouble to arrange for a couple of really good meals during the day. If you have to work hard, you will need *good* food.

I enquired yesterday about *Juno and the Paycock*. It has not come out yet. As soon as it appears I will send a copy to Miss R[obinson].* I shall get Joseph Bedier's book.

Yes, the result of the English elections did surprise me, tho' I was quite prepared for a Tory victory. The Tories had luck on their side this time. But the result, instead of converting me to proportional representation, confirms me in my objections to that system. On the whole I am of opinion that the decisive victory of the Tories is the best thing that [could] have happened for England, and for Ireland too. It makes a collapse into chaos less likely here.

I am delighted to learn from your post card that your work is interesting and that you are enjoying your life. I want to hear all about your proceedings. All well here, except poor Nicholas, who is suffering from cold and the appearance of his teeth. Enclosed cutting from *E[vening] Telegraph* will amuse you.[35]

---

31 Between 18 and 20 November five by-elections took place, among them North Mayo and South Dublin. In both constituencies, Republican candidates were elected by a small majority, Seán Lemass in Dublin. The polls were, however, strikingly poor, less than 43 per cent in South Dublin. 32 Mayo was fairly strongly anti-Treaty. The Republican candidate J.A. Madden was elected by a small margin, the poll being 53 per cent of the total electorate. 33 Admiral Alfred von Tirpitz (1849-1930). Backed by Kaiser Wilhelm II, Tirpitz was the driving force behind the massive enlargement of the German Navy from 1897 onwards with the intention to rival the British fleet. During World War I Tirpitz was commander of the German Navy. His *Politische Dokumente* were published in 1925. 34 He had a large collection of these, some of which are still in the family's possession. Sir Richard Burton was one of his favourites. 35 Unfortunately lost.

In this month's *Irish Rosary*[36] there is a ferocious attack on Æ and "his infidel gang", and on the *Irish Statesman*. I shall send you a copy.

144
[Myles to John Dillon] 22. xi. '24

That my postcard arrived so late made it more miserable still, but it was prompted only by anxiety to acknowledge the cheque, and that is why it was a postcard. I wrote to Maria since and mentioned Lloyd Jones's book. I shall write to him myself, but I don't believe I have it, and anyway I could not find it from here. The news of Ballagh is cheering, and that James is having peace of mind. He has the quality of efficiency anyway, if that can help.

This ought to be a strenuous time for me, but perhaps it is for the good—I have no gift for overwork. The new philologian[37] is very encouraging, and is reading Greek, Gothic and Latin inscriptions, and Thurneysen* is holding a seminar on a law text, which is a great pleasure, as he is now one of the few who know the Irish Laws. McNeill[38] is the other, but Thurneysen is everything that McNeill is not. For the rest, I am reading Sanskrit and doing my thesis, and I wish I had time for it all. I confess it is like waking up again to be back here amongst the learned. The only difficulty is to avoid distraction, because so much is said and done. Tonight I went to hear Werfel[39]—one of the best known poets at present—reading his own poems, but he forgot to turn up, so we were merely lectured about him by someone else.[40] Tomorrow Strauss[41] from Vienna is giving a concert, and on Monday, for a change, Marx[42] is coming to address the Centre Party.

36 Since its inception in 1897, the *Irish Rosary* was published by the Dominican order. It regarded itself as the Catholic spearhead in the ongoing fight against the perceived moral and cultural decay in Ireland. The anonymous article in question attacked "the Plunkett House clique of pagans, theosophists and log-rollers, who largely control the *Irish Statesman* and the Abbey Theatre" (Nov. 1924, p. 373). The quotation gives an insight into the style and the aggressively illiberal mind-set of the authors who wrote for the *Irish Rosary*. 37 That is, Professor Ferdinand Sommer. See Letter 134. 38 Eoin MacNeill, Prof. of Early Irish History at U.C.D. and Minister for Education in Cosgrave's cabinet. See also Letters 96 and 121. 39 Franz Werfel (1890-1945), German poet, novelist and playwright, born in Prague, and resident subsequently in Hamburg, Leipzig and Vienna. The war, and subsequent political troubles, gave his work a strongly revolutionary tinge. His most recent volume of poetry had been *Der Gerichtstag* in 1919, but he had just in 1924 produced a play, *Juarez und Maximilian*, and a novel on the opera, entitled *Verdi*. 40 The Bonn daily, *Generalanzeiger*, critized Werfel strongly for his "unreliability and immaturity" and judged that Prof. Oskar Walzel's lecture on Werfel and Stefan George, another famous German poet, was superior to whatever Werfel might have said anyway (*G*, 24 November 1924). 41 Richard Strauß' *Lieder-Abend* received enthusiastic reviews in the local press. 42 Wilhelm Marx (1863-1946), German politician, born in Cologne, entered the political branch of the civil service, and became a judge. In 1899

I have just finished Newman's *Grammar of Assent*, which Theo had lent me, a great book, and very well worth reading in this country, where learning is the only religion one is taught. Still, I like the learning too. My regret is that I did not come here two or three years sooner, and have time to go through the school, instead of hastening through my work, and merely seeing what others can spend time on. But something is better than nothing. I have got a book on Greek religion which has delightful things in it. It is wonderful that one gets through so many years at school and knows so little at the end, but perhaps it would not be worth so much now if I had known it before.

Have you seen Wickham Steed's new book?[43] The review of it interested me particularly on account of his impression of Paris after Jena and Berlin, for in spite of my admiration for wise men here, I really expect to have the same experience in Paris. Living here is as comfortable as it always was, so there is no danger of my starving, and my hostess is as kind. She sends greetings, and declares that she expects to have the pleasure of meeting you again next summer.

Please let me have the *Rosary* attack on Æ. I'm sorry they have done it, and they are probably on a false track. I should not be surprised if they suspect him of "Tomorrow",[44] and he was nearly as vexed by it as they were. I wrote to him

he was elected to the Prussian Diet, and in 1910 entered the German Reichstag, where he soon became prominent among leaders of the Centre Party. He was elected president of the Centre Party in 1921, and on 30 November 1923 succeeded Stresemann as Chancellor of the Reich. In August 1924 he took part in the Conference of London which determined the acceptance of the Dawes Plan. In the autumn of 1924 Marx dissolved the Reichstag in the hope of getting a government majority, and after the elections retired from the post of chancellor. He ran unsuccessfully against Hindenburg in the 1925 Presidential elections. See Introduction and Letter 156.   43 Henry Wickham Steed (1871-1956), British journalist. He had studied economics, philosophy and history at Jena, Berlin and Paris universities, and in 1896 joined the staff of *The Times* as acting correspondent in Berlin. He was sent to Rome in 1897, and in 1902 to Vienna as correspondent for Austria-Hungary. He remained there till 1913 when he returned to London, and was appointed Foreign Editor of *The Times* in January 1914. In 1913 he published *The Habsburg Monarchy*, in which the internal condition of Austria-Hungary was critically examined and the possibility of a European war discussed. During World War I, Steed was mainly responsible for the foreign policy of *The Times*, and, in 1918, was chosen to frame the policy of Lord Northcliffe's Department for Propaganda in Enemy Countries. He was sent on an official visit to the Italian front, where he was authorized by the Allied Governments to promise independence to the subject Habsburg peoples. He helped also to arrange, in April 1918, the Rome congress of the oppressed Austro-Hungarian races. In February 1919 he was appointed editor of *The Times*, and held this post till November 1922 In 1923 he acquired control of the *Review of Reviews*, of which he became editor. After leaving the editorship, in 1924, he published *Through Thirty Years, 1892-1922* (2 vols. London: Heinemann) in which he related his experiences of European politics between 1892 and 1922; this is the book Myles is referring to.   44 The short-lived journal *To-Morrow* was edited by Lawrence K. Emery (pseudonym of Dr A.J. Leventhal) and numbered most of the radical, free-thinking and/or left-wing intellectuals in Ireland among its contributors, such as Yeats, Liam O'Flaherty, Francis Stuart, F.R. Higgins and Cecil Ffrench Salkeld. It only lasted for two issues (August and September 1924).

the other day a rather bold exhortation to plead the cause of an Irish Collège de France, or some institution under the aegis of the universities, where the Seminar system could be introduced and only higher studies pursued.[45] That is one of the most effective parts of university work here, and it is attractive in a special way on account of the men who turn up. There are six of us in one of the Seminars here, one of them mainly interested in the philosophy of language, another in Classics, another in Semitic, another in Comparative Philology and Celtic, one who is still young, and myself, but we all have some reason for reading Latin inscriptions.

Forgive the wandering of this letter, but I have been rather distracted today, and can neither write nor not write at present. I hope that Nicholas has recovered by now.

With love to everyone,

[PS] What I said about the value of Newman here is hardly fair to the Catholicity of the Rhineland, which is everywhere to be seen—everywhere except in the university. But that seems to be often the way with Catholicity. A stranger easily passes it by.

My thesis has been behaving rather well for a week or so, and I hope to show a part of it to Thurneysen next week. It looks as if I saw the end in the distance, but I don't dare say that yet.

145

[John Dillon to Myles] Tuesday, 2nd December, 1924.

Your letter came last week—a very pleasant, and *very* interesting letter. No need to apologise for wandering. It is just the kind of letter I like to get. I am relieved to hear that you are comfortable and being well fed, because I feel sure that your misfortunes during the Summer were to some extent due to starvation at Heidelberg.[46]

Your account of the life you are leading is most cheerful, and I have not the slightest doubt that the distractions are exceedingly good for you and make your brain work better. I should like to have the name of that book on Greek religion, a subject in which I take an intense interest and about which I know practically nothing. I can quite understand your sensation on leaving Dublin and getting back amongst the learned. Poor Dublin! I greatly fear it will be a considerable time before we can set her feet on the path to a really intellectual and artistic life.

45 Some such institution did eventually emerge as the Dublin Institute for Advanced Studies, of which Myles ultimately (in 1949) became a member, in the School of Celtic Studies. 46 It sounds as though Myles had been ill while at home during the summer.

Things here, political, educational, etc., etc., are very bad, and going from bad to worse. I sent you the *Irish Rosary* and in this letter you will find some further cuttings on the Irish language controversy.[47] Father Quinlan's[48] speech was a very sensible one. I agree with all he said, except compelling boys to study Irish whether their parents liked it or not. There can be no doubt that a very formidable reaction is being stirred up by this system of trying to force Irish down the throats of all the people. I suppose you have seen Sean O'Casey in last Saturday's *Irish Statesman*.[49] It is poor stuff for him. Nevertheless, I have no doubt that it speaks the mind of a large section of the Dublin working people. What I fear is that, just as the S.F. campaign has killed all enthusiasm in Irish public life and politics, so the rabid Irish language enthusiasts will kill enthusiasm for the language, and provoke a bitter and cynical reaction.

I am afraid we are not nearly ripe for your ideal of a Collège de France. What is really needed is a thorough reorganisation of Trinity College and the National University, so as to make real provision for the teaching and civilisation of the youth of the country, and as things stand I do not see how this is to be brought about.[50]

Enclosed you will find a notice for the Convocation,[51] with some very silly notices of motion. The political situation is getting more and more mixed. Cosgrave is, I am told, really very ill[52]—he went off yesterday for a month's holiday in the South of France—and O'Higgins seems master of the field. But I do not believe O'H. will be able to hold the Govt. Party together for long, and what is to happen when the smash comes, no man can foretell.[53]

47 Lost, but various items appear in recent issues of both the *Irish Independent* and the *Irish Times*. The language aspect of the new Educational Programme virtually dominated the letter pages of both papers. The *Irish Times* pointed to the effect the new regulations would have for classical and even more so modern languages. This proved to be particularly true for German, which almost disappeared from Irish secondary schools after 1922, right until the late 1960s. 48 This was Harold Quinlan's brother, the Very Rev. Michael Quinlan S.J., who was rector of Belvedere College. Addressing the annual College dinner, he emphasised that schools would do their duty in the revival of the Irish language, if the new regulations did not affect the more rounded programme of education which was currently on offer (incl. the classics) (*IT*, 28 November 1924), Myles had been a student at Belvedere before changing to Mount St Benedict. 49 In his short story "Irish in the schools" (*IS*, 29 Nov. 1924, pp. 361-2) Sean O'Casey dealt with the language question from a Socialist point of view. He has one of the unempoyed workers queuing up in the Labour Exchange say: "The problem of havin' enough food to eat is of more importance than that of havin' a little Irish to speak. The Gaelic spoken by the Ard-Breitheamh for the first time in Dublin Castle is very different to the Gaelic spoken in the Labour Exchange." 50 It is not clear what he has in mind here. Presumably he is not anticipating Donogh O'Malley's 1970 proposal of a merger—just separate reorganisations. 51 Presumably of the Senate of the National University. 52 Cosgrave's illness which effectively meant that he was running the country from his hospital bed indeed aggravated the problems which the Free State Government was facing. 53 Like all of John Dillon's apocalyptic predictions, this was unfulfilled, but there were strains in the government at this time between O'Higgins and Cosgrave which caused Cosgrave to take over the Ministry for Defence himself after Mulcahy's resignation, rather than hand it over to O'Higgins (Lee 1989, p. 105) .

Nicholas has got over all his troubles. He was here on Sunday in an extremely sunny and agreeable mood.

Enclosed you will find your dividend (£25). Sign it and send it on to your Bank to be placed to your credit.

The weather is awful—deluges of rain—large tracts of the country are under water. Business very bad. I fear we are in for a hungry winter.

A very funny cable arrived for James yesterday from Chicago: "We expect you in January. A grand wedding. Dodo Badger."[54] So Badger's mission to Europe has proved a success.

Write soon.

[PS] Remember me very kindly to the Gräfin and her sisters.

146

[Myles to John Dillon] 14. xii. '24

Many thanks for your letter with cuttings, and also for the *Rosary*. The paragraph on the pagans was a deplorable performance, and, as I supposed, a very misdirected attack, as Æ* had as little to do with "Tomorrow" as I had, and disliked it greatly. The idea of calling on the priests and nuns of Ireland to save Irish literature before it is too late! It is unfortunate, because the *Rosary* was said to be quite a good magazine.

It is strange that the New Movement[55] has remained so entirely in the hands of a distinctly non-Catholic group in Ireland. I have been asked to lecture on the Irish Literary Renaissance here during Easter week, and though it has thrown me into great confusion of mind, I agreed. If my thesis is not finished before March—which is hardly likely—I may have to postpone my exam. for some weeks, but as I don't think of going to Paris till the Autumn and shall remain here in any case, it does not much matter. This question of the history and position of the movement is one of my problems. I am inclined to see in Yeats, Æ, Synge, Lady Gregory and Hyde,* a group parallel in their own day to Davis and Mitchel in theirs. The parallel is, of course, very loose, but both are protestant, and of a similar social surrounding. I mean no more than that.[56] As regards details, even Yeats and Hyde could not be taken together at all. But ever since 1792 there have been protestant nationalists, sometimes half literary, never— excepting Parnell—popular leaders as the Catholic nationalists were, O'Connell, Davitt, O'Brien and the Irish Party group. At earlier times those others found a place in politics—the Catholics had hardly begun to fight—but at the time of the literary renaissance there was hardly room in politics for these men. I see that

54 A lady friend of James Dillon's from Chicago. 55 This term appears to be largely synonymous with the Irish Renaissance, judging by the members of the movement Myles lists below. 56 It is interesting that Yeats himself liked to see some such connection. Cf. Hone 1962, p. 148.

the words I am writing suggest that Yeats and Synge would have been politicians if they could, which is ridiculous.[57] All I mean is that they resemble Davis in this much, that they felt themselves not members of an Anglo-Irish protestant community, but of the whole Irish people. The literature they have made, and the fact that so few of the Irish people themselves have been able to follow them, is probably a result of their better tradition of intellect. Please let me know what you think. Perhaps someone would send me Æ's *Candle of Vision*,[58] which is in the bookshelf in my room—2nd or 3rd shelf near the window, I think. By the way, Dibelius,* who asked me to give these lectures, has agreed to supply me with the necessary books up to a figure. Perhaps in emergency you could send me out one or two. Two points on which I am vague are the biography of Yeats himself and also of Standish Hayes O'Grady.[59] Boyd's[60] book is here, and may tell something. I should like to have Yeats' *Early Memories*, 1923.

I find it difficult to get back to work, since I have been wondering and imagining about the lectures I am to give, but there never was more need for industry. And I daresay if I start seriously to prepare the lectures towards the end of February, I should have them more than ready by the middle of April. But not having tried it before I don't know. A paper which one can read is simpler.

My book on Greek religion is called *Greek Religion from Homer to the Age of Alexander*, by Cornford,[61] in the *Library of Greek Thought*, edited by Ernest Barker. The books are all anthologies, so that one has simply a collection of fragments from the writers themselves, and many of them are delightful, but there must be a good religious history of Greece from the Oxford Press. The most exciting thing to have appeared recently is Stephen McKenna's translation of Plotinus.[62] Did you see Æ's review of it in the *Statesman*?[63] If he stuck to

57 And yet Yeats did have a political dimension to him, as we know, which fully developed, admittedly, only after this was written. **58** London, Macmillan and Co., 1919. **59** (1832-1915), scholar and antiquary, son of Admiral Hayes O'Grady. Born at Erinagh House, Castleconnell, Co, Limerick. Brought up and fostered in the Irish-speaking barony of Cloonagh. Received his formal education at Rugby and T.C.D. Appointed President of the Ossianic Society in 1856, but shortly afterwards emigrated to the United States, and worked there for thirty years as an engineer. On his return, he turned to scholarly activities, and compiled a catalogue of Irish manuscripts in the British Museum. Otherwise, his most notable work is *Silva Gadelica* (1892), a valuable compilation of tales from old Irish manuscripts, with translations and notes. **60** Presumably Ernest A. Boyd (1887-1946). The book in question would be either *Appreciations and Depreciations* (Dublin: Talbot 1917) or *Ireland's Literary Renaissance* (Dublin and London: Maunsel 1916). **61** F.M. Cornford (1874-1943), distinguished historian of Greek philosophy and religion, later (from 1931) Laurence Professor of Ancient Philosophy in the University of Cambridge. *Greek Religious Thought* was published in 1914. **62** Stephen McKenna (1872-1934), Irish journalist and man of letters. A thorough romantic, he taught himself Greek in order to translate the *Enneads* of Plotinus, a task to which, with the financial support of an English businessman, Sir Ernest Debenham, he devoted the latter part of his life, from 1916 on. In 1923, disillusioned by the Civil War, he went to live in England. Myles was certainly acquainted with him in later years, but possibly not at this stage. By this time only four of the six volumes of his great translation had appeared, Vol. IV in 1924. **63** This enraptured review of

that and left the leading articles to someone else both he and the paper would probably benefit. I'm sure he would.

One gets into the habit of abusing Dublin and the ignorance of Ireland, and perhaps it is more foolish than I think.[64] The current number of the *Handbuch der Literaturwissenschaft* discusses the Celtic Renaissance and in another section points to the Abbey Theatre as having succeeded where many attempts in England failed. The other night, in a lecture here, Dibelius gave the Abbey the same praise. And from the *Statesman* I gather there is as much and as good music to be heard in Dublin at present as in most cities of its size. All the queer things which have happened may make us think we are worse than we are. But I believe it is true about the university. It is about as bad as possible.

I sent off Kern's book yesterday. 9Fr. 10 is the total cost = 10/- or 9/6.

I have not succeeded in saying exactly what I mean about the Yeats-Æ company. The point is that a German would be inclined to say that this literary revival is a result of the recovery of the Irish people—Catholic emancipation and especially the freeing of the tenants—and that is probably true enough of the Gaelic League; but the leading figures of the Anglo-Irish movement belong to a class who were hardly affected by these happenings. I suppose freedom was in the air, but land or no land Yeats and Synge and Lady Gregory would have gone their way.

Could you tell me which of Moore's *Ave, Salve, Vale*[65] tells most of these things, or is there any choice?

The cold weather has come here now, and it requires courage to go out, but it remains as dry as a bone.

[PS] I got the warrant and have lodged it. M.

147

[Myles to John Dillon] [*Postcard*] Bonn, 22 December 1924

Please allow this card with my good will, as I am expecting another letter from you. Many thanks for your letter and the most welcome enclosures. One of my fellow Celtists here was examined yesterday,[66] and this has left me in a state of

Stephen McKenna's translation has Æ philosophise on the art of translation in a style which is as inimitable as it appears to us nowadays over-the-top, where he sees the translator as "that impalpable shepherd who can make one sentence light as air and another solemn, and these act as an incantation evoking in us the mood in which the thought was born" (*IS*, 6 December 1924). 64 Does this perhaps constitute a mild reproof of his father's Eeyore-like complaints in the previous letter? 65 George Moore's autobiography *Hail and Farewell* (1911-14) was divided into these three books. All three provided vital insights into the background to the Celtic Renaissance. 66 Kathleen Mulchrone?

excitement about my fate. The exam does not seem to be too awful. Father Coghlan enquired for you yesterday. He gave me an excellent supper after the opera, insisted on my taking a tin of cigarettes and, that seeming not enough, he added a further packet of the same cigarettes. Finally he implored me to bring a bottle of whiskey, but I could not consent.

148

[Kathleen Cunningham to Myles] Ballymore, Dec 30th, 24

Dear Mr Dillon,

Isn't this awful? Just think of me, caged up here in Ballymore, thinking hourly of my age. And the worst of it is, there seems to be no escape. Already I find myself reading the *Daily Independent* with deadly regularity. Notice that I never read a paper for over three years in Bonn. As for the way I pass my days, it would be ludicrous to describe. I feel like Mark Twain who wrote in his Diary for over twenty years "got up, washed, ate my breakfast, dinner and supper and went to bed."

I am afraid I started badly. In order to get back into the spirit of things, I began reading *The Valley of the Squinting Windows*[67] und fand, dass es stimmt,[68] and that you, Yeats, Æ and the rest of the poets were all in a conspiracy to tell amicable falsehoods about this country. However, I shall do my best, when the holidays are over to run away again and pitch my tent in some one of the European capitals.

Your realistic little sketch of Dublin when one arrives proved quite true in my case. I got into Westland Row at 6 a.m. and spent the next hour, accompanied by a rather humorous cabman, knocking and ringing at doors. Some people had lights on, pretending they were up, but of course, they weren't.

I met K. Mulchrone* at Mullingar ("where you have to get tea into the train"). She was bubbling over with an awful desire to talk, having been corked up tightly for the last four months.

I had a touching little note from M.K. MacNevin,[69] referring in morbid terms to her strange post in the West. I hope to have more accurate information in a few days, as I have summoned her and K. Mulchrone to visit me.

---

67 The novel by Brinsley Macnamara (1890-1963), published in 1918, deals in a rather humorous yet scathing way with Irish village life. It resulted in public burnings of the book in Macnamara's home town of Delvin, Co. Westmeath and the author was driven from the town in fear of his life. 68 "and found that it was true". 69 Two articles by M.K. MacNevin from the 1930s on library matters seem to indicate that she obtained a post in the library service. A post in a county library somewhere in the west of Ireland would probably tally with Kathleen Cunningham's description. See Letters 42 and 51.

Well, how are things going in Bonn? For Heaven's sake stay there as long as you can, or at least somewhere in Europe. Life on an island is impossible.

By the way, I found that book I was telling you about in connection with Lennox Robinson's[70] story. The title is *Without Sin* by Martin J. Pritchard. London 1896. If you think of exposing [?] him you can have it.

As regards posts there is nothing to relate. The modish sort of one would seem to be a connection, distant or otherwise, with the "Shannon Scheme".[71]

Give my love to Tiff and my best regards to Edwards.* I am somewhat afraid of the latter.

Best wishes for 1925

Yours v. sincerely
Kathleen Cunningham

149
[John Dillon to Myles] 30 Dec., 1924

I ought to have written this letter a week ago, but Christmas days are not favourable to the writing of long letters. Enclosed in this you will find various communications which ought to have been forwarded to you before now. Also a sonnet by Dr Sigerson[72]—a marvellous production from so old a man. It will please you, I think. Return it to me, as it is the only copy I have.[73]

Your card arrived on Christmas day, and was very welcome. Please remember me most warmly to Father Coghlan when next you see him.

What was [the] fate of your fellow Celtist?

I got a very cheerful letter from Theo. They have had wonderful weather at Leysin since Ist. Nov., and I am hoping Theo may be allowed to get out of bed soon.

70 Lennox Robinson (1886-1958), playwright and director, associated with the Abbey Theatre for almost 50 years of his life. The story Kathleen Cunningham is talking about may have been contained in his *Eight Short Stories* (Dublin: Talbot 1919) which was the only prose collection he had published so far. 71 This was the hydro-electric power station which was due to be built by the Berlin company Siemens-Schuckert at Ardnacrusha near Limerick. Work on the scheme started in September 1925 and the sluice gates were opened in 1929. The Shannon Scheme marked the beginning of electrification of Ireland on a national scale. Thomas McLaughlin, whom Myles had met in Berlin (see Letter 31), had established the initial contact between the German firm and the Free State government. 72 George Sigerson (1836-1925), physician, scientist and man of letters. In the midst of his medical studies in the 1850's, he had taught himself Irish, and became quite an authority on Irish language and literature. His first book, *The Poets and Poetry of Munster*, was published in 1860, and was followed by many others. He engaged in political journalism for many years, contributing regularly to the *Freeman's Journal*. He was one of the founders of the Feis Ceoil, and was one of the original members of the Free State Senate. His house at 3 Clare Street became a gathering place for all interested in Irish literature and music. He actually died not long after this, on 17 February 1925. 73 The cutting is lost.

Jim was with us for Christmas. He seems to be getting on well in Ballagh, and brought rather cheering news of the Christmas business. It has been something of an improvement on last year, whereas I had expected a further slump. I have now decided to put off my departure to take up residence in Ballaghaderreen to Ist. March.

If Theo is able to travel in May, I shall join him and take him to Italy. If he is not allowed to move around by that time, I shall hope he may be fit in October. Possibly you may see your way to joining us in May or October.

By the way, I forgot to remind you to send your application for the extension of your scholarship for another six months. I spoke to Coffey* on this matter about a fortnight ago, and he said he was confident it would be granted. The Senate meets about the end of January, and Coffey said your application should be in time for that meeting.

Now I come to your letter of 14. Dec., and your course of lectures. I shall gladly help in every way I can, and shall send you any book you may require. I sent off *The Candle of Vision* a few days ago.

It is not easy in the compass of a letter to make any attempt, even, to answer the questions put in your letter. The parallel between Davis and Mitchel, and Yeats, Lady G[regory] and Hyde, is by no means as clear as you indicate. Davis and Mitchel were *primarily* politicians—politicians with a strong literary tendency—whereas Yeats, Lady G. and Hyde are purely literary and absolutely non-political. That is, they have no real understanding of politics, no appreciation of the realities of Irish social conditions.

Again, within these groups of the '48 men and the contemporary Irish writers there are subdivisions. Duffy[74] (who was one of the best writers of the '48 Movement), Davis and Mitchel were primarily politicians. Duffy was a Catholic, of the old Celtic stock. I doubt whether either Davis or Mitchel would have written the "Muster of the North". Mitchel [was] really of Scotch stock, Davis of Welsh, and both Mitchel and Davis belonging to the English garrison class. Then through all the history of Irish literary movements from the 16th century down runs the division into those who lived in the atmosphere and wrote from the point of view of the English garrison, and those who lived in the atmosphere of the old Irish Celtic tradition. A book has been published a few weeks ago by Corkery[75] called *The Hidden Ireland*, which deals with the subject. I do

74 Charles Gavan Duffy (1816-1903), co-founder, with Davis and John Blake Dillon (John Dillon's father), of *The Nation,* and of the Young Ireland Movement. He was imprisoned during the 1848 Rising, and so avoided exile, but in 1855, disillusioned, he emigrated to Australia, where he flourished, becoming, in 1871, Prime Minister of Victoria, and being knighted in 1873. He wrote extensively in later life about Thomas Davis and the Young Ireland Movement. In 1880 he retired to the South of France, but visited Ireland occasionally. 75 Daniel Corkery (1878-1964), writer and teacher. Learned Irish in his late twenties, and with Terence MacSwiney and Con O'Leary founded the Cork Dramatic Society in 1908, and wrote plays for it in both Irish and English. In 1916 he

not yet know whether it is any good, but I shall send it on to you, if it is any good.

Swift, Lecky,[76] Grattan, Flood, etc., were Anglo-Irish. The '48 men were a reaction against this Anglo-Irish school, inspired by the Repeal agitation and Catholic emancipation. The modern Celtic revival was, perhaps unfortunately, much more divorced from politics, but it was, all the same, though probably unconsciously, the outcome of the Home Rule movement and the Land League. But this modern movement having started on a basis of more or less veiled hostility to the political movement of the day, the breach widened, and then the influence of Plunkett[77] and Æ on the one hand, and the Gaelic League on the other[78]—the two branches of the Celtic revival were *used* as political weapons to strike at the Irish Party and the National Movement.

Plunkett was working in the interest of ... [*illegible*] and the preservation of the landlord system, and Æ and Co. more or less consciously supported him in this campaign; and the Gaelic League crowd were working in the interest of the I.R.B. and the Clan na Gael.[79] The results we have seen. Owing to the War, etc., the I.R.B. and the Clan came out on top, and the Plunkett-Æ crowd and even Hyde and the sincerely non-political set of the Gaelic League, were swept away in the flood, and the present crowd placed on top—an ignorant, intolerant gang for the most part—with, I fear, the inevitable result that there will be a severe set-back to the Celtic revival. The atmosphere of present-day Ireland is not nearly so favourable to the Celtic revival as was the atmosphere of the days when the much-abused Irish Party was on top. After a few years, I have no doubt, things will begin to mend, but there is no sign of improvement yet.

You are too hard on the University.[80] You must remember how young it is, the material it has to deal with, the atmosphere in which it has [had] to exist during the last ten years, and the fact that it has been financially starved ever since its foundation. Your generation will have to take it in hand and reshape it.

Dibelius* is right about the Abbey Theatre. It has been a *marvellous* success, and I am glad to say it seems now to be in a more flourishing condition than ever. Brian and I went a fortnight ago to see *The Playboy of the Western*

had published his first collection of short stories, *A Munster Twilight*. At the time of this letter he was teaching art for the Cork County Technical Educational Committee, but in 1930 he became Professor of English at U.C.C., a post which he held until his retirement in 1947. *The Hidden Ireland* (1924) is perhaps his most famous work. 76 W.E.H. Lecky (1838-1903), historian and Fellow of Trinity College, seems the odd man out here, as being of a later generation than the '48 men, but he certainly represents the Anglo-Irish tradition. 77 Dillon's objection to Sir Horace Plunkett (1854-1932) was that he saw him as part of a sinister British plot to "kill Home Rule by kindness", which was certainly the policy of the British administration during the Chief Secretaryship of Gerald Balfour at the beginning of the century. 78 The syntax rather breaks down at this point. 79 This is quite unfair if taken as referring to Douglas Hyde himself, but not, of course, to Pearse and others. 80 Dillon had, of course, been intimately involved in the setting up of the University. Hence his rather protective tone here.

World. Admirably acted—the theatre was packed. And on Friday James, Brian and I went to see an extremely amusing farce by Lady Gregory, *Aristotle's Bellows*[81]—the acting again quite admirable, and again the theatre was quite full.

We have had terrible weather, storm and terrific floods. Write a good long letter soon.

[PS] Enclosed is cheque for 10/- for the book you sent me.[82] If you have any difficulty in cashing cheque, you can lodge it to your credit in London Bank.

150

[Myles to John Dillon] Bonn, Schedestrasse 3, Wednesday, 28. i. '25

It is a long time since I last wrote, and my excuse is always the same. There is a lot to be done, and it takes me all my time to do it.

Many thanks for your letter. I have never felt that I knew much about '98, or the United Irishmen of '82, but I have a feeling that the latter were almost exclusively protestants, and that it was primarily part of the history of Grattan's parliament which had very little in common with the old Ireland. Were the United Irishmen of '82 joined and supported by the Catholics? And am I quite wrong?

I was very glad to have Corkery's book, but I have only had time to look at it yet. He probably did not feel equal to attempting a general history of Irish Ireland in those times. I imagine it would be a difficult book to write, and he is not a historian, but I do agree that it would be well worth writing. The account of the Gaelic League attempt at reunion interested me very much, though it was hardly encouraging.[83] All the news of Ireland is bad now, and I feel in myself a foolish pessimism. It becomes hard to believe that we are good for anything in the material world. We seem to have no money and no trade and practically no population and have lost the most valuable part of the country (for its size).[84] The material world is not the most interesting or the most important, but all soul and no body have proved with us a very unpleasant prescription.

Theo sent me O'Hegarty's book[85] which I read with much satisfaction, though it is horribly written and altogether unpleasant. But it is a blessed thing that these things have been written.

81 This was first produced in March 1921. It is a three-act surrealist farce, written for children as well as adults. It concerns Conan, a Trinity College graduate, who makes himself unpleasant and unhappy by constantly wishing for perfection. He finds a magic bellows which, for seven times only, will change the things they are blown upon. The changes turn out to be unpleasant. Finally, he reverses the magic spell, and uses the last blow to make himself content. It is remarkable for a Gregory play in that music and song are extensively used to create atmosphere. 82 The book by Kern, see Letter 146. 83 This does not figure in his father's last letter, though possibly in an enclosed cutting. 84 That is to say, the six counties of Ulster, as a result of the Boundary Commission. 85 P.S. O'Hegarty (1879-1955) had just published *The Victory of Sinn Fein*. From

I had a letter from Inis Meadhoin the other day. My friend was gone before my letter reached there, but it appears that he was well looked after in Dublin.

There are hardly more than two thoughts in my head at present, as my thesis is not anxious to get finished, and I am persuading it diligently, and Sanskrit and other things remain undone. The lectures of Easter week come into my mind every now and then and vanish again, but I shall have to devote myself to them soon. Have you been able to trace Standish James O'Grady's *History of Ireland (Heroic Period)*?[86] The Irish Bookshop has not answered me. And I should be glad to have *Reveries over Childhood and Youth* of Yeats (1916) too. I told Dibelius* to order a number of books from the Irish Bookshop and he sent me the order before Christmas, but there has been no reply.

Please give my thanks to Shaun for the *Independent,* which arrived this morning. Dr Hickey[87] was a delightful man, and I suppose more or less of a saint himself, though he did not care for living saints.

Please write when you have time.[88] I wrote to the Senate some time ago. Perhaps you will hear what the result has been. By the way, was Hyde elected recently or not?[89]

I shall be interested to hear what happens to the Free Staters in these elections. Is there any hope of anything taking their place?

I read a most laudatory review of Father Nicholas' book[90], which he has published despite all our discouragement.

151

[Myles to John Dillon] Monday, 23. ii. '25

These weeks have passed very quickly, but I have managed to complete the first proof of my thesis, so that all it will need now is a few additions and corrections and some rewriting, most of which I will put off until after Easter. It is a relief to have got even to that stage, and I am browsing on the Irish revival now.

We have had no winter here this year, and are now enjoying the first spring. I hear strange birds for the last week or so, and an owl and another night bird

1922 to 1944 he served as Secretary of the Department of Posts and Telegraphs. He edited a number of journals, and published five other books, of a polemical nature. **86** Standish James O'Grady (1846-1928), historian and novelist, cousin of Standish Hayes O'Grady, had published this work in 1878-80. **87** Dr Michael Hickey, President of Clonliffe College. See also Letter 32. **88** No more letters from John Dillon survive, unfortunately, until 25 March. **89** Douglas Hyde was not successful in the Seanad elections. See Letter 175. **90** This will have been a little pamphlet, *Four Rainbows and Four Questions,* by Nicholas Dillon, O.F.M., published in January 1925 by the Irish Dominican Printing Press in Lisbon. It is certainly a curious little work, mainly about St. Francis of Assisi, but not without interest.

cried last night. The shoots are out, and leaves in some places, and it is bright and delightful. This is the last week of term, and then holidays till May. I rejoice at the prospect of free days, but I will have a lot to do—besides Yeats and Æ and Synge—if there is time for it. I left Sanskrit and other things to look after themselves until my work was finished.

The Senate have graciously extended my extension, which is really very generous. It is to be hoped that they will not feel taken in.

You wrote from Bealach, but I like to think that the war is over by now[91] and that Duff's has been restored to life. Please give me the news of the strike if it is over. You promised a paper with the speeches of the patriots, but it did not come. All my efforts to find Standish O'Grady's *History of Ireland* have failed, which leaves me at a loss. However, there are some later reprints which I may fall back on. Another book I badly need is Lady Gregory's *Our Irish Theatre*.[92] It appears to be out of print, but it is in the study, I believe. I would be very glad to have it if you could send it, and I should return it by post as soon as the affair is over.

—Tea—

They are almost too good-natured here, and life is very comfortable. Still, I could not live in this country—without fireplaces, and bacon, and tea, and with flats and civil servants and paganism and cutaway coats all over the place. It is queer how different everything can be. I thought I smelt Ballagh a moment ago on the balcony, but the smell only reaches here occasionally.

It appears there are to be more elections.[93] Have you no prophecy yet as to what is before us? I gather from the *Statesman* that that deplorable person McGrath[94] has collapsed and his party is broken. The Free State seems to find conventions as embarrassing as you found them of old.

I had a letter from Inis Meadhoin the other day, and my poor friend, having sunk his fortune in an outfit for America and travelled to Dublin, and then to Cork, was held up at the harbour on the ground that his heart was weak. He says two other doctors had vetted him already, and why his heart shouldn't be weak if it liked one doesn't see.[95] What can this have to do with the American constitution? Anyway, he had to wander home again, and is very unhappy. Is it true that conditions are so bad in the West?[96]

91 This is actually a reference to a strike which had broken out in Monica Duff's which continued for many months, until it was finally broken in October 1925. 92 New York, 1913. 93 In March 1925, there were by-elections in seven constituencies in order to fill nine Dáil seats. See Letter 153. 94 Joseph McGrath (1887-1966), Sinn Féin revolutionary and politician. Fought in the 1916 Rising. Took the Treaty side, and became, first, Minister of Labour and then Minister of Industry and Commerce in the Free State Government, but resigned in sympathy with the army faction involved in the abortive coup of April 1924, and vacated his Dáil seat in the following October. Later, in 1930, he founded the Irish Hospitals Sweepstake, and became a very rich man, and a prominent racehorse owner. 95 Myles got the story from a letter written in Irish by this friend, Partholon Ó Flaithbheartaigh. Myles stayed in his house whenever he visited Inishmaan. 96 The Government was

By the way, what have people been doing for provisions during the strike? Were the markets held outside closed doors?

Thurneysen* enquires for you often.

[PS] I tremble to ask such a question in view of the strike, but did James finally send off my gift to the two sages of Inis Meadhoin? And what do I owe for the transaction? Please give the enclosed cheque to Brian. I owe it to him for months.

152

[Myles to John Dillon] 6. iii. '25

Your reproach was I am afraid well earned, but I should have escaped it if I had not addressed my last letter to Dublin. It must have reached you immediately after you had written. However, these are days of leisure, and I will try to improve my record.

The term came to an end on Saturday, and we have two months holiday. I hear of people going to walk through Bavaria into Switzerland and another is going to Paris. Edwards,* whom you met last Autumn, has gone home to Belfast; and I felt the Wanderlust in myself for the first few days, but I cannot stir till I have made up my mind what I am going to say about the Irish revival at Easter.

I get now and then into a foolish panic with nightmare imaginations of myself stammering speechless before the crowd, and when that happens my inspiration fails me, but it is only a mood. Lady Gregory's book arrived yesterday to my great satisfaction, sent by Maria, and in the cover a strange matter-of-fact review from a Chicago paper by Uncle Willy, which could have been written by Father Nicholas.

I am sorry that my ignorance of modern Irish history showed itself so plainly, though I have to confess that it does not surprise me. I think we are not altogether to blame for knowing so little, as one was taught nothing at all, but the worst of it is that I have sometimes pretended to know more than I do. I searched for Lecky here and found that they have neither his nor any other decent book on Irish history, except—strange to say—the *Two Centuries* ... [97] and Spenser's *View*.[98]

It is disappointing that the strike is so hard to settle. I only hope that James and his three lieutenants are able to do a good trade. I suppose most of the strikers have gone home. Perhaps the saving in salaries almost balances the

reacting to the dismal conditions in the West by appointing the Gaeltacht Commission. See Letter 153. **97** *Two Centuries of Irish History*. **98** An edition of Edmund Spenser, *A View of the Present State of Ireland* (1596).

injury to the business, for the moment at any rate, as the profits have been so small for the last two years.

I got the paper with Father O'Flanagan's performance in it.[99] He is coming very near to the borderline. Do you know whether he still lives as a priest, or if he has repudiated all mere superstitions?

I was asked to tea by a fellow-sanscritist last Sunday, and found myself, to my joy, for the first time in Bonn in a house where there was no trace of the wretched formality of the German middle class. I never knew what bourgeoisie could amount to until I experienced it here in a form so stupid and shameless as would be unthinkable with us. And what makes it more puzzling and more horrible is that it arms itself with a very high standard of education, so that the names of Raphael and Bach and Beethoven, and above all Goethe, can be taken in vain by people whom these men would have made outlaws. I read an essay of Symonds[100] yesterday in which he distinguished education and culture, and it seemed to give me words to explain the miserable self-deception which is so common here. Everyone is educated, education is enormously valued, people run to concerts and theatres and picture galleries, and collect aesthetic experience by the ton, and then with unwholesome flatness they talk about culture, a word which we seldom use. But they have mistaken quantities of things seen and heard and read for something quite different, and culture is the very thing that is so rare here. When I came here first, this *Bildungswille*[101] impressed me enormously, in contrast to the ignorance and indifference at home, which often amounts to hostility towards intelligence. But now I begin to wonder where the true wisdom is. I can imagine that if the divine Beauty and eternal Truth were posted up on hoardings at every street corner it would do more harm than good, and something similar seems to have happened here. Over-education seems to make culture impossible—since I have to use the word—because people forget how little they know.

Another evil thing in the air here is that one can become avaricious of knowledge—I have felt it often myself—and avarice of knowledge is as ugly a feeling as avarice of any other sort.

99 Fr Michael O'Flanagan (1876–1942), priest and Republican. In 1917 he had managed Count Plunkett's successful election campaign, and became Vice-Chairman of Sinn Féin. Said the prayers at the opening of the first Dáil in January 1919, and was "silenced" by his bishop. Campaigned for the Republic in the United States, until de Valera invited him back to formulate a new electoral policy. Speaking in Ballina on 1 March 1925, Fr O'Flanagan challenged the bishops who "wanted to turn us into a helpless people altogether" and one day latter at a meeting in Sligo he even talked about a new religion: "There were only two articles in the new religion. One was belief in an independent Irish Republic, and the second was belief in the duty and the right of every citizen of the Republic to serve it according to the best of his ability" (*IT*, 3 March 1925). No wonder the bishops were alarmed. 100 John Addington Symonds (1840–1893), English essayist, poet, biographer and expert on the Italian Renaissance. The essay Myles is referring to must have been in the collection entitled *In the Key of Blue* which Theo had sent him. See Letter 127. 101 Will or eagerness to be educated.

But I was forgetting the pleasant tea-party. There was a singer there with whom I came home, and she told me that she holds a session every Wednesday evening, and has asked me to come, so that I am looking forward to something new and pleasanter.

I have written to Blackwell in Oxford for the other books I want, and if they are to be had I daresay he will send them. The review of Fr Nicholas was in a paper Shaun sent me containing a poem on Father Hickey.[102] I have no idea of the date, but he probably has the paper.

153

[John Dillon to Myles] 25 March 1925

Your letter of 23 Feb. reached me the day after I posted my letter reproaching you for your prolonged silence, and since that I received your letter dated 6 March. I am now very anxious for news of you again. How has your thesis got on? When will you learn [the] result? What progress are you making in preparation of your lectures? And when are they to begin? Has the Wanderlust prevailed, and have you set forth on your wanderings? Or have you decided where you will go? I fear from what I have seen in the papers that the weather of the last few weeks has not been favourable for walking tours.

About the books you wanted, I found here a copy of Standish O'G.'s *Story of Ireland* and sent it to you. The history is out of print and costs 30/- 2nd hand, when it turns up. The *Two Centuries of Irish History* ought to be a very valuable book. The contributors were first-rate men. By the way, I suppose you heard of the death of Dr Sigerson.[103] Douglas Hyde* has written an article on him in the March number of *Studies*. I shall send it to you when I have read it myself.

You will have seen the result of the elections.[104] Much as I distrust and dislike the present Government, I am glad their candidates won. If the Republicans had won, Ireland would soon have become uninhabitable. As it is, it is bad enough, but there is some attempt to maintain law and order. The elections were won largely by the priests, who worked hard for the Govt., using the argument that a victory for the Republicans would mean a fresh outburst of murder, robbery, destruction of roads, bridges, etc., etc. This frightened the people and induced them to vote for the Govt. as the lesser of two evils. Father O'Flanagan's outrageous speech[105] did a good deal to help the Government, and

102 Possibly on Dr Michael Hickey, President of Clonliffe College, where Shawn studied for the priesthood. 103 See Letter 149. He died on 17 February 1925. 104 In the by-elections of March 1925, seven out of the nine contested seats went to the Government parties, including the one in North Mayo. 105 See previous letter (152).

the distribution of coal and promise of large relief works helped also. We had several meetings in Ballaghaderreen, and they were all miserably small, and without the slightest sign of enthusiasm.

The strike continues, and it looks now as if it would be a long and bitter struggle. We were closed entirely for 3 weeks. After that, about the end of Feb., we opened, and have since then been doing quite a good business. All our yard men and bakers remained loyal, and the shop is run by the four Partridges, James, and five apprentices who have returned to work. The strikers are very active. They keep pickets walking up and down in front of Gordon's and Beirne's, but the country people take no notice of them, and, strange to say, they have so far made no attempt to picket us or Flannery's. But four weeks ago they attacked our place and Flannery's and would, I have no doubt, [have] used violence, had it not been for the prompt action of the Civic Guards, who charged with batons, knocked down the organisers and the ring leaders, and subsequently arrested the organisers and ten of the rioters. Since then peace has prevailed. As you suggest, I believe we are doing better financially than before the strike started, and, unpleasant as it has been, I am inclined to think that the strike will turn out to be a blessing in disguise, as it will enable me to considerably reduce the staff, and to get rid of some very undesirable and troublesome employees. James is doing splendidly. Without his help I never could have carried on.

I was in Ballaghaderreen for 7 weeks up to yesterday week, when I came up here for a short visit. I return to Ballaghaderreen next Tuesday, and shall be there till the middle of May. I have put off closing up the house for the present owing to the uncertain position created by the strike. This morning I had a letter from James, enclosing a letter from your aunt K. In it she says your Grandmother got a sudden attack of bronchitis, and was very near dying, but when your aunt wrote, her mother was better, and the doctor thought her out of danger.

Your disquisition on Culture and Education in Germany in your letter of 6 March interests me extremely. Read Wickham Steed's *Through Thirty Years*.[106] He has something to say on the subject which will interest you. And another book I recommend to you very much is Brandes[107]—the Danish author's— *Recollections of Childhood and Youth*.

106 See Letter 144.   107 Georg Morris Cohen Brandes (1842-1927), Danish critic and literary historian, born in Copenhagen, son of a Jewish merchant. In 1871 he became reader in Belles Lettres at the University of Copenhagen, but was passed over for the professorship of Aesthetics, because of his modernism and championing of self-determination, as well as his Jewishness. His *Main Streams of Literature in the 19th Century*, published in four volumes in 1872-5, was translated into most European languages and became a classic. He lived in Berlin from 1877 to 1883, and published a number of works while there. He was an early champion of Ibsen, on whom he published a study in 1899. In 1902 he was at last appointed to the chair of Aesthetics at Copenhagen. During

By the way, did you get Yeats' *Reveries over Childhood and Youth*? I don't remember a copy of it in the house.

Enclosed is a cutting from the *Irish Times* which will interest you. A Commission has been appointed by the Govt. to consider how best to deal with the Gaeltacht.[108] I shall send you a report of its proceedings.

Eimar O'Duffy* and his wife are dining with us here tonight. Poor Eimar has got 3 months' notice of dismissal. His department is to be abolished,[109] and he is in the woes of the world looking for a job, with a wife and two little children depending on him.

Write a full account of your proceedings.

[PS] Remember me very kindly to Prof. Thurneysen,* and to your hostess.

154

[Maria O'Reilly to Myles] 2 Nth Gt Georges St., Palm Sunday, 5th April
1925

My dearest Myles,

I feel I cannot allow your Birthday to pass without conveying my best and fondest wishes for all you desire in this life and the next.

Did you get the Shamrock I sent you for St Patricks day? I had a post card from Gerard's[110] wife saying he is much better. Dr Maginnis rang me up last Friday asking Theo's address as he was going to advise Mr Murphy an old school friend of Theo's to go to Leysin. So I gave his address.

We celebrated Nicholas's 1st Birthday on 1st of this month. We were all invited to tea but your father had to return to Ballagh that day as James wrote him requesting him to come at once. The strikers have published leaflets denouncing him and declaring he was the cause of the strike which is only of course their last resource [*sic*] to try to get your father to take them back.

World War I he sought to be impartial, but he openly quarrelled with his friend Clemenceau, and displeased the Allies by his criticism of their colonial policy, and by his faith in post-revolutionary Russia. He published a host of literary studies between 1905 and 1925. The Danish original of *Recollections of My Childhood and Youth* was published in 1905, the English translation appeared one year later. 108 This Commission was appointed on 27 January 1925 and submitted its report on 14 July 1926. Its members were Pádraig Ó Cadhla, L.O. Moriarty, P. Baxter, T.D., Tadhg Ó Scannaill, General Richard Mulcahy, the Rev. J. Cunningham, Risteard Ó Foghludha and Joseph Hanly. 109 He was employed in the Department of External Affairs. This was certainly not abolished, so the reference must be to the particular programme he was involved with. His losing his job probably had to do with the Ministers and Secretaries Act of 1924 which recommended a slimming down of the administrative system of the Free State. O'Duffy went off after this to work in Paris as a journalist, and then gravitated to England, where he lived by writing. 110 I.e. Gerard Murphy.*

I am glad to say he has decided not to give in to them. Imagine May Rush striking! She certainly ought to be ashamed of her action in doing so.

When are you coming home? Have you had you[r] exam. yet? [...]

Brian has gone down to Gorey to day with J. Sweetman[111] in his motor. He may stay a few days and he may return tonight. I enclose a photo to keep you in mind of one who never forgets you. Also a Poplin tie for to greet you on your Birth Day.

With best love from

Your loving nurse
Mary O'Reilly

155

[John Dillon to Myles] Ballaghaderreen, Co. Mayo, Tuesday, 8 April, 1925

I have been looking out for a letter from you for some days. You have not answered my last letter in which I put some questions about books. Since I wrote I have been in Dublin for a fortnight, and one day I came across Yeats' *Reveries over Childhood and Youth* in the study. I had not remembered that I possessed it. Do you still need it, or have you procured it? I gave you particulars about O'Grady's history. You will be pained to hear that the Irish Bookshop has gone bankrupt, and has been bought by a Jew (I think). I do not know what he proposes to do with it.

This letter will, I hope, reach you on your birthday,[112] and will carry to you my best love, and all good wishes for the coming year. I hope you will be brilliantly successful with your Thesis, and your lectures on the Irish Renaissance. I confess I feel rather proud of a son of mine being asked to lecture in a German University.

After you have finished your lectures, and by way of corrective to a too unbridled enthusiasm for Irish Ireland, I would recommend the perusal of three books:

The Real Ireland,
    by Bretherton[113]—
a very scurrilous and poor production, but nevertheless with some elementary truth;

The Shadow of the Gloomy East
    by F.A. Ossendowski;[114]
and *The Dark Horse*
    by Savinkoff.[115]

111 John Sweetman, son of the Irish Party M.P. John Sweetman of Drumbaragh. 112 11 April. 113 C.H.E. Bretherton, *The Real Ireland*. London: A. & C. Black 1925. 114 Ferdinand Anthony

I think I told you in my last letter of our altered plans with regard to my visit to Theo. I now propose to go about the middle of October. You will have heard that Theo is not to be allowed to get on to his feet till July, so there is no chance of his being [able] to travel before October. What are your plans for the Autumn? It would be very pleasant if you could arrange to join us.

The Strike here is still going on, and likely to last for several weeks to come, altho' it is now universally recognised that the strikers are hopelessly beaten. We are open every day, and doing a very good business. It is amazing how we have been able to carry on. James, the four Partridges, and six apprentices form the staff. But of course all the yardsmen, Farrell, John Harmon, and the Baker have remained loyal. The Boots and Hardware are closed, but all the rest of the establishment is running normally. We are doing about ⅓ of the business we did with the whole staff, and I calculate that, instead of losing by the Strike, we are doing better so far as net profit goes, so that we could hold out for a year if necessary. However, if the Strike does not break up within the next few weeks, we shall get in a new staff. About half the number will be quite sufficient.

Enclosed you will find my usual birthday gift, and also some strange communications which have been lying here for some time. I spent a fortnight in Dublin and returned here last Tuesday week. I found all well in Dublin. Nicholas has got over his troubles, and is now flourishing exceedingly, and beginning to talk, to the immense delight of his parents.

156

[Myles to John Dillon] Bonn, Schedestrasse 3, Holy Thursday, 9. iv. '25

Your letter was much enjoyed. I hope you have forgotten how long it is since I wrote, but in spite of nominal holidays I have not had much peace in these weeks. I did not go away at all, as the forthcoming event—the lectures—were in my mind, and I have kept promising myself other things instead, but I shall hardly do any of them. One was to spend these days at Maria Laach with the Benedictines and that has not happened, and the other is to travel to Trier as

Ossendowski, Polish traveller and writer. Born in Witebsk in 1876. After the October Revolution, Ossendowski joined the staff of General Kolchak in Siberia, fighting the Bolsheviks. Following the collapse of Kolchak, he made his way through the forests to Mongolia disguised as a peasant, a journey recounted in *Beasts, Men and Gods* (1923). *Men and Mystery in Asia* followed in 1924, and *The Shadow of the Gloomy East* in 1925. He later travelled in Africa, producing further works. 115
Boris V. Savinkov, *The Black Horse*. London: Williams & Norgate 1924. A novel.

soon as the lectures are over, and walk down the Mosel for a few days. But it may end with my sticking to my job. Many thanks for Standish O'Grady. I thought the other book would be out of the question. However, the lectures are more or less ready now, and I think they will be intelligible and will tell something about our great men. If I could only persuade myself I was Napoleon for the few hours it would be of value to me, as it makes a good deal of difference if one has plenty of confidence.

It is unpleasant that the strike is lasting so long. It is late now to be asking how it arose at all, but I find myself a bit curious. Someone told me that it started in Flannery's, and you had to lock-out in sympathy, so that it was evidently not immediately a dispute about wages. I shall be glad to hear when it is over. James must have been doing great work. He is at least rescued from boredom, I suppose, and will have learnt a new field of trade activity uncharted in the maps of Marshall Fields'.[116] It is at least to the credit of the Civic Guard that they rescued Bob from the violence of the rioters. The *Roscommon Herald* delighted me. There are paragraphs in it which deserve never to be forgotten, and when someone gets polite in a row it is often good. I remember someone before a court in Collooney or Ballysodare, and it was asserted that he received a kick, "whereupon he delivered a box"—a dignified phrase.

I had a splendid letter from Kathleen the other day, and she says that Grandmother is rapidly recovering, and that they will soon go to Rye.

Indeed I am anxious to read Wickham Steed,[117] though I hear he is villainously conceited. There was a rather happy satire on his book in a recent *Punch* (I think 6 March) which I was given by someone. But all the same I cannot help feeling that much of what he says of Germany and France would please me. I wish I could make up my mind about Germany, though it sounds foolish when I say it that way. Their science impresses me so much that I often doubt that it isn't simply my own superficiality which makes me dislike it, but I really don't believe it is. There is something lacking here, without which I could not live as a scientist. A man can come into the first rank in Germany and yet be a mediocre person without a shred of personality, if only he takes on the yoke of German method, and is industrious. Men are judged by what they do. No one can hope to advance until he has published his book, or at least some considerable work, and this is the test. And, after all, these mounds of work done are imposing. I have often felt in me the question: what is the use of it? And I believe that, to many of the workers themselves, it is of no spiritual value whatever. They have lost themselves in the wheels of the machine and will never be able to overlook the field of knowledge. But even so, what they do remains. It is a service to humanity.

116 The department store in which he had been working in Chicago. 117 See Letter 144.

And that is the question—is it? My mind has been racing over this again today, because I read, in a review of Gooch's[118] *Germany* in the *Supplement*,[119] a statement that nine-tenths of the writers and philosophers here "are a hindrance to thought and clearness of expression." In spite of the impertinence of such a dismissal of the mass of German scientists I felt a sort of sympathy with it. But I would rather ask this question: is the mere discovery of detailed knowledge— I mean literary and philosophic and historical and so on (not industrial)—a service to mankind in itself?—apart from the mood in which it is discovered, and the form in which it is given to others? Everyone admits that it is not how much a man knows which matters, but how he knows it. And I'm sure we are not as much better off than the people of the 15th and 16th centuries—or than the Greeks, for that matter—as our heads are fuller of knowledge.

And if it is not knowledge, but the other less tangible thing which really matters, the German science comes badly out of it on the whole—though I am told their philosophy is still untouchable—and I feel that English and French criticism and scholarship is superior. Perhaps it is more a question of tradition or taste than I think. The English and French when they write seem to me to overlook, to look from above or outside, and to be simple and wise, but the Germans look from within—unfortunately my phrase is often used as a compliment—and from underneath, and I often don't know what they want or what they mean.

By the way, I breakfasted with the Rabbi the other day, a remarkable man and one of the prominent men amongst the Jews here at present. He spoke with enthusiasm of Newman and prophesied a great future for Catholicism. There is good hope of Marx[120] being elected, which is very good indeed. I confess, apart from my political sympathies, it is hoped that somewhere in Europe there should be a Catholic head of the State. And if Marx can save the German Republic from internal and external enemies, he might do a great deal for Christianity as well. I hope these politics are not too religious for you.

118 George Peabody Gooch (1873-1968), English historian, educated in London and Trinity College, Cambridge, he continued his studies in Berlin and Paris. He was Liberal M.P. for Bath (1906-10), and for Reading (1913). He was joint editor of the *Contemporary Review* from 1911 to 1960; President of the Historical Association (1922-5); and joint editor of the *British Documents on the Origins of the War, 1898-1914* (1926-1938). He made a special study of modern German history, and was the major English authority on the subject. His most important works include *Germany and the French Revolution* (1920), *History of Modern Europe, 1878-1918* (1923); *Franco-German Relations, 1871-1914* (1923); and *Recent Revelations of European Diplomacy* (1927). In 1955 he received the German order *Pour le mérite*. The book in question, *Germany*, was published by Benn in London in 1925. 119 I.e. the *Times Literary Supplement*. 120 See Letter 144. In 1925 Wilhelm Marx (1863-1946) became Prussian Minister-President for a short period. He is now standing for the Presidency of the Reich, following the death of Ebert. Myles' hopes for him were not realised. He was defeated by Hindenburg. He went back into politics in Jan. 1926, becoming Minister for Justice and the Occupied Territories in the second Luther cabinet, and later in the same year succeeded Luther as Chancellor. He remained Chancellor through the reshuffle on the entry of the German National Party representatives into the cabinet, but resigned on 13 June 1928, partly owing to ill health.

157

[Myles to John Dillon] [*Postcard*] Tuesday, [15 April 1925]

Ever so many thanks for your letter and the enclosure. They arrived this morning, delayed by the holidays. I daresay my letter will reach you today too. Your
words of encouragement were welcome, and I am beginning to feel more confident about the lectures. The festivities in connection with the courses commence
tonight and I am to talk on Thursday and on Friday. Many thanks to James
for copying out the poems, but the volume arrived together with his copies, and
I rejoice to have them. I had forgotten the other wonderful things in it. I have
been reading the terrible and delightful poem on the Desmond War to myself
and to others this morning. (I have Yeats' *Reveries*. I got it some time ago from
England.) Is Ossendowski good? I was rather put off by *Beasts, Men and Gods*,
which was one of the sensations here last year.[121] I did not read the book. By the
way, the unpublished parts of Wilde's document,[122] which is not to be published
in England till 1950, have appeared here this Spring—at the request of his relatives—and are talked of a good deal.

There seems to be good news from Ireland at last. Say what you think of
Devlin's[123] success and the Ulster position when you write. Are there any
rumours from the Boundary Commission?[124]

I hope to be in France in the Autumn if all goes well with my exam here, as
I shall have to learn some French before starting at the Sorbonne. Miss Robinson has asked me to spend some time with friends of hers and I may wander a
bit afterwards, but I have no plans. It will be splendid to go with you to Italy
when you come out.

I had a cheerful letter from Gerard [Murphy]* this morning, but he said
hardly anything about himself. Theo has written too. He and his lady[125] made me
a splendid chocolate cake, and he has set me reading Plato, which I find consoling.

121 On Ossendowski see Letter 155. *Beasts, Men and Gods* was published in 1923, and concerned
his travels in Central Asia. 122 Oscar Wilde, *Epistola. In carcere et vinculis*. Berlin: S. Fischer,
1925 was the first complete edition of *De Profundis*, translated into German by M. Meyerbeer.
The first complete and accurate English edition did not come out until 1949. 123 Joseph Devlin
(1871-1934), Nationalist politician from Belfast. Started as a journalist on the *Irish News*, and
showed gifts as a public speaker. Was elected unopposed as Nationalist M.P. for North Kilkenny in
1902, and then won a seat in West Belfast in 1906. Had been offered leadership of the Irish
Parliamentary Party in 1918, on Redmond's death, but declined in favour of John Dillon. Survived
the collapse of the party in 1918, defeating a challenge from de Valera in West Belfast, and then
continued to sit in the Northern Parliament until his death. On this occasion, Joseph Devlin topped
the poll in West Belfast. The new Northern Parliament had 32 Unionists, 4 Independent Unionists,
10 Nationalists, 2 Republicans, 3 Labour members and one Independent, 52 *in toto*. For Devlin the
elections were a great victory since his party increased its strength from 6 to 10 deputies. 124
The elections meant no changes to the Northern government's opposition to participation in the
Boundary Commission. 125 This would be his nurse and future wife, Marie Benninger.

The Spring is in triumph here, and the café verandahs and orchestras and steamers and motor boats on the Rhine are in full swing. Salutations to James. I wish he was nearer, and I might persuade him to type some of my thesis. I have to write it all out, and my fingers will need to be repaired when it is over. I am glad the strike is not as terrible as it might have been.

[PS] Thanks for the paper and *Rosary*. I read "Imaal",[126] but he did not help much. The Bishop of Killaloe remains.[127] However, it is interesting that the article was published. M.

158

[Myles to John Dillon] [*Postcard*] Saturday, [19 April 1925]

The last lecture was yesterday, and they seem to have been really enjoyed. I had a big crowd, perhaps 130, and they were full of interest and friendliness, so that I am in good spirits. I would ask no greater pleasure than to be allowed to speak of one's own enthusiasm to an audience anxious to understand and share the enthusiasm. And that is perhaps a special virtue of a German audience, that they are never indifferent or unreceptive. I found rather to my surprise that I had no difficulty in speaking freely all through, and never needed to look at my script except for references. These days have been full of interest, as there were a number of interesting people about in connection with the lectures, one a Petersburg professor who interested me because he was so clearly indifferent to Bolshevism, or rather anything but indifferent, but absolutely apart from it. He simply did not know how they managed their affairs, or what the exact trouble is between Trotsky and the others,[128] and it reminded me so much of the position of many in Ireland during the last years. But he seems to have had a bad time. I lunched with a Russian lady and a German friend of hers today—she wanted to hear something about Irish music, and I tried to sing her some folksongs, to her great delight. They were both charming and I hope to see more of them. I shall send you the programme of the holiday course here, and a copy of the bibliography I gave the listeners. I will write again.

126 The article in question was entitled "Morality in Irish politics" and was a review of P. S. O'Hegarty's book *The Victory of Sinn Féin*. The author was critical of O'Hegarty's acceptance of violence under certain circumstances, a rather odd position given the verbal violence to be found in other articles in this journal. See Letter 143. 127 Reference unclear. 128 Leon Trotsky (1879–1940) had been Commissar of Foreign Affairs and War from 1917 to 1924 when factional infighting after Lenin's death in January 1924 resulted in Stalin seizing control of the party machine. He denounced Trotsky and removed him from the War Commissariat in January 1925, after Trotsky had attacked the violation of democracy in the party and its failure to develop adequate economic planning. Stalin denounced Trotsky's idea of the "permanent revolution" as a heresy and eventually exiled him from the Soviet Union in 1929.

159

[Myles to John Dillon] [*Postcard*] Bullay, Saturday, [26 April 1925]

We came to Trier on Thursday, a splendid city. I don't remember any other with so much of interest and so little pretension. And yesterday we walked all day through the Mosel country, in vineyards and woods and meadows. It is an ideal life, and as lovely a country as I have ever seen. There is every kind of beauty, on the hills and in the valleys—and the wonderful Mosel everywhere. We came here across the mountain last night and found ourselves on a high ridge in an opening in the forest with the Mosel on both sides, and the little towns with their lights below us. The path to Bullay got lost in the dark, so we got down to Alf and crossed in the ferry. On to Cochem this afternoon and then somewhere else and home on Monday.

160

[John Dillon to Myles] 2 North George's St., Dublin, Thursday, 7 May 1925

I was much interested and rejoiced by your two post cards, received last week and the week before. I gather that the lectures were a great success, but I should very much like to have a more detailed account of how they went off. I suppose you had to speak in the German tongue. It must have been a very trying task to address a number of Germans in their own language. Write the full details.

I was delighted to hear that you had gone to Treves and walked the Moselle Valley. That used to be a dream of mine fifty years ago. I am not surprised that you are full of enthusiasm over it. I suppose you drank an immense quantity and variety of Moselle.

I find I received three post cards, besides your letter written on Holy Thursday. I was much interested by your account of your Russian friends. I see Trotsky is apparently coming back to power.[129] I am hoping that the days of Bolshevism are nearing an end.

Miss Robinson* is certainly extremely kind. It will be most useful and interesting to stay with her friends. I had an extremely cheerful letter from Theo on Monday last. In it he tells me that Dr Rollier's[130] chief assistant made a most careful examination, and after having done so said he advised him to get up immediately and try a little cautious movement. This is very pleasant news, and makes me hope that we may be able to carry out our project of a trip to Italy together in October. Gerard has arrived in Leysin.

I came up here on Monday, after spending all the month of April in Ballaghaderreen fighting the Strikers. The Strike is still in full blast, tho' I have

129 This was a misconception. See Letter 158.   130 See Letter 91.

to say that they have never up to this attempted to picket either our place or Doyle's. The idea has been to concentrate on Gordon and Beirne, to create jealousy and break up the combination of the employers. So far this policy has completely failed, and the four houses are standing loyally together. We are carrying [on] and doing a good business. We have 4 Partridges, James, 8 apprentices, and a non-union paid hand in Drapery, whom we took in on Monday last, and it is astonishing how well we are able to get on. James is working hard, and is invaluable. He presides at the Grocery and Drapery in turn.

Vigorous efforts are now being made to induce the Sligo Transport Workers to refuse to handle our goods. But even should these efforts succeed, we shall be able to carry on quite well, as we can easily get all we want from Dublin and Belfast. I expect to return to Ballagh at the end of May, and then stay on there till October, by which time I hope the Strike may be over.

Have you formed any definite plans for the Vacation yet? When does it commence? Are you thinking of coming to Ireland? And when may we expect you? If you are coming, as I hope you will, I shall insist on your giving Lough Derg a wide berth.

Enclosed you will find your scholarship cheque, which you can sign and send to the Charing Cross Nat. Bank. Also some communications which have come for you, and a cutting on the great question of Irish teaching, which will interest you. I opened a parcel from Blackwell's directed to you, which has been lying here for some time, and found in it two books, with enclosed bill. What do you wish done with the books?

Yesterday I sent your French periodical.

I shall write again in reply to your letter of 9 April. In it I see you express yourself hopeful that Marx would be elected. I am not in the least surprised or disturbed by the election of Hindenberg [*sic*]. Once he was persuaded to stand his election was almost inevitable. He had an enormous advantage in personality over Marx, and I have no doubt that the fact of Marx having been a Catholic cost him a considerable number of votes. I do not believe that the election of Hindenberg will lead to a change in the foreign policy of Germany, or in the long run do any harm to Germany, notwithstanding the outrageous violence of the Paris Press.[131]

161

[John Dillon to Myles] Monday, 11 May 1925

I find I forgot to enclose Blackwell's bill in my last letter. Here it is now.

Enclosed you will also find some cuttings which will interest you, including a letter from S. Gwynn* on the Mount St. Benedict situation from yesterday's *Observer*—rather good. His Reverence is once more in very hot water. [132]

131 John Dillon obviously read French papers as well. 132 Fr John Francis Sweetman,* headmas-

In one of your post cards you asked me to say what I thought of Devlin's victory.[133] I was very much gratified by it, and pleased that he has taken his seat in the Ulster House. His very striking victory in Belfast will, I feel sure, have far-reaching results in the Irish situation. I am sending you by this post a copy of the *Irish News* with a full report of the Dublin banquet.[134] D. made a good speech. I was glad to have an excuse for not attending, as the audience was bound to be too mixed for my taste. However, it went off very well, and was a decided success.

I have been reading over again your letter of 9 April, and am very much interested by what you say about German learning and German Philosophy. I advise you *strongly* to read the three books mentioned in my last letter, Gooch's *Germany*, Wickham Steed, and Brandes' *Recollections of Childhood and Youth*. On the question of German learning and culture compared with that of other countries these books will be extremely interesting to you.

I continue to receive good accounts from James. No fresh developments in the Strike. It will, I expect, go on for another 3 or 4 months, and gradually peter out. No settlement is possible, as we are unanimously determined not to take back ring-leaders into our employment, and for two reasons: one, that our places were grossly over-staffed; and two, that we are convinced that if we re-employed the men who organised the Strike, and the attack on our premises, we would be simply laying the foundations for fresh and worse trouble in the near future, and it would be quite impossible to trust these men to act loyally by the business.

I hope to be able to remain here till the first week in June.

Nano and Smyth dined here yesterday, in excellent form.

[PS] I am expecting a letter.

162

[Myles to John Dillon] 15. v. '25

Your two letters were a great pleasure. The silence had been so long that I often imagined terrible things, but consoled myself in the knowledge that these imaginings are never true. I enclose the first and second announcements of the Ferienkurs,[135] and a copy of the bibliography I gave the audience. It saved me a

ter of Mount St. Benedict's, the Benedictine school in Gorey, Co. Wexford where Myles, James and Brian had all gone, was frequently in hot water with the Bishop of Ferns because of his pronounced Republican views. The Bishop actually had the school closed down in 1925. **133** See Letter 157. **134** On 30 April 1925 a complimentary banquet was held at the Dolphin Hotel in Dublin to celebrate Joseph Devlin's victory in the Northern elections (see Letter 157). In his address Devlin appealed to the Republicans to drop their policy of abstention. **135** "holiday course".

lot of trouble and may be of some use to them later. You will have an idea from it of the ground I tried to cover, but I made the discovery, as soon as the first hour was over, that it would need twice as long to tell my tale, so I had to stick to Yeats, Æ and Synge, and simply praise the others at the end. My job was to speak in English. That—and not any special virtue in me or the Irish Revival—was my raison d'être, but it was much pleasanter. I don't think I should have cared to talk in German. I would have had to read from a paper, and it would have sounded horrible, as foreigners reading a language always do. However, it is well over, and not the least pleasant part of it was a cheque for 150M., which was generous.[136]

But much more terrible things are before me. My dissertation is at last mercifully bound, and ready to be presented, and I still hope to take the oral exam at the end of June. There is a great deal to be prepared between this and then, and as we are now in the glorious heat of summer, it is hard to do much. I spent a great part of today and yesterday taking off clothes, and cooling myself with water, and work has been only a pretence. My mind wanders enviously to the tennis courts (altho' I can't play tennis)[137] and to the Rhine.

The Rhineland millenium festivities are beginning here tomorrow.[138] Some of the greatest conductors and musicians are to come during the celebrations, the greatest in Köln, the less great greats here, but I don't know how much I will have time for. The Köln exhibition, which is to be open for three months, will be a great affair from the historical point of view, but you will hardly be near Köln until later.

What you say of Hindenburg is optimistic. I'm sure it's true that the plan of restoration will fail, but the election was a great disappointment all the same. It's hardly true that Hindenburg's election was inevitable.[139] It was even unexpected. His name was a good deal, but all anti-militarist feeling, all republican feeling, all hope of reconciliation with France—everything moderate—ought to have been against him. I hear the *Kölnische Zeitung*—wh. afterwards strongly supported him—wrote a few days before he agreed to stand that his candidature was unthinkable.[140] As regards military glory, Ludendorf and he are companions, but poor L. did much worse. Marx's Catholicity did him harm, it seems. In Saxony and Wurtenburg—both socialist but protestant—Hindenburg did far better than was expected. Anyway, H. is only a postponement. In a few years they will have to choose again.[141]

136 The exchange rate at this time was 20RM to the £1stg. 137 He learned to play only later, during his years in America, at the University of Wisconsin at Madison, from 1937 to 1946. 138 See Introduction. 139 Hindenburg polled 48.3 per cent of the vote, Marx 45.3 per cent and Ernst Thälmann, the Communist candidate, 6.4 per cent. If the Communist party had decided to withdraw its candidate, Marx would almost certainly have been elected. There was a typically Weimar irony in the fact that it was the Communist candidate Thälmann who brought the ultra-right-wing Hindenburg to power. 140 This is perhaps less surprising if we consider that until three weeks before polling day Hindenburg himself consistently denied in interviews that he would stand as a candidate. 141 Myles

Many thanks for the *Roscommon Herald* and the *News*. I read both with interest. The end of the trial seems to have been most satisfactory.[142]

Please let me know when you write again what has happened to the Mount and to His Reverence.[143] Is the school closed? I know nothing, but I have heard the most extraordinary things. Someone wrote about His Reverence being kicked out of Ireland. Who in the world is kicking him out, and what has Cosgrave got to do with it, and is there no hope of Downside carrying on?[144] Have you heard from His Reverence at all?

The night I came back from the Mosel I heard the first nightingale, and they have sung at night ever since. There is one opposite my window, and she has just begun. We have been having a full moon, and I was down on the Rhine a few nights ago listening to four or five singing together.

It is good that James's bulletins are favourable. I hope that some infusion of grace will bring the thing to an end before long.

As regards plans, I have made none yet, and still have a good many. After the exam, I shall go to Theo, and then probably back here for the end of the term. The great part of the holidays I shall have to spend in France somewhere, learning French. I might go to Bavaria at first—Rotenburg—Nüremburg—München. I even thought of Vienna, but it is a bit remote. If you are coming out in October I might go home for a while before that, and we could come out together. But the plans are easily made if all goes well with the exam. Are you by any chance tempted to come through Bavaria too?

[PS] Love to Maria. I believe she is the person who owes a letter. Many thanks for the cheque and the *Bulletin*.

163

[John Dillon to Myles] Saturday, 13 June 1925

I have been for several days projecting a letter to you, and now on looking at your last letter, which arrived in due course, I find it is dated 15 May.

All my plans were a bit upset by a summons to Ballaghaderreen from James. The Bishop, Dr Morrisroe,[145] had written a very unpleasant letter to Doyle, calling on the employers to go into a conference with the Strikers. I had to go to

---

was wrong here. Hindenburg was re-elected President in 1932. After paving the way to power for Hitler, he died in 1934, making way for the latter as both chancellor and head of state. **142** That is, the trial of the rioters. See Letter 153. **143** That is, to Mount St Benedict and its rumbunctious headmaster, Dom John Francis Sweetman.* **144** That is, Downside Abbey, a Benedictine foundation in Somerset, which was the mother house of Mount St Benedict. Downside did in fact hold on to the Mount, but never reopened the school after it was closed down in 1925. **145** I.e. the Bishop of Achonry, Dr Morrisroe.

Ballaghaderreen on Thursday week to meet my colleagues. We met and found ourselves unanimous and firm in deciding to reject the Bishop's invitation, and sent him a joint communication to that effect. But for this intervention on the part of His Lordship the Strike would have petered out in the course of a few months. Two of our best men have returned to work, and profess themselves thoroughly disgusted with the Strike and the Union, and three other Strikers have found other jobs and departed from Ballaghaderreen. But of course the Bishop's intervention will encourage the Strikers who remain and seriously prolong the struggle. It is very difficult to understand the ecclesiastical mind. His Lordship had all along expressed himself as most hostile to the Strike, and I was informed that he had expressed the hope that we should stand firm and smash the Union.

I returned to Dublin on Monday, but we sent our reply to the Bishop on Sunday last, and up to yesterday no fresh developments had taken place.

About a fortnight ago the pickets were withdrawn from Gordon's and Beirne's, and now ours is the only place picketted. They march up and down all day long in front of our shop door and in front of the hardware, shouting "Strike on here!", very noisy and aggressive, but the customers pay no heed to them, and we are doing nearly as much business as before the Strike started, and find no difficulty in attending well to all customers with about half the previous staff.

James is very active and very effective, and is of course an object of great animosity to the Strikers, who have circulated several scurrilous attacks on him, and indeed on all of us. I should not be surprised now, thanks to the intervention of His Lordship, if the Strike continued another six months.

I was very much gratified and interested by the account of your lectures. I gather they were quite a success. I wonder what proportion of your audience were able to follow you fully in the English tongue.

I was disappointed you did not give me more details of your tramp though the Moselle country. It must have been most delightful. It was an old project of mine 50 years ago, never carried into effect.

I need not say that I shall be eager to have news of your fortunes in the examination. Write me full particulars. We have been getting very cheering news of Theo. You will find him, I hope and expect, wonderfully improved. He is now able to get round again, and I have every hope he will be fit to travel by October. I am very pleased with the plan suggested in your letter. If you can arrange to come home about the middle of September, we might set out together about the 15 Oct.—that is if the Strike has reached a stage which will make it possible for me to leave Ireland. I am arranging to partially close this establishment at the end of this month, leaving Maria in solitary occupation, keeping house for Shawn and Brian, when he returns to Dublin for his examination in September.

I am going to Ballaghaderreen at the end of June, and intend to reside there permanently till after Christmas, except while away with Theo. After Christmas I hope to be in a position to open this house again.

We have been having the most glorious summer weather here since this day week—a cloudless sky, and blazing hot sun. No such weather has visited Ireland for the last three years. On yesterday week there was a deluge, and we were all in despair. The crops were three or four weeks late all over the country, and it seemed as if we were to have no crop in Ireland this year. And as the cattle and sheep have been dying by thousands from ... [*illegible*] rot, the prospect was bleak in the extreme. But this last week has changed all, and everyone is in much better spirits. So far there is no sign of a break in the weather.

The affairs of the Mount are so complicated that I cannot undertake at the end of a long letter to unravel them for you. Brian is down there at present, having gone for Corpus Christi. He will be back on Monday, and I shall ask him to write you a full account. He has been in close touch with Father Sweetman all along. I am very much afraid that the school is doomed. Father S. is fighting hard, but I very much fear not very wisely.

Enclosed is your Dividend Warrant. You can lodge it in the Bank yourself. I was much edified to hear of the cheque for 150 marks, wh. I agree with you was generous, in view of the condition of Germany. Write soon and at length.

164

[Myles to John Dillon] 20. vi. '25

Your letter was a long expected relief. I am very glad that you are surviving the strike, and that it seems to be approaching an end. You say that some have come back, and that the hardware is open as well as the big house. James is the hero of the occasion and is to be admired, for it is rather a horrid position. Please let me know when there is better news.

I do not like writing in this state of suspense, but there will—Deo gratias— be some time yet before my exam., and anyway I have enough of grammars for the moment. I was informed the other day that I may not be called till the middle of July, but it seems impossible to me now that I shall be able to satisfy the philology man[146] even by that time. However, he has promised to be reasonable, and these things always seem impossible just beforehand, so I hope on. One great stage has been passed since I wrote last—I think—in as much as I handed in my thesis before Whitsuntide, and Thurneysen* has had it for some weeks. This leaves me freer for other things.

But I am impatient to have it past. My mind is sometimes full of other things. I have been so long here now that I am half German, without being able

146 Ferdinand Sommer. See Letter 134.

to get any further, and it will probably be better to get back instead, and take all the good I can with me. I have often found myself forgetting my purpose here, through distractions in other directions of learning, but I believe that what Inis Meadhoin and Tourmakeady[147] can give me is more vital than what I can find here in Celtic Studies, tho' I hope I shall be able to make even more of it now. Still, this is a difference between my work and that of a German Celtist. Indeed it would be true for a German too, if he could get to Ireland, because a language and a culture can only be studied satisfactorily in the country itself, and Irish spoken dialects are largely unknown to science—the spoken languages are the centre of interest now—but it is more true for us, because we can get from Irish what they cannot, and what we can get nowhere else. I look forward with joy, when I get home, to spending a year or so in Galway working on the dialect there. It will teach me the language at last, and there is a lot to be discovered, words, syntax, folklore, placenames, phonetics and the delightful life. But that is still well into the future.

Theo and his guardian have written and he seems to be doing well. I expect to be with him early in August and then I shall go to France. I daresay I could go home some time in September and see everyone, and then it would be excellent if we could start together.

By the way, did you ever send O'Casey to Mabel Robinson* and did she answer?[148] I shall be writing to her soon, to know whether I may invade her castle in the holidays. Did I dream that you ordered shelves to be put in my room last Autumn? I hope to be sending home the great part of my books in a month or so, and it would be well to have some place for them. There will be two or three hundred. I hardly dare to read anything apart from my special occupation now, so that I sometimes feel a bit empty. Sanscrit is the one consolation. It is an amazing world and I am resolving to do some special work on it after the exam. At last, this term I am attending sessions with the great old Sanscritist here,[149] who retired some years ago, and only reads more advanced work. And one seems to learn something each minute, and it is always something delightful. The literature itself, and the strange and wonderful forms of the language—if only I could read it better—and above all, the philosophy and religion are so good that it is impossible to have enough of them.

Love to everyone. I haven't been able to develop much pressure up to now, as the date of the exam has been vague, but I shall have to do more for the next few weeks if disaster is to be avoided.

[PS] Please write when you have time. Thanks for the dividend.

---

147 A village in the Irish-speaking area of Co. Mayo, where Myles spent a considerable time improving his spoken Irish. 148 See Letter 141. 149 Prof. Hermann Georg Jacobi (1850-1937) who had retired in 1922.

With many thanks
& best wishes.
m-d

NOMINAL PREDICATES IN IRISH

I

PRESENTED AS A

DISSERTATION

FOR

THE DOCTORATE IN THE PHILOSOPHICAL FACULTY

OF THE

FRIEDRICH-WILHELM UNIVERSITY BONN

BY

MYLES DILLON

$PF10 cl 2$

HALLE (SAALE)
PRINTED BY KARRAS, KRÖBER & NIETSCHMANN
1928

Title page of Myles' doctorial thesis.
This particular copy was presented to Thurneysen by Myles and eventually found its way into the departmental library of the Sprachwissenschaftliches Institut of Bonn University, hence the two stamps at the bottom of the page from two different periods of German history.

165

[Myles to John Dillon] Saturday, 18. vii. '25

Many thanks for your wire, which arrived with extraordinary speed. I thought it fairer to send you the somewhat glorious name for my Prädikat[150] in advance, before unfolding the modest details. It is the second grade of merit, into which I was only just elevated by the oral. My thesis seems to have been lacking in arrangement and in deeper searchings on some points, so that it was placed in the third-cum laude. However, the arrangement at least can be improved before it is published.[151] In the oral Thurneysen declared "sehr gut", and the Sanskrit man[152]—mirabile dictu—"sehr gut", the philology man "gut". The oral in philology was the least pleasant part of it, and it is a pity, as I had done more work for it than for any other. For the first time—as far as I remember—I was rather shattered in nerve before the exam, having worked to the last moment; as it was in German, there was no question of the readiness which is so valuable in an oral. But I even managed to forget things I knew, in the excitement of the moment. It is queer to be more foolish in that respect in one's old age[153] than when I was in Dublin, but a German Doktorprüfung seemed a very terrible thing, and I had never been through that sort of exam before. When it came, I discovered, of course, that I was aiming too high, and stuffing my mind with knowledge, and some of the necessary things got left out.

But it is well over, and I suppose I am at last free to work as I like. I congratulated myself three years ago that I would never have another exam, and there has been another, but this must be the last.

I am trying to catch up now what I have missed of swimming and walking out all the Summer, and in a fortnight I expect to leave for Leysin. I am not sure what will happen after that—I may have to come back here for a while to put my thesis into order—but I hope to be in France in September.

Salutations to James and thanks for his goodwill. I shall write again when I have recovered peace of mind, but perhaps I shall hear from you in the meantime.

[PS] I had forgotten to thank you for various cuttings and a most welcome letter. The speeches of the good bishop[154] and of Flower* I thought extremely good. I should agree—I think—with all the bishop said. It is a pity the Celtic Congress was not a success,[155] but it seems never to have attracted the right people.

---

150 That is, the result of his examination. **151** Publication was, as it is still is, a requisite condition of the award of the doctorate in Germany. The thesis was finally published in 1928, by Karras, Kröber and Nietschmann of Halle (Saale), with the title *Nominal Predicates in Irish.* **152** Probably Prof. W. Kirfel who succeeded Jacobi. See previous letter. **153** He was now 25. **154** Since the cuttings are lost it remains unclear which speech Myles is referring to. **155** The Celtic Congress took place from 30 June to 5 July 1925 in U.C.D. and was attended by over 120 delegates from Scotland, Wales, the Isle of Man, Cornwall, Brittany and Ireland. Among the participants and speakers was Robin Flower, which would explain Myles' reference to his speech.

The review of Æ's* poems was a queer performance. The man had evidently got very little out of them, but he would have done better to say nothing. Unfriendly criticism of Æ is especially perverse because he is so very kind himself. I daresay you saw the review in the Statesman—I think by Bridges[156]—which didn't amount to much, but there was a better one in the *Supplement* of June 25th.

The Galway plan is interesting.[157] I think it ought to be tried, but they would have to take care to placate the Munster people. I think it could be done by giving special attention to Munster dialects and literature in the Galway school— with special chairs. The reasonable Munsterman would not deny that Galway and Connemara behind it are a better field than any in Munster, and in that field even a Munsterman could practise his Irish with advantage. And the Connaught fellows would have a special chance of living their own dialect and studying the other. Whatever mixture there would be would be no harm, as we shall have to develop a *Schriftsprache*[158] out of the dialects some time. Indeed that might be the very way to do it.

But I was forgetting an important problem. I shall be having my books sent home soon. There is a company here who will send them for me, so that they will arrive in Dublin in about three weeks from being sent. A summons would then be sent to me at George's Street to declare contents, and then the books will be delivered at the door. Then, and not till then, they are paid for, and the cost may be seven or eight pounds. Who could undertake to reply to the customs and receive the case of books? I hardly think Maria would be the best person. You expect to be in Bealach for some months from now? I shan't do anything until I hear from you anyway.

153

[Osborn Bergin to Myles] 10 Grosvenor Place, Rathmines, Dublin, 21 July 1925

Lieber Herr Doktor!

Heartiest congratulations! I have told Æ that you can now afford to fall in love. (Was this premature? Anyway, your mind is at ease now.) He asked me

---

156 The review of *Voices of Stones* (London: Macmillan 1925) was actually by Robert Graves and Æ had asked Graves to write it. Graves' review is very flattering and contains interesting comparisons between the Irish and the English poetic genius of the 1920s. 157 This refers to the proposal to make University College, Galway, an Irish-speaking university. The plan was not in fact carried into law until 1929. The suggestion for consoling the men of Munster made here was never acted upon. Dillon's own chosen dialect was that of Connaught. 158 That is, a literary language. It is interesting to have this expression of Dillon's views on the development of the Irish language. He remained interested in this all his life, but objected strongly to the policy of compulsion, which he regarded as a recipe for the destruction of love and practice of the language. It is noteworthy that, when an official written language was ultimately developed, it was based rather on the Munster dialect. See also the "Lehmacher controversy" in Letter 61.

about your dissertation, and I said you had been investigating the problem of the agreement of the subject and the predicate, at which he sighed deeply.

A couple of months ago you sent an interesting card in which you asked, among other things, about Munster accentuation. The standard work on this subject—if it were published—wd. be O'Rahilly's[159] M.A. dissertation. It is a most valuable collection.

By the way, Sommerfelt[160] has sent a paper for *Ériu* on the Cork and Kerry dialects based on the material collected the year before at the School of Irish Learning. He even classifies the diphthongs. There is good stuff in it, but of course he admits that it is tentative. O'Rahilly maintained at the time, and still does so, that a phonetician who knew no Irish working at lists drawn up by us, wd. have given better results. Certainly the Torr lists[161] were not the best fitted to illustrate the dialects studied. And at times it is evident that Sommerfelt heard, not what the men said, but the corresponding Donegal form. e.g. *Táim a' rith* he heard as *tá mé rith*, which no Corkman would say. The diphthongs wd. have taken at least another week, even for a rough classification. However, this is a beginning.

Looking forward to a long talk in September, and hoping that in the meantime you will enjoy yourself in glorious weather—

Yours very sincerely,
Osborn Bergin.

167

[Myles to John Dillon] [*Postcard*] Bonn, Friday, [24 July 1925]

The University of Belfast has published an advertisement for applications in Celtic, and the question arises whether it would be well to apply for it. It would mean sacrificing Paris and having to start work in Belfast in October, which I am little inclined to do. But the opportunities in Celtic Studies are so few that I am in doubt. One plan would be to insist on a year's leave of absence now or after the first year, if they were inclined to give me the job. But I have no idea who else may be on the list, or whether I should be likely to get it.[162]

I had been thinking of seeking employment in the British Museum for a while, after I am finished in Paris, as there is a lot of Irish material there, and I

159 That is, T.F. O'Rahilly (1883–1953), linguist and Gaelic scholar. Some of the material of his M.A. thesis was published in his seminal work *Irish Dialects Past and Present* of 1932. **160** Alf Sommerfelt (1892–1965), distinguished Norwegian Celtic scholar, subsequently a good friend of Dillon's. This paper does not seem to have been published, but an article entitled "Munster Vowels and Consonants" appeared in the *Proceedings of the Royal Irish Academy* 37. C. 1927, pp. 195–244. **161** Published in Alf Sommerfelt, *The Dialect of Torr, Co. Donegal. I. Phonology.* Christiania 1922. **162** He did not pursue this application, on the advice of Osborn Bergin (see Letter 173). In the event, the job went to Michael O'Brien,* whom Myles had met in Berlin.

Facsimile of letter from Douglas Hyde, 6 August 1925.

want to go on with Sanscrit, which I could do well in London and hardly at all in Ireland—the period of spiritual revival in Galway would have to fit in between somehow. But I would be glad to know what you think of the Belfast business. I shall be here till Thursday.

[PS] Did James ever send the things to the sages of Inis Meadhoin? He told me at Christmas that he had some of them ready. I daresay the strike upset things, but maybe he could find time to send them now.

168

[Myles to John Dillon] [*Postcard*] Heidelberg, Tuesday [4 August 1925]

It has been good to be back here for a while. I am going on to Munich tonight for a week, and then to the Lake of Lucerne. Till Monday a letter wd. find me at Munich, 31 Nymphenburgstrasse II, bei Schilling, and after that at Eden Hotel, Brunnen, Schweiz. I expect to be with Theo on the 15th. Have not heard from you for weeks, but perhaps you wrote to Leysin.

169

[Douglas Hyde* to Myles] 1 Earlsfort Place, Dublin, Lughnas 6, '25[163]

A Chara,

Chualas an deagh sgéal od' thriail cheana, is tá mé ag déanamh *míle comhgháirdeachas* leat.

Cuirim chugad ann so sórt teistis, acht tá faitcheas mór orm gur ab Ulltach atá a teastáil ó na hUlltachaibh, is chualaidh mé go raibh Séamus Ó Searcaigh[164] ag cur isteach ar an áit.[165]

163 Dear friend, • I had already heard the good news about your exam.; my heartiest congratulations to you! I am sending you a sort of reference, but I fear very much that the Ulstermen want someone from Ulster, and I have heard that Séamas Ó Searcaigh is applying for the post. • Did you see the book on "Phonetics" which he brought out? He renders the Irish in German characters! But it looks nice nevertheless. • I saw your father and James three days ago in Ballaghaderrin. I never saw him looking better. We are now all in Ratra Park, but I had to go to Dublin yesterday and thus got your letter to me. • Give my regards to Theobald. It is good to see that he is finally improving. • Yours sincerely • An Craoibhín. 164 Séamus Ó Searcaigh (1886–1965), Gaelic scholar. Born in Donegal, he taught Irish in various schools before going to university. He completed his B.A. at Queen's University Belfast in 1914; his M.A. thesis was published under the title *Foghraidheacht Ghaedhilge an Tuaiscirt* in 1923, which is the book Hyde is referring to. In 1932 Ó Searcaigh gained his doctorate from U.C.D. and was appointed Lecturer in Irish the following year. He held this post until 1955. 165 This is in relation to the post of Lecturer in Celtic in Queen's University Belfast.

An bhfaca tú an leabhar thug sé amach ar "Fhoghruigheacht"?[166] Tá sé tar eis a thabhairt amach i litreachaibh Gearmánacha Gaedhilge! Tá sé go deas mar sin féin.

Chonnaic mé t'athair agus Séamus trí lá ó shoin i mBealach a Doirin a' Chrainn. Ní fhacaidh mé riamh é ag féachaint níos fearr. Támuidne go léir ag Ráth Treágh, is b'éigin damh-sa dul go 'Blácliath indé is fuaireas do litir rómham.

Tabhair mo mhíle meas do Thiobóid. Is breágh an rud é go bhfuil feabhas ag teacht ar san deireadh.

Mise do chara
An Craoibhín

170

[John Dillon to Myles] Ballaghaderreen, Co. Mayo, Saturday, 8 August, 1925

From your last letter I gathered that you would arrive in Leysin about the end of last week, so I posted a letter to you directed to Leysin on July 30th.[167] Since then Maria has shown me a letter received from you saying you did not expect to reach Leysin till the 12th August. I shall be anxious to hear from you about your future movements. You say in your letter to Maria that you intend to return to Bonn for a few weeks. Have you abandoned your project of spending a month in France before you return home?

I am still hoping to get away about the 15 October, and calculating on your company. Enclosed is your scholarship cheque. Please acknowledge receipt.

Brian has been here since this day week and Maria arrived on Tuesday last. She has been suffering from a very sore finger, and is to stay here for ten days or a fortnight to recuperate. She is already much improved. No. 2 George's St. is locked up. Shawn is for the present resident in the Presbytery, Harlston [?] Street.

The Strike is still going. But there are signs of disintegration. Tell Theo that I am writing fully to him.

171

[Myles to John Dillon] Monopol Hotel, Simplon. Wednesday, 12. vii. '25

These wanderings have been as delightful as any. I spent a few days in Heidelberg and found various people again, and then a week in Munich. It is an ideal city, I think the most beautiful and pleasantest I have seen, and I have left

166 See note above. 167 This has not survived.

half of it unseen till the next time, as well as the wonderful country around it. I was able to see two of the galleries and a show of modern pictures, and attend the Mozart festival one night, and swim in a wonderful open-air bath, and to walk through the streets rejoicing. On Monday two of us went out to one of the lakes and bathed again and again, so that we missed a last steamer and had to walk for hours to the station—so that we missed the last train to Munich and had to spend the night in an inn.

I left Munich this afternoon and have got thus far. Zurich seems to be a pleasing town, and I was told there were some things worth seeing here, so I tumbled out on the way. Tomorrow I hope to be in Luzern, and on Saturday in Leysin. It is happiness to be in Switzerland again. Whenever I come here I have a feeling of health and freedom and joy more than anywhere else, and the journey is somehow always pleasant, and the first sight of the mountains so exciting.

Theo has announced that a letter from you has come to Leysin, so I am looking forward to it on Saturday. Please write again when you have time. Salutations to James.

172

[John Dillon to Myles] Ballaghaderreen, Co. Mayo, Friday, 28 August, 1925

My dear Myles,

I must apologise to you for not having written before today. This is a most amazingly sleepy place—the days slip over before you know where you are. Every day for the last week I have been determined to write to you, and somehow the day was over and at night I realised I had not written.

Your letter from Zurich arrived on Monday, 17 Aug., and your letter from Leysin on this day week, Friday 21st.[168] Both were read with the greatest possible pleasure. You certainly have had a glorious time during your wanderings, and coming after your long spell of hard work and all the anxiety over your examination, and after your success, it must have been as delightful [an] experience as one could desire.

Your account of Theo gave me the keenest pleasure. It is delightful to hear that he is fairly on his legs again, and able to take long walks. There can now be very little doubt that he will be well able for our proposed tour in Italy in October, wh. I am looking forward to with much pleasure—if I can manage to get away from here.

The Strike is still going on, and the picket marches up and down in front of both our establishments shouting "Strike on here". But its numbers diminish every week. More than half the strikers have left town, and others are going. I

168 Both of these seem to have disappeared.

have great hope that the whole business will be at an end by October. No one takes any notice of the shouting now.

—Since I wrote above a letter from Theo arrived in which he urges the view that I should go out to join him and you at the end of September. I am afraid this will not be possible, as I have very urgent reasons for wishing to be present at the stock-taking here which begins on 6 Oct., and will be finished about the 10th Oct. Moreover, I am hoping to see the Strike definitely at an end before I set forth.

Now about your own future—I strongly advise you to drop the Belfast business, and make up your mind to spend a full year in Paris. I think it would be a great mistake to break in on the continuity of your studies and miss the year in Paris, even if there was a chance of getting leave of absence. I can quite understand and sympathise with the desire to get established in a living, but somehow I feel confident that when you do come home you will be able to get some post wh. will give you a decent living, and it will be far more satisfactory for you to work in Dublin or in some part of Southern Ireland than in Belfast. Pessimist though I am, I feel also that as time goes on Ireland will be getting to be a pleasanter place to live and work in than it has been for the past 10 years, or is at present.

I am afraid it will not be possible for me to start for Italy before the 12 Oct., but even if you have to be in Paris on the 1st Nov., you might join us for ten days or a fortnight. I agree with your view that it is hardly worth your while to come all the way home, as you would have such a very short time to stay. We could meet in Paris. I shall be able to make my way so far alone very comfortably.

Maria went back to Dublin on Monday, quite recovered. She is staying at Clondalkin at present. George's St. will be opened again about the 14 Sept. I have arranged that a cook-general is to be engaged, as it has proved quite impossible for Maria to run the place single-handed.

Have you heard any talk of Count Keyserling's *Travel Diary of a Philosopher*?[169] A very strange book. I am reading it at present. It appears to have created a considerable stir in Germany, but it is not an easy book to understand.

Read enclosed. It will show you that many are suffering this year as you suffered last year. Yesterday I read of a man in Belfast who has been blinded and is in danger of death from the sting of a gnat.

169 Count Hermann Keyserling (1880-1946), German philosopher, born at Könno in Livonia. Studied natural sciences in Russia, Switzerland and Germany, and lived for a time in Paris, where he wrote criticism of art and philosophical essays. During the years 1907-11 he travelled in Europe, and in 1911-12 round the world, where he acquired an appreciation of Oriental philosophy which, blended with his scientific and political studies, contributed to his strongly individual philosophical attitude. *Das Reisetagebuch eines Philosophen*, his principal work, was published in 1919, and had just appeared in English translation.

James and Brian had good sport amongst the grouse on the 12 and 14, but since then they have had no luck. The birds are so wild that they cannot be shot. [...]

[PS] I am sending this to Leysin as Theo says in his letter received today that you are not leaving for Bonn till the 2nd Sept. I do not know what letters after your name you are entitled [to] in respect of your new degree. Let me know.

173

[Myles to John Dillon] Bonn, Schedestrasse 3, Friday, 4. ix. '25

Theo has sent on your letter to Geneva, whither I had wandered on Monday. Dr Bergin had written meantime, sending me a testimonial in case I should apply to Belfast,[170] but he too rather advised against it, so I decided to leave it, and go to Paris.

While in Leysin I heard that various things were happening in Geneva, and a number of Irishmen were there, so I went there for a few days on my way home, and had a very interesting time. There are endless conferences and lectures and discussions going on, some of which I attended, and the council of the League assembled on Wednesday.[171] An Indian professor had been lecturing in one of the halls, and in the course of the discussion which followed he asked me to meet him the next day at the League of Nations library. I went down and had a very pleasant talk with him. He asked eagerly for literature and information about the Irish land settlement, and I ventured to suggest that he should write to you. It appears that the worst miseries of the Indian peasants are due to their having no fixity of rent or tenure, and being at the mercy of their native absentee landlords, and this man—Prof. N. Gangulee[172] of Calcutta—hopes to be on the Indian Council soon, and is anxious to bring about some reform. He introduced me to a lady who, he said, is the mother of Sir Frederick Whyte, the last President of the Indian assembly, and she appears to have known you well, and asked me to come and see her; but I had arranged to leave last night, and could not do it.

---

170 See Letter 164. **171** The League of Nations had been established in 1919, but the Irish Free State had not been in a position to join until 10 September 1923. **172** Nagendra Nath Gangulee (1889-1954), agricultural scientist and author. Educated at the University of Calcutta, the University of Illinois and London. While in England, he travelled widely in Europe, including Ireland, to observe modern agricultural methods. After his return to India, he became Professor of Agriculture and Rural Economics in the University of Calcutta, a post he held for many years. He married a daughter of Rabindranath Tagore. In 1929 he was made a Commander of the Indian Empire.

After the professor left me I was able to view the proceedings of the Council from the garden unmolested, Briand[173] in the middle with Chamberlain[174] beside him, and the official translator droning out his version of the Turkish speech on the Mosul question.[175] I confess that, having been there, and heard something of the League's work, I feel that cynicism is rather futile. They have failed often enough—where under the circumstances one must expect them to fail at this early stage—but wonderful things have been done. The American Chairman of the Greek Refugees Commission[176] lectured last night, and claimed the successful treatment of that event as the most remarkable performance in migration and in finance in history, and from what he said it seemed to be a fair claim.

By the way, I met MacWhite,[177] the Irish representative, one afternoon and he is a very interesting fellow, and impressed me very much. He has served in the British civil service and the French Foreign Legion, travelled all over Europe and married a Danish artist, and he is a most reasonable man with few illusions, and still fairly optimistic. He seems to be quite equal to the situation, if only the Free State government would pay any attention.

I left Geneva at a quarter to one this morning and got here at five in the afternoon, rather feeling as if I had fallen down a hole, for Geneva was the centre of things yesterday, and now I am well out towards the circumference.

I will be very glad to join you in Paris, tho' it is perhaps a pity that it must be so late. But I suppose the stocktaking had to be seen to. I had intended seeing Theo up the mountain again, as he will be better off with someone at

---

173 Aristide Briand (1862-1932), prominent French Socialist politician, was at this time Foreign Minister in the government of Paul Painlevé. He and Chamberlain were soon, on 16 October, to be instrumental in the passage of the Locarno Treaty, which seemed to settle the peace of Europe, and this greatly enhanced his reputation. In November, on the resignation of Painlevé, Briand became Prime Minister, but his government only lasted till the following March, when he returned to being Foreign Minister. **174** Austen Chamberlain (1863-1937), prominent Conservative politician, was at this time Foreign Minister in the government of Stanley Baldwin. He was a staunch supporter of the League, and assiduously attended its meetings. **175** This concerned the boundary between Turkey and Iraq, which was a British mandated territory. No agreement had been come to at the Conference of Lausanne in 1923, further negotiations also failed, and the question was put to the Council of the League in Aug. 1924, which appointed a commission. The Council were at this moment considering their report. In December they came to a decision (which Turkey refused to accept) that Mosul should go to Iraq, subject to a continuance of the British mandate for 25 years. **176** This was indeed a success of the League. About 1,500,000 Greek refugees from Turkey, more than a fifth of the existing population of Greece, were transported back to Greece, with the aid of a £10 million loan, which helped to settle them in productive employment. **177** Michael MacWhite, a Corkman, was one of the first recruits to the Irish diplomatic service. He had served in the French Foreign Legion during World War I. In 1919, after his return to Ireland, he was sent on diplomatic missions on Sinn Féin's behalf to France, to negotiate Ireland's inclusion in a European peace settlement. As early as 1922 MacWhite had opened an Irish Bureau in Geneva and he became the Free State's first permanent diplomat at the League of Nations. He was later posted to Washington and to the Vatican and remained in the diplomatic service until 1949.

hand. But if I have to leave you in Italy, someone could come down to Aigle to meet you if necessary. Have you planned anything about the way you will go? There's not much point in going into the cities, as Theo could not walk about museums and galleries to any extent. Perhaps the pleasantest thing would be to spend most of the time in one place—on the Lago Maggiore or the Lago di Garda—and we could make expeditions from there, and perhaps see Venice, which can largely be done in gondolas, I imagine.

I left Theo in excellent form, and expecting Aunt Anna on Wednesday and Ralph Barry* about the same time. My love to all and good wishes for your birthday.[178]

174

[Myles to Theo Dillon] Saturday, 19.ix.'25

Dear Theo,

Both your letters are here and call for an answer, but I am not yet sure whether I am going to answer them this time. I have been in good humour this afternoon. It was fine and even warm after the dreary autumn days and I resolved solemnly to go for a walk, feeling as if it had been the first time for months. But I was alone, which made it more important. And the point is that the walk has been delightful.

What is wrong with walks in Bonn is that you always go up the Rhine or into the forest, both of which are pleasant but made a little fearsome by the absolute alternative. And I went into the forest today and took a new path, and came out again into the open on the mountain, with heather and bracken around me, and cows mooing down below and wandering about in the fields, which they hardly ever do here, and I followed one of the Landstraßen along the hill and finally lay down in the heather and ate chocolate and smoked a cigarette, and a rabbit came and sat in front of me for a moment, and I got up long afterwards and walked through the bushes into a valley where the fields were full of boys and men and women and dogs, and I found another Landstraße and followed it into the village of Ippendorf, and walked through the village till I got to the chapel, and I went in and the priest was not yet in the box but there were people waiting, and I came out again and marched out of Ippendorf and down the hill back to Bonn.—

Sunday. The papal choir sang here last night, the same splendid maestro whom we saw in Dublin and the same wonderful choir, and I came back so excited and full of joy that I did not attempt to write any more.

I have been reading Gilson[179] and am telling people about it. I don't know any books for years, perhaps since the "Dark Night", which I have enjoyed so much.

178 4 September. **179** Étienne Gilson (1884-1978), French Christian philosopher and historian of

I would like to lie in a field and consult with you or with Gerard about bits of it, the extraordinary Scotus and St. Anselm with his to me invaluable—non intelligo ut credam, sed credo ut intelligam, which is the answer to the desperate questions of modern philosophy so far as I know them, and the reason why the Age of Enlightenment has been the first real dark age,—and then as a relief from syllogisms St. Bernard, and perhaps better the Augustinian of St. Victor who said such marvellous things about learning and knowledge, though he thought mysticism greater still. Weren't we saying at Leysin that science is killing itself by specialisation, and valuing knowledge merely for itself, and in the specialisation always searching for problems to discuss till the object itself is forgotten (I heard last week that the first volume of a history of the history of literature has appeared)?—and this man says—I must repeat what I know you have read—that the trivium and quadrivium are so-called because they are *as paths* leading the soul to wisdom, and the ancients possessed them so perfectly and were so wise that they have written more than we can read, but our scholastics do not know how to learn, and that is why we have so many students, and so few wise men; and then he says the one other thing which requires to be said, that these seven are inseparable, and that one is always wrong in thinking to attain to true wisdom by devoting oneself to one of them and neglecting the others.

I had been looking for that for a long time, and it makes me sure of myself as regards the modern spirit of method and research. I was hoping that Croce had said it in that book of Gerard's, but we read the thing and it remained unsaid. But as my enthusiasm was subsiding I came to Abelard which made things wilder and wilder, so I shall say no more. The Arabs and Jews have sobered me somewhat.

But I am going to try to answer your letters. First, the three questions: 1 it was the modern heathen, agnostic, pantheist, and so on whom I had in mind, 2 and I meant a standard of absolute good, 3 and I felt that the heathen was absolutely better than the Christian, apart, as you say, from the sin against the light. The last point is the point, and does involve the reflection that the Christian is absolutely right at least formally, and the heathen wrong which is a danger for me. But I don't think it affects the subjective position. The issue [*something missing here*] he wills it. Surely a man who will steal as much as he can get for a venial sin would steal more if only he could get a better bargain—if the "mortal" level were put up. He has the letter without the spirit, and is keeping his eye on the rules. But the man who simply regards stealing as out of the question will not steal at all. If neither steal, the man who is honest because it is God's will and sees the whole universe as created to do His will, and out of

medieval thought. Educated at the Sorbonne where he gained his doctorate in 1913. He was appointed Professor of History at the University of Strasbourg in 1919, moving to the Sorbonne in 1921. From 1932-1951 he was Professor of History of Medieval Philosophy at the Collège de France and from 1951-1968 Professor in Toronto.

that spirit regards stealing as unthinkable, is far better off than the heathen, but if he only sees the rules and spends his time trying to get round them I believe he is absolutely worse off. There remains one large item on the credit side, that, when all comes to all, he will avoid the mortal, and I suppose, if he does, he will in fact have to abandon the bargaining, or your threat of ultimate disaster would come in. Isn't there a great difference between knowing one's weaknesses and hoping they will be judged lightly, and deliberately doing something, and intending to go on doing it, on the ground that it is not a mortal? In one case you will the good, and in the other you seem to will the evil.

Love to Anna, thanks for her card.—And to S. M. and Gerard and Mary. I suppose the Choresians have gone. Else give them my salutations too

With love
Myles.

175

[John Dillon to Myles] Ballaghaderreen, Co. Mayo, Monday, 21 September, 1925

Your letter from Geneva came in due course. It was extremely interesting, and it ought to have been acknowledged and answered long ago, but the delay was due partly to the fact that I went up to Dublin on Wednesday last to vote in the Senate election[180]—not from any patriotic motive, or indeed that I took the smallest interest in the result of this absurd performance, but because poor Paddy Hooper[181] was a candidate with an off chance of success, and I felt bound to do anything in my power to help him. So I travelled all the way to Dublin, and voted for Hooper, Hyde[182] and a few others, and secured Morris' [?] vote for Hooper also.

Maria is quite well again and is comfortably established in George's Street with a cook-general of her own selection to aid her. Nano and her son Nicholas were in George's St. to see me, both in splendid form. A new member of the Smyth family is expected to arrive within the next few days.

Now about my arrangements. Theo wrote suggesting that we should meet in Italy, but I do not like the idea of travelling alone so far, and shall expect you to meet me in Paris. I am writing to Theo that we can stay in Montreux, and you could go on from Montreux and fetch him back there, when we could go on

---

180 All citizens over the age of thirty were eligible to vote for the Free State Seanad. 181 Patrick J. Hooper, a staunch supporter of the Irish Parliamentary Party, and former editor of the *Freeman's Journal*, He was not successful on this occasion, but was elected to fill a vacancy in March 1927, and held his seat in the subsequent general election, until his death in Sept. 1931. In May 1931 he was elected Vice-Chairman of the Senate, defeating a Cumann nanGaedheal candidate. He embarked on a biography of John Dillon, which survives in manuscript. 182 Douglas Hyde had been elected to the Senate to fill a vacancy on 4 February 1925, but he was not re-elected on this occasion.

together to Italy. He is nervous about facing the road alone, and I entirely sympathise with him in that feeling. He ought not to run any risks. He may possibly be able to ... [*illegible*] of someone going to Montreux or as far as Aigle, or to make an arrangement with one of the attendants in La Valerette to travel with him, when he could join us in Montreux. I am writing to him fully on this matter. I heartily agree with what you say about our programme in Italy. My plan was to settle down on Lake Maggiore or Lake Garda, visit Venice if we felt disposed, and if the weather were reasonably fine, and the winter should set in early, take refuge in the Italian Riviera, south of Genoa, which I have heard described as an extremely charming and delightful region.

I have succeeded in moving the date of stock-taking a week earlier. It will begin on this day week, and I expect to be free to go to Dublin on Saturday week, the 3rd Oct. I want to spend two days in Dublin. On Wednesday I go to London and on Saturday 10 Oct. I expect to cross to Paris, where I hope to meet you. I should like to take a day's rest in Paris; then on to Montreux on Monday 12th. It seems to me that you might like to come to Paris a few days before I was due to arrive, and carry out some investigations preliminary to settling down there. It would be a great advantage, I should say, to have your quarters secured and to make the acquaintance of your Professor before you started for Italy. You will have to select an Hotel in Paris, as our stay will be a very brief one. I am rather inclined to go to the Continental, the big Hotel at the Place de la Concorde, end of the Rue de Rivoli. One is sure to be comfortable there. The situation is ideal, and altho' rather expensive it is not, I fancy, so extortionate as some of the newer Hotels. You could establish yourself there, and secure a room for me for Saturday and Sunday. I shall of course pay your bill.

Now to come to your letter. I was keenly interested by your account of your experiences in Geneva. I am not at all surprised at the extent to which you were impressed by the proceedings and by the atmosphere of Geneva. It is a very wonderful and most interesting development in the history of the world, and indirectly, and in the long run, it may do some good. But I confess I remain utterly sceptical and unconvinced as to the capacity of the League of Nations to control Europe at present, or to prevent wars, and to me it appears the very climax of hypocrisy and humbug to see the League of Nations in solemn session considering how to procure peace and prevent war, while one of the most iniquitous and cowardly [?] wars that has ever been waged is raging in Morocco.[183] Two of the leading members of the League, having combined forces and put in all the most diabolical machinery of modern war to crush a few gallant tribes

183 This refers to the "Riff War", the campaign being waged jointly by France and Spain against the nationalist leader Abd el Krim, who had inflicted many defeats on them. He was finally suppressed the following May. This is a remarkable example of Dillon's continued informed concern with world affairs.

who have maintained their independence for over a thousand years, bombing villages, killing and wounding women and children, and, if one can believe the newspapers, refusing repeated applications to send doctors, nurses and medicines—an act of savagery unparalleled in modern times—and not a single voice is raised at Geneva. I thought the Irish very foolish in choosing to have the Treaty registered ... [*illegible*] by the League, but as they have gone in, I think Mr MacWhite would be well occupied in making a claim that the case of the Riffs should be examined by the League.

I was much interested by your account of your meeting with the Indian Professor. Mrs Whyte is a great friend of mine. Her husband, the Rev. Alexander Whyte,[184] was the leading Presbyterian clergyman in Edinboro' in 1888, when I visited Edinboro.[185] He entertained me in his home, and came on the platform at my meeting, to the great indignation of a very large part of his very fashionable congregation.

By the way, Theo has suggested that we should stop first at a place called Baveno, on Lake Maggiore, recommended him by a friend in Leysin. I shall leave the choice to him.

The Strike here goes on still. Today the pickets are very noisy and aggressive, but they have very little influence on the business. Business is extremely bad, but that is due to the general poverty of the country, not to the pickets.

I am sending you two Irish papers, wh. will give you some idea of the state of affairs here. Poor Hyde has had a nasty blow, to get so few 1st prefs. He will be horribly mortified.[186] It is a most significant sign of the extent of the revolt against compulsory Irish, and he no doubt lost a great many votes by the attack made on him by the Catholic Truth Society on account of his vote for [the] Douglas divorce motion in the Senate.[187] Anyway, the Senate election was a mon-

---

184 Alexander Whyte (1836-1921) was educated at King's College Aberdeen and graduated in 1862. He entered the Free Church of Scotland and became minister of St. George's Free Church in Edinborough in 1866. In 1881 he married Jane Elizabeth Barbour whom John Dillon also knew well. Whyte was appointed principal of New College, Edinburgh in 1909; he retired in 1918. He was the author of numerous biblical studies. 185 This visit, not recorded in Lyons' biography of John Dillon (1968), took place in the midst of the Plan of Campaign, and was doubtless for the purpose of raising funds. 186 While the poll topper Thomas Toal polled 14,181 first preferences, Douglas Hyde received only 1731. He came 54th out of a total of 76 candidates, which was the second worst result of all outgoing Senators, a disastrous result indeed (*II*, 21 September 1925). It has to be borne in mind that the turn-out was exceptionally low, especially in the West. The *Irish Independent* reported on a constituency in Clare, from where the ballot box was brought to Ennis at a cost of £10, only to discover that it was empty. Nobody had bothered to vote. In Tuam, Co. Galway, 15 out of 400 registered voters went to the poll (*II*, 19 September 1925). 187 Senator James G. Douglas, a prominent member of the Protestant minority (actually a Quaker), who was Vice-Chairman of the Senate, introduced a motion in response to an order from the government seeking to bring to an end the facility for Private Bills of Divorce being introduced in the Senate. His concern was simply to maintain the essence of the status quo, but, owing in part to an intem-

strous farce. I am afraid poor P. Hooper has very little chance, but it is impossible to forecast the result till there have been 15 or 20 counts. It will take weeks.

Write soon and give me a full account of your plans. It might be well to communicate with Miss Robinson* and ask her whether she can give you any hints as to getting room. I believe it is extremely difficult to get tolerably comfortable quarters in Paris at present.

176

[Myles to John Dillon] 24. ix. '25

It was the restoration of peace, and the renewal of purpose, and the filling of the gap to get your letter this morning. I had been trying without success to give up expecting one. The papers were very welcome too, though I am shut out from the mysteries at present. It appears that Hyde has already been elected to the Senate, and been misbehaving on it, and is now in the field again, which is perplexing.[188] And you say the elections are an absurd performance, which makes things worse. The list looks a bit long and confusing. I should have thought it better to attempt some division into constituencies. Was it an unnecessary flourish as well? Mannix[189] and Fr O'F.[190] are at large again, but I suppose they are not much listened to. But of these things I shall hope to hear something when I see you. Do you follow the strange duel between Æ and Mary MacSwiney?[191] Æ does get the better of it, but I wonder that he crosses pens with her at all.

It is very good that you have been able to take stock a bit earlier. What you have arranged will suit me very well. I had planned to go to Paris in the first week of October and await you there. I had an idea that the Continental was somewhere near the Opera and not where you say, but that doesn't much matter. If I am more than a few days ahead of you I may go first to Foyot's opposite the Luxembourg, which is good and cheap, as I hear, and near my future field of activity, but I shall move over to the other place before you

perate speech by Senator W.B. Yeats, the issue became extremely fraught, and the atmosphere poisonous. This was certainly not helped by the efforts of the Catholic Truth Society to discredit Yeats, Hyde, Douglas and other Senators. **188** Hyde had been elected to the Senate, to fill a vacancy, the previous February. His "misbehaviour" had consisted in supporting Sen. Douglas' very reasonable motion on divorce. See previous letter (175). **189** Daniel Mannix (1864-1963), Archbishop of Melbourne. Before going out to Australia in 1911, he had been Professor of Theology in Maynooth, and from 1903 President of the College. He was a strong supporter of Irish independence. **190** Fr Michael O'Flanagan. See Letter 152. **191** Mary MacSwiney had written a letter to the *Irish Statesman* which was published on 19 September 1925. She argued that the results in the by-elections only proved how effective the scare tactics of the clergy against the Republican candidates had been. Æ replied that such statements sounded rather hollow coming from a party which refused to abide by elections and tried to force the majority to submit to them. He also insinuated that Mary MacSwiney had actively encouraged Irishmen to kill their compatriots.

appear unless Foyot's is all that can be desired. Kathleen writes that Baveno is an ideal place, and has various further suggestions as she has been over the ground, but you will hear them if you see her in London. They are promising themselves some days of you, but please do not be persuaded to stay longer than Saturday the 10th, as then time will not be as long as it is.

Robert[192] is to arrive here on Monday and intends to occupy my room and work at the university. I shall be here for the first week and shall probably move on to Paris on Saturday or Monday. Mabel Robinson* is there and has a lodging for me in view, which is very kind. I hope to be able to find a roof and dump my possessions somewhere during the days I am there.

After I came back I wrote to Mrs Whyte, without knowing who she was, and got this very kind answer.[193] I am hoping to find her again in London when I have a chance. It is true that the poor Peace Conference is feeble at present, and one is amazed at the accepted silence about Morocco. But on the other hand there was—as a matter of fact while I was at the window—the open discussion of the Mosul business, and the extraordinary work for the Greeks too, which does mark the change. The treatment of the Riffs is horrible. A Quaker woman stated at a Congress in this part of the world the other day that they were unable to go to the help of the Riffs as the import of their stuff is forbidden. It is sensational, perhaps, to be discovering great secrets in such things, but if one tries to be objective, doesn't it look as if it means a great conflict between Islam and European culture, and that the English feel that? Professor Gangulee prophesied that the Indians were bound to get rapidly increasing measures of freedom now, mainly for the reason that the English must try to cool the temper of the Mahomedans in India, so as to cut them off from the rest of Islam, which was the big danger. I see that Garvin is on this line,[194] and with the war in mind, and Spengler,[195] and the state of Christianity at present, and the apparent collapse of democracy which was, I suppose, thought to be the golden future of Europe, one begins to wonder. But I expect a reproof for lightmindedness, as the Germans say.

Which reminds me of Keyserling.[196] I heard him speak last year in Heidelberg, and was rather impressed, though some things seemed wild. He developed the thesis that Germany in 1914 simply stood for a creed which was in conflict with the whole trend of world feeling at the time, and that her whole conduct for 50 years had been calculated to produce that result. That pleased me well, but he went on to explain that it was an obvious case of subconscious

192 His cousin, Robert Mathew (1906-54), son of Theobald, and younger brother of Toby. He subsequently became a solicitor, and died comparatively young. **193** This has not survived. **194** J.L. Garvin. See Letter 99. **195** Oswald Spengler (1880-1936), German philosopher and prophet of doom for Western civilisation. His chief work *Der Untergang des Abendlandes* was completed in 1914, but not published till 1918 (2nd revised ed. 1922). The English translation, *The Decline of the West*, was first published in 1926-28. **196** See Letter 172.

deliberate suicide, if that is not a hopeless mixture. He maintains that living beings commit suicide or, perhaps better, drive themselves to suicide almost unconsciously, but so that the blame is on themselves, and this was what Germany had done. That was not so clear to me, but his conclusion was that salvation lay in trying to get back into harmony with the world spirit, and not in singing "Deutschland über Alles", and that seemed sound. His book was read a lot here, but I have not read it.

I have just read a delightful little book on mediaeval philosophy by a Frenchman whose lectures I hope to hear next winter,[197] and I have got some essays of Croce[198] now, but they have disappointed me a bit. All the same, he is more pleasing than the professors who philosophise, from what little I know of them.[199]

I rejoice that we may expect another niece or nephew. I hope it will be nephew. Nano and Paddy seem to flourish in the distressful country. Theo says they have a new car and a large new house. The strike is longlived. I had an idea that most of the malcontents had scattered. But if the pickets consist of persons who have no prospect of getting back on any terms, they might walk up and down for years.[200]

It is splendid that I shall see you in a fortnight. I often want to say something or ask something, but as I cannot shout loud enough to reach you and the problems don't always turn up when I am writing, some of them remain floating about.

I would be very grateful if you would bring out Thurneysen's book *Die irische Helden- und Königsage* with you, if you remember it. It is much too expensive to buy again. I brought it back to its place in the big bookcase in the backdrawingroom when I was home last Autumn.

Give my love to James, and a special tribute of devotion and admiration on his birthday.[201] I should write to him, but perhaps he will read this and forgive me. Salutations to Sarah and Felix and Bob and the rest.

[PS] I intend to confer with a carrier tomorrow about my books and shall have them sent to Brian at George's Street. I hope he will be well enough disposed to sign whatever is to be signed and make the statement of contents "books", and pay the enormous bill, but I shall appeal to him someday soon.

---

197 Probably Étienne Gilson, see Letter 174. **198** Benedetto Croce (1866-1952), Italian philosopher. His Philosophy of the Spirit was enjoying wide influence at the time. In 1920-1, he had briefly been Minister of Education in the Giolitti cabinet. **199** Croce had enrolled in the University of Rome in 1886, but dropped out shortly afterwards, and returned to his native Naples. **200** The strike finally faded out during the month of October. It plainly caused Myles a good deal of pain and embarrassment, though he is too tactful to dwell on this. It may, however, have been a factor in discouraging him from returning home during the summer. **201** 26 September.

APPENDICES

LONG SILENCE BROKEN

Mr Dillon's Views on Present Situation

We have been requested by Mr John Dillon to publish the following letter, which appeared in the "Melbourne Argus" on April 2nd. It was written by Mr Dillon in response to a cablegram announcing the dissolution of the United Irish League of Australia in December last:

M.P. Jageurs, Esq.,
President United Irish League of Australia.
2 North Great George's Street, Dublin, December 27, 1922

My dear Mr Jageurs,—It was, of course impossible for me to hear of the dissolution of the old League without a certain feeling of sorrow, or without the awakening of many memories. It called up in my mind a vivid recollection of the vast services which had been rendered to the Irish cause as represented by the Parnellite movement during nearly forty years, and of my own visit to Australia and the happy months I spent there in 1889, when, under the auspices of the old League, I travelled through South Australia, Victoria, New South Wales, and Queensland, and met everywhere hosts of very kind friends. And, looking back on those years I am irresistibly tempted to contrast the results of that movement, in which the Australian League co-operated with the Parnellite Party in Ireland, with the results of the policy which has dominated Irish public life for the past four years.

In 1879, when the Land League was founded, and the Parnellite Party was formed, we found Ireland in rags, famine stricken, disarmed, coerced, and quite at the mercy of her masters. After 39 years of patient labour, every stage of which was marked by some substantial gain for the people, we left in 1918, when control passed from the hands of the old party, an Ireland in possession of all the reforms mentioned in the programme of the Land League, and many others not mentioned in that programme, with a settlement of the National demand on the Statute Book, which, had it been allowed to stand, would undoubtedly have united Ireland, and which was unquestionably in all essential particulars a much better settlement than that acquired under the Treaty signed on December 6, 1921. All this had been achieved with a minimum of sacrifice and suffering to the people. In fact, I do not believe that there is another case recorded in history in which so great an emancipation has been wrought for a people, in face of great and powerful interests and desperate difficulties, at so slight a sacrifice of blood and wealth.

In 1918 after 39 years' control of the old party, Ireland was, with the possible exception of Holland and Sweden, the most prosperous nation of Europe, having been raised to that status from an age-long condition of famine. She had in her hand a settlement of the National question substantially better than the Home Rule Bill of 1886, which had been received with gratitude and enthusiasm by the Irish race throughout the world, a settlement which I shall always be prepared to maintain was a much better settlement than that which at such fearful cost had been effected under the Treaty of December, 1921. And during those 39 years of successful struggle we had succeeded in securing for Ireland the sympathy and friendship of nearly every civilised nation throughout the world, an invaluable asset which has now to a large extent been lost.

Contrast that record with the record of the last four years, since, in December, 1918, the control of the Irish movement passed into the hands of the leaders of Sinn Fein. In four years more than twice as much money has been spent on the conduct of the movement as was spent by the old party during 39 years. Many hundreds of valuable lives have been lost, civil wars have continuously devastated and demoralised the country, and between direct destruction of property and consequential destruction of trade and industry the loss inflicted on the country cannot, I think, be estimated at less than 150 millions sterling, a sum in proportion to the resources of the Free State equivalent to a loss of six thousand millions to Great Britain. I say nothing of the wide-spread demoralisation, the inevitable result of civil war, though in my judgement the demoralisation caused in Ireland by the events of the last four years is a more grievous injury to Ireland than even the huge material loss.

And what has been the result of all this colossal sacrifice? A settlement less satisfactory than that which has already been won by peaceful means, and without any of these terrible sacrifices, the signing of a solemn treaty with Great Britain which recognises the permanent partition of Ireland, and sets up an Orange Parliament for North-East Ulster, which has, I fear, saddled this country with an impossible financial burden; which has started a new civil war in Ireland, led to the most ferocious and sanguinary split among the Nationalists of Southern Ireland that has occurred for many generations; has alienated the sympathies of foreign nations, and given to all the critics and enemies of Ireland an unparalleled opportunity of piling insult and contumely on her; and, finally, has dug wider and deeper than ever since 1641 the gulf between the South and the Protestants of North-East Ulster—a gulf which, during 39 years of patient effort, we had nearly succeeded in obliterating. A poor result it seems to me for all the bloodshed and ruin of the last four years.

Personally nothing would have induced me to sign the Treaty of December 6, 1921, or to accept any share of responsibility for the policy which led up to it. And the members of the Old League in Australia, who, under the most difficult circumstances, remained faithful to the Parnellite policy, have, I think, good reason to feel grateful that they also are free of responsibility for all that has happened in Ireland during the last four years. Since the election of 1918 I have taken no part in Irish politics. I never admitted and I do not admit, that the result of that election was a free decision of the Irish people. Nevertheless, having seen in the course of my public life so much of the horrors of Irish faction, I decided that the best course was to accept the verdict of the election in spite of the methods by which the verdict had been secured, and to place no obstacle in the path of the party that had won. I have adhered to that decision, and have remained silent for four years, leaving, so far as I was concerned, the country absolutely in the hands of the Sinn Fein leaders. And neither by word or act have I done anything to embarrass them or increase their difficulties. I cannot pretend that I think they have made good use of their opportunities.

But, you may ask me, what of the future? I have no responsibility for the present situation, and I do not know whether I shall ever again take any part in the public life of Ireland. But I give you my opinion for what it is worth. The Treaty has been signed on behalf of Ireland by men who were, at the time, recognised without protest as the representatives and plenipotentiaries of the Irish race. And there can be no doubt that the majority of the Nationalists of Ireland approved their action in signing the Treaty under the circumstances obtaining in December, 1921. Much, therefore, as I dislike the Treaty, I am of opinion that the only hope for Ireland, in face of all that has occurred during the last four years, is to accept the Treaty, work it loyally, and extract from it whatever good it contains. As for the present Government I cannot say that I am favourably impressed by the results of their rule up to date, or that I approve of all their methods. But it must be recognised that they are faced by terrible difficulties. They have been compelled to set up their Government in the midst of fierce civil war. Their Republican opponents are brave and fanatically devoted to their ideals, and in fighting them the members of the Government are desperately handi-capped by their own past. The finances of the country are in confusion; a deficit of twelve million on this year's Budget, without taking into account the payments contracted by the Treaty, for Ireland's share of the war debt—and every prospect of a larger deficit next year; trade nearly ruined by the civil wars; the country sinking into poverty as a result of the losses inflicted on it during the last four years; the credit of the country is utterly ruined, the whole machinery of law and police smashed and thrown away, leaving to the Government the task of creating a new system in the midst of a civil war. No Government surely was ever up against more terrible difficulties. Sometimes I think that they are insuperable. But so far as I am concerned, I think that the Government should get a fair show and I shall certainly be no party to any attempt to weaken them or increase their difficulties. You will say that this is rather a disheartening estimate of the present situation in Ireland and that I am a pessimist. That is true; I am not, and never was, a believer in the Treaty settlement, and I am not san-guine as to the outcome of the present situation. But time is a great healer, and doubtless time will mend the ills of unhappy Ireland. And when that healing comes I am convinced that Irishmen will look back on the four years from December, 1918 to December, 1922 as one of the darkest and most unhappy periods of all her tragic history.

Yours sincerely,
John Dillon

[*Freeman's Journal*, 12 May 1923]

B. MYLES DILLON'S ARTICLES IN THE 'IRISH STATESMAN'

LIFE IN GERMANY

Returning to Germany from Ireland one has the same feeling, only much more deeply, as when entering a hospital or a prison. I came last year to Prussian Berlin, but as a stranger one's first impressions there were of the strangeness of life and dress and manners, and of the difficulty of the language, rather than of the misery of the people. I have come back to Bonn in the Rhineland, before the war I should think one of the happiest and handsomest countries in Europe, but now under a shadow of despair.

The chief cause of the despair is want of food, with no prospect of relief. Of my own acquaintance here I know hardly anyone who is getting enough to eat, excepting foreigners. The professors and people in a similar position can afford meat, as a rule, only once a week. They can never have milk or butter or eggs, and I should think rarely any white bread. Owing to scarcity I never have any milk myself, except occasionally through the kindness of a friend, and I am practically alone amongst those I know in the enjoyment of butter. With the condi-tions of the workers I am less familiar, but such luxuries must be quite out of the question for them. There are fewer here than in the industrial world of the Ruhr, but from Essen and Düsseldorf one hears of tuberculosis and rickets amongst children, and general hunger and despair.

I spoke about our recent adventures in Ireland to one of the University people here the other day, and he said: "We would have war here, too, if it were not that the people are educated."And this is perhaps near the truth. It makes a queer impression to find lectures being delivered on art and music and literature, on the interpretation of the Septuagint, and on the religion of the Indogermanic people, as besides the more ordinary subjects, while neither the lecturer nor his hearers have had enough to eat, nor can afford a suit of clothes.

The Germans are being starved, but, as our hunger-strikers have now proved, it is a slow process; and when one considers how much Germany suffered during the war, their endurance is amazing. An American lady in Berlin told me that during two months of the year 1917 there was no food of any kind to be had there but turnips and black bread. One of the professors here was so exhausted from want of food when he returned from the war that he did not recognise even the names of the books he had studied before going out, and had practically to begin again. After the peace followed a period of recovery for two years, and people began to get fat and feel happy, and then came this second war against starvation and humiliation. In the houses of the hungry live French families, the wives and children and nurses of the officers, who are well fed at the expense of the people, and since the Ruhr deadlock hundreds have been driven out of their homes either as a punishment for sedition or merely to make room for the conquerors. In these cases four hours notice is given, and nothing may be brought away from the house except personal luggage. For five years the French and Moroccan soldiers have been in the Rhineland, and as the French do not admit that the period of occupation has yet commenced, they intend to remain at least fifteen years longer.

The suffering here is such as Ireland in modern times has not known, and one feels that in such conditions the Irish would not remain passive. But there are two reasons why the Germans will endure as long as their sanity endures, apart from the main reason that resistance is hopeless. The first is that they are more civilised than we are. Culture is a very large element in German life, and in Ireland rather a small one. In Bonn there is the University atmosphere, and there are museums and libraries and book shops. There is a school of music, and very good concerts are given in the Beethovenhalle all through the term. If one has little food, there are other forms of consolation available, and there is a reason for not letting loose the rage of the French.

The second reason is similar, from the material point of view. The Germans have too much to lose. The Rhineland is crowded with what once was prosperous towns and wealthy cities only a few miles apart. Cologne and Bonn, within half an hour of each other are both University cities; Cologne larger than Dublin and full of interest and charm, and Bonn, its summer residence, built almost in a garden; and on south to Coblenz and Mainz and Wiesbaden, the signs of wealth are everywhere. The destruction of beautiful houses and the beautiful things they contain, which was so readily undertaken in Ireland recently would be too big a sacrifice in this country.

Another contrast, pleasant to an Irishman, is the lack of interest in politics amongst Germans. They seem to know little and care less about political questions, and being accustomed to efficient government political freedom has no magic for them. A professor speaking of the English liberal watchword, "Good government is no substitute for self-government," said: "That doctrine would be impossible for us."

How many of the people manage to live is a problem, I have given up trying to solve. It has been announced in the local papers that more than half the population of Bonn are receiving support from public funds. A friend who is a clerk in the post office told me that his week's wages in one unlucky week amounted to about three shillings, and he has a wife and child; but this is, of course, not normal. For the moment things have improved on account of the rapid rise in the mark, which caused a fall in prices, but it has been followed by a reduction of salaries and pensions to what is regarded as a starvation level. One match box costs more than a thousand million marks an egg, two hundred and twenty thousand millions, a pound of margarine (the standard by which rents and wages are often reckoned now) still seven hundred and fifty thousand millions, and these are considerable prices now as a patient arithmetician will discover.

What hope is there of improvement? How long can the Germans hold out? No one can give an opinion. I can only borrow the phrase of Nevinson, writing in the *Manchester Guardian*, who sees the only prospect of relief in the "unsure hope that the majority of any nation will not remain crazy for ever."

O.I.

[*Irish Statesman*, 5 January 1924]

CHANGING GERMANY

To the Editor of the *Irish Statesman*

Dear Sir,—When I wrote in the *Irish Statesman* six weeks ago, a change was coming; it has since developed and maintained itself. A policy of strict economy is being energetically pursued by the Government in all its departments. The printing presses appear to have ceased work, and the floods of Notgeld, which every town and district had been allowed to issue, are gradually disappearing.

From the post office in Bonn alone thirty-six men have been dismissed, and the windows are no longer cleaned, but my friend gets each month a hundred and twenty-five billions of marks which retain their value (over £7), and on this he can live, though I believe prices here are mostly far above world prices.

The worst evil is gone now that the exchange has become steady. What made things impossible before, but particularly in November, was that shop-keepers dared not accept for goods what would have been a fair price on the day they sold them. They had to replace their stock, and could not always get rid of the paper money at once, so the reckoning was—what may the price be in two or three days time? And it is obvious that this gave free play to rogues. But since the stabilisation confidence is gradually returning, and views with satisfaction the fall of the franc at the moment when the Renten mark is the highest valuta in Europe.

Dr Schacht, the president of the Renten bank, seems to be mainly responsible for the change.—Yours faithfully,

O.I.

Bonn, 4th February, 1924

[*Irish Statesman*, 16 February 1924]

LIFE IN GERMANY (II)

Coming to Germany from Ireland for the first time, one finds much that is difficult to understand—dogmatism, sentimentality, a sort of broadness, which remains unsympathetic even when it has become familiar. But more interesting is the philosophic mood which is, I think, peculiar to Germans. These differences are probably nowhere more to be felt than in the student life here as compared with our own.

During my first days in Berlin I went by chance to a lecture on Gerhardt Hauptmann, the literary hero of the new republic. I had never heard of him before and was surprised to find a large hall crowded to the doors when I came in. In the hope of finding my ground I asked my neighbour in halting German when Hauptmann died, and retreated in confusion on being told that he was still living. But what impressed me was the attitude of the students, who received the professor with applause as he came, and applauded frequently during the lecture, and again at the end. I went every week afterwards, and the enthusiasm was always the same.

This was not exceptional, but characteristic of the German students' attitude towards the university and the professors. For him the university is a sort of Hall of Wisdom, and the professors are the prophets. He is free to go from one university to another to hear the great men, and is free to hear them or not as he likes, which is a much more reasonable arrangement than our compulsory attendance. He is a serious person and has acquired a Weltanschauung, and is, I think, incapable of laughing at himself. A man said to me apologetically the other day that he enjoyed music, but was unable to talk about it. The naiveté which is common here would perish under the cynicism of Dublin, and in this I think Germans might borrow a little from Ireland with advantage, but their real enthusiasm for science carries them far.

The fencing and beer-drinking Verbindungs studenten lead a separate life. For them their particular Verbindung is their university. *Esprit de corps* is their fundamental, to some of us an unwholesome principle. Courage, manliness, patriotism are the rather appalling articles which they commonly recommend as their creed. Indeed, they might be quite other than they are. They are sometimes picturesque, and preserve a tradition, but at present they are at best objects of interest, and are regarded with scorn by the intellectuals.

In a country where life is so varied and culture so general as it is in Germany, the universities play a large part, and are themselves at a great advantage. It is interesting in these hard times to see the figures of the four faculties in Bonn for this semester. Out of a total 3,126 students, Theology has 431; Law, 476; Medicine, 506; Philosophy, 1,713. The last include over 600 agricultural students, and for the rest, one sees the largest crowds at lectures on literature and on the history of art. Many of the literary people, I imagine, intend to become teachers and librarians and so on. One wonders what becomes of all the art historians. They have at any rate pleasantly avoided the dilemma which faces nearly all of us in Dublin—whether to become a lawyer or a doctor. How many in Ireland of each profession have tried both in their time?

In the good days that are coming when the idea of a university enlivens the dreariness of University College, Dublin, we shall have an interesting choice of examples between this system and the very different English system, where men learn in conversation with each other, and the professors are in disfavour; and perhaps we shall borrow from each of them.

Lest anyone should say it, let me at once protest that borrowing of this kind will not endanger Gaelic culture. A varied, interested university life would be a most powerful medium for promoting it.

O.I.

Bonn.

[*Irish Statesman*, 15 March 1924]

LIFE IN GERMANY (III)

The Prussian Ministry of Instruction has issued a memorandum on the new reform of secondary education (*Die Neuordnung des preussischen höheren Schulwesens*: Berlin, Weidmannsche Buchhandlung. 1mk.), which is an interesting illustration of the past and present attitude towards education in Prussia. Secondary schools in Germany are of four kinds: the

Gymnasium, which is specially devoted to the classics, and where Greek is an essential part of the programme; the Realgymnasium, which is a modern language school, and here Greek gives way to an additional modern language; the Oberrealschule, where mathematics and natural science are the main interest; and the Deutsche Oberschule, about which I know very little. I do not remember having met anyone who had been there. These have represented up to the present different aspects of knowledge, but all were supposed to endow their pupils with an Allgemeinbildung, and the leaving examination from any one of them qualifies a man to study at a university.

The present reform is important in three of its clauses, which, however, it is claimed are a direct development of the reforms of 1893 and 1901, and of the tendencies which have shown themselves since then. The three main points are the improvement of the ladder of education by bringing the secondary school more into line with the primary school; secondly, the definite abandonment of the idea of an Allgemeinbildung in each school; thirdly, wider freedom to schools in drawing up their programmes, and to teachers and pupils in carrying them out.

The former idea was that each of the four types of school should plan a general education, from its own standpoint, but covering the whole field of knowledge. This was the highest end of secondary education. But "with the defeat of Hegel's philosophy the appearance of new realistic tendencies, the variation of cultured interests, the specialisation of the sciences, the great widening of the horizon of knowledge, and the changed political and economic condition of Germany," the new scheme recognises the impossibility of this general education. " The leading spirits of Germany have recognised that a unified comprehension of the entire content of culture is no longer possible and, therefore, an education the same in content for all individuals is forbidden by our present condition." Accordingly it is planned to build up in the four types of school as one whole a programme of general education (Allgemeinbildung), but each must supply only a part of the whole.

There is a great deal of self-reproach. The schools are accused of having too varied, and at the same time too stereotyped a programme, and of being too much controlled. The effect is to produce men who have learnt *multa non multum*, and who have little they can call their own, and Goethe is called to witness that those who stray from their own way are often worth more than those who remain in a way which is strange to them. An interesting recognition is given to the now widely-spread Youth Movement, as showing that the spirit of modern youth insists on being free.

The principle is abandoned on which the sovereign state "with clear purpose educated in the pupils its own instruments, had for its chief object the qualities of an official, and compelled from the school what it required from its officials." It gives one rather a shiver to hear that such a principle had existed.

The memorandum goes on to outline the changes in view: less definite programmes, less examination, and a reduction of the hours of class-work. This reform accepts the saying of Kant: "That does not ripen to freedom, which is not sown in freedom." One sentence recalls the Irish report of three years ago: "The (official) programmes will be indications and suggestions for the school programmes, from which the particular school will decide for itself its department of work, its choice of material, and its own peculiarity."

The "cultural" subjects of education: German, history, philosophy, religion, art and music, are separately treated. (The Socialist attempt of last year to secularise the schools has evidently been abandoned.) In all four types of school these subjects have a special importance, as being the medium of culture, and they are to be taught so that in their history and interpretation they express the spirit and cultural development of Germany. Here there is much of interest, but I have written too much already. I wonder whether the declared purpose of making the whole content of education as German as possible is not a faulty view, but since Irish education has erred in the opposite direction all its life there is no reason to stress this.

I mentioned before the philosophic tendency, without saying much about it, and so much has been said already that it was perhaps the safest plan, but the temptation is very strong.

Richard Jeffries, in *The Story of My Heart* prophesies that in a thousand years whole new regions of knowledge will be familiar to men, and Renan says: "What would we not give to be able to glance furtively at a book for primary schools a hundred years from now?" When these revelations come, one feels that they must come first in Germany. Is it not true that in England and in Ireland the inclination is rather to enjoy and meditate on what is known? In Germany there is a constant search for more. Every department of knowledge is being searched, every appearance is tested and explained, and one unsuccessful theory evokes corrections and new theories in an unending sequence. Most discussions of literature or politics turn to psychology before long.

In such an atmosphere the question often suggests itself, whether all of this is genuine thought, and whether it leads anywhere. To ask such a question about the immense work of the recognised masters of science would be pointless except from someone wiser or as wise as they, and as regards manners of criticism in literature or politics one comes to realise that the national or rather racial mood is philosophic; but I am thinking of a particular fashion which is often puzzling. An obvious subject for this ceaseless analysis and enquiry in Germany is the life of the spirit, and the meaning of life itself, and in many book shops these are the books which I seem to see all around me. I must at once confess that I have as yet read none of them. They are books in which such words as "inner life," "conflicts in the soul," "efforts towards a new life-freedom" frequently occur, and they are of various grades in form and price. In the last few days I have noticed two series specially devoted to them, *die Engelhorn-Bücher* and *die Blauen Bücher*. This afternoon I went in search of them to collect some of the titles, and fragments of the challenging summaries which appear on each cover, but the shop had not got them, so you are spared; and the man told me that the chief attraction of the *Engelhorn* series are translations of books by an American named Martin, which slightly weakens my case. But do these broodings really bring people much further? I have heard them attributed to an inclination towards Indian thought here at present. Such a manner of thinking in the West would flourish most, at any rate, where institutional religion is weak.

Perhaps this is all part of one tendency. With the development of psychology and psycho-analysis, one can imagine a literature of the future which will tell only of adventures in the minds and souls of the characters. Marcel Proust and Joyce are a beginning, and the life of pure thought in *Methuselah* will be the realisation. But Pelmanism of the soul, which seems to be the method of die *Blauen Bücher*, is rather a disquieting plan.

It is somewhat confusing, when writing about German life, to find oneself noting only the things one wants to criticise, but I hope that this is not meanness of spirit, but rather because we learn in Ireland to be shy of enthusiasm. If I had to choose another country than Ireland to be born in, I think I would choose Germany. It is rather a world than a nation, and you feel that you need not go abroad in search of anything. Art, music, science, and beautiful cities and hills and woods are here. Two things which I should like to praise are the universities and the theatres, but I have not the courage to commence.

O.I.

Berlin.

[*Irish Statesman*, 10 May 1924]

LIFE IN GERMANY (IV)

The quality of life which strikes one particularly in Germany might be expressed as intensity. The way from Bonn to Heidelberg is through a country of vineyards and fruit farms along the Rhine. From Mainz you can come by Frankfurt, one of the wealthy cities, but charming, and with memories of Goethe and of the old emperors who were crowned there till the eighteenth century; or you can go up the Rhine through a number of large towns to Ludwigshafen, and across the bridge to Mannheim, which was till 1918 one of the residence cities of Baden, and has, I am told an intellectual society all its own. And when you arrive, Heidelberg is a new charm.

It is summer here now, and people live in the streets and cafés, and in and on the Neckar. The warmer it is the less one wears, and in this there is the pleasantest freedom of choice. Here are three Naturmenschen coming up the Hauptstrasse, who have taken to the road in linen jackets and short trousers, with canvas slippers, and rucksacks on their backs, and going towards them is a portly gentleman with cut-away coat and silk hat, but even he has yielded, and carries his hat in his hand.

Everything is possible in Germany. You can be a millionaire, and build a bathroom of marble with a vaulted ceiling, and marble stairs into the bath, like one I saw in a house in Köln, or you can wander through the woods, clad almost like primitive man, and sleep in Jugendherbergen. (These are huts built for the Wandervögel wherever the country attracts wanderers.) And the youth movement itself, though it is only one feature of German life, reflects in its way the life of the whole country. Anyone may be a wanderer, from the Communists to the Hitler group. If you meet such a man on one of the Wanderwege—he will be unmistakably dressed, and will be carrying a rucksack—he may belong to one of the Catholic organisations, of which there are two or three, or he may be a pagan Hellenist. Hellenismus is, I imagine, one of the strongest creeds in Germany at present, and, if one only knew it, is perhaps due to Winckelmann, and Goethe and others who were influenced by him.

This is the individualism of Germany, which is often deplored by those who long for a second Bismarck to bring unity. A wise man said to me that whereas in England the aim in society is to be like other men, to be normal; in Germany it is the reverse. A man feels that he must be peculiar or die. Of the wanderers he said: "One could understand a reaction against social formality, against religion, or against marriage, but a reaction against becoming anything at all.... Some of these fellows wander about the whole time."

This quality of intensity explains the ceaseless research in Germany, too, and it is apparent in conversation about literature. There is Gerhardt Hauptmann, rather arid and satirical, and Sudermann, and the merry Schnitzler from Vienna, and another Austrian named Unruh, a pacifist, who I am told denounces women for bearing children to kill each other. Büchner is grotesque and improper (the theatre was nearly empty, before the last act of his Woyzeck in Bonn the other day), and Wedekind is supposed to be influenced by him. And there is Thomas Mann, who used to write very pleasant rococo short stories, but now he is fifty and has a family, and seems to have settled down. There are lyricists, Rilke, Stefan George, and Hofmannsthal, who makes German a beautiful language. But I may not write of literature as I am only repeating gossip. Problems perhaps more tedious occupy me at present. But these men occupy a place in the life I am living here, which was a vacuum in Dublin University life. Not for want of poets and writers, perhaps, but of people who read them.

Schopenhauer taught that the escape from human misery was through asceticism to the subjection of all desire, but he lived according to a different plan, and was capable of saying that there was no more need for a saint to be a philosopher than for a philosopher to be a saint. Here I discover a quality in Irish men as opposed to Germans which I did not expect. I think I may generalise a little and say that Germans rejoice in philosophising, but can quite contentedly live outside their theories. An Irishman lives more according to his belief. It is an unhappy moment to praise this quality. If an Irishman believes that he is an Irish Republic, he establishes himself, and assumes the duties and privileges of his State. But it is the quality of heroism, and if we had a similar devotion to philosophy, something great might happen.

Schopenhauer said, "the world is my idea." What does Saint Thomas say? Is the world an idea in the Divine Mind which is reality for us? If Germany were Catholic or Ireland philosophic, there would be a splendid intellectual life.

O.I.
Heidelberg.

[*Irish Statesman*, 31 May 1924]

Æ see RUSSELL, GEORGE WILLIAM

BARRY, RALPH BRERETON, (1899-1943), barrister-at-law. School friend of Myles Dillon, and subsequently best man at his wedding in 1937. Youngest son of Judge Brereton Barry. Educated at Mount St. Benedict and Oratory School, subsequently attending Sandhurst and Trinity College Dublin, where he graduated in Law in 1922. Called to Bar Michaelmas 1922, having won the Brooke Scholarship at the King's Inns. Went on to a distinguished career at the Bar, becoming a Senior Counsel and Bencher of the King's Inns in 1935. Rather quixotically contested the post-Treaty General Election in 1922 for Co. Wexford as an Independent, but was not elected. Tried again in Wicklow in 1943, in the Fine Gael interest, but was once again unsuccessful. Died of typhoid fever on 2 December 1943, while on circuit in Letterkenny. He was unmarried.

BERGIN, OSBORN J. (1873-1950), distinguished Irish Celtic scholar, first Professor of Early and Mediaeval Irish at U.C.D., from 1909 to 1940, and Dillon's chief mentor. He had himself gained his doctorate under Thurneysen, in Freiburg, in 1906. It was Bergin who, following on the initiative of Kuno Meyer, established the scientific study of Old Irish in Ireland on a sound basis, from his vantage-point in U.C.D. training, besides Dillon, such distinguished scholars as Gerard Murphy, Daniel Binchy and Michael O'Brien. In 1940, Bergin became the first director of the School of Celtic Studies in the Dublin Institute of Advanced Studies (a position that Dillon himself later held), but he resigned within a year, over policy differences, and thenceforth devoted himself to research. He contributed many learned articles to *Ériu* and *Studies*. His paper on "Bardic Poetry" *(Journal of the Ivernian Society,* 1913) opened up new aspects of Irish literary history. His *Stories from Keating* (1909) became a standard textbook, and he edited Keating's *Three Shafts of Death* (1931), other mediaeval texts, and many previously unpublished poems. He became general editor of the Royal Irish Academy's *Dictionary of the Irish Language,* and he had an immense and accurate knowledge of Irish at its various stages of growth and neglect.

BOYLAN, MGR PATRICK A. (1887-1974). Ordained a priest of the Dublin diocese in 1903. Studied Egyptology and Semitic Languages in Berlin and returned to Berlin at regular intervals until the 1920s. Professor of Scripture in St. Patrick's College, Maynooth, from 1905 to 1922, when he became Vice-President of the College. His *Thoth, the Hermes of Egypt* (Oxford Univ. Press) appeared in 1922. Seconded as Parish Priest of Dun Laoghaire in 1934, but served also on the Governing Board of the School of Celtic Studies of the Dublin Institute for Advanced Studies from its inception in 1940 to his death in November 1974, Dillon being his colleague on the board from Sept. 1949 to his death in June 1972.

COFFEY, DENIS JOSEPH (1864-1945). Born in Tralee, Co. Kerry and educated by the Christian Brothers and at the Dominican school of Holycross, Tralee. In 1883 he went to the Catholic University of Ireland in Dublin to study medicine and eventually obtained a scholarship to go to Louvain, Madrid and Leipzig. Professor of Physiology in the Royal University, 1893-1905; Dean of the Medical School, 1905-8. After the foundation of the

National University in 1908, he became the first President of University College Dublin in 1909, and continued in that position until 1940. He was an old friend of John Dillon's, and to some extent owed him his position as president. Later, in 1930, he persuaded Myles Dillon to leave Trinity College for U.C.D. on the understanding that he would be a strong candidate for the chair of Modern Irish, which became vacant in 1932, but in the event Dillon's stance of opposition to the policy of compulsion ensured that the position was not offered to him. One of Coffey's sons was the poet Brian Coffey (1905-1995).

COMERFORD, MÁIRE (1893-1982), republican activist, and journalist. Born in Wicklow, her father, a wealthy mill-owner, was a friend and supporter of Parnell. Sent to school in London, she reacted by becoming strongly nationalist, and, following on 1916, joined Cumann na mBan, taking part in its anti-Conscription campaign. She was active in the War of Independence, and took the anti-Treaty side after 1921, being a member of the Four Courts garrison in June 1922. She escaped arrest then, and went on the run, but was arrested while plotting to assassinate W.T. Cosgrave, and lodged in Mountjoy, where she went on hunger-strike in Nov. 1922, and was finally released from jail on a stretcher. Later, she refused to join Fianna Fáil, remaining loyal to Sinn Féin, but in 1932 found employment on *The Irish Press*, and remained on the staff for the next thirty years. Strangely, she remained all her life a friend of both Myles and James Dillon.

COX, ARTHUR (1891-1965), distinguished lawyer and confidant of statesmen. Son of the physician Sir Michael Cox, an old friend of John Dillon, and the Dillon family doctor. After an illustrious career in U.C.D., became apprenticed in 1915 to the solicitor F.J. Scallan, and founded his own firm in 1920, which Myles briefly joined as an apprentice, before realising that this was not for him. Was closely involved with the leaders of Cumann na nGael, Cosgrave, O'Higgins, and John A. Costello, and gave them much useful advice on legislation. Later married the widow of Kevin O'Higgins. After his wife's death, became a Jesuit, and went out to work on the missions in Rhodesia.

CURRAN, CONSTANTINE PETER (1883-1972), civil servant and litterateur. Had been a class-mate of James Joyce at university, and remained a friend of his. He joined the Four Courts staff, attached to the Accountant-General's Office, and later became Registrar of the Supreme Court. He was also one of the driving forces behind the Georgian Society of Ireland and contributed numerous articles on art history and literature to *Studies*. His book *Dublin Decorative Plasterwork of the Seventeenth and Eighteenth Centuries* appeared in 1967.

DELARGY, SEAMUS (Séamus Ó Duilearga) (1899-1980), Celtic scholar and folklorist. Born in Cushendall, Co. Antrim. Studied Celtic in U.C.D. under Douglas Hyde and Eoin MacNeill, graduating with B.A. in 1921, and gaining his M.A. degree in 1923. A college contemporary and lifelong friend of Myles Dillon, he joined the Department of Celtic in U.C.D, in 1924 as assistant to Hyde. In 1926 he helped to found the Folklore of Ireland Society, and became editor of its journal, *Béaloideas*, of which he remained editor until 1973. On the setting up of the Irish Folklore Institute in 1930, he became its first director, and in 1934 he was appointed to a lectureship in Irish Folklore at U.C.D., which became a professorship in 1946. When the Folklore Commission was established in 1935, he became director of that. His best known work is *Leabhar Sheáin Í Chonaill*, an edition of the stories of a Co. Kerry storyteller, a classic in Irish folklore studies. In 1937 he visited Berlin and gave lectures on Folklore Studies in Ireland .

DIBELIUS, WILHELM (1876-1931), Professor of English Philology at Bonn from 1918 to 1925 and one of the most eminent English scholars in Germany at the time. He studied in Berlin, spending a period in Cambridge in 1895. In 1903, after his 2nd doctoral exam., he became Professor of English at the Royal Academy in Posen (Poznán, Poland). In 1911 he visited Scotland. From 1911 to 1918 Dibelius was Professor at the Colonial Institute in Hamburg, but during World War I he was attached to the *Kriegspresseamt* (War Press Office) where he had particular responsibility for Ireland. He moved to the University of Bonn in 1918 after his appointment to the chair of English. From 1919 onwards, Dibelius started to organize *"englische Abende"* to introduce the Bonn public to English culture at a time when such ventures would have been politically highly sensitive. His special interest after the war was the English novel, but contrary to mainstream English Studies in Germany, he placed the literary work firmly in its social and political context. His main work *England*, 2 vols. (Stuttgart 1923-25) was widely read in Germany, and, as we can see in the letters, in Britain as well. Dibelius moved back to Berlin in 1925 where he died in 1931.

DILLON, ANNE ELIZABETH (Nano) (1897-1986), John Dillon's only daughter to whom he felt particularly attached in the last years of his life. In 1923 she married Patrick J. Smyth (q.v.), a rising Dublin surgeon. After his death she went to live in Washington, D.C., with her son Nicholas and daughter Roma.

DILLON, BRIAN (Fr Matthew) (1905-1979). Educated like three other Dillon boys at Mount St. Benedict and at U.C.D. Showed great academic promise by becoming a Brooke scholar. Qualified as a barrister and served at the Irish Bar for two years. Studied in Rome at Beda College to become a priest. He was ordained in 1933 and entered the Benedictine Order at Glenstal Abbey in 1934. Headmaster of Glenstal School 1937-1948 and 1953-1961. Went to Dublin in 1948 to set up Balnagowan House, a student residence along Glenstal lines; he ran the house between 1948 and 1953 and again from 1961 to his retirement in 1966. Died on 25 October 1979.

DILLON, HENRY (Fr Nicholas) (1856-1939), younger brother of John Dillon. After being called to the Bar in 1883, entered the Franciscan Order, of which he served as Minister-Provincial, 1912-1918. He published a small number of religious books, one of which, *Four Rainbows and Four Questions*, is mentioned in the correspondence.

DILLON, JAMES MATHEW (1902-1986). Educated at Mount St. Benedict, U.C.D. and the King's Inns. After spending a period at London and Chicago studying modern business methods, he took over the family business in Ballaghaderreen. He was elected to the Dáil as an Independent T.D. for Donegal in 1932, but changed his constituency to Monaghan in 1938. Founded the National Centre Party which coalesced with Cumann na nGael to eventually form Fine Gael. During World War II he resigned from the party because he advocated Irish participation on the Allied side. After the war he became Minister for Agriculture in two governments (1948-1951 and 1953-1956), first as an Independent and later as a member of Fine Gael, after he had rejoined the party. He was leader of Fine Gael from 1959 to 1965. He was an imposing orator and had a reputation for eccentricity.

DILLON, JOHN (1851-1927), Irish nationalist politician and son of John Blake Dillon. Educated at University School, Harcourt St., Dublin and at the Catholic University of Ireland, where he studied Arts until 1870. After a spell as an apprentice in Manchester he re-entered the medical school of the Catholic University and graduated with a licentiate from the

College of Surgeons. Went into politics and was elected Nationalist M.P. for Tipperary in 1879 and in 1885 for East Mayo. Involved in agrarian struggles in Ireland and arrested several times. After the Parnell split, he became leader of the anti-Parnellites in 1896, though always advocating the unity of the party. Retired from the chairmanship, allowing Redmond to be elected leader of the united party in 1900. While Redmond limited himself to parliamentary leadership, Dillon more or less controlled the party in Ireland, and together with Joseph Devlin and T.P. O'Connor (q.v.) remained one of the most influential Irish politicians until 1918. The Universities Bill of 1908 largely adopted Dillon's proposal of linking the Queen's Colleges to University College Dublin, but his opposition to making Irish a compulsory matriculation subject was overruled. He shared Redmond's position of support for the Allied cause at the outbreak of World War I, but did not participate actively in the recruiting campaigns. On Redmond's death in 1918, Dillon was unanimously elected Chairman of the Party. Joined de Valera in the struggle against conscription, but in the ensuing elections the Party was wiped out and Dillon lost his seat in East Mayo to de Valera. Withdrew from public life after that.

DILLON, MYLES (1900-1972). Educated at Belvedere College and Mount St. Benedict in Gorey, Co. Wexford, a school run by the unconventional educator Dom John Francis Sweetman (q.v.) before studying Irish at U.C.D. mainly under Osborn Bergin (q.v.) and Douglas Hyde (q.v.). He obtained a travelling scholarship from U.C.D. enabling him to undertake the sojourn on the Continent which is documented here. After his return to Ireland from Paris he lectured in Sanskrit first at T.C.D. (1928-1930) and then at U.C.D. (1930-1937), during which time he competed unsuccessfully for the chair in Modern Irish in 1932. It is generally presumed that his opposition to the government policy of the compulsory teaching of Irish, amply documented in these letters, made him virtually unappointable to this highly prestigious and influential academic position. He also shared his father's view that Home Rule would have been a better political solution for Ireland than what emerged after 1922, a view which was not particularly popular either. He finally took up the offer of the chair of Irish at the University of Wisconsin, where he taught until 1946. After a spell at the University of Chicago and the University of Edinburgh, he returned to Ireland in 1949 and became Senior Professor at the School of Celtic Studies at the Dublin Institute of Advanced Studies. He held this position until his death.

DILLON, JOHN MATHEW (SHAWN) (1896-1970). Educated at Downside, Somerset. Attended Clonliffe College where he was ordained priest in 1923. He never rose very high in the hierarchy, mainly due to a certain degree of laziness and eccentricity. He ultimately became Parish Priest of Chapelizod, where he ended his days.

DILLON, THEOBALD WOLFE TONE (1898-1946). Attended Belvedere College, before he was sent to Mount St. Benedict in 1908. In 1915 he won a scholarship in classics and mathematics to go to U.C.D., where he graduated with first place in 1921. The following year he won a travelling scholarship in Pathology, but was unable to take it up due to suspected tuberculosis. Instead, he had to be lodged first in a sanatorium at Berck-Plage in Normandy, before moving to Leysin in Switzerland, where he was to spend almost four years. At Leysin, he was first a patient and later an assistant to Dr Rollier, the pioneer in heliotherapy. He also met his future wife Marie Benninger there whom he married in 1926. In 1928/29 he studied medicine in Vienna before returning to Ireland. He first became a research scholar in the U.C.D. medical research laboratory, then an assistant, before being appointed Professor of Pharmacology and Therapeutics in 1932. During the 1930s he became involved in refugee issues and was a member of the Irish Catholic Council for Refugees. He published numerous articles of a medical as well as a philosophical nature.

DUCLAUX, AGNES MARY FRANCIS (1856-1944). Born Agnes Mary Francis Robinson in Leamington, England, she was a respected poet and literary critic in her own right, publishing no less than five collections of poems, and a friend of Browning and Walter Pater, Sargent and George Moore. In 1885, she moved to Paris, where once again she became a member of literary circles, befriending such distinguished figures as Ernest Renan (whose life she later wrote), Taine, Gaston Paris and Bourget. In 1888 she married the distinguished orientalist and philosopher James Darmesteter (1849-1894), author of a definitive translation of, and commentary on, the *Zend Avesta*. Darmesteter, sadly, died rather young, in 1894, and after an interval, in 1902, Mary Robinson married Émile Duclaux, a noted biologist, favoured pupil of Pasteur, and his successor as head of the Pasteur Institute. Tragically, this marriage only lasted two years, as Duclaux died in 1904, and she spent her last forty years as a widow. However, at the time Myles Dillon knew her, she and her sister enjoyed active social lives, and gave most interesting parties, so they constituted an ideal introduction to Parisian society. She also kept up her writing, both in English and French, into old age, her best known books, after her early poetry, being *The Life of Ernest Renan* (1897), *The End of the Middle Ages* (1888), *Vie d'Émile Duclaux* (1907), *Madame de Sévigné* (1914), *Twentieth Century French Writers* (1919), *La Pensée de Robert Browning* (1922), and *A Portrait of Pascal* (1926). A friend of hers, and later a friend of Myles Dillon's, the author Daniel Halévy, wrote a charming memoir of her after her death, *Les Trois Mary*.

EDWARDS, OLIVER (1900-1980). Studied in Queen's University Belfast where he obtained his BA in 1920 and his MA in 1923 with a thesis on the Austrian dramatist Grillparzer. He went to Bonn in 1923 from where he proceeded to Vienna. In 1925 he lived in Erlangen in Franconia. In 1930 he gained his doctorate at the University of Bonn with a thesis on *Englische Dichtung aus Goethes Zeitalter im Lichte deutscher Kunstlehre* (Bonn: Röhrscheidt). Taught in various English and Welsh universities before returning to Northern Ireland to become Lecturer and later Senior Lecturer in German at Magee University College, Derry until his retirement in 1965. An expert on Yeats and Ezra Pound, he published a number of poems which show the influence of Yeats in Northern literary magazines; he also helped to organize the Yeats Summer School in Sligo. He died in Queen's University Belfast in Autumn 1980 while attending a conference.

FLOWER, ROBIN (1881-1946), Celtic scholar and folklorist. After graduating in Classics from Oxford, he joined the Manuscripts Department of the British Museum in 1906 where he began to learn Irish; he was commissioned to complete the catalogue of Irish mss. begun by Standish Hayes O'Grady. In 1910 he came to study Irish at the School of Irish Learning in Dublin. Discovered the culture of the Blasket Islands, and became the friend and backer of Tomás Ó Criomhthain, encouraging both him and Peig Sayers to record their memoirs. Ó Criomhthain's *An t-Oileánach* was published in 1929 and translated by Flower as *The Islandman*, published in 1934. The memoir *The Great Blasket* (1945) and a survey of Irish literature entitled *The Irish Tradition* (1947) are further works from his pen. He was awarded a Hon. D.Litt from the N.U.I. in 1927 and from Trinity College in 1937.

GWYNN, STEPHEN LUCIUS (1864-1950), historian and poet; grandson of William Smith O'Brien. Born in Dublin and educated at St. Columba's College, Dublin and Brasenose College, Oxford. Married Mary Louisa, daughter of Rev. James Gwynn in 1889. Returned to

Ireland from Britain in 1904 and was elected Nationalist MP for Galway City in 1906, he lost his seat in 1918. In World War I he joined the Connaught Rangers and served in France until 1917. Wrote biographies of Dean Swift (1933), Oliver Goldsmith (1935) and others. In 1936 he published his *Irish Literature and Drama*. He was honoured with a D.Litt. by the National University of Ireland in 1940 and by Trinity College in 1945. His son Aubrey Gwynn SJ was Professor of Medieval History at U.C.D. A copious correspondence from Stephen Gwynn to John Dillon survives. Gwynn contributed the biographical note on John Dillon to the *Dictionary of National Biography*.

HAYES, MICHAEL (1889-1976). Educated at the Christian Brothers School in Synge St. and U.C.D., obtaining his BA in English, Irish and French in 1909. Assistant to the Prof. of French in U.C.D. from 1912 to 1922. M.A. in French in 1920. Joined the Irish Volunteers in 1913 and took part in the Easter Rising. While interned during the Anglo-Irish War he was elected to the Second Dáil and was released after the Truce. Voted for the Treaty and became Ceann Comhairle of the Dáil on 9 September 1922, a post which he held until 1932. Returned to academia in 1932 when he became Lecturer in Modern Irish Language and Literature in U.C.D. Appointed Professor in 1951 and retired in 1960. Member of Seanad Éireann 1938-1965.

HENEGHAN, THOMAS (Tomás Ó hEighneacháin) (1897-1983). From Knockloss, Ballinrobe, he was educated at the Christian Schools, Ballinrobe. He studied Arts in University College Galway from 1917 to 1920, when he graduated with First Class Honours. He obtained his H.Dip. in Education in 1921 and his M.A. in 1922. In 1922 he went to Bonn on a travelling scholarship from Mayo Co. Council and returned to Ireland one year later. In 1923, he founded Cumann Liteardha na mBeanna mBeóla together with Pádraic Óg Ó Conaire and Pádraic Ó Conaire and brought out a little textbook of Irish entitled *Droichead na Gaedhilge* one year later. In 1923 he found employment as a translator in the Houses of the Oireachtas, and transferred to the Dept. of Education in 1931, becoming Publishing Editor with the Department's Irish language publications branch, An Gúm. During the 1930s he translated Spanish works by G.M. Sierra and S. and J.A. Quintero and a French play by Molière into Irish. In 1944 he became Chief Editor of An Gúm. He retired from this post in 1962.

HYDE, DOUGLAS (1860-1949), Celtic scholar. Born in Frenchpark, Co. Roscommon, son of the Rev. Arthur Hyde. Educated at T.C.D., where, among his many other accomplishments, he developed an expertise in Irish. Took his LL.D. in 1888, and, after a year as a visiting professor in Canada, settled down in 1892 in Ratra Park in Roscommon, and devoted himself to literary pursuits and the revival of the Irish language, which was still spoken in the area by old people at that time. *Beside the Fire* (1889) was his first collection of folk-tales, followed by *Love Songs of Connaught* in 1893, and A *Literary History of Ireland* in 1899. That year saw the founding of the Gaelic League, with Hyde as its moving spirit and first president. The League flourished, and by 1905 had 500 branches. When the National University was founded in 1908, Hyde became first Professor of Modern Irish, a post which he held until his retirement in 1932. He served in the Senate of the Irish Free State in 1925-6, but otherwise held no political position, until de Valera, with the assent of all parties, invited him to become the first President of Ireland in 1937, a post which he held until his retirement in 1945. He died in Dublin on 12 July, 1949. Hyde had been friendly with, in particular, Dillon's mother Elizabeth in the 1890's, since she took a great interest in the revival of Irish, and had visited the house in Ballaghaderrin regularly, and, when Myles went to College, Hyde became one of his mentors and supporters.

MULCHRONE, KATHLEEN (Caitilín Ó Maol-Chróin) (1895-1973). Educated at Loreto Convent, Mullingar and U.C.D. B.A. in 1916, H.Dip. and M.A. in 1917. She won a travelling scholarship to study under Thurneysen and completed her Ph.D. in Bonn in 1924. According to Proinséas Ní Chatháin she was Thurneysen's favourite pupil. From 1928 to 1938 she worked on a catalogue of the Irish mss. in the Royal Irish Academy. In 1939 she published a revised version of her doctoral thesis *Bethú Phátraic. The Tripartite Life of St. Patrick*. Other publications include *The Book of Lecan* (1937) which she co-edited and *Cathréim Cellaig* (1933). In 1938 she was appointed to the new chair in Celtic Linguistics and Old Irish at University College Galway, from which she retired in 1965.

MURPHY, GERARD (1901-1959), Celtic scholar. Born in Clones, Co. Monaghan, second son of Henry Murphy, solicitor (and later County Registrar). A contemporary of Myles Dillon's at Mount St. Benedict, where he developed a taste for Irish and Classics. Again as a contemporary with Dillon, entered U.C.D. with a scholarship in Classics in 1918, though (like Dillon) he turned more and more to Irish, studying with Osborn Bergin and John Lloyd-Jones and graduating with First Class Honours. He went on to take an M.A. in 1922, and then got a position in the National Library, under R.I. Best, where he worked for two years. In 1924 he married Máire O'Neill, but he then, like Dillon's brother Theo, fell victim to T.B., and had to spend the years 1925-30 in Switzerland, where, as with Theo, a cure was ultimately effected. On his return to Dublin, he was appointed to the staff of U.C.D., ultimately, in 1948, being given a special professorship in the History of Celtic Literature. His favourite Gaeltacht was Cúil Aodha in West Cork, from which he collected much material. Among his books were the completion of the edition of the *Duanaire Finn* (The Book of the Lays of Finn), begun by Prof. Eoin MacNéill (Vol. II, 1933; Vol. III, 1954); and his most important work, *Early Irish Lyrics* (1956; reissued Dublin 1998).

O'BRIEN, MICHAEL (Micheál Ó Briain) (1896-1962). Born in Clonmel, he studied at U.C.D. where he graduated in 1916 with First Class Honours. He joined the Republican Army and was involved in the Anglo-Irish War. In 1920 he received a travelling scholarship to go to Berlin and study under Julius Pokorny (q.v.) Together with Pokorny he worked on the German edition of the *Irish Bulletin* published by the Irish office in Berlin under the editorship of Nancy Power. In 1924 he gained his doctorate under Pokorny. Worked as an English Lector at the University of Leipzig; during that time he married his German wife Thora. He was appointed Lecturer in Celtic at Queen's University of Belfast in 1925, a position which Myles Dillon also considered for a while. After a brief spell as Professor in the Dublin Institute of Advanced Studies (1942-1945) he went back to Belfast to a newly created chair in Celtic. He returned to Dublin only two years later to become Senior Professor and Director of the School of Celtic Studies in the Dublin Institute of Advanced Studies. For many years he was a colleague of Myles Dillon at the Institute, well respected and highly regarded for his vast knowledge of modern Irish literature and language. Sadly he published only little; the *Corpus Genealogiarum Hibernici* which appeared in the year of his death is his only major published contribution to Celtic Studies. His wife died only three days after him.

O'CONNOR, THOMAS POWER ("T.P.") (1848-1929) journalist and politician. Born in Athlone, and educated at the Queen's College, Galway. Became a journalist, working first for *Saunders' Newsletter* in Dublin, and then joining the *Daily Telegraph* in London. Elected Parnellite M.P. for Galway in 1880, and in 1885 won the Scotland division of Liverpool, a seat which he held till his death. In 1902 he started *T.P.'s Weekly*, a popular literary paper which flourished for many years. His books include *The Parnell Movement* (1886) and

Memories of an Old Parliamentarian (1929). In 1917 he became the first British film censor, and in 1924 a Privy Councillor. In his last years he held the position of "Father of the House of Commons". He was an old friend of John Dillon, and his chief confidant in the years after 1918, when T.P. held the remnants of the Irish Party together at Westminster.

O'DUFFY, EIMAR ULTAN (1893-1935), writer and patriot. Born in Dublin, son of the dentist-in-ordinary to the Viceregal Lodge. Educated at Stonyhurst, and U.C.D., where he graduated in dentistry. Took an active part in the Volunteer movement, and was one of the couriers sent out by Eoin MacNeill to countermand Pearse's order for the Rising. In 1920 he married the sister of Frank Cruise O'Brien. During the Civil War took a liberal pro-Treaty position, and was afterwards employed for a time in the Department of External Affairs. In 1925, spent a short period in Paris as a journalist, where Dillon saw a good deal of him and his wife, and then moved to England, where he sought to make his living as a writer. Already in 1919 he had produced his best-known novel, *The Wasted Island,* a largely autobiographical reflection on the period of the "troubles". His main work of the later period was *King Goshawk and the Birds* (1926). He died in New Malden, Surrey.

O'FARRELLY, AGNES (Una Ní Fhaircheallaigh) (1874-1951). Lecturer in Irish Language at U.C.D., 1909-32; Professor of Modern Irish Poetry, 1932-46. Born near Virginia, Co. Cavan, into a prosperous farming family, with a long tradition of Irish learning. She was a notable figure in the College, and a regular member of its governing body from its inception. With Mary Hayden, she was prominent in the campaign for women's rights in the University, and co-founder, with Hayden, of the Irish Association of Women Graduates. She was also a prominent member of the Gaelic League, and a close friend and loyal supporter of Douglas Hyde, whom she succeeded in the chair of Modern Irish Poetry. She is satirised by Nano Dillon in a number of letters as "The Lamb of Ulster", based on her adopted pen-name "Uan Uladh". She produced two short novels in Irish, and two volumes of verse, the first of which, *Out of the Depths,* had appeared in 1921. She remained unmarried, living with her brother Alphonsus.

O'NEILL, JOSEPH (1884-1953), distinguished public servant and literary figure. Born in the Aran Islands; educated at Queen's College, Galway (1898-1902), and afterwards at the University of Freiburg, where he met and formed a life-long friendship with Osborn Bergin (q.v.). He also from 1920 on became a good friend of Æ's (q.v.). His chosen career was educational administration. He became inspector of Primary Schools in 1907, of Secondary Schools in 1909, Civil Service Commissioner for the Irish Free State in 1923, and also in 1923 (the appointment Myles Dillon is referring to, and sending congratulations to him on) Permanent Secretary to the Department of Education, a post which he held until 1944, and which gave him a key role in the development of the indigenous educational system. He wrote a number of novels in the 1930s (notably *Land Under England,* 1935), and was also an occasional contributor to the *Dublin Magazine,* but he was in general a rather shy and retiring man. He married, in 1912, the poet Mary Devenport, and she survived him.

POKORNY, JULIUS (1887-1970), Celtic scholar. Born in Prague, Pokorny grew up in Austria and studied in Vienna where he obtained his doctorate. In 1920 he was appointed to the chair in Celtic at the University of Berlin which had become vacant after Kuno Meyer's death in 1919. Pokorny was in close contact with the Irish legation in Berlin and collaborated on the German edition of the *Irish Bulletin.* Among his many publications were an anthology of Old Irish poetry into German, *Die älteste Lyrik der grünen Insel,* published in 1923 with a grant from the Dept. of Foreign Affairs in Dublin, and *Die Seele Irlands* (1922) containing translations of short stories by Pádraig Pearse, Pádraic Ó Conaire and others. After Meyer's death he also took over as editor of the *Zeitschrift für celtische Philologie*. Because of his Jewish ancestry, Pokorny lost his chair in 1935, but did not leave Germany until 1943 when he escaped to Switzerland. He settled in Zurich but never obtained another permanent academic appointment. He lectured part-time in Zurich and in Munich after the war. In 1970, he was killed in a road traffic accident. Pokorny had a rather flamboyant and eccentric personality which made him quite a rare bird among the generally rather staid community of Celtic scholars. His linguistic theories were sometimes equally unconventional: in Dublin he raised quite a few eyebrows during a visit in November 1925 when he gave a lecture on the close kinship between the Irish and the Esquimos. Among Pokorny's students in Berlin was Michael O'Brien (q.v.), later Myles Dillon's colleague in the Dublin Institute of Advanced Studies..

PURSER, SARAH HENRIETTA (1848-1943), artist and patron of the arts. Born in Kingstown (Dun Laoghaire) she became a fashionable and wealthy portrait painter. In 1911, she acquired Mespil House near the Grand Canal where she held regular afternoon salons for leading literary and artistic figures. Together with her cousin Sir John Purser-Griffith she established a travelling scholarship in the history of art at U.C.D. and Trinity College.

QUINLAN, HAROLD (1898-1978). Educated at Clongowes, he studied Medicine at U.C.D. from 1915-1921. Went to Berlin in 1922 and obtained his medical doctorate there in 1924. Distinguished physician, attached to Vincent's Hospital. Articles of his on medical subjects appeared the *Irish Journal of Medical Science* during the 1930s.

REDDIN, NORMAN (*c.*1890-1942), solicitor and man about town, with literary and theatrical interests. Brother of Kenneth Reddin, judge and playwright. Educated at Clongowes, and went into the law. In the period 1922-early 1923 he was the accredited swain of Nano Dillon, but she dropped him suddenly, to the family's great surprise, in favour of P.J. Smyth (q.v.). He never married, but not, it would seem, out of pining for Nano, since he was accounted quite a ladies' man in later life. Like his brother, he was much interested in the theatre, and was a director, and for a time secretary, of the Gate Theatre. He died of pneumonia on 10 March 1942.

ROBINSON, MABEL, sister of Marie Duclaux (q.v.), also with a strong interest in literary matters. Translated *The Great Literary Salons* from French into English in 1930.

RUSSELL, GEORGE WILLIAM (Æ) (1867-1935), poet, painter, theosophist, and writer on economic and political questions. Born in Lurgan, Co. Armagh, and, when the family moved to Dublin, was educated at Rathmines School and the Metropolitan School of Art, where he began his life-long friendship with W.B. Yeats. After working as a clerk in Pim's drapery store from 1890 to 1897, he joined the Irish Agricultural Organisation Society under Sir Horace Plunkett, and became the editor of its organ, the *Irish Homestead*, where his gifts as a writer and publicist gained it a wide circulation. His first book of poems, *Homeward: Songs by the Way*, appeared in 1894, and established him in the Irish Literary Movement. His interests were wide: he became a theosophist, and wrote extensively on economics and politics, besides continuing to paint and write poetry. His *Collected Poems* appeared in 1913, with a second edition in 1926. From 1923 to 1930 he edited the *Irish Statesman*, and it is this organ to which Myles Dillon makes a number of contributions from Germany (see Appendix). Dillon had become something of a protegé and an admirer of Æ's, although his father did not much approve of him or his politics, as the correspondence shows. After his wife's death in 1932, Æ moved to England, where he died in Bournemouth on 17 July 1935.

RYAN, FR JOHN, S.J. (1894-1973), Celtic scholar and historian. Born in Castleconnell, Co. Limerick. Educated at Crescent College in Limerick, where he entered the Jesuit novitiate in 1911. Graduated from U.C.D. in Celtic Studies in 1917, studying under Eoin MacNeill, and won the travelling studentship in 1918, but postponed it. He completed his studies in philosophy in Louvain and Valkenburg, and then resumed his Celtic studies in Bonn in 1921-3, studying under Thurneysen. As Myles Dillon arrived in Bonn, he departed for Burgos in Spain, and was ordained back in Dublin in 1926. In 1930, he was appointed lecturer in Early Irish History in U.C.D., and in 1942 succeeded Eoin MacNeill in the chair, retiring in 1964. His main work, *Irish Monasticism: Origins and Development,* was published in 1931; its most recent edition is in print, Dublin 1995 He served on the Board of Celtic Studies in the Dublin Institute of Advanced Studies in the 1960s, when Myles Dillon was chairman of the School of Celtic Studies.

SMYTH, PATRICK J. (1891-1958), surgeon. Born in Ballybay, Co. Monaghan as the son of Solomon Smyth. Studied medicine at U.C.D., and then served during World War I in the Royal Army Medical Corps, where he saw service in the Balkans, developing a special expertise in dealing with trauma. On his return, he joined the staff of the Mater Hospital, where his experience with bullet wounds led to his being frequently approached secretly to patch up wounded I.R.A. men, which he never refused to do, though he had little sympathy for their cause. Married Nano Dillon after a brief courtship in June 1923. After their first son, Nicholas, whose birth on 1 April 1924 is mentioned in the letters, they had four more children. "Paddy" Smyth continued to occupy a prominent place in the Dublin medical scene to the end of his life, with a house and consulting rooms in Fitzwilliam Square.

SWEETMAN, JOHN FRANCIS (1872-1953). According to the *Irish Times* obituary "one of the foremost educationalists in the country" (*IT,* 30 March 1953). Born in Clohammon, Co. Wexford, he was educated at Downside, Somerset where he entered the Benedictine order in 1890. After a few years in Rome he joined the staff of his old school, before he went to South Africa to serve as British army chaplain during the Boer War (1900-2). He returned to Downside and eventually, in 1907, came to Ireland to found Mount St. Benedict, an experimental school, in Gorey, Co. Wexford. Throughout his life he was a keen supporter of Sinn Féin ideals which ultimately was the reason for his school being closed down by the local Bishop in 1925. He was also an authority on questions of agriculture and became one of the most successful tobacco growers in Ireland. He was no man for compromises, though, and stopped producing tobacco when the Irish government would not grant him a remission of duties.

THURNEYSEN, RUDOLF (1857-1940). Born in Basle, Switzerland, he attended Basle university, where Jakob Burckhardt and Friedrich Nietzsche were among his teachers. He continued his studies at Jena, Berlin and Leipzig, where he obtained his doctorate under the Celtic scholar Ernst Windisch. Lecturer and Professor of Romance Philology in Jena until 1887 when he was appointed to the chair in Comparative Philology at Freiburg University. He moved to Bonn in 1913 to become Professor of Comparative Philology and eventually retired from this post in 1923. Thurneysen dominated the field of Celtic Studies in the early decades of this century and was the chief authority on Old Irish. In 1909, he published his *Handbuch des Alt-Irischen,* the revised English edition of which, translated by Michael

Duignan, Osborn Bergin (q.v.) and Daniel Binchy and published in 1946, is still the standard textbook for students of Old Irish. His equally famous work on the Irish sagas, *Die irische Helden- und Königsage* was published in 1921 with a grant from Dáil Éireann, but remains as yet untranslated. Among his many Irish students apart from Myles Dillon were Osborn Bergin (q.v.), Tomás Ó Máille, John Ryan (q.v.) Kathleen Mulchrone (q.v.) and Nancy Power. Thurneysen visited Ireland twice, in 1911 and in 1929; in the latter year he held seminars on Old Irish law tracts in the Royal Irish Academy. Daniel Binchy wrote of him: "He was not merely the last of the great line of foreign scholars who, ever since the days of Zeuss, have contributed so powerfully to our knowledge of Old and Middle Irish; he was also the greatest of them all" (*Eigse* Winter 1940).

WULFF, WINIFRED (1900-1946), Celtic scholar. Graduated in Celtic from U.C.D., contemporary with Myles Dillon, and did postgraduate studies with Osborn Bergin, gaining her Ph.D. in 1930. In 1942 she published a book called *Archaeology without Tears,* but her main work, an edition of an Irish herbal *Hortus Sanitatis Hibernicus,* in two volumes, was published by the Irish Texts Society only after her untimely death.

BIBLIOGRAPHY

1. NEWSPAPERS AND PERIODICALS

ZCP *Zeitschrift für Celtische Philologie*
St   *Studies*
G   *Generalanzeiger* (Bonn)
KZ   *Kölnische Zeitung*
BT   *Berliner Tageblatt*
II   *Irish Independent*
IT   *Irish Times*
IR   *Irish Rosary*
IS   *Irish Statesman*
College Calendars for Bonn, Berlin, Heidelberg and University College Dublin

2. BOOKS AND ARTICLES

Breathnach, Diarmuid and Ní Mhurchú, Máire, *1882-1982. Beathaisnéis 1-5*. Baile Átha Cliath: An Clóchomhar 1986-95

Bewley, Charles, *Memoirs of a Wild Goose*. Dublin: Lilliput Press 1989

Cullen, L.M., *An Economic History of Ireland since 1660*. London 1972

Cullingford, Elizabeth, *Yeats, Ireland and Fascism*. London: Macmillan 1981

Davis, Troy, "The Irish Civil War and the 'International Proposition' of 1922-23". In: *Éire-Ireland* 29 (2). 1994, pp. 92-112

Delmer, Sefton, *An Autobiography*. 2 vols. London: Fecher & Warburg 1961-62.

de Jonge, Alex, *The Weimar Chronicle*. New York & London: Paddington Press 1978

de Róiste, Liam, A Trip Abroad. In: *The United Irishman* 28 April-28 July 1923

Drüll, Dagmar, *Heidelberger Gelehrtenlexikon 1803-1932*. Berlin: Springer 1986

Dunleavy, Janet E. and Dunleavy, Gareth, *Douglas Hyde. A Maker of Modern Ireland*. Berkeley: Univ. of California Press 1991

Erenburg, Ilya, *People and Life*. 6 vols. London: Macgibbon & Kee 1961-6 (esp. vol. 3: *Truke 1921-1933*).

Fischer, Joachim, *Das Deutschlandbild der Iren 1890-1939. Geschichte - Form - Funktion*. 2 vols. Dublin: Trinity College 1996(a)

Fischer, Joachim, "Periphere Perspektiven. Zum Deutschlandbild irischer Reisender zwischen 1919 und 1933". In: *Runa* (Coimbra) 25. 1996(b), pp. 447-55

Freyer, Grattan, *W.B. Yeats and the Anti-Democratic Tradition*. Dublin: Gill & Macmillan 1981

Friedrich, Otto, *Before the Deluge. A Portrait of Berlin in the 1920s*. London: Michael Joseph 1974

Hogan, Robert [et al.] (eds.), *The Macmillan Dictionary of Irish Literature*. London: Macmillan 1985 (paperback edition.)

Hone, Joseph, *W.B. Yeats 1865-1939*. London: Penguin 1971

Hopkinson, Michael, *Green against Green. The Irish Civil War*. Dublin: Gill and Macmillan 1988

Hünseler, Wolfgang, *Das Deutsche Kaiserreich und die Irische Frage 1900-1914*. Frankfurt am Main, Bern, Las Vegas: Lang 1978

Isherwood, Christopher, *The Berlin Novels*. London: Minerva 1993.

Keogh, Dermot, *Ireland and Europe 1919-1989.* Cork & Dublin: Hibernian University Press 1990
Keyes McDonnell, Kathleen, *There is a Bridge at Bandon. A Personal Account of the Irish War of Independence.* Cork and Dublin: Mercier Press 1972
Kluge, Hans-Dieter, *Irland in der deutschen Geschichtswissenschaft, Politik und Propaganda vor 1914 und im Ersten Weltkrieg.* Frankfurt am Main, Bern, New York: Lang 1985
Köhler, Henning, Berlin in der Weimer Republik (1918-1932). In: *Geschichte Berlins. Zweiter Band: Von der Märzrevolution zur Gegenwart.* München: Beck 1987, pp. 793-923
Kolb, Eberhard, *The Weimar Republic.* Tr. from the German. London and New York: Routledge, 1988
Laqueur, Walter, *Weimar. A Cultural History.* London: Weidenfeld and Nicolson, 1974
Lee, Joseph J., *Ireland 1912-1985. Politics and Society.* Cambridge [usw.]: Cambridge University Press 1989
Lerchenmüller, Joachim, »*Keltischer Sprengstoff«. Eine wissenschaftsgeschichtliche Studie über die deutsche Keltologie von 1900 bis 1945.* Tübingen: Niemeyer 1997
Lyons, F.S.L., *John Dillon. A Biography.* Chicago: University of Chicago Press 1968
Lyons, F.S.L., *Ireland since the Famine.* London: Fontana 1973
Lyons, F.S.L., *Culture and Anarchy in Ireland 1890-1939.* Oxford, New York: Oxford University Press 1982
MacArdle, Dorothy, *The Irish Republic. A Documented Chronicle of the Anglo-Irish Conflict and the Partitioning of Ireland, With a Detailed Account of the Period 1916-1923.* 4th ed. Dublin: Irish Press 1951
McElligott, Tom, *This Teaching Life. A Memoir of Schooldays in Ireland.* Mullingar: Lilliput Press 1986
Moore, Sara, *Peace without Victory for the Allies 1918-1932.* Oxford, Providence: Berg 1994
Morrissey, Thomas J., *Towards a National University. William Delany SJ [1835-1924]. An Era of Initiative in Irish Education.* Dublin: Wolfhound Press 1983
Murphy, Brian P., *John Chartres. Mystery Man of the Treaty.* Blackrock, Co. Dublin: Irish Academic Press 1995
Oidtmann, E. von, "Das Geschlecht Gymnich". In: *Zeitschrift des Aachener Geschichtsvereins* 30. 1908, pp. 155-234
Ó Lúing, Seán, *Kuno Meyer 1858-1919. A Biography.* Dublin: Geography Publications 1991
O'Neill, Marie, *From Parnell to de Valera. A Biography of Jennie Wyse Power 1858-1941.* Dublin: Blackwater Press 1991
O'Neill, Patrick, *Ireland and Germany. A Study in Literary Relations.* New York [etc.]: Lang 1985
Overesch, Manfred and Saal, Friedrich Wilhelm, *Die Weimarer Republik.* Düsseldorf: Droste 1982
Smith, Denis Mack, *Mussolini.* London: Phoenix 1994
Snoddy, Theo, *Dictionary of Irish Artists. 20th Century.* Dublin: Wolfhound Press 1996
Tormin, Walter (ed.) *Die Weimarer Republik.* 18th ed. Hanover: Fackelträger 1973.
Tristram, Hildegard, L.C., "150 Jahre deutsche Hibernistik". In: Tristram, Hildegard L.C. (ed.), *Deutsche, Kelten und Iren. 150 Jahre deutsche Keltologie. Gearóid MacEoin zum 60. Geburtstag gewidmet.* Hamburg: Buske 1990, pp. 11-53
Tynan, Katherine, *Life in the Occupied Area.* London: Hutchinson [1925]
Valiulis, Maryann Gialanella, *Portrait of a Revolutionary. General Richard Mulcahy and the Founding of the Irish Free State.* Dublin: Irish Academic Press 1992
Vogt, Helmut, "Bonn in Kriegs- und Krisenzeiten (1914-1948)". In: Dietrich Höroldt (ed.), *Bonn. Von einer französischen Bezirksstadt zur Bundeshauptstadt 1794-1989.* Bonn: Dümmler 1989, pp. 437-638
Wenig, Otto, *Verzeichnis der Professoren und Dozenten der Rhein. Friedrich-Wilhelms-Universität zu Bonn 1818-1968.* Bonn: Bouvier / Röhrscheidt 1968

INDEX